PEOPLE AND ORGANISATIONS

People and Organisations

Edited by Graeme Salaman and Kenneth Thompson
at The Open University
(assisted by Mary-Anne Speakman)

Published by Longman
for The Open University Press

LONGMAN GROUP LIMITED
London
*Associated companies, branches and representatives
throughout the world*

Selection and editorial material
copyright © The Open University 1973

First published 1973
Second impression 1975

ISBN 0 582 48668 · 8 cased
ISBN 0 582 48669 . 6 paper

Printed in Great Britain by
Western Printing Services Ltd
Bristol

Contents

Acknowledgements

People and Organisation by the Open University Course Team.

We are grateful to the following for permission to reproduce copyright material:
Authors and Administrative Science Quarterly for excerpts from 'A Strategic Contingencies Theory of Intraorganizational Power' by D. J. Hickson *et al.*, in *Administrative Science Quarterly*, Vol. 16, No. 2 (June 1971), pp. 216–29 and 'A Convergence in Organization Theory' by D. J. Hickson in *Administrative Science Quarterly*, Vol. 2, No. 2 (Sept. 1966), pp. 224–37; author and Aldine Publishing Company for excerpts from 'The Practicalities of Rule Use' by Don Zimmerman in *Understanding Everyday Life* ed. Jack D. Douglas. Reprinted from Jack D. Douglas, editor, *Understanding Everyday Life* (Chicago: Aldine Publishing Company, 1970); Copyright © 1970 by Aldine Publishing Company; reprinted by permission of the author and Aldine Publishing Company. Author and Aldine Publishing Company for excerpts from 'Society as a Complex Adaptive System' by Walter Buckley in *Modern Systems Research for the Behavioral Scientist* ed. Walter Buckley. Reprinted from Walter Buckley, editor, *Modern Systems Research for the Behavioral Scientist* (Chicago: Aldine Publishing Company, 1968); Copyright © 1968 by Walter Buckley. Reprinted by permission of the author and Aldine Publishing Company; American Psychological Association for excerpts from 'Role, Personality and Social Structure in the Organizational Setting' by Daniel Levinson in *Journal of Abnormal and Social Psychology*, Vol. 58, 1959, pp. 170–81; The American Sociological Association for excerpts from 'Role Activation Conflict: A Study of Industrial Inspection' by Derek Pugh in *ASR*, Vol. 31, 1966, pp. 835–42; author and The American Sociological Association for the article 'The Police on Skid-Row: A study of Peace Keeping' by Egon Bittner in *ASR*, Vol. 32, pp. 699–715; author and The American Sociological Association for the article 'Professionalization and Bureaucratization' in *ASR*, Vol. 33, No. 1, Feb. 1968, pp. 92–104; authors and The American Sociological Association

for 'Organizational Goals and Environment: Goal-Setting as an Interaction Process' by James D. Thompson and William J. McEwen in *ASR*, Vol. 23, No. 1, 1958, pp. 23–31; Basic Books Inc. for Chapter 12 of *The Sructure of Organizations* by Peter M. Blau and Richard A. Schoenherr, © 1971 by Basic Books Inc., Publishers, New York; Cambridge University Press for excerpts from *The Applicability of Organizational Sociology* by C. Argyris; The Clarendon Press for an adaptation of the article 'Organizational Structure, Environment and Performance: The Role of Strategic Choice' by John Child in *Sociology*, Vol. 6, 1972, pp. 1–22, © 1972 Oxford University Press, and 'by permission of The Clarendon Press, Oxford'; Collier-Macmillan Publishers for excerpts from 'The Social Organization of Industrial Work' in *The Sociology of Work in Industry* by Allen Fox, London: Collier-Macmillan, 1971, pp. 28–47; author for excerpts from 'Behaviour in Private Places: Sustaining Definitions of Reality in Gynaecological Examinations' by Joan Emerson in *Recent Sociology*, No. 2 ed. Hans Peter Dreitzel, New York, Macmillan 1970, pp. 73–100; Holt, Rinehart & Winston for an extract from 'Religious Organization' by Kenneth A. Thompson in *Processing People: Case Studies in Organizational Behaviour* ed. J. McKinlay, Holt, Rinehart and Winston, London, 1974; Alfred A. Knopf, Inc. for excerpts from 'Integrative and Adaptive Uses of Autonomy: Worker Autonomy in Factories' in *Autonomy and Organization: The Limits of Social Control* by Fred Katz; Copyright © 1968 Random House, Inc. Reprinted by permission of the publisher; Macmillan, London and Basingstoke for an extract from *Exploring The Industrial Subculture* by Barry A. Turner; Macmillan Publishing Co., Inc. for excerpts from 'The Hospital and its Negotiated Order' by A. Strauss *et al.* in *The Hospital in Modern Society* ed. E. Friedson © The Free Press of Glencoe, a Division of The Macmillan Company; Penguin Books Ltd for excerpts from 'The Comparative Study of Organizations' by D. S. Pugh and D. J. Hickson in *Industrial Society* ed. Dennis Pym (Pelican 1968), pp. 374–96, Copyright © Penguin Books, 1968, and the article 'The Study of Organization—Objectivity or Bias?' by Martin Albrow in *Penguin Social Science Survey 1968* ed. Julius Gould, pp. 146–67, Copyright © Penguin Books, 1968; Routledge & Kegan Paul Ltd for excerpts from 'The Practicalities of Rule Use' by Don Zimmerman in *Understanding Everyday Life* ed. Jack Douglas, 1971; Scott, Foresman and Company for an extract from *Complex Organizations:* A Critical Essay by Charles Perrow. Copyright © 1972 by Scott, Foresman and Company. Reprinted by permission of the Publisher; Society for Applied Anthropology for excerpts from 'Banana Time: Job Satisfaction and Informal Interaction' by D. F. Roy in *Human Organization*, Vol. 18, No. 4, 1960; and author and The Society for the Study of Social Problems for excerpts from 'Normal Crimes: Sociological Features of the Penal Code in a Public Defender Office' by David Sudnow in *Social Problems*, Vol. 12, No. 3.

Introduction

This book is devoted to the restoration of *a sociology of organisations*, rather than merely supplying yet another collection of what are taken to be significant contributions to *organisation theory*. As has been noted elsewhere the orthodox approach to the study of organisations (called organisation theory) tends to adopt theories and models of organisational functioning, and to focus on areas of empirical investigation, that are highly oriented towards managerial conceptions of organisations, managerial priorities and problems, and managerial concerns for practical outcomes (Silverman, 1968; Albrow, reading 26 in this book). This sort of perspective is often misleading and unduly restrictive.

As comparative newcomers to the area of organisational studies the editors[1] can still remember having experienced something of a surprise as they studied the major works and classical reports in this area. They found it difficult, in some cases, to know why a certain approach was given so much attention or why a particular problem was considered salient, since, in their view, these approaches and problems were not necessarily highly interesting from a sociological point of view. The reason for the rather strange directions that organisation theory has sometimes taken is not hard to find: this sort of analysis is centrally concerned with management issues and problems—or 'organisational' problems—rather than sociological ones.

Furthermore they were dissatisfied with the rigidity of the demarcation lines drawn between the various sociological sub-disciplines or

---

[1] Kenneth Thompson has done research on the sociology of religious organisations (Thompson, 1968, 1970, 1973) and Graeme Salaman's work has been on occupational communities (Salaman, 1971 a and b, 1973 a and b).

specialities which could have been considered to have had some interest in the study of organisations. Thus it was clear, in considering industrial sociology, the sociology of occupations, and organisation theory, that these specialities typically asked different questions and employed different models and theories, and that they were concerned with different groups of people—industrial sociology with workers, organisational theory with managers, executives and professionals, occupational sociology with all members of an occupation. Each of these subdisciplines also tended to consider its subject matter (managers, workers, professionals or whatever) as a relatively homogeneous group whose most significant characteristic is that covered by the speciality. Thus organisation theory tends to see membership of the organisation as crucial while industrial sociology apparently typically considers membership of the category 'workers' as highly salient. And, of course, occupational sociology considers membership of a particular occupation and its subculture as being of determinate significance. The point that is missed by this academic division of labour is that people are typically members of all these groups or categories, and that to restrict one's attention to just one is unnecessarily limiting. So, in this Reader attempts have been made to view with indifference the established distinctions and to avoid any *a priori* assessment of the significance of organisational, occupational or group membership, and to reject any necessary commitment to what could be seen as the 'normal' approaches, theories, considerations and problems of any particular sub-discipline.

Such a rejection is in favour of an attempt to apply a sociological perspective to the study of organisation. That is, this book represents an effort to view organisations in terms of the way in which they are problematic with reference to sociological theory and discussion (cf. Albrow, reading 26).

At the same time, however, the editors were aware that a great deal of academic theorising about organisations was surprisingly irrelevant to the practical concerns of those who worked in organisations, or who were clients, victims or patients of organisations. And that, therefore, an attempt should be made to ground the academic discussions in matters of everyday experience and concern of all those exposed to, or involved in, organisations. It was also appreciated that in this way it should be possible to enable students to use the sociological repertoire of concepts, models and perspectives with reference to their own experience. It has been suggested elsewhere by Charles Perrow (Perrow, 1972) that a great deal of sociological investigation of organisations tends to ignore the urgent political and social realities of these phenomena. Crucially important issues of organisational control over, and manipulation of, their social environments, their attempts (usually successful) to achieve the interests and priorities of those who run or own them, their invulnerability to outside or government control and the ways in which organisational, financial, political and military power overlaps or coincides, have been, irresponsibly, extremely cursorily covered in the sociological literature, while considerable attention has been devoted to what could be considered trivial issues, and what Perrow terms 'trivial organizations'.

We have a great deal of sympathy for this view. However, we have chosen mainly to focus our attention on certain fundamental processes of social control within organisations, in the belief that these are no less serious with regard to the predicament of 'organization man in an organizational society'. The analysis of such processes and their repercussions fits into the tradition stemming from the founder of the sociology of organisations, Max Weber. We are convinced that a return to the spirit of Weber's work on rationalities of organisation, as exemplified in his discussion of bureaucracy, might help to bring about the restoration of a sociology of organisations. The theoretical and practical implications of this approach are evident in the first two readings of the book. Blau and Schoenherr (reading 1) examine the insidious and unobtrusive controls exercised by modern organisations; controls which are all the more powerful and dangerous because they are so deceptive. They are deceptive, for example, because they do not entail for participants the experience of being oppressed by a despot, but often simply the experience of conforming to the logic of a situation or performing according to an internalised standard. McMillan (reading 2) in a piece specially written for this volume, shows how the logics and strategies of multinational corporations give rise to organisational control across national boundaries. Both these articles are in the spirit of the Weberian tradition in their efforts to bring a sociological perspective to bear on the most pressing problems that the modern forms of organisation pose for individuals and societies today.

But what is meant by 'the sociological perspective'? And what theories and approaches should be employed and discussed? This Reader eschews commitment to any one sociological dogma, but eclectically utilises what is available in order to explicate and discuss the main overarching theme of the Reader: organisational processes of control. This theme has been chosen for a number of reasons.

First, it is maintained that interest in control in organisations or elsewhere is central to sociological theory. Opinions vary as to the true nature of sociological activity, but few would deny that sociology is and should be concerned with the explanation of meaningful social action.

As such, sociology is oriented to uncovering the determinants of action, and therefore with attempts to control that behaviour. Now it is clearly absurd to consider that all such behaviour is determined by official, legal, formalised demands and expectations (though such a view is implied by some studies of organisations); but clearly any interest in the causes of action must attend to such constraints—while avoiding any excessive commitment to official conceptions of obedience, deviancy or other troubles. Simplifying grossly, it can be argued that two primary approaches to the determinants of social action can be discerned within sociology: one starts with a view of society and social life as inherently ordered and searches for shared agreements and convictions through an analysis of apparently mutually interlocked and adjusting systems and structures; the other focuses on the everyday conflicts, interactions and negotiations that give rise to this appearance of large-scale structured regularity. These two perspectives, which typically differ in their application and methodology, can be termed the structuralist (or systems) approach, and the action (or interactionist) approach. And they have important implications for the study of organisations.

There exists an enormous body of work on the nature and determinants of organisational structure and the relationships between significant aspects of this structure. The readings in Section 2 of this book are relevant to this sort of approach. Considerable work has been done on organisations as arenas within which members negotiate, bargain and compromise with each other—and with their respective ideologies, definitions and values. Such work is represented in Sections 3 and 4. It will be clear that the distinction between these two approaches is merely another way of viewing the perennial and recurrent conceptual distinctions between formal and informal processes, activities and forms of control within organisations. As has recently been noted, it would not seem that there is any advantage in retaining this distinction since, not only has it been used to refer to a number of different phenomena, but it also may derive from, and perpetuate, a view of the organisation that is empirically unrealistic and biased towards an 'official', formal account of organisational activities and processes. As Fox (reading 21) has commented, the distinction can lead to the—unwarranted—conclusion that there exist two different and opposing systems of behaviour, whereas in fact there is only one. And it seems unfortunate that sociologists should concern themselves with defining some events and actions as proper and others as deviant. However, the distinction does have some utility if it is seen as a warning to treat official definitions and descriptions as being problematically related to actual observed behaviour.

The selections in this Reader have been chosen to make the point then that to the extent that the behaviour of members of organisations is controlled and determined (i.e. appears to be regular and predictable) such regularity may derive from sources other than the official rules and prescriptions. It may, for example, follow the norms and definitions of subcultural groups within the organisation as Roy's article suggests (reading 13), or follow from a constantly on-going series of negotiations and definitions, as Strauss and his colleagues argue (reading 20). Certainly the conception of organisational rules as blue-prints for actual behaviour is critically considered by many articles in this selection.

Another reason for choosing control as a unifying theme lies in its importance to those who have studied organisations, or theorised about them, as well as its central significance to those who are employed or treated by them. For Weber the orientation of members of a bureaucracy towards the power of those who attempted to control and regulate their behaviour was a primary distinguishing feature of organisations; and others have followed his seminal insights into this matter. However, it has also recently been noted that the most significant form of power within organisations is the power to limit, guide and restrict the decision-making of organisational personnel, such that even when they are allowed, or obliged, to use their own judgment, they do not deviate from official expectations. This matter is introduced by Blau and Schoenherr (reading 1) and Perrow (reading 18). It is also discussed by Child (reading 6) who argues that organisational structure itself—which may be seen as a series of limitations and controls over members' decision-making—is a result not of the working out of some inexorable organisational logic, but of senior, powerful organisational personnel choosing what the structure of the organisation should be like.

A third reason for this decision to concentrate on organisational control and power systems relates to the interest, noted above, to consider not just those who work *for* organisations but also those who are worked *on* by them. As its title suggests, this Reader is about people and organisations; people who are exposed, as we all are, to actual organisational treatment and processes in their everyday lives, people who constitute the raw material of the organisation, or who are its customers, clients, inmates or victims. For this reason the Reader includes a number of accounts of the way in which organisational personnel interpret and utilise organisational procedures in their application to practical situations. These articles explore and describe the processes involved in turning a person or event into a 'case'. In so doing they demonstrate the point made earlier: that formal controls and organisational rules are not, cannot be, adequate as guides to action or determinants of it; in their actual organisational behaviour the policemen, bureaucrats and lawyers described in Section 3 show their concern not for the goals of the organisation as adumbrated by senior organisational spokesmen, but for what *they*, the people actually facing the difficulties of rule application, see as their problems and difficulties. Thus the rules are used to justify and legitimise a particular behaviour as a normal one under the circumstances, rather than as determinants of that behaviour.

This Reader includes work done under the theoretical rubric of what is variously known as ethnomethodology, the sociology of everyday life, or phenomenological sociology. These inclusions need no particular justification since it is clear that anyone with an interest in sociology, or the sociology of organisations, must be interested in, indeed fascinated by, the ethnographic accounts of Zimmerman (reading 16), Bittner (reading 22), Sudnow (reading 23) and Emerson (reading 24). Whatever the epistemological status of this theoretical approach, no one can deny that in their dogged concern for unravelling and describing the complex procedures and negotiations of everyday life, and the knowledge and assumptions that underlie the perpetual construction of 'normal' orderliness and routineness, those who can be classified as ethnomethodologists have contributed significantly to sociological thought.

A fourth reason for focusing on processes of organisational control stems from recent work in sociological theory which points to the paradoxical way in which society—or an organisation—is both an objective and subjective reality. Regularity is only possible because persons are convinced of its existence; they consequently experience their own and others' expectations and values as constraining, and in complying with expectations of typical or proper behaviour recreate the objective regularity within which they live. Such a view can be applied to organisations, especially when it is remembered that the ability to impose definitions, to tell the way things are, is an important source of power (indeed Weber would argue it is a necessary basis for any stable power system). What is more, some organisations attempt to define the world in a more deliberate way than others. Some organisations are, apparently, overtly concerned with spreading ideas (churches, schools, psychiatric hospitals, prisons, public relations organisations, political parties), others merely attempt to structure reality for those who work in them, or who are worked on by them. Often the most important object of this activity is that the organisational hierarchy should be justified in the eyes of those who are disadvantageously placed within it.

The theme of control is developed in the various sections of the book according to the following plan:

Section 1, *The problem of organisations*, concentrates on presenting examples of the serious individual and social problems posed by organisations. It discusses some of the new forms of power exercised within organisations and through them in contemporary society. There is also a discussion of one of the most potent new forms of organisation, the multinational corporation.

Section 2, *Structure and system—basic concepts and theories*, considers the theme of forms of organisational control with reference to the concept organisational structure and the systems approach to organisations. As well as containing a classical formulation of the structural approach this section also includes critical articles, particularly with reference to orthodox thinking on the determinants of organisational structure. It is also argued that organisations consist of groups (and cultures) that hold different conceptions of the organisation, its rationality and structure.

Section 3, *Organisational control, rules, roles and power*, addresses the question of organisational control both directly in terms of determinants of intra-organisational power, and more generally through an investigation of the utility of the concepts role and rule in organisational analysis. The view of an organisation as a structure of compatible, explicit and accepted expectations and prescriptions is rejected in favour of an awareness of differing, possibly conflicting subcultural value systems, and role conflicts.

Section 4, *Knowledge and information* considers the ways in which members of organisations hold views of themselves, their clients and their organisation in common. Particular attention is paid to the nature of the definitions and expectations held about those who constitute the raw material of the organisation and the ways in which these definitions are constructed, negotiated and maintained. These articles argue for an emphasis on the negotiated, situational nature of shared organisational assumptions and definitions, rather than on the officially propounded rules and rationalities.

Section 5, *Perspectives on organisations*, provides an overview of different approaches to the study of organisations and considers the question of whether it is possible to avoid bias and attain objectivity in this field.

This book originated with a specific purpose—to form part of an Open University 'third level' course, *People and Organisations*. It is one component of a course which also includes personal tuition, a basic correspondence text, BBC radio and television programmes and other prescribed books.[2] We have deliberately avoided including pieces which already appear in these prescribed books. We are also able to send some offprints (for instance of journal articles) to Open University students. Consequently in editing this Reader we have tried to select recent articles which do not appear in other Readers on organisations (although there are exceptions). In two cases, where there was no existing article which was suitable for our purpose, we commissioned new articles.

In preparing the book we have been greatly helped by suggestions and comments from fellow members of the People and Organisations Course Team: Martin Albrow, Hedy Brown, John Beishon, David Elliott, David Hickson, Jill Jones, Arthur McCullough, Charles McMillan, Charles Perrow, Ken Patton (BBC), David Silverman, Eric Wade and David Weeks.

We are particularly indebted to another member of the Course Team, Mary-Anne Speakman, who did a great deal of the detailed editing and research that went into the preparation of this book.

At the Open University we have had the excellent assistance of our secretary, Kathy Tyrell.

GRAEME SALAMAN

KENNETH THOMPSON

[2] In addition to this volume the other prescribed texts for the course are: Oscar Grusky and George A. Miller, eds, *The Sociology of Organizations: basic studies*, New York, The Free Press, 1970; David Silverman, *The Theory of Organizations*, London, Heinemann, 1970; Peter M. Blau, *The Dynamics of Bureaucracy*, University of Chicago Press, revised edition, 1972.

REFERENCES

PERROW, CHARLES (1972) *Complex Organizations: a critical essay*, Illinois, Scott Foresman.

SALAMAN, GRAEME (1971a) 'Some sociological determinants of occupational communities', in *The Sociological Review*, **19**, no. 1, 53–77.

SALAMAN, GRAEME (1971b) 'Two occupational communities: examples of a remarkable convergence of work and non-work', *The Sociological Review*, **19**, no. 3, 389–407.

SALAMAN, GRAEME (1973a) *Community and Occupation*, Cambridge University Press.

SALAMAN, GRAEME (1973b) 'Occupations, community, culture and Consciousness', Martin Bulmer, ed., *The Occupational Community of the Traditional Worker*, Routledge & Kegan Paul.

SILVERMAN, DAVID (1968) 'Formal organizations or industrial sociology: towards a social action analysis of organizations', *Sociology*, **2**, 221–38.

THOMPSON, KENNETH A. (1968) 'Bureaucracy and the Church', in David Martin, ed., *A Sociological Yearbook of Religion in Britain*, London, SCM Press, pp. 32–46.

THOMPSON, KENNETH A. (1970) *Bureaucracy and Church Reform*, Oxford, Oxford University Press.

THOMPSON, KENNETH A. (1973) 'Religious organizations', in J. McKinlay, ed., *Processing People—Studies in Organizational Behavior*, Holt, Rinehart and Winston.

SECTION I

The problem of organisations

We begin this book with a piece by Blau and Schoenherr which sets the theme for all that follows. It examines the paradox that modern man is freer from coercion through the power of command of superiors than most people have been, yet men in positions of power today probably exercise more control than any tyrant ever had. This is seen as being due to the new forms of power exercised within organisations and through them in contemporary society.

It is firmly within the Weberian tradition in that, like Weber's work, it contributes to the understanding of modern organisations by discerning incipient trends in their developing mechanisms of control and makes analytic distinctions between them. Blau and Schoenherr claim that the emerging trend seems to be a decreasing reliance on control through a fixed chain of command and an increasing tendency to rely on indirect kinds of control. Probably the most prevalent mechanisms of organisational control are those based on incentive systems and machine technologies, but even more significant may be the growing emphasis on controls through recruitment of qualified personnel and the prior allocation of resources by top decision-makers, which set the premises which all subsequent lower level decision-making must follow.

These unobtrusive or indirect forms of control have the advantage of seeming to be more compatible with democratic values than a system based on direct commands by superiors. Not only do they excite less resistance from subordinates, they are also more efficient. As Blau and Schoenherr put it: 'Slave drivers have gone out of fashion not because they were so cruel but because they were so inefficient.'

The growing dependence of organisations on professionals and their expertise is based on an awareness that the efforts of men can be controlled more efficiently by mobilising their professional commitments to work than by physical coercion or even wages. This can lead to insidious organisational control over participants, because the more unobtrusive controls are not easily identifiable as power. Such control and power is also dangerous to democracy, for two reasons, according to Blau and Schoenherr: first, the complex structures of decision-making make it difficult to locate the individuals whose judgments were the ultimate source of a given action. Second, when they are located, they are usually specialised experts whose judgments rest on technical grounds of efficiency.

The pressure to make the most rational decision in terms of the interest of the organization requires that the recommendations experts make on the basis of their technical competence govern as much as possible such decisions of organizations as whether to shut down a plant and lay off its workers; in which city to build a new plant; whether to back the British pound against inflation or not; or in which company's stock to invest funds (Blau and Schoenherr, pp. 354-5).

It is precisely this problem that is discussed by Charles McMillan in the second reading in Section 1. It is sadly revealing of the present priorities of organisation theory that so little attention has been paid to the phenomenon of the multinational corporation. McMillan shows that none of the existing schools of thought in organisation theory 'come remotely at the real dimensions of this giant organisation, especially the structure of power and technology which underlie organisation growth; and the means of preserving control once it is achieved'. His discussion of the decision-making framework surrounding the operations of multinational firms illustrates very well the issues raised by Blau and Schoenherr.

I

Peter M. *Blau and*   New forms of power
Richard
A. *Schoenherr*

Excerpts from Peter M. Blau and Richard A. Schoenherr, *The Structure of Organizations*, New York, Basic Books, 1971, pp. 347–57.

Middle managers in large organisations do exercise more authority and more influence than those in small ones, and the discretion of employees on lower levels also may well be greater in large organisations. Similarly, there can be no doubt that the citizens of modern democracies are more affluent, have more political rights, and are less dominated by the arbitrary will of a ruler than the subjects of a feudal lord or of a tribal chieftain. But does this mean that the top executives of the largest organisations exercise less control either within the organisation or outside it than the executives in small organisations or feudal princes or tribal chieftains or even political tyrants? Is not the power of control over our lives and destinies that the heads of the military establishment and of giant corporations exercise far greater than the power a Caligula or a Genghis Khan has wielded? This is the paradox: we today are freer from coercion through the power of command of superiors than most people have been, yet men in positions of power today probably exercise more control than any tyrant ever has.

New forms of power have been emerging that are exercised within modern organisations and through them in contemporary society. These new forms of organisational control can be clarified by contrasting them with old-fashioned bureaucratic power. Weber's great contribution to the understanding of modern organisations is that he discerned incipient trends, which have only become manifest since his time, and that he recognised that organisations take advantage of a variety of mechanisms of control, ranging from obviously bureaucratic ones, such as command authority and discipline, to quite unbureaucratic ones, such as the controlling power rooted in expert knowledge (Weber, 1946, pp. 196–244 and 1947, pp. 324–41). His limitation is that he failed to make explicit analytical distinctions between these different control mechanisms and subsumed them all under his ideal type.[1] This failure prevented him from exploiting his profound insights fully and from realising that traditional bureaucratic controls were in the process of becoming transformed into different ones. To be sure, several mechanisms of control occur together in organisations, but the anaytical distinctions between them are necessary to examine how they combine and which ones become predominant in certain places and at certain times.

The prototype of bureaucratic control is the authority exercised through a chain of command, in which superiors give orders subordinates are obligated to obey. This is the mechanism of organisational control Weber emphasises most, and its polar example is the Prussian army of his time, which lends some justification to Friedrich's (1958) criticism that Weber's analysis of bureaucracy 'vibrates with something of the Prussian enthusiasm for the military organization' (p. 31). An essential element in the exercise of control through a chain of command is rigorous discipline enforced through coercive sanctions. Weber (1946) explicitly states 'that military discipline is the ideal model for the modern capitalist factory' (p. 261), and he implies that Puritanism is an important source of the discipline in modern armies (pp. 256–7). Discipline is the means that transforms the simplest kind of human control—that of a man who gets others to do what he wills, which is limited to a single person's span of attention—into a control mechanism for large organisations. The transmission of orders through a long chain of communication links in an organisational hierarchy is likely to be a slow process and to distort these orders unless strict discipline reigns. But though there are similarities between the command authority of the general and that of the factory manager, and between the disciplined performance required of soldiers and of workers, the rigid obedience the general demands of his troops, the virtually unrestricted power of sanction he has over them, and the deference he

[1] Talcott Parsons has emphasised the advantages of analytical over type concepts and specifically criticised Weber for failing to distinguish between the authority based on administrative position and that based on professional competence; for the first, see Parsons (1937), pp. 27–42, 606–10; for the second, see his 'Introduction' to Weber (1947), pp. 58–60, note, and Alvin W. Gouldner (1954), pp. 22–4.

expects of them are quite unlike the conditions characteristic of the management of modern factories.

A second mechanism of control in organisations discussed by Weber is the establishment of explicit regulations and procedures that govern decisions and operations. Discipline refers to compliance with rules and regulations as well as to compliance with orders from superiors. Moreover, standing orders of those in positions of authority become rules or, as they are called in the army, 'standard operating procedures', which must be regularly followed. Hence, there is a close connection between conformity with rules and control through a chain of command in organisations, which is illustrated by the strong emphasis on strict compliance with detailed rules as well as on the chain of command in military organisations. Nevertheless, rules restrict the arbitrary exercise of power by the dominant group, because rules are relatively general in two senses of the term, both of which Weber notes: they refer to the principles underlying decisions rather than a particular decision, and they tend to apply to everybody in the system, rulers as well as ruled. Freedom of action is less restrained if superiors establish rules stipulating criteria for decision-making than if they issue commands as to how specific decisions must be carried out. Besides, once a management or dominant group has established a rule that is to its advantage, its individual members cannot easily escape from being bound by the rule even if they would like to in particular instances, because it is to the advantage of the group as a whole to uphold the rule (Lenski, 1966, p. 55). Hence, a rule, though it be established purely in terms of the self-interest of an elite, limits the arbitrary exercise of power by the members of the elite.

A control mechanism of special importance in modern work organisations is the incentive system. Weber discusses the significance of salaries and of career advancements for making employees dependent on the organisation and thus constraining them to submit to the authority exercised in it. But his focus on public bureaucracies has the result that he pays no attention to the ways these rewards are directly tied to performance as incentives in many private firms and in recent times increasingly also in government bureaux. Pure cases of this control of performance through incentives are piece rates in factories and sales commissions in merchandising firms. A modified form, applicable to any type of work, is the systematic periodic review of the performance of employees, often on the basis of statistical records of performance, and the use of this information in adjusting salaries and in making promotions. The control exercised through the chances for an impending promotion clearly is more indirect and entails less imposition of another's will on one's action than that exercised through a chain of command with coercive sanctions to enforce disciplined compliance.

The technology enters the control system of an organisation in two different respects. First, the machine technology constrains the performance of workers and is a tool in the hands of management for controlling operations. A clear example is the regulation of productivity by the speed of the assembly line in a factory. A more complex illustration is provided by the design of the automated set-up in a white-collar office, which constrains the work of the employees preparing the input and those processing the output of the computer. Automation in factories plays a similar role. Second, the technical knowledge of the experts employed by an organisation is the source of their ability to perform complex tasks and keep in control of the situation. By hiring the appropriate professionals with the expert knowledge required for the performance of various responsibilities, management indirectly controls operations and reduces the need for alternative mechanisms of control, such as close supervision through a chain of command or detailed rules for less skilled employees to follow. In addition, employing experts makes it possible to discharge responsibilities that otherwise simply could not be undertaken. Weber (1947) placed much stress on the significance of expert knowledge in organisations: 'The role of technical qualifications in bureaucratic organizations is continually increasing' (p. 335). And again: 'Bureaucratic administration means fundamentally the exercise of control on the basis of knowledge' (p. 339).

From the perspective of management, the importance of expertise in modern organisations means that the recruitment of employees with the required technical skills becomes a crucial responsibility and a major mechanism of control. An organisation can be governed by recruiting anybody and everybody and then using a chain of command to rule them with an iron hand or installing a technology that harnesses them to machines. But an organisation can also be managed by recruiting selectively only those employees that have the technical qualifications and professional interest to perform on their own the various tasks for which the organisation is responsible and then give them discretion to do what needs to be done within the broad framework of basic policies and administrative guidelines. This is how research institutes and universities are run. Though the specialists in these organisations are never told how to do things and rarely what to do, senior administrators maintain long-range control over operations by recruiting certain specialists rather than others. As a matter of fact, administrative control becomes still more indirect if the organisation is large and comprises specialists in many different fields, because under these conditions top administrators cannot make recruitment decisions themselves but must delegate responsibility for them too.

The allocation of personnel and other resources is the ultimate mechanism of organisational control, not only in the sense that it is fundamental and nearly always complements other mechanisms, but also in the sense that reliance primarily on it is the polar opposite of Weberian bureaucratic control through a chain of command backed with coercive sanctions. Take major universities as an extreme example. The faculty's responsibilities for teaching and research are not supervised by administrators; tenure provisions make it impossible to discharge senior faculty members whose performance fails to meet expected standards; and most personnel decisions are in effect made by departmental faculties, because senior administrators cannot easily, and rarely do, exercise their veto power over these decisions. Nevertheless, senior administrators control the direction in which universities are moving and the work that is being done in them in the long run, because they allocate the funds that determine which fields can expand and which ones must contract. Whereas major universities are atypical organisations, of course, and most other organisations are not administered as they are, they provide an extreme instance of indirect forms of administrative control in organisations.

Combinations of several of the mechanisms of control outlined are found in most organisations, but the emerging trend seems to be a decreasing reliance on control through a chain of command and an increasing tendency to rely on indirect kinds of control. While incentive systems and machine technologies are probably the most prevalent mechanisms of organisational control today, controls through recruitment of qualified personnel and allocation of resources assume major significance in organisations with the most specialised personnel, which may well be indicative of their growing future importance. These indirect forms of control are more compatible with democratic values than is the bureaucratic authority exercised through a chain of command in which subordinates are compelled to obey the orders of superiors. However disagreeable the need to keep up with a piece-rate system or a machine is, it does not violate the democratic conception of man, as submission to the commands of a drill sergeant does. In the extreme case, these constraints disappear too, and employees are free to do the work they are professionally trained to do and interested in doing in their own way, and managerial controls are primarily exercised indirectly through selective recruitment and through decisions that determine the expansion and contraction of various personnel complements. That type of power suffices to govern the organisation, though there is virtually no domination of any individuals in it. The extreme case of organisations composed of specialised professionals working with dedication and free of external constraints, though rare, is a polar example of a more general principle: in as much as indirect forms of control are more compatible than army-type submission to commands with our values of human freedom and integrity, they reduce resistance, which makes them more effective means of control.

The new forms of power that are developing in modern society are closely connected with the great efficiency of indirect mechanisms of organisational control. Slave drivers have gone out of fashion not because they were so cruel but because they were so inefficient. Men can be controlled much more effectively by tying their economic needs and interests to their performance on behalf of employers. Calling this wage slavery is a half-truth, which correctly indicates that workers dependent on their wages can be exploited as slaves can be, and which conveniently ignores the basic differences between economic exploitation and slavery. The efforts of men can be controlled still far more efficiently than through wages alone by mobilising their professional commitments to the work they can do best and like to do most and by putting these highly motivated energies and skills at the disposal of organisations. There is a tremendous gain in freedom for individuals, just as there is in the step from slavery to working for wages, and there are simultaneously great advantages that accrue to organisations and give them new potentials for expanded power, just as did the change from slaves to employees. The professionalisation of organisations, by which is meant that decisions are made by technical experts both interested and qualified in specialised fields of competence, enhances the internal efficiency and the external power of organisations. In speculating about the implications of this, we have in mind the power exercised by giant organisations, such as the US Army or US Steel.

Power on a large scale, and thus excepting that in small tribes and small groups, is indubitably always exercised with the aid of organisations. The new forms of power, however, are not so much exercised by individuals through organisations as by organisations through individuals. This is not anthropomorphism; on the contrary, attributing the power of organisations to strong leaders is. Administrative decisions are naturally made by individuals, and the decisions of senior administrators of large organisations entail the exercise of much power. But we suspect that even top corporation or military officers are tools of their organisation, not the other way around, in the specific sense that their administrative decisions are made to further the interests of the organisation rather than their immediate self-interests, which they can ignore because their own long-range interests are linked to those of the organisation. Besides, not all important administrative decisions in an organisation are made by one individual at the top, and it is often impossible to say which individuals wield the power exercised by an organisation without being completely arbitrary. The power is rooted in the structure of the organisation. No individual has it, and individuals merely make the decisions through which this power is exercised as incumbents of positions in the formal structure.

The new forms of power rooted in the structure of organisations pose a serious threat in a democratic society. For democratic institutions have been designed to curb the power of individuals or political institutions, such as the federal government, and not that of organisations, such as corporations or military services. How serious the threat is is indicated by a well-known warning of the late President Eisenhower, who hardly can be accused of harbouring an ingrained prejudice against the military or against private enterprise:

> In the councils of government we must guard against the acquisition of unwarranted influence, whether sought or unsought, by the military-industrial complex. The potential for the disastrous rise of misplaced power exists and will persist. We must never let the weight of this combination endanger our liberties or democratic processes (Eisenhower, 1961).

It is the contention here that we shall not be able to meet this danger until we recognise its basic nature and realise that what is required is a readjustment of our democratic institutions to make them capable of controlling the power of organisations.

INSIDIOUS CONTROL

The power exercised in new forms within and by big organisations rests on insidious control—control that is 'more dangerous than seems evident' (*Webster's New World Dictionary*, 1960) for democracy and that is not readily identifiable as power. It is deceptive, because it does not entail the experience of being oppressed by the arbitrary will of a despot and sometimes not even the need to comply with directives of superiors, but merely the internalised obligation to perform tasks in accordance with standards of workmanship. It is elusive, because there is usually nobody who can be held accountable for the actions of powerful organisations that may harm thousands or millions. It is unresponsive to democratic constraints, because it is often not recognised as power and has developed historically more recently than our basic democratic institutions, which are not constituted to protect people's freedom against it. The insidious character of the new forms of power is the source of their strength and of their danger.

The surmise that the controlling influence of giant organisations in modern society is insidious is not meant to imply that a sinister power elite conspires to subdue the populace. Nor is the suggestion that the persons responsible for influential decisions can frequently not be located intended to imply that bureaucratic buck-passing and the shielding of the real powers behind the throne by underlings keep decision-makers from public view. Quite the contrary, the position taken here is that to blame in such manner the diabolical plots of selfish men for the basic problems of power in contemporary society is completely mistaken. There are undoubtedly corrupt and power-hungry men in high places who conspire to dominate others at any price. But evil men are not what produces the fundamental problem of power in today's society in our view. What does is the structure of organisations and the systems of interrelated organisations in modern society, including the fact that these organisations command the loyalties of many decent men who often quite selflessly discharge their responsibilities in the interest of their organisation.

... [It] must be remembered that the giant organisations comprising the military-industrial complex we are discussing now are more than 100 times as large as employment security agencies. The considerations advanced here apply to the power that exists in organisations with the most benign objectives, for example, the Roman Catholic Church, which is more than 100 times as large as the corporate giants. The power wielded by a huge and complex organisation does not simply rest on the decisions of its top executive, regardless of how dominant a person he is, but it is the joint result of the judgments of many officials, past and present. Furthermore, there is a tight web of intricate connections among big corporations and between them and the dominant military or political organisations, with the stocks of most companies owned by others, interlocking directorates, consultation arrangements, and senior military officers and government officials being often recruited from private corporations or moving later to lucrative posts in corporations. The outlawed trust of companies is a horse and buggy by comparison with this powerful combination.

There are two reasons why the search for the men to be held accountable for the actions of powerful corporations is a chimera: first, as just noted, the complex structures of decision-making make it frequently impossible to locate the individuals in diverse places whose judgments were the ultimate source of a given action; second, when they can be located, they are usually specialised experts whose judgments rest on technical grounds of efficiency, which makes it almost meaningless to hold them responsible for any deleterious consequences that may result from their judgments. The pressure to make the most rational decision in terms of the interest of the organisation requires that the recommendations experts make on the basis of their technical competence govern as much as possible such decisions of organisations as whether to shut down a plant and lay off its workers; in which city to build a new plant; whether to back the British pound against inflation or not; or in which company's stock to invest funds.

Decisions like these have far reaching implications for the lives of people, and sometimes they have deleterious consequences for society. But if experts have reached their recommendations on the basis of technical judgments, they cannot be censored for having arrived at these conclusions, because there is no animus in them, technical criteria govern them, and other experts would have reached the same conclusions. Whereas not all administrative decisions are based on purely technical grounds and exclude all political considerations, it is in the interest of organisations to make most decisions largely on these grounds.[2] In as much as experts judge issues in terms of universal criteria of rationality and efficiency, they cannot be blamed for the conclusions they reach, even though these conclusions may lead to actions of powerful organisations that are contrary to the interest of most people. We must stop looking for villains to blame for the ills of modern society. But as a democratic nation, we must at the same time protect the interest of the commonweal against the actions of powerful organisations and their combinations by finding ways to regulate these formal structures themselves without worrying which particular individuals in them to hold responsible.

Selective recruitment and allocation of personnel resources as mechanisms of internal control in organisations also pose a problem for a democratic society. The employees in an organisation benefit from the greater freedom they have if management resorts little to control through a chain of command or detailed rules and relies primarily on this kind of control through gate-keeping, that is, determining how

[2] Although Weber has been justly criticised for failing to make the analytical distinction between the authority based on administrative office and that based on professional competence . . . and one of us (Blau) has previously joined in this criticism, he foresaw correctly that the merger of the two kinds of authority is what makes the modern administrative organisation such an efficient tool for power.

large a personnel complement to recruit for each of the various responsibilities and the qualifications required, and then letting those hired largely work at their own discretion. Surely, these are the organisations in which most of us like to work. But the advantages the insiders gain entail some cost, and those who are kept out pay the cost, simply by being kept out of these preferable places of employment. If a management mistreats its own workers in some ways, they may organise themselves and jointly force management to make concessions, as the union movement illustrates. But if the persons who suffer from the treatment of management remain outside the organisation, they have no such recourse. It would appear to be the responsibility of a democratic society to protect these outsiders. Indeed, laws prohibiting discrimination in employment against ethnic minorities do precisely that in one area.

These speculations are not entirely unrelated to the inquiry into organisations that has been presented. A main theme emphasised throughout the book has been that the formal structure of organisations exhibits regularities of its own. Although organisations are made up of people, of course, and what happens in them is the result of decisions of human beings, regularities are observable in their structure that seem to be independent of the personalities and psychological dispositions of individual members. [. . .]

. . . [This] is supported by the very fact that a large portion of the variance in structural characteristics could be accounted for by organisational antecedents without taking into account differences between individuals at all. Hence, a common theme of the sociological analysis . . . and the political speculations in the last few pages is, in short, that organisations are not people.

Democratic institutions are established to maintain the sovereignty and protect the liberty of people against encroachment by other people and particularly by the institutionalised structures other people have built. In the eighteenth century, the main threat to popular sovereignty and individual freedom were tyrannical governments (except for slavery, which was essentially ignored), and the democratic institutions Jefferson and the other fathers of the American Revolution developed were primarily designed to deal with this threat. These men could not have anticipated the threat to human freedom in the twentieth century created by the military-industrial complex, by giant corporations with millions of dollars at their disposal and a military establishment that devours many billions every year. Instead of adapting democratic institutions to this growing threat, we have perverted them and used the very provisions intended to protect people against domination by powerful impersonal structures to protect these structures against people, through legal fictions like the one that corporations are persons.

Marx and his followers have criticised all along the exploitation of people by capitalistic enterprises, imperialist armies, and government bureaucracies. Though true enough, what needs to be added is that economic exploitation is not the only issue, and neither is it the main one in technologically advanced countries near the end of the twentieth century. The oppression of Manchester workers by sweatshop owners and that of Russian soldiers by the tsarist army were blatant. Nowadays the control exercised by organisations is generally more insidious, but regardless of how subtle and easy to take these indirect controls are and how little economic exploitation they involve, the domination of society by combines of huge organisations is a threat to democracy.

Unless we take seriously the simple fact that organisations are not people, we as citizens shall not be able to meet this threat to democracy, and we as sociologists shall not be able to meet the main challenge our discipline poses. To put it another way: in our sociological analysis as well as our political thinking, it is time that we 'push men finally out', to place proper emphasis on the study of social structure in sociology, and to recognise the power of organisations as the main threat to liberty in modern society. The enemy is not an exploitative capitalist or an imperialist general or a narrow-minded bureaucrat. It is no man. It is the efficient structure of modern organisations, which enables the giant ones and their combinations to dominate our lives, our fortunes, and our honour. To restore the liberty of men, we must free them from the domination of powerful organisations, just as eighteenth-century men needed to be freed from domination by tyrannical governments. To do so requires that we stop pretending that organisations are people and protecting them as if they were people. It also requires that we stop looking for villains on whom to place blame and begin to realise that a democratic society is entitled to prevent organisations from engaging in actions that are harmful to the commonweal whether the men who decide on such action are evil or well-intentioned. Their intentions are irrelevant: what is important is to reassert the sovereignty of the people over organisations by instituting democratic restraints on these organisations.

REFERENCES

EISENHOWER, DWIGHT D. Farewell Address to the Nation, 17 January 1961.
FRIEDRICH, CARL J. (1958) *Authority* (Nomos I), Harvard University Press.
GOULDNER, ALVIN W. (1954) *Patterns of Industrial Bureaucracy*, New York,
The Free Press of Glencoe.

HOMANS, GEORGE C. (1964) 'Bringing men back in', *American Sociological Review*, **29**, pp. 809–18.

LENSKI, GERHARD (1966) *Power and Privilege: A Theory of Social Stratification*, McGraw-Hill.

PARSONS, TALCOTT (1937) *The Structure of Social Action*, McGraw-Hill.

WEBER, MAX (1946), *Essays in Sociology*, New York, Oxford University Press.

WEBER, MAX (1947) *The Theory of Social and Economic Organization*, New York, Oxford University Press.

2

Charles J. McMillan Corporations without
citizenship: the emergence
of multinational enterprise

An original article prepared for this volume.

Modern industrial economies have long been familiar with very large
corporations, high market concentration, and very powerful business
interests. What is not so familiar is the extension of the corporate network across political boundaries, so that the power of the corporate
boardroom extends far beyond the citizenship of the legal charter. In a
world accustomed to the computer, satellite television, credit cards and
jet travel, i.e. the instant communications of McLuhan's global village,
a new organisational form emerges, the multinational corporation.
Larger in sales than the gross national product of many countries,
controlling more resources than most governments, multinational
corporations are a very new institution, 'islands of conscious power in
an ocean of unconscious cooperation', to borrow Dennis Robertson's
apt phrase (Robertson, 1956).

The sociology of organisations has not caught up with the newspapers and the consumer movement in recognising the scope and
power of the multinational corporation, yet it has been praised and
damned alike, praised as the harbinger of a new economic order and
business statesmanship in the aftermath of the cold war, damned as
the newest form of industrial imperialism and unchecked power. The
multinational firm has also been viewed largely as an American phenomenon, a byproduct of the first trillion dollar economy and good
management practice.

Despite the paucity of analysis provided by sociology, considerable
attention has been given to the multinational firm by students of

economics and business administration, although the emphasis of each discipline has been clearly different.[1] In economics, the central themes have involved such well developed lines of thought as international trade, international capital flows and technology transfers, and the resulting implications for the division of the international market. In business administration, the central themes have focused on the international division of the firm, in the context of organisational structure and strategic choice, resulting from changing market conditions and technology. It is this latter approach which forms the basis of the present analysis. This paper has four aims: (1) to demonstrate the emergence of multinational corporations on an international scale; (2) to identify the principal organisational features of the multinational firm; (3) to present a dynamic hypothesis for corporate growth in terms of the product cycle and the rationale for foreign investment; and (4) to discuss the decision-making framework surrounding the operations of multinational firms.

THE NON-AMERICAN CHALLENGE

One has only to check the daily newspapers to find the multinational corporation. Names like IBM, Ford, Esso, and Coca-Cola are household words in the four corners of the world, and appear on the editorial page as well as in the advertising columns and stock market reports. These are well-known American corporations, but they can also be seen on the billboards of Europe, South America, Africa and Asia. In his well-known book, *The American Challenge*, Servan-Schreiber (1968) presents his view of the economic trends: 'Fifteen years from now, it is quite possible that the world's third greatest industrial power, just after the United States and Russia, will not be Europe, but American industry in Europe.' What he describes, with considerable insight, is not just the magnitude of American investment in European industry, but the fact that this investment has two important characteristics. Firstly, the investment is concentrated in the technologically advanced sectors of the economy. Secondly, American investment involves equity capital, i.e. capital which involves ownership in the corporation (in contrast to portfolio or lending capital, which can be paid back) and therefore has decision-making power.

Although Servan-Schreiber's analysis is very dramatic, pointing as it does to American multinational firms dominating European industry, the perspective taken is basically narrow and myopic, in at least two

[1] See, for example, the articles in Brown (1970), Dunning (1972), Kindleberger (1970), and Paquet (1972).

basic points. First, American investment outside the United States is not new, although the amount of foreign investment has never before reached the current levels. As early as 1901, a British writer, Fred A. McKenzie, called attention to the American challenge:

> The most serious aspect of the American industrial invasion lies in the fact that these newcomers have acquired control of almost every new industry created during the past fifteen years. . . . What are the chief new features in London life? They are, I take it, the telephone, the portable camera, the phonograph, the electric street car, the automobile, the typewriter, passenger lifts in houses, and the multiplication of machine tools. In every one of these, save the petroleum automobile, the American maker is supreme; in several he is monopolist (p. 31).

The second point is more fundamental: the spread of multinational corporations is not just an American phenomenon alone but a worldwide pattern of economic development (Roche, 1969). A recent study presents data which suggests that what appears to Europeans as an American 'challenge' in Europe is in fact a challenge to American corporations in the United States market. On the one hand, there has been the growth of American firms in Europe, faster in fact than the growth of the European organisations. On the other hand, European corporations have increased their total production (at home and abroad) faster than the growth in total sales of American firms. As Hymer and Rowthorn (1971) note:

> To the short-sighted European firm, whose markets are mainly European, U.S. investment seems to be an aggressive move to dominate Europe. To the long-sighted American firm, on the other hand, this investment appears to be a desperate attempt to defend its existing world share and keep up with the dynamic Europeans (p. 72).

When one adds to this trend the overseas investment of such countries as Canada (which is host to more foreign investment than any other single country, but also has more money invested around the world, relative to population, than the United States), and Japan (which has the fastest growing economy in the world), the change in economic relations is truly an international phenomenon. This change is a fundamental one and has no historical precedent. In this respect, as Peter Drucker (1968) has noted, the whole world has become one economy. Drucker states that this evolving world economy requires an appropriate monetary and credit system to replace the present institutions which developed from World War II. In addition, what is needed is a producing and distributing institution which is not purely national in its operation and point of view.... An institution which has a genuine self-interest in the world economy, rather than any one of the individual national economies.... Such an institution we already have at hand. Its development during the last twenty years may well be the most significant event in the world economy, and the one that, in the long run, will bring the greatest benefits. This institution is the 'multinational corporation' (p. 84).

Some figures which give an index to the size and growth of multi-national firms are provided by a recent study published by the Canadian government (1972). This study indicates there are 300 multinational firms dominating the field of direct foreign investment, of which 100 are not American owned (e.g. Nestlé, Shell, Unilever). Non-American subsidiaries result in approximately $100 billion production in the United States market and $150 billion in other countries, while American subsidiaries account for $200 million in sales. The book value of American investment abroad increased from $7.5 billion in 1929 to $70.8 billion in 1969. Sixty-two of the largest 100 American corporations have each got production facilities in at least six foreign nations. Table 2.1 lists the extent of foreign investment by non-American corporations.

STRATEGIC CHOICE AND CORPORATE DEVELOPMENT

To list the magnitude of multinational corporations is one thing, to understand how they have emerged is quite another matter. Unfortunately, much of present economic analysis and organisation theory, with the emphasis on general equilibrium analysis and static models, fails to come to grips with the slow, evolutionary development of the modern multidivisional corporation, and the changing tools used by management to confront crisis and avert disaster (Brook and Remmers, 1970).

Recent contributions to business history have made significant contributions to this void, and it is these analyses which best explain the corporate development process.[2] As a general definition, the multinational firm can be viewed as 'a cluster of corporations of diverse nationality joined together by ties of common ownership and responsive to a common management strategy' (Vernon, 1968). In this 'business' definition, the emphasis is on the link between the separate operating units or subsidiaries and an overall, unified strategy. In this respect the multinational firm epitomises the large multidivisional federated structure of management theory. For example, Ford Motor Company, an

[2] See Chandler (1962), Neufield (1971), and Wilkins (1970).

TABLE 2.1. *The 200 largest non-American corporations by country* (the majority of which are multinational)

	No. of companies	Ranked 1–100	Ranked 101–200	Largest company	Sales ($000)	Rank
Argentina	2	0	2	Yacimientos Petroliferos	537,025	111
Australia	2	2	0	BHP	1,386,334	31
Austria	1	0	1	Voest	293,000	198
Belgium	3	2	1	Petrofina	888,440	63
Brazil	1	1	0	Petróleo Brasileiro	667,669	89
Britain	47	22	25	British Petroleum	3,260,160	3
Canada	12	4	8	Alcan Aluminium	1,000,341	48
France	21	15	6	Renault	1,733,061	19
Germany	28	17	11	Volkswagenwerk	2,925,000	5
India	1	0	1	Hindustan Steel	292,447	199
Italy	8	5	3	Montecatini Edison	2,315,680	8
Japan	45	18	27	Hitachi	2,281,728	10
Luxembourg	1	1	0	Arbed	997,000	49
Mexico	1	1	0	Pemex	883,629	65
Netherlands	5	2	3	Philips' Gloeilampen	2,685,277	6
Neth. Antilles	1	0	1	Schlumberger	409,085	146
Portugal	1	0	1	C.U.F. Group	298,909	196
S. Africa	2	1	1	De Beers Consol. Mines	600,310	100
Sweden	6	2	4	Volvo	747,080	76
Switzerland	8	5	3	Nestlé	1,938,715	15
Zambia	1	0	1	R.S.T. Group	360,332	167
Neth.–Britain	2	2	0	Royal/Dutch/Shell Group	9,215,772	1
Germany–Belg.	1	0	1	Agfa-Gevaert Group	371,200	162

Source: *Fortune*, 15 August 1969, p. 111.

American based multinational, has sixty separate operating units, of which forty are located outside the United States and account for 36 per cent of the company's 8 billion dollars total assets, invested in twenty-seven countries. More than 150,000 of the firms' 388,000 employees work outside the United States (Rose, 1968).

Neither Ford nor any of the other 500 multinationals in existence today evolved overnight; in fact, the historical evidence points to a very painful trial and error process, an evolution highlighted by tremendous personality conflict, plain stupidity, often huge financial losses, and in some cases, very good luck (Neufield, 1971).

One of the seminal studies of corporate development is the work of Alfred Chandler (1962), who has identified four phases of organisational transition:

> Four phases or chapters can be discerned in the history of the large American industrial enterprise: the initial expansion and accumulation of resources; the rationalization of the use of resources; the expansion into new markets and lines to help assure the continuing full use of resources; and finally the development of a new structure to make possible continuing effective mobilization of resources to meet both changing short-term market demands and long-term market trends (p. 385).

Chandler notes that it was the growing US population, the resulting new markets, and technological virtuosity which provided the impulse for corporate expansion.

> The prospect of a new market, or the threatened loss of a current one stimulated geographical expansion, vertical integration, and product diversification. Moreover, once a firm had accumulated large resources, the need to keep its men, money and materials steadily employed provided a constant stimulus to look for new markets by moving into new areas, by taking on new functions, or by developing new product lines (p. 15).

In his case study of four corporations (Dupont, General Motors, Standard Oil, and Sears Roebuck), Chandler develops his central theme: 'Strategic growth results from an awareness of the opportunities and needs—created by changing population, income and technology—to employ existing or expanding resources more profitably. A new strategy required a new or at least a refashioned structure if the enlarged enterprise was to be operated efficiently' (p. 15). A direct corollary of this theme is that organisation structure follows from strategic choice, and that the most complex kind of structure results from a constellation of several basic strategies. Organisational strategy can be defined as: 'the determination of the basic long term goals and objectives of an enterprise, and the adoption of courses of action and the allocation of resources necessary for carrying out these goals' (p. 13). In short, then, successful exploitation of strategic opportunities comes as a result of devising an organisational form which provided for top management the separation of strategic or long run decisions from the concentration on operational or day to day decisions.[3]

What was the consequence of not allowing this separation? According to Chandler:

> The failure to develop a new internal structure, like the failure to respond to new external opportunities and needs, was a consequence of overconcentration on operational activities by the executives responsible for the destiny of their enterprises, or from their inability, because of past training and education and present position, to develop an entrepreneurial outlook (p. 15).

In order to understand organisational structure, therefore, it becomes necessary to examine the factors which define strategic choice. For corporations, strategic choice involves defining the product-market mix, that is, the variety of products to be produced and sold, and the location and penetration of markets to be served. The range of options in the product-market mix defines the complexity of corporate structure, in terms of the number of operating units, the communications network, and the policy-making system. The evolutionary stages of this pattern are shown in Table 2.2.

What emerges from this discussion is a model of the multidivisional corporation, the early prototype of the multinational firm, which is highly structured, but streamlined to take maximum advantage of changing environmental conditions, such as access to cheap labour, raising capital in the cheapest markets, changing technology (including adoption of new product lines, but also assuring continuity after old products), tax allowances, etc. The critical development is the internal division of labour for decision-making. In the approach of policy analysis (Ansoff, 1965), large corporations display three categories of decisions: strategic,[4] which are directed towards the organisation-

---

[3] This notion parallels Gresham's Law of Planning: 'Daily routine drives out planning' (March and Simon, 1958, p. 185).

[4] The discussion of strategic and operating tasks given here closely parallels Selznick's (1957) analysis of organisation building and institutional leadership. He cites four tasks of leadership: (1) definition of mission and role, (2) institutional embodiment of purpose, (3) defence of institutional integrity, and (4) ordering of internal conflict.

TABLE 2.2. *A model of strategic choice and corporate development*

	STAGE 1	STAGE 2	STAGE 3	STAGE 4
STRATEGY PRODUCT-MARKET MIX	1. Simple product line related technology, single channel of distribution.	1. Single product line large scale production, product lines related by technology, one major market.	1. Diversification of product lines, new channels of distribution, accumulation of resources.	1. Complex range of products, sold in different markets, multiple channels of distribution.
ORGANISATIONAL STRUCTURE	1. Small firm, owner-manager, single unit firm, simple communications (this is surrogate entrepreneur model of economic theory). 2. Informal control system.	1. Team management (not professional) single operating unit. 2. Increased use of rules for task coordination.	1. Development of operating units by geography, structure like Stage I or II. 2. Centralised management to integrate operating units and adjudicate conflict at lower levels.	1. Multidivisional product structure, headed by functional managers. 2. Divisions run as a separate profit centre with highly elaborate communications system, often used to train and test executives. 3. Highly centralised policy unit at headquarters, concentration of finance, planning, and research and development.

environment nexus (product-market mix); operating, which involve the implementation of strategic decisions by way of production and scheduling; and administrative, which involve coordinating mechanisms to relate long run strategy and short term operations, especially in terms of acquiring and allocating resources, including personnel, finance, and equipment. Within the administrative structure the most important device is the budget,[5] which represents a control feature to check performance against agreed criteria and a planning tool to specify feasible programmes. In most respects, the budget specifies the degree of freedom or autonomy and the terms granted the subsidiary by central headquarters. It is in this sense that the multidivisional structure is said to be 'decentralised', since it allows many features of an artificial market or price system within the firm. This artificial pricing system, allowing management to administer transactions among divisions, has a variety of applications, including transfer pricing, management licensing, and technology fees, all of which provide a 'negotiated internal environment' for the firm.[6]

Such a web of decision-making processes, when located within one country, subject to a common tax structure and legal system, and existing in a single political culture, does function with minimal strategic conflict and crises of legitimacy, as Chandler's study indicates. In the real world of the multinational, there are a number of national jurisdictions, each with its own political, legal and cultural environment. The right to initiate and to innovate therefore become important policy weapons, for they effectively determine the ability of the firm to adapt to a local jurisdiction. Yet the type of decisions which are delegated to the subsidiary and those which are centralised at headquarters is a matter left to the parent company and therefore causes a shift in the locus of decision-making. As a Canadian government task force noted: 'Foreign direct investment is not an economic phenomenon alone. It is a political phenomenon. Foreign control means the potential shift outside the country of the locus of some types of decision making' (Watkins *et al.*, 1968, p. 51).

The potential conflicts of interests between the subsidiary and parent

---

[5] The budget is viewed here as a constitution of negotiated rules and operating procedures: see Cyert and March (1963), especially pp. 270–9. Elsewhere they note, 'Although budgets can be flexible, they cannot help but result in the specification of a framework within which the firm will operate, evaluate its success, and alter its program' (p. 111).

[6] See Schulman (1967), and Thomas (1971) for a discussion of the basic issues, and the references cited for more technical treatment of transfer pricing.

company, and of the national interest of each raise a variety of questions, two of which are crucial to the present analysis. Why do multinational firms become multinational, since they could, alternatively, export their products from the domestic market? Secondly, why do multinational firms exist in some industries and not in others: for example, computers but not machine tools, electronic equipment but not steel? In part, at least, the answer to these questions lies in the role which technology and institutional innovation play in the structure of multinational enterprise.

INNOVATION AND THE PRODUCT-CYCLE

In the same way that orthodox economists and organisation theorists regard the division of labour in the firm from different perspectives, so also do they part company on the analysis of innovation and change. Economic theory, building on a model of the surrogate entrepreneur (depicted in Stage I of Table 2.2), acting on the premises of rational choice, does not make any formal distinction between the continuation of ongoing programmes of actions (e.g. existing product lines) and the establishment of new programmes (March and Simon, 1958). In multinational enterprise, as in the large multidivisional firm of the domestic economy, the process of innovation, of changing the organisation's technology, is institutionalised into the decision-making structure of the firm, and innovation in turn relates to the growth pattern of the firm.

Recent studies provide very strong evidence that multinational enterprises engage in direct foreign investment in high technology industries. The meaning of high technology refers to the knowledge factor in producing a particular product, a technology which may be discovered and developed or purchased by the organisation. Vast sums of money are spent by multinational firms in research and development departments as a means of searching for distinctive products. For example, a recent study shows that between 1958 and 1964, the four American industries (computers, instruments, electronics, chemicals) which spent the most money on research and development also invested two and a half times the amount on new plant and equipment in Europe as fourteen other industries (Gruber *et al.*, 1967).

The relationship between technology and growth was first given prominent theoretical formulation by the Austrian economist, Joseph Schumpeter (1950). For Schumpeter, innovation is defined as change: change in product, technology, or market, and the instrument of change is the entrepreneur. The process of introducing change in the organisation is creative destruction:

In capitalism, reality, as distinguished from its textbook picture, it is not (pure) competition which counts, but the competition from the new commodity, the new technology, the new source of supply, the the new type of organisation—competition which commands a decisive cost or quality advantage and which strikes not at the margins of the profits and the outputs of the existing firms but at their foundations and their very lives (p. 84).

What Schumpeter describes is a process whereby once a new technology is discovered, it carries a distinctive entrepreneurial advantage (at least temporarily) and thus it commands certain monopoly price features, since no competitive product exists. In the multinational enterprise, research and development expenditure is directed towards such technology, and once discovered, can be exploited in the home market, or among existing customers. The particular advantage that knowledge technology creates is that once it has brought financial returns in the home market greater than the discovery costs, it may be applied to new markets without incurring any new sunk costs (Johnson, 1970).

More specifically, consider the case of a large multidivisional firm located, say, in the United States. It has expended a very large sum of money in research and development, and over time gets rewarded with the discovery of new technology. The firm can then exploit this technology by introducing a product in the home market, the United States. The firm normally undertakes market research studies, develops an advertising campaign, and gains experience with customer response. In short, the activities of the firm shift from the entrepreneurial functions to managerial functions, from tasks which originate as being unique to tasks which become essential but recurrent. In this way the firm develops 'a distinctive competence', an experience of undertaking tasks committed to an institutional goal (Selznick, 1957).

From the perspective of the competitive position of this firm, there are two critical advantages. The first factor is the availability of the existing technology, developed for the home market. The second competitive advantage is an organisational one, the entrepreneurial experience of innovation in the home market which, with relatively easy transferability of skills, can be applied to entry into a new market. The combination of these two factors, technology transfer and entrepreneurial experience, amount to what is called, in the language of business administration, synergy. Synergy in fact is a measure of joint effects, or in more common language, the $2+2=5$ theorem. It demonstrates that for complex organisations such as multinational firms, the combination of two or more products and/or two or more markets, can create advantages greater than the sum of the parts. As Ansoff (1965) notes, 'in synergy, joint effects are measured between two product-markets: in strength and weakness evaluation, the firm's competences are rated relative to some desired performance level. The former contributes to the decision to make a new entry: the latter, to the decision to exploit certain strengths or to remedy certain deficiencies within the firm' (p. 76).

The analytical insights of the synergy can be shown by a simple growth diagram where products and markets are cross-tabulated to indicate the product-market mix or organisation strategy. The firm may move from the stage of market penetration, i.e. selling to as many customers as possible a single product, to product development (adding a new product to existing customers), or selling to customers in a different market the same product. These stages represent growth by expansion. The fourth stage represents a significant change for the organisation since diversification requires knowledge about markets and product lines which are not directly related.

Market \ Product	Present	New
Present	MARKET PENETRATION	PRODUCT DEVELOPMENT
New	MARKET DEVELOPMENT	DIVERSIFICATION

FIG. 2.1. *Product-market strategy.*

What is really involved here is an organisational process of strategic choice, choice first between product concentration or market concentration and then diversification. Over a period of time markets become saturated and products age and lose their competitiveness. The innovative advantage which confers monopolistic privilege loses out to competition, and slowdown and decline of sales: a sequence of introduction, spread, maturation, and senescence—in short, the product life-cycle (Levitt, 1965).

The shift in the product life-cycle requires an organisational response, if the firm wishes to grow or even to survive. As markets extend by geographical dispersion, the organisational structure itself becomes changed, giving rise to separate quasi-independent divisions headed by divisional managers, each with flexibility to develop a particular market segment, as discussed earlier, and shown in Table 2.2. But in the multi-national firm, the quasi-independent operating unit is in fact a national subsidiary, tied to headquarters by the technology and capital of the parent firm.

Product \\ Market	Present	New
Domestic	(1) Saturation	(3) Diversification
Foreign	(2) Export	(4) Direct Investment

FIG. 2.2. *Market strategy and foreign investment.*

Applying the innovation product-cycle model to the multinational firm, the sequence of growth can be traced according to the stages of Fig. 2.2. First, a firm operating within a country develops a unique product and ultimately reaches market saturation of the domestic outlet. If the product technology remains competitive (hasn't been perfected or copied by competitors in the home market or overseas market), the firm can then enter a new foreign market by export. Concurrently, this firm, given the strategic outlook for entrepreneurial changes, will intro-duce a new product in its home market to take up the slack caused by market saturation of the first product. By the strategy of diversification, the firm protects itself in the domestic market and at the same time provides an aggressive strategy of entry into the foreign market by export. The final stage of development is the foreign investment decision.

In fact, the model outlined here has been simplified for explication. Moreover, the process of market saturation in the home market and technological innovation do not in themselves explain why firms establish production facilities in the foreign market, i.e. direct invest-ment. It is to this question the next section is directed.

STRATEGIC CHOICE AND DIRECT INVESTMENT

The foregoing analysis of the structural features of corporate development, and of the product cycle and technological innovation, must now be linked to the critical issue: why do multinational firms cross the threshold of entry to new markets by export, to entry to new markets by production and direct investment? The exigencies of foreign investment involve considerable risk, and not every entry has proved profitable. Yet corporations do extend their geographical boundaries of operations, even where such expansion involves political and cultural entanglements in the foreign market.

The answer to this question is by no means immediately obvious, and simple explanations such as the pursuit of profits hardly add much enlightenment to the analysis. On the surface, it would appear that by entering new markets by direct investment, corporations are actually deliberately increasing the amount of uncertainty and turbulence they face in the environment. To increase the amount of uncertainty in this way is a tendency which appears to contradict much of the current view of organisations as attempting to avoid uncertainty and risk, and to seek a 'negotiated environment' (Cyert and March, 1963). The key to understanding this issue lies in the logic of organisation and technology discussed earlier. Multinational firms are multiplant federated organisations which are structured to take advantage of a number of scarce commodities—labour, capital, managerial skill and experience, technology, and access to customers—and huge size provides economies of scale and synergy to exploit these advantages. Moreover, the corporate structure is designed expressly to do so.

The foreign investment decision is a logical outcome of domestic expansion arising from product innovation, and market saturation. As competition increases in the home market, and as profit margins decline as a result, corporations seek to exploit the monopoly gains first accrued in the home market in new markets where a competitive product does not exist. As Kindleberger (1969) notes: 'Monopoly, then, is one basis of direct investment and of international growth of the national corporation.' In some cases, monopoly privileges can be achieved without foreign investment, but by export alone. However, monopolies, except perhaps those established by government edict, do not exist in a vacuum, and monopoly profits, like many prized possessions, soon attract suitors.

In a dynamic world, therefore, direct investment often occurs not necessarily, or solely, from the aggressive strategies of growth, but instead, from a defensive posture intended to forestall entry by competitors to a captive market. In other words, direct investment can occur from the attempt, real or potential, of other corporations which threaten to enter the captive market and by use of size, technology, or even initial entry, gain comparative advantage over any rival firm. Direct investment provides a presence of the multinational firm in the host market which export alone does not provide, namely, that once established, withdrawal is very costly, both for the firm, but also for the host country. From the perspective of uncertainty and predictability, multinational firms in oligopolistic markets must weigh the risk of staying put in existing markets, even when they are very profitable, as against the risk of entering new markets not necessarily as profitable, but as a means of forestalling competition or the erection of possible barriers to future entry (Caves, 1971).

This motivation for direct investment demonstrates a very subtle but critical issue in the analysis of foreign investment and the multinational. The subtlety rests in the fact that it is the barrier to trade through export, not the removal of barriers, which lies at the heart of the multi-national corporation. As noted, there are the obstacles presented by the possible location of one or more multinationals in a foreign market, to the competitive detriment of any rival multinational, which motivate entry by direct investment of additional firms. A further factor, how-ever, is the action of host governments, most notably in the case of tariff barriers, but also in the case of differential monetary and fiscal policies, and a battery of industrial policies (e.g. tax advantages, subsidies to investment, etc.) which can provide a motivation for multinational firms to exploit local opportunities by entry into the host market. In other words, in a world of very high factor mobility, multinational firms are capable of moving from one jurisdiction to another, and if economies of scale are great enough, as they usually are, they can exploit the differ-entials created by national policy to their own profitable advantage.

An additional consideration in discussing the emergence of multi-national corporations generally concerns the constellation of organisa-tions to which any corporation is committed in established markets. These organisations include what has been termed the 'organisational set' (Evan, 1966), i.e. a variety of social actors providing sources of inputs and channels for outputs. Once one important corporation makes the breakthrough to overseas investment, other organisations follow. These organisations range from suppliers, advertising agencies, bankers and consultants, to hotels, food and entertainment organisations, and eventually, perhaps, labour unions, all of which are involved in the evolutionary stages of corporate development from domestic operations to the multinational arena. In other words, overseas investment by the larger corporations has a spillover effect on secondary organisations (Hollander, 1971).

SUMMARY AND DISCUSSION

To paint a picture of the multinational firm with a few brush strokes is very difficult and hazardous; its many facets cover a broad landscape, and while the essential features have been discussed here, much has been left out. This is an important caveat, for it might be tempting to conclude that the decision-making process in the multinational firm represents the penultimate form of organisational rationality, a model of computer-like exactness and precision. After all, what other type of organisation has at its disposal such immense resources, a huge labour force of highly educated and company trained professionals, and a worldwide network of contacts that can rival the best on any diplomatic corps?

Indeed, critics of the multinational firm can see in its operations the exploitation of undeveloped countries, the ransom of resource-rich developed economies, tax evasion and the corporate ripoff; in short, the strong arm of imperialism and hinterland dependence for the corporate metropolis. Or is the multinational firm a giant sprawling octopus, capable of extending its tentacles into new markets while protecting existing ones, owing loyalty neither to a flag nor any national interest, all in the pursuit of global profits and growth? From a political and legal perspective, it seems difficult to avoid the conclusion that both saints and sinners occupy the multinational arena, but it is even more striking that governments, labour unions, and consumer movements seem singularly hesitant to catch up with current economic realities and the need to provide countervailing power to check the multinational. If it is true that the multinational firm has been able to mobilise labour, management skills, technology and capital wherever they may be found, to produce and sell commodities at an unparalleled level of output and sophistication, it happens to be also true that much of the third world and the Communist bloc now want a piece of the action. However repugnant it may appear to some ideological purists, the underdeveloped nations and the East bloc states have opened their doors to the multinational firm for the goods, technology and organisational knowledge only it can provide.

As noted earlier, organisational sociologists have not been concerned with the study of the multinational enterprise. Given the present stage of the organisational field, where would the multinational firm be fitted? In the human relations school? With systems theory? From an analytical perspective neither of these 'schools' of thought come remotely at the real dimensions of this giant organisation, especially the structure of power and technology which underlie organisational growth; and the means of preserving control once it is achieved. As for the school of thought which offers bureaucracy with a human face, or Beyond Bureaucracy, this view, much like the Marxian notion of the withering away of the state, seems curiously out of touch. The multinational firm is bureaucracy with a vengeance, large, hierarchical, and very centralised.

Perhaps the only perspective in organisational sociology which comes to grips with the reality of the multinational firm as organisation is the institutional school, often associated with the works of Philip Selznick. To this perspective, however, must be linked the insights of industrial economists, with well developed analyses of market structure and organisational environment which far surpass anything in the sociological literature.

The concept of changing markets has been emphasised in the corporate development of the multinational firm, but to it should be added Innis's, and later McLuhan's, insights on communications as a means of integrating separate operating units located in geographically dispersed markets. It is sometimes suggested that the multidivisional corporation has been 'decentralised', a word which is as misleading as any in the organisational field. The division of labour within the giant firm is both horizontal and vertical, horizontal in terms of operating divisions, vertical in terms of strategic and operating decisions and the tasks that accompany them. In a world of changing markets, rapid innovation and the technology of instant communications, corporate management can carry the principle of divide and rule to a very refined precision. Furthermore, the strategy of creating within each division dependencies on headquarters for resources and information, and of developing reciprocal interdependence among the subunits for inputs and outputs, assures top management control even while allowing for delegated responsibility.[7]

But the multinational firm is not an omnipotent actor, and sometimes makes costly mistakes. Moreover, it is not without defensive weaknesses, as when the central control structure is challenged by govern-

---

[7] As an executive observed: 'When you have a joint venture in Turkey, with engines from Germany, chassis from the US, together with a local source of components, you just have to be centralized. You'd probably have to call us pretty well centralized as far as design, product development, purchasing, and financing are concerned ... from an operations standpoint we don't attempt to run the subsidiaries in day to day operations' (Rose, 1968, p. 104.)

ments insisting on joint ventures within their jurisdiction, i.e. 50 per cent ownership. An even more difficult dilemma is created when the trade obstacles which provided the impetus to entry into new markets in the first place, such as building plants in each nation of the European Common Market, get torn down and the company suddenly has too many plants in too many locations.

However, when innovation and change are institutionalised, as in the multinational firm, a mistake is a lesson learned, and such lessons can provide future dividends beyond the costs of tuition. It is this ability to learn, to adapt, and to avoid direct confrontation which makes the multinational firm such a successful institution, but also such a tantalising subject of analysis. Indeed, as nationalist sentiments increase public awareness of the benefits and costs of the multinational corporate presence, this corporate flexibility can reach surprising dimensions: equity participation by locals, recruitment of local managers and directors, listing on the local stock exchange, government partnerships, etc. (Macmillan, 1973).

The trend of multinational corporate development is pretty clear, although the full implications are less visible at this stage. At the moment multinationals are at the forefront of global economic integration of high technology industries, and to adopt an organisational perspective from within one political jurisdiction is to miss the organic whole. For those who view the multinational trend as a positive shift for world welfare, the balance of economic forces has been on their side. For those who take up a different perspective, who see in the nation state something which must be preserved, who see in the centralised bureaucracy a global hierarchy of power stratified in favour of the developed countries, the challenge is enormous indeed.

REFERENCES

ANSOFF, H. IGOR (1965) *Corporate Strategy*, McGraw-Hill.

BROOKE, MICHAEL Z., and REMMERS, H. LEE (1970) *The Strategy of Multinational Enterprise*, Longman.

BROWN, COURTNEY C., ed. (1970) *World Business*, New York, Macmillan.

CAVES, RICHARD E. (1970) 'International corporations: the industrial economics of foreign investment', *Economica*, **38**, 1–27.

CHANDLER, ALFRED (1962) *Strategy and Structure*, Cambridge, Mass., M.I.T. Press.

CYERT, RICHARD M. and JAMES G. MARCH (1963) *A Behavioural Theory of the Firm*, Prentice-Hall.

DRUCKER, PETER F. (1968) *The Age of Discontinuity*, Harper & Row.

DUNNING, JOHN H., ed. (1972) *International Investment*, Penguin Books.

EVAN, WILLIAM (1966) 'The organization set: towards a theory of interorganizational relations', in J. D. Thompson, ed., *Approaches to Organizational Design*, University of Pittsburg Press.

Foreign Direct Investment in Canada (1972) Ottawa, Information Canada.

GRUBER, W. *et al.* (1967) 'The R & D factor in international trade and international investment of United States Industries', *Journal of Political Economy*, **75**, 20–37.

HOLLANDER, STANLEY (1971) 'The internationalization of contractual marketing systems', in Donald N. Thompson, ed., *Contractual Marketing Systems*, D. C. Heath.

HYMER, STEPHEN, and ROBERT ROWTHORN (1970) 'Multinational corporations and international oligopoly: the non-American challenge', in Kindleberger (1970) pp. 57–91.

JOHNSON, HARRY G. (1970) 'The efficiency and welfare implications of the international corporations', in Kindleberger (1970) pp. 35–56.

KINDLEBERGER, CHARLES P., ed. (1969) *American Business Abroad*, Yale University Press.

KINDLEBERGER, CHARLES P., ed. (1970) *The International Corporation*, Cambridge, Mass., M.I.T. Press.

LEVITT, T. (1965) 'Exploit the product-life cycle', *Harvard Business Review*, **43**, no. 6, 81–94.

MARCH, JAMES G., and SIMON, HERBERT A. (1958) *Organizations*, Wiley.

MACKENZIE, FRED A. (1901) *The American Invaders*, New York.

MCMILLAN, CHARLES J. (1973) 'Public policy and the multinational corporation', Bradford Management Centre, Working Paper.

NEUFIELD, E. P. (1971) *The Global Corporation*, University of Toronto Press.

PAQUET, GILLES, ed. (1972) *The Multinational Firm and the Nation State*, Collier-Macmillan.

ROBERTSON, DENNIS H. (1956) *Economic Commentaries*, Staples Press.

ROCHE, JOHN B. (1969) '"The American challenge" challenged', *Harvard Business Review*, **47**, no. 5, 45–57.

ROSE, SANFORD (1968) 'The rewarding strategies of multinationalism', *Fortune*, **78**, no. 4.

SCHUMPETER, JOSEPH A. (1950) *Capitalism, Socialism, and Democracy*, 3rd edn, Harper & Row.

SELZNICK, PHILIP (1957) *Leadership in Administration*, Row Peterson.

SERVAN-SCHREIBER, JEAN JACQUES (1968) *The American Challenge*, New York, Atheneum.

SCHULMAN, JAMES (1967) 'When the price is wrong—by design', *Columbia Journal of World Business*, **2**, 69–76.

THOMAS, ARTHUR L. (1971) 'Transfer prices of the multinational firm: when will they be arbitrary?', *Abacus*, **7**, no. 1, 40–53.

VERNON, RAYMOND (1968) 'Economic sovereignty at bay', *Foreign Affairs*, **47**, 110–22.

WATKINS, MEL, *et al.* (1968) *Foreign Ownership and the Structure of Canadian Industry*, Ottawa, Queen's Printer.

WILKINS, MIRA (1970) *The Emergence of Multinational Enterprise*, Harvard University Press.

SECTION 2

Structure and system— basic concepts and theories

After cataloguing the ways in which bureaucracies threaten the established liberties of democratic societies Blau and Schoenherr write, in Section 1 of this Reader:

> Unless we take seriously the simple fact that organisations are not people, we as citizens shall not be able to meet this threat to democracy, and we as sociologists shall not be able to meet the main challenge our discipline poses. To put it another way: in our socio-logical analysis as well as our political thinking, it is time that we 'push men finally out', to place proper emphasis on the study of social structure in sociology, and to recognize the power of organiza-tions as the main threat to liberty in modern society.

It appears then that these authors are suggesting that to adopt an interactionist perspective on organisations, or one that focuses on the day-to-day activities and negotiations of members of organisations (instead of the overall patterned regularities of organisational division of labour) is irresponsibly to abdicate from concern about the most important aspects of organisational activity: their increasing dominance over all areas of political, social, economic, military and educational matters, both at home and abroad. And, as has been noted, these authors employ the concept of organisational structure to explore the development of what they consider to be new and insidious forms of organisational control.

But what is organisational structure? How is it to be described or measured? And what determines inter-organisational variations in structure? These questions, which typically arise in discussions about the utility of the concept are considered by the writers in this section. The fact that they might to some extent be seen to undermine confidence in the concept should not be taken to imply that the sorts of questions considered by Blau and Schoenherr are in any way rejected or dismissed. Rather, it is held that it is first necessary to consider critically one's conceptual and theoretical tools. It is intersting, as the contributions by Child (6) and Argyris (5) suggest, that it is possible to argue that some approaches to the study of organisational structure have pushed men so completely out of the organisation that its structure— the way in which activities, responsibilities and authorities are distributed and coordinated—is seen as an inevitable outcome of the fulfilment of an inexorable organisational logic, and the responsibility of no one. If men are pushed out, who takes responsibility for the consequences of organisational activity—with respect to organisational members, clients or customers?

The article by Pugh and Hickson (3) represents a refreshingly thorough and systematic attempt to operationalise the concept organisational structure. Their conclusions, and the methodology they employed have proved to be extremely influential. But the problem remains, as Argyris notes: it's not just *how* you measure, it's *what* you measure that matters, and when Turner in his article (4) refers to, and emphasises the importance of 'the multiplicity of levels of symbolic interpretations of the industrial environment which appear as each individual attempts to attribute meaning to his situation', he is warning us that to attend only to the way in which senior members know the organisation can be misleading. It will be seen that Argyris, in his article, addresses this same issue with respect to Blau's work.

Argyris criticises Blau for taking too seriously the descriptions and accounts of organisational structure as supplied by senior members of management. This results, Argyris claims, in a confusion of intention and reality, and can lead to a distressing situation whereby any observed or imputed discrepancy between the way things are and the way things 'should' be (as defined by senior members of the organisation) is regarded as deviance and explained through persons' irrationality, or their attachment to some subcultural group. Although starting from a different view of organisations both Argyris and Child focus on the processes whereby organisational structure is constructed. Argyris notes, in passing, that Blau seems to explain the correlations he discovered in terms of an implicit conception of the nature of man, in terms of which such correlations are necessary. For otherwise, why should they exist? Argyris suggests that one explanation could be that organisational structure is not something that sociologists should merely accept as the outcome of vague social forces, but as the planned and deliberate consequence of decisions and choices of senior organisational personnel. Thus what is really being studied is how a certain view of the 'proper' organisational structure is actually applied (or rather how it is seen to have been applied by top management).

The same point is made in a more thorough way by Child who, after considering the variety of factors that have been seen to determine organisational structure (and which could thus be used to argue for the inevitable necessity of any organisational property—say a minute and repetitive organisation and division of work on an assembly line), suggests that organisational structure is an outcome of 'choice by whoever have the power to direct the organisation. We shall argue that this "strategic choice" extends to the context within which the organisation is operating, to the standards of performance against which the pressure of economic constraints has to be evaluated, and to the design of the organization's structure.' Although not denying the existence and importance of constraints Child directs attention to the area of choice that remains either within such constraints, or in evaluating them. It could also legitimately be inferred from Child's article that organisational structure is a sort of story, an account generated by top management, to explain, justify and realise their priorities and aspirations, and their knowledge of organisations and society. In short, as a type of ideology.[1]

Both Child and Argyris then argue that a radical critique of organisations, or an approach that considers organisation in terms of their

---

[1] This is not to suggest that Child himself follows this line, but it could be argued that by pointing to the ways in which organisational structure (as seen and described by senior managers, that is, 'formal' structure) is a product of managers' decisions and choices based upon what they see as their priorities and goals, Child is hinting at a sense of organisational structure that is developed by Bittner in his contribution in Section 3 (reading 17). Bittner considers organisational structure in terms of how this concept is *used* by organisational members, in routine and methodical ways, for 'information, direction, justification, and so on'.

impact on members and on society, should not start by accepting organisational structure (which is the central focus of such a critique) as an outcome of some sort of organisational imperative, but as itself a political phenomenon, having to do with interests, values and the strategies of power. In short a radical approach to organisational structure itself (or the implicit views of man underlying it) is demanded.

It has long been argued that organisations typically employ two forms of control, one of which relies on tightly defined rules and prescriptions, the other on the discretion of the trained, expert employee. It has been claimed that these two forms are observable and relate to the organisation's technology, personnel, markets and so on. (Reading 1, by Blau and Schoenherr, is relevant to this distinction.) Interest in structural forms of organisational control is also displayed in Hickson's article (7) on organisation theory which nicely summarises a great deal of work in the area of organisational typologies. Hickson argues that this work tends to reveal a concern for the two types of control mentioned above. He writes that there is evident a preoccupation with 'the specificity (or precision) of role prescription and its obverse, the range of legitimate discretion'.

The article by Hall (8) considers the claimed dichotomy between professional, occupational control and bureaucratic, procedural forms with reference to an empirical study of professionalisation and bureaucratisation. Notable for its rigorous and concise statement of this perennial distinction, it also leads to some considerable revision of the established, rather simplistic view. Hall argues that forms of organisational control are a result of adjustment between the existing organisational procedures and the expectations and demands introduced by professionals who 'import standards into the organization to which the organization must adjust'. Once again organisational structure is viewed as a result of negotiations and compromises between powerful groups, a view that is more fully developed in later readings (for example, by Strauss, reading 20).

Throughout this and later sections of the Reader a suggestion of conflict and contradiction between what may be called the interactionist and systems view may be apparent. The article by Buckley (9) presents an impressive attempt to save the systems concept from some of the attacks that have been made on it by arguing for its ability to include the sorts of approach and findings of two classical interactionist studies of organisation, one of which, that by Strauss, is excerpted in this Reader. Buckley does this by arguing that negotiation, bargaining and role-making (i.e. interactive behaviour) is a morphogenic process which is perfectly compatible with a conception of organisations not as equilibrium systems, but as complex adaptive systems, open to 'significant changes in the nature of the components themselves'.

Finally, this section includes an article which directly addresses a central concept of the systems approach to organisations: organisational goals. The difficulties attendant on the employment of the notion of organisations as goal attaining systems have been well documented elsewhere and are also discussed by Albrow later, in reading 26. The article by Thompson and McEwen (10) considers organisational goals in terms of organisations' relationships with their environments, a relationship which is never stable, but always undergoing change. Furthermore the authors also note the difficulties of assessing whether or not a goal has been attained.

3

D. S. *Pugh and*
D. J. *Hickson*

The comparative study of organisations

Excerpts from D. S. Pugh and D. J. Hickson, 'The Comparative Study of Organizations' in Denis Pym, ed., *Industrial Society*, Harmondsworth: Penguin, 1968, pp. 374–96.

It is a commonplace of discussions among administrators and managers to hear that all organisations are different. Frequently the implication is that there can be little in common between them and consequently no coherent description of organisations. Even so, administrators continue to forgather to discuss their problems in a way which suggests that, after all, they find they have common interests and value each other's experience and advice.

For even if all organisations are indeed different it is possible to state these differences and to classify them so that something useful can be said about various kinds of organisations and the ways in which they function. This field of study has become known as 'organisation theory'. It is a meeting ground for the managers of privately owned business, administrators of state-owned ministries and agencies, economists, sociologists, and psychologists. The practitioner wants to know how to run his organisation to best advantage, and how to cope with the human problems that arise in doing so. The attention of social scientists has been caught by the proliferation of work organisations in modern society. Problems of size have been investigated; the characteristics of organisation known as bureaucracy are increasingly studied; and there has been research on a variety of human behaviours at work.

ANALYSIS OF ORGANISATION STRUCTURE

All organisations have to make provision for continuing activities directed towards the achievement of given aims. Regularities in activities such as task allocation, supervision, and coordination are developed. Such regularities constitute the organisation's structure, and the fact that these activities can be arranged in various ways means that organisations can have differing structures. Indeed, in some respects every organisation is unique. But many writers have examined a variety of structures to see if any general principles can be extracted. This variety, moreover, may be related to variations in such factors as the objectives of the organisation, its size, ownership, geographical location, and technology of manufacture, which are associated with the characteristic differences in structure of a bank, a hospital, a factory, etc.

The concept of structure is thus central to modern organisation theory. Yet despite its importance it remains primitive in empirical application. So far neither manager nor researcher has any means other than personal intuition of knowing how far the structure of Company A is the same as, or different from, that of Company B, or State Agency C. Very often differences are assumed or taken to be obvious; whereas the crucial question is exactly how much they differ. In what respects do they differ, and in each characteristic do they differ a very great deal, a lot, a fair amount, a little, or hardly at all? Even then, phrases like 'a fair amount' or 'a little' are extremely vague. What is needed is precise formulation of characteristics of organisation structure, and development of measuring-scales with which to assess differences quantitatively.

The Industrial Administration Research Unit at the University of Aston in Birmingham . . . has been concerned with the problems of such measurements. This has involved (*a*) discovering in what ways an organisation structures its activities and (*b*) seeing whether it is possible to create statistically acceptable methods of measuring structural differences between organisations.

Measurement must begin with the ideas as to what characteristics are to be measured. In the field of organisation structure the problem is not absence of such ideas, for there are many books and papers discussing what organisation is, but rather disentangling from such discussions those variables which can be clearly defined for scientific study. We will take three influential writers, Fayol, Brown, and Weber, as representative sources for our variables.

Henri Fayol (1949) was managing director for thirty years, until

1918, of a French mining and metallurgical combine. From his long experience he distilled a time-honoured definition of what management is: to manage is to forecast and plan, to organise, to command, to coordinate, and to control. In discharging these functions, management should abide by certain principles, one of which is the Principle of Centralisation. But Fayol did not mean by this that organisations should always be centralised, for he argued that: 'The question of centralization or decentralization is a simple question of proportion, it is a matter of finding the optimum degree for the particular concern.' Here, then, is an interesting variable capable of empirical study: *Centralisation of Authority*. Which organisations in what circumstances are more centralised, and which less so?

Wilfred Brown (1960), like Fayol, writes from his own experience of management and organisation. For over twenty years until 1965 he was Chairman of the Glacier Metal Company, which manufactures bearings, and he was also Managing Director for most of this period. As a theorist he aims at clarifying what he believes happens in organisations by stressing that they carry out three distinct functions, executive, representative, and legislative. Discussing the executive or working organisation, he subdivides its activities into operational work, which is development, production, and sales, and specialist work, which is in general terms personnel, technical, and programming. Specialists such as personnel officers, engineers, production controllers, chemists support the development, production, and sales departments. There are also specialists in operational work—specialists in research and development and specialist salesmen, etc. Here is a second interesting variable: *Specialisation of roles*. Which organisations in what circumstances break down their activities into the most, or the least, number of specialisms?

Pride of place among sociological theorists in this field goes to Max Weber (1947). He presented a typology of organisations in terms of the sources of the authority on which they are based. Why do subordinates accept the power of their superiors as legitimate? In 'charismatic' organisations, Weber suggested, it is because they have faith in the superlative personal qualities of the leader. In 'traditional' organisations it is because they accept long-standing custom without question. In 'bureaucratic' organisations it is because they submit to the law of rules and procedures. Each source of authority corresponds to a type of organisation.

Weber sees his third type, bureaucracy, as the dominant institution of modern society. In common usage bureaucracy is synonymous with inefficiency, emphasis on red tape, and excessive writing and recording, but Weber pointed out its strengths. In it authority is exercised through the official positions which individuals occupy by a system of regulations. These official positions are arranged in a hierarchy, each successive step embracing in authority all those beneath it. Rules and procedures are drawn up for every conceivable contingency. There are 'bureaux' for the safe keeping of all written records and files—it being an important part of the rationality of the system that information is written down. The system thus aims to develop the most efficient methods by depersonalising the whole administrative process. Written rule-books, routine procedures, formal training and qualifications for appointment, fixed salary scales, all minimise capricious differences in the handling of the same problem at different times, eliminate nepotism in promotion, and set and maintain standards of efficiency. In modern computer jargon, a bureaucracy is an organisation which is completely 'programmed'.

Weber's description of bureaucracy as an 'ideal' or perfect type (very much as economists often postulate 'perfect competition' whilst recognising that this never occurs in practice) has led to a tendency to assume that an organisation either *is* or *is not* bureaucratic. But thinking need not be so confined. It is far more useful to regard organisations as ranging from *more to less* bureaucratic in their activities, so that some have more routines and procedures and paper-work and files, and some have less. Here then are two further variables: *Standardisation of procedures and Formalisation of documentation*.

All three authors, Fayol, Brown, and Weber, assume a structure of related roles or positions. Fayol has his principles of 'one man one boss' and limited span of control. Brown has his executive system, Weber, his hierarchy of offices. They all have in mind what is usually summed up in the organisation chart. This, too, can be regarded as a variable—or rather a series of variables. It has a 'height', from the man at the top to the man at the bottom; it has varying spans of control of subordinates to each superior, and so on. This 'shape' of the role structure we call its *configuration*.

Thus we have elucidated five primary variables or dimensions of organisation structure:

Specialisation
Standardisation
Formalisation
Centralisation
Configuration

RESEARCH DESIGN AND METHOD

The dimensional method of analysis has a major advantage over classification by types. If scales are devised to measure the dimensions, then the position on these scales of a particular organisation forms a 'profile' of its structure. Even with a comparatively crude analysis we obtain a very large number of theoretically possible profiles (with five dimensions each a ten-point scale, for example, there are 100,000 theoretically possible profiles). Of course, many of these theoretical profiles may never appear in reality, and those that are found may cluster into bunches of similarly structured organisations. These bunches may well be labelled 'types', but with the knowledge that these types have not been postulated *a priori* but have been evolved with reference to the empirical data. We can now go beyond individual experience and scholarship to the systematic study of existing organisations.

To begin with, and for convenience, we have limited ourselves to work organisations in the West Midlands employing more than 250 people. A work organisation is defined as one that employs (that is, pays) its members. We have constructed scales from data on a cross-sectional sample of fifty-two such organisations. These include leading firms making motor-car bumpers and milk-chocolate buttons, municipal organisations repairing roads and teaching arithmetic, large department stores and small insurance companies, and so on.

We have written first to the chief executive of the organisation, who may be a works manager, an area superintendent, or a chairman, and begun by interviewing him at length. There has followed a series of interviews with department heads of varying status, as many as were necessary to obtain the information we required.

. . .

Since organisation structure is a construct derived from activities, some concepts of the activities of work organisations are needed which can be applied to both manufacturing and non-manufacturing organisations. We have found the analysis given by Bakke in *Bonds of Organization* to be very useful as a generalised description of the processes of work organisations, and we have relied considerably upon his formulations of the work-flow, perpetuation, and control processes, among others (Bakke, 1950). Bakke's concepts have the merit of being applicable to every work organisation whatever its purpose, whether industrial, commercial, retail, public service, etc. So the danger that we would only be concerned with work-flow activities (those involved in the direct production and distribution of the product or service) is avoided if attention is also drawn to perpetuation activities (such as those about buying materials or engaging employees) and to control activities (quality, inspection, budgeting, scheduling, etc.), and so on. By this means a list of items pertinent to each variable was built up. The method was then to ask of each organisation, for which of the given list of potentially specialisable functions it had in fact a specialised role, for which of the given list of potentially standardisable routines it did have a standardised procedure, and so on.

THE MEASUREMENT OF THE FIVE PRIMARY DIMENSIONS

Specialisation
Analysis of data from a pilot survey of organisations in terms of the

---

TABLE 3.1 *Functional specialisation*
$(n=52)$ Scale No. 51·01

Specialism number	Activities to:
1	develop, legitimise and symbolise the organisation's charter (Public Relations and Advertising)
2	dispose of, distribute, and service the output (Sales and Service)
3	carry outputs and resources from place to place (Transport)
4	acquire and allocate human resources (Employment)
5	develop and transform human resources (Training)
6	maintain human resources and promote their identification with the organisation (Welfare and Security)
7	obtain and control materials and equipment (Buying, Stock Control)
8	maintain and erect buildings and equipment
9	record and control financial resources (Accounts)
10	control the work-flow (Production Control)
11	control the quality of materials and equipment and outputs (Inspection)
12	assess and devise ways of producing the output (Methods)
13	devise new outputs, equipment, and processes (Design and Development)
14	develop and operate administrative procedures (O and M)
15	deal with legal and insurance requirements (Legal)
16	acquire information on the operational field (Market Research)

Scores: Range – 0–16
Mean – 10·19
Standard deviation – 5·19

Bakke activity variables enabled construction of a list of sixteen activities which are assumed to be present in *all* work organisations, and on which any work organisation may therefore be compared with any other. These activities or functions exclude the work-flow activities of the organisation, and so are not concerned with operatives in manufacturing, sales clerks in retailing, etc. The question is whether an organisation has a specialism responsible for an activity, that is, whether it is performed by someone with that function and no other, who is not in the work-flow superordinate hierarchy (line chain of command, in management terms). Table 3.1 lists these specialisms, which form a functional-specialisation scale from which a score for each organisation can be derived. A range of organisations is found from those where all sixteen activities are performed by non-specialists (for example, in an agency of a central Government department) to those where all the activities are performed by specialists working in a functional relationship to the work-flow management who are left with considerably restricted duties (for example, in the vehicle industry and electrical equipment manufacturing).

Given that an organisation has a specialism for an activity (that, for example, it has salesmen for Activity 2, or personnel officers for Activity 4) and so it scores on the functional-specialisation scale, then scales of role specialisation indicate how far the tasks *within* a functional specialism are differentiated and the role of the specialist narrowed down. . . .

Standardisation

The empirical problems here revolve around defining a procedure and specifying which procedures in the organisation are to be investigated. A procedure is taken to be an event that has regularity of occurrence and is legitimised by the organisation (no assumption is made whether the procedures are used or not). We have used the Bakke (1950) activity headings to guide the construction of a list of potential procedures. For example:

Control. Quality inspection, ranging from none at all, through haphazard inspection and random sampling, up to the extreme of standardisation, 100 per cent inspection of all outputs; and standardised techniques such as statistical quality control.

Financial control, ranging from historical costing through job costing, budgeting, and standard costs, to marginal costing.

Maintenance of equipment from repairs as needed to standardised routines of planned maintenance and programmed replacements.

Perpetuation (of necessary resources). Buying routines such as standardised procedures for seeking and evaluating tenders for supply of materials.

Employment procedures such as standardised interviewing by central boards, automatic internal advertisement of vacancies. A range of scores from 30 to 131 is obtained, the extremes being marked by a chain of retail stores and a metals processing plant.

Subdivision of the overall standardisation scale enables further differences to be traced among organisations. Bringing together from among the items in the original scale those procedures concerned with selection, discipline, and the like, a scale is constituted of Standardisation of Procedures Controlling Personnel Selection and Advancement, etc. This is found to make a crucial distinction between kinds of organisations which will be discussed later. It is constructed in such a way that a high score on it signifies both that an organisation *does* standardise procedures controlling the recruitment, selection, advancement, and the discipline of employees, and that it *does not* have standardised procedures such as routine quality inspection, production scheduling, and work study.

Formalisation

Formalisation denotes the extent to which rules, procedures, instructions, and communications are written down. How does the weight of documentation vary from organisation to organisation? Definitions of thirty-eight documents have been assembled each of which can be used by any known work organisation. They range from (for example) organisation charts, memo forms, agendas, minutes, to written terms of reference, job descriptions, records of maintenance performed, statements of tasks done or to be done on the output, handbooks, manuals of procedures.

Further analyses can be made, such as the number of categories of employees using documents. Scores are found to range from 4 in a single-product foodstuffs factory where there are few such documents, to 49 in the same metals processing plant that heads the standardisation scores and where documentation parallels the routine procedures. As with standardisation, this dimension can be broken down into various aspects. The data suggest three which are conceptually separate: formalisation of role-definition, of information-passing, and of role-performance recording. Linked together in the formalisation of role-definition sub-scale are all those documents whose primary purpose is the prescription of behaviour . . . Information-passing documents are those which are intended to pass from hand to hand (memo forms, house journal, etc.). Role-performance records notify or authorise the accomplishment of some part of a role (carrying out inspections, maintenance of equipment, etc.).

Centralisation

Centralisation concerns the locus of authority to make decisions. 'Authority to take decisions' is defined and ascertained by asking 'who is the last person whose assent must be obtained before *legitimate action* is taken—even if others subsequently have to confirm the decision?' This picks out the level in the hierarchy where executive action can be authorised, even if this remains subject to a 'rubber stamp' confirmation later by, for example, a chairman or a committee. A standard list of thirty-seven recurrent decisions has been prepared covering the range of organisational activities. . . .

For each organisation the lowest level in the hierarchy which has the formal authority to take each decision is determined. . . . This overcomes the endemic problem of deciding whether a foreman in factory A is at the same level as a shop-buyer in retail store B or a head clerk in commercial office C. Levels are equated in terms of the scope of the work-flow segment (the proportion of the production activities) which they control. Centralisation scores are formed by scoring a decision taken outside the unit of organisation (at the head office of an owning group, for example) as 5, a decision taken at chief executive level as 4, and so on, down to 0 for a decision at operating level. Thus a high score means high centralisation, and a range has been found from the most decentralised organisation with a score of 108 (an independent manufacturer of transporting equipment) to an extremely centralised organisation, where a considerable majority of the decisions are taken right at the top or above, which has a score of 173 (a branch factory).

Configuration

Configuration is the shape of the role structure. Its data would be contained in a comprehensive and detailed organisation chart that included literally every role in the organisation. The assessment of the configuration of this hypothetical chart requires the use of a combination of selected dimensions. Each of these provides a measure of the development of a particular aspect of the structure.

The vertical span of control (or height) of the work-flow superordinate hierarchy (line chain of command) is measured by a count of the number of job positions between the chief executive and the employees directly working on the output, and by the proportion of managers and supervisors (work-flow superordinates). Lateral 'widths' can include the chief executive's span of control; the ratio of subordinates to first work-flow superordinates (first-line supervisors) and the percentage of direct-output employees to total employees. Note that in a savings bank, the cashiers are direct-output employees, as are drivers in a bus company, and so on. The total of work-flow employees (those directly responsible for the output, including management) can be compared with the number of those engaged in other activities ('functional specialists' or 'staff' departments). Totals of employees in each of the sixteen special-isms (cf. specialisation) can be calculated and related. Here the size of the specialism in terms of the number of those engaged in it is taken account of, as distinct from their specialisation which is measured under that heading. And so on.

STRUCTURAL PROFILES

Equipped with scales for the analysis and measurement of organisation structure, we can now construct 'profiles' characteristic of particular organisations. (For comparative purposes, all raw scores are trans-formed into standard scores based on distributions with a mean of 50 and standard deviation of 15.) Figure 3.1 shows the profiles of six organisations which we have studied and it will be seen that they each have a distinctive pattern.

Organisation A is a municipal department responsible for a public service. But it is far from being the classic form of bureaucracy as described by Weber. By definition such bureaucracy would have an extreme high-score pattern on our scales. That is, it would appear as highly specialised with many narrowly defined specialist 'offices', as highly standardised in its procedures, and as highly formalised with documents prescribing and recording all activities and available in the files as precedents. If everything has to be referred upwards for decision, then it would also score highly centralised. In configuration it would have a high proportion of 'supportive' or administrative or 'non-work-flow' personnel. But of fifty-two organisations, *none* shows such a profile. Perhaps extreme total bureaucracy exists only among the bureaux of central government—which are not represented in our provincial sample.

Organisation B represents a relatively unstructured family firm, relying more on traditional ways of doing things. Although it has the specialisms usual in manufacturing industry (and hence a comparatively high specialisation score) it has minimised standardised procedure and formalised paperwork.

Organisation C represents 'big business'. It is the subsidiary of a very large company, and its profile shows the effects of size; generally very high scores on specialisation, standardisation, and formalisation, but *de*centralised. The distinctively different relationship of centralisation is typical. Centralisation correlates *negatively* with almost all other structural scales. The more specialised, standardised, and formalised the organisation, the *less* it is centralised, or to put it the other way round, the more it is decentralised. Therefore these scales do not confirm the common assumption that a large organisation which develops specialist offices and the routines which go with them 'passes the buck' upward for decision; in fact, such an organisation is relatively decentralised.

But it is not only a question of size, as the profile of Organisation D shows. It has the *same* number of employees as Organisation B and yet its structure is in striking contrast and is more nearly that of a much larger firm. Clearly the policies and attitudes of the management of an organisation may have a considerable effect on its structure, even though factors like size, technology, form of ownership, etc., set the framework within which the management must function.

Organisation E is an example of a manufacturing unit owned by the Government, and is characterised by a high centralisation and a high formalisation score. Comparison of the profiles of D and E brings home the fact that two organisations may be 'bureaucratic' but in considerably different ways.

Organisation F is included as an example of the relatively low scores often found in retailing.

Scrutiny of all the profiles suggests that there are numbers of organisations which have similar structural characteristics, a suggestion which reflects the associations between measures shown by intercorrelations among them. . . . This impression is confirmed by the statistical method of principal components analysis, as a result of which the structural characteristics of each organisation can be summed up in a comparatively few composite scores. Plotting the composite scores for all the organisations discloses various clusters which have certain pronounced features in common. These distinctive clusters extend from a core of comparatively undistinguished 'average' organisations which tend to have scores around the mean points. As might be expected, the one third of the total fifty-two organisations which can be roughly classed as 'average' make a very mixed collection. There are retail shops, a brewery, an omnibus undertaking, a development organisation, and a variety of factories manufacturing anything from gears to machine tools. On the other hand, the clusters of organisations with more pro-

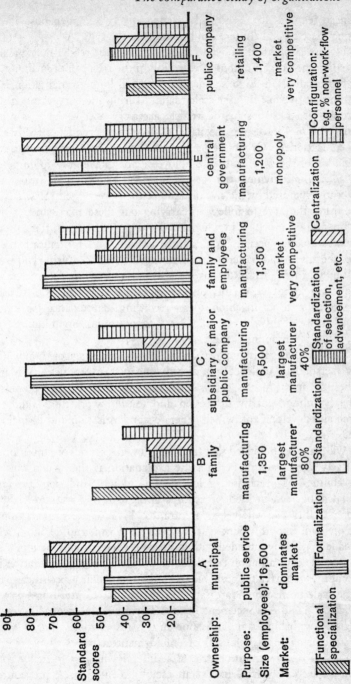

Ownership:

A	B	C	D	E	F
municipal	family	subsidiary of major public company	family and employees	central government	public company

Purpose:

A	B	C	D	E	F
public service	manufacturing	manufacturing	manufacturing	manufacturing	retailing

Size (employees): 16,500

B	C	D	E	F
1,350	6,500	1,350	1,200	1,400

Market:

A	B	C	D	E	F
dominates market	largest manufacturer 80%	largest manufacturer 40%	market very competitive	monopoly	market very competitive

Standard scores

Functional specialization

Formalization

Standardization

Standardization of selection, advancement, etc.

Centralization

Configuration: e.g. % non-work-flow personnel

FIG. 3.1. *The structural profiles of six organizations.*

nounced features are found to be comparatively homogeneous. Three among these several clusters will be outlined.

The first is sufficiently obvious in the data that the reader may already have discerned organisations of this kind in the six profiles in Fig. 3.1. High specialisation, high standardisation, and high formalisation is a pattern that prevails in large-scale manufacturing industry. Among the examples are factories in the vehicle accessory and vehicle assembly industry, those processing metals, and those mass-producing foodstuffs and confectionery. Organisations like this have gone a long way in the regulation of the work of their employees. They have gone a long way in *structuring* activities; that is, the intended behaviour of employees has been structured by the specification of their specialised roles, of the procedures they are to follow in carrying out these roles, and of the documentation involved in what they have to do. In short, the pattern of scores among specialisation, standardisation, and formalisation denotes the range and pattern of *structuring*. So manufacturing industry or 'big business' tends to have highly structured work activities— production schedules, quality inspection procedures, returns of output per worker and per machine, forms recording maintenance jobs, etc., etc. We can call this the *work-flow structured* kind of organisation (see Fig. 3.1, Organisations C and D).

This kind of organisation usually has a high percentage of 'non-work-flow' personnel (employees not directly engaged in production). Many of these are in the large specialised sections such as production planning and scheduling, quality inspection and testing, work-study, and research and development, which generate standardisation and formalisation.

It will have been noticed that the work-flow structured organisation is relatively *de*centralised. Perhaps the explanation is that when the responsibilities of specialised roles are laid down, and activities are regulated by standardised procedures and are formalised in records, then authority can safely be decentralised because the organisational machine will smoothly run, as it has been set to run, and decisions will be made in the way intended with less need for referring to the top.

But while centralisation correlates *negatively* with standardisation in general . . . , it correlates positively with that particular aspect measured by the scale termed Standardisation of Procedures Controlling Personnel Selection and Advancement, etc. . . . Therefore high centralisation is associated with high standardisation in this respect *only*, that is, with the structuring (or regulation) of employment activities. This means central control of recruitment, central interviewing by formally constituted selection boards, fixed staff establishment figures, procedures laid down in writing which are to be followed in cases of employee discipline or dismissal, etc. Such an organisation we call *employment structured*. It should be remembered that it has not structured the *daily work* of its employees to the same extent as is found in work-flow structured organisations. This kind of structure is especially common in local and central government, for example, a municipal education department or public department. Its centralisation is accentuated by public ownership, where the need for public accountability requires many decisions to be referred upwards to committees and councils. Probably for similar reasons, the same structure also occurs in the smaller branch factories of large companies (see Fig. 3.1, Organisation A).

The cartoonist's stereotype of bureaucratic public departments proves to be very near the mark in so far as they are employment structured. Here are all the desirably equitable *but* unavoidably cumbersome procedures for control of employment and for uniform practices in taking decisions. But if public departments have a characteristic brand of bureaucracy, what the cartoonists have *not* spotted is that so has work-flow structured 'big business'. However, here we are interested not in lampooning bureaucracy but in exploring the different forms structure takes in organisations with different tasks to perform.

One question that jumps to mind is: 'What is manufacturing organisation like if it is also publicly owned?' The hypothesis being that it will be *both* work-flow structured and employment structured. Our sample includes only one such organisation, a medium-sized state-owned engineering factory (see Fig. 3.1, Organisation E). Examining its scores, we do indeed find that it shows both these forms of structuring—though one case does not justify generalisations, and further work is needed.

Thirdly, a number of organisations are found to have relatively low scores all round. Low on specialisation, low on standardisation, low on formalisation, and low—but not too low—on centralisation. Typical of this cluster of organisations are smaller factories in the size range from 250 to 750 employees, whose ownership is concentrated, that is, a comparatively small number of individuals are large shareholders and often are also directors. The low scores of such factories do not mean that they have no structure and career along in a state of anarchy. Rather, their kind of structure gives low scores on the characteristics measured and with the particular scales used. To label them unstructured would be a misnomer, for it is rather that for these measures their structure is latent. We might therefore cautiously call them *latent structured* (see Fig. 3.1, Organisations B and F). A hypothesis would be that these organisations are run not by explicit regulation but by implicitly transmitted custom, a hypothesis which appears very plausible but is not adequately tested by these results alone.

FURTHER DEVELOPMENTS

All scientists, and particularly social scientists, are continually faced with the problem of having to identify with some precision the characteristics they have described and measured; that is they have to tackle the problem of validity of data. To some extent this is a semantic problem, as is illustrated by the famous non-definition that 'intelligence it what intelligence tests measure'. At this level, if it is thought that our scales of, say, specialisation and centralisation do not in fact tap these characteristics then other names would have to be found for them (since they have an *internal* consistency which makes it unlikely that they would be complete artefacts). But this is hardly adequate and some form of *external* validation is required. This we are at present undertaking.

The way that we obtain external validity is by testing acceptable hypotheses that there are relationships between the characteristics of structure that we have measured and other characteristics of organisations. Figure 3.2 gives a paradigm which relates an organisation's

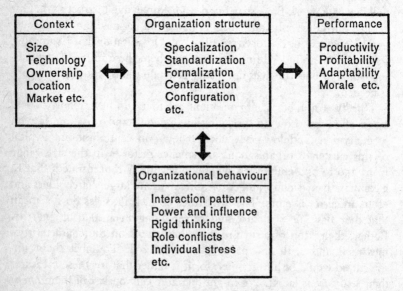

FIG. 3.2. *A scheme for organisational functioning.*

structure to aspects of its context, its performance, and to the behaviour within it. If we can postulate relationships between the four boxes shown and obtain data to support our hypotheses, then we have gone a considerable way towards demonstrating that our scales do measure aspects of structure which are relevant to organisational functioning.

If we can predict to a considerable degree, from a knowledge of an organisation's context (for example, its size, technology of manufacture or service, ownership pattern), what its structural scores will be, then we have evidence that its scores are meaningful. Again, if we can demonstrate that in given contexts an organisation's structural scores will be directly related to its performance (productivity, profitability, etc.), then we can have that much more confidence in our scales. If, in addition, we find that given structural forms are correlated with characteristic behaviour (specialisation with interaction patterns, centralisation with power and influence, standardisation with rigid thinking etc.) then we have added to the data on the external validity of our measures. Our work is geared to an examination of these topics.

POTENTIAL APPLICATION

The manager of the future will have available to him ever increasing amounts of information, and will be anxious to know what signals he should primarily attend to. If he knows what is crucial to organisation functioning he can manage by exception. What types and amounts of environmental change can occur before internal adjustments must be made in order to maintain performance? How much internal change will be required, and in what direction? What sequence of compensatory changes is likely to be triggered off by any specific decision? The precepts of the classical management theorists have proved inadequate to deal with such questions as these. The contemporary social science approach to organisation theory may yield a more useful set of criteria to help the manager to take important decisions. Use of the profiles as developed here enables direct comparison between organisations, as shown in Fig. 3.1. Closer analysis of typical organisations may lead to a better understanding of the patterns we have found. At least it should enable future theory to be firmly grounded in fact.

Many possibilities are opened up if relatively exact means of comparison are available. There is, of course, no political or geographical limit to their use. It would be feasible to measure the specialisation of structures in French as against German organisations, or for that matter Indonesian and Soudanese. If degrees of bureaucratisation can be represented by scores on empirically based measures, then the development of bureaucracy can be systematically studied. As a further instance, the businessman interested in systems of costing may have to rely completely on guesswork as to whether such a system will succeed: but if measurements of centralisation have shown that such costing systems have a high rate of failure in decentralised organisations, then he has something to go on. If Company X's structure is more centralised than Company Y's, Company X may provide the most favourable setting for a new system.

To take another example, many researchers have studied 'restriction of output' among workers. We would like to be able to relate this type of behaviour to the sort of factory and the sort of economical and social context in which it does, or does not, occur. The same approach is possible for studies of many other kinds of behaviour—absenteeism, labour turnover, sociability among fellow employees, or neuroses among managers. The incidence of the factor studied can be related not merely to a vague description of the work-place in which it occurs, but to a precise and standardised characterisation. We can then consider another firm, perhaps identical or perhaps different, and, knowing precisely the identity or difference, can see whether the same behaviour occurs. In this way the causes can more clearly be pin-pointed.

If these processes can be better understood, then a manager can predict better what changes are likely to take place in the structure of an organisation and plan for them. Knowing which structures operate more efficiently in which situations, we can look forward to designing organisations appropriate to the tasks they face.

REFERENCES

BAKKE, E. W. (1950) *Bonds of Organization*, Harper.
BROWN, W. (1960) *Explorations in Management*, Heinemann.
FAYOL, H. (1949) *General and Industrial Management*, Pitman.
WEBER, MAX (1947) *The Theory of Social and Economic Organization*, New York, Free Press of Glencoe.

4

Barry A. Turner   The industrial subculture

Excerpt from Barry A. Turner, *Exploring the Industrial Subculture*, Chapter 1: 'The industrial subculture', Macmillan, 1971, pp. 1–8.

A subculture is a distinctive set of meanings shared by a group of people whose forms of behaviour differ to some extent from those of the wider society (cf. Wolfgang and Ferracuti, 1967). The distinctive nature of the set of meanings is maintained by ensuring that newcomers to the group undergo a process of learning or socialisation. This process links the individual to the values of the group, and generates common motives, common reaction patterns and common perceptual habits. Distinctiveness is also maintained by the use of sanctions which are operated against those who do not behave in appropriate ways.

There is not necessarily a clearcut disparity between, on the one hand, a single cultural pattern which characterises the wider society, and on the other, a series of separate subcultural patterns. Both culture and subculture may be made up of a large number of groups, each differing slightly from the next, over a broad range. It is not necessary for all of the groups within a culture or a subculture to be identical, nor even for all of the members of these groups to be totally committed to their groups, or to the values which their groups perpetuate. But even though there is some overlapping of the groups, it is still useful to class some of the groups together as 'the main culture', and other groups together as 'a subculture', because this concentrates attention on broad differences between the two aggregates of groups. It is important, however, to be satisfied that the similarities of behaviour ascribed to a subculture really arise from the subculture, and are not merely some form of statistically modal behaviour. A sociological analysis is only appropriate if it is clear that we are dealing with sociological phenomena.

In moving from one industrial organisation to another, it is possible to observe certain similarities of behaviour which can be contrasted with behaviour elsewhere in society, and in considering these similarities it is useful to regard them as aspects of an industrial subculture. This industrial subculture is not a monolithic entity which can be readily identified and closely delimited, for industrial life itself is complex and variegated. But there are different manifestations of the subculture in different industries, and in different companies. Outside the main industrial organisations, there are a host of subsidiary groupings—trade unions, manufacturers' associations, professional bodies and so on— which partake of, and contribute to, the subculture. Within industrial organisations there are what might be called 'micro-cultures' made up of the distinctive normative patterns, perceptions and values associated with departments, work groups and other social subdivisions of the organisation.

But it is reasonable to use one comprehensive term, 'the industrial subculture', to refer to all of these social groupings because of the pervasive similarities found in all forms of industrial life. And the use of this term has the advantage of drawing attention to certain aspects of industrial life which need to be more fully examined and understood before industrial sociology can proceed much further.[1] The existence of such a subculture has already been acknowledged by certain sociologists, significantly those who have considerable personal acquaintance with a range of industrial and non-industrial organisation; but because their preoccupations lie elsewhere, they merely note the fact in passing, and move on to carry out analyses *within* the subculture.

We might expect, for example, to find a detailed discussion of the nature of the cultural aspects of industry in Jaques' book *The Changing Culture of a Factory*. But instead, we find that apart from two or three brief comments, he takes the existence of this cultural setting as given:

> The culture of the factory is its customary and traditional way of thinking and doing things, which is shared to a greater or lesser degree by all its members, and which new members must learn, and at least partially accept in order to be accepted into service in the firm. Culture in this sense covers a wide range of behaviour: the methods

---

[1] Shull and Del Béque (1964) point to the existence of gaps in organisation theory, in the area which they refer to as that of the 'symbolic culture'.

of production; job skills and technical knowledge; attitudes towards discipline and punishment; the customs and habits of managerial behaviour; the objectives of the concern; its way of doing business; the method of payment; the values placed upon different types of work; beliefs in democratic living and point consultation and the less conscious conventions and taboos. Culture is part of second nature to those who have been with the firm some time. Ignorance of culture marks out the newcomers, while maladjusted members are recognised as those who reject or are otherwise unable to use the culture of the firm. In short, the making of relationships requires the taking up of roles within a social structure; the quality of these relationships is governed by the extent to which the individuals concerned have each absorbed the culture of the organisation so as to be able to operate within the same general code. The culture of the factory consists of the means or techniques which lie at the disposal of the individual for handling his relationships, and on which he depends for making his way among, and with, other members and groups (Jaques, 1951).

Jaques thus states the cultural issue, from the organisational point of view, at least, in a single paragraph, and apart from two brief comments about the effects of the culture of the community upon the patterns of behaviour which are accepted as reasonable within the industrial concern,[2] he does not return explicitly to the topic again. For his own purposes, he clearly did not need to, but sociologists who wish to follow him would benefit greatly from an elaboration of the paragraph cited above.

Burns, too, while aware of the existence of subcultural forms in industry, is sufficiently accustomed to stepping in and out of different organisations to accept the existence of these forms as a social 'given'

[2] On this, Jaques (1951) comments: 'The more the members of the concern intuitively understand, and can also consciously put to use, the established practices of British culture before seeking new practices, the greater their freedom to experiment' (p. 258).
'Members of the concern, having been brought up within British culture, are unconsciously limited in the extent to which they can deviate from its traditional practices. Moreover, patterns of behaviour and organisation within the concern must remain consistent with the patterns of behaviour and expectations of a community that carries this culture' (p. 260).
Burns (1967) has also made this point: 'Variation and developmental change in the value system of society . . . profoundly affect not only the institutional pattern and structure of organisations, not only the capacity of society to meet demand and use resources, but the *kinds* of organisations which are brought into being and the social characteristics of the entrepreneurs and administrators who try to start organisations and run them' (p. 133).

which does not of itself call for further comment. Thus in *The Management of Innovation*[3] he refers at different points to a 'code' or 'style of conduct' (pp. 10, 11), to the 'firm's way of doing things' (p. 143), to a 'code of practice which defines the kind of conduct appropriate to managerial roles' (p. 252), and, following Parsons, to a 'common culture':

> Guides for action, epistemic moduli, or institutions are not wholly private to the individual. They are, as Parsons has pointed out in another connection, functions of interaction between persons. As such, their existence depends on a pre-existing *'common culture'*, that is, a commonly shared system of symbols, the meanings of which are understood on both sides with an approximation to agreement. Non-verbal conduct, as well as objects and language, is involved in such symbol systems (p. 118).

Clearly, Burns has perceived or experienced subcultural features, which are useful in his analysis, but his main focus of attention lies elsewhere.

There are two ways in which the industrial subculture is different in kind from other subcultures studied by sociologists: firstly, it is a *segmental* subculture; secondly, it is a *stable* subculture. It is segmental because, in general, it is found away from the participants' home and leisure areas.[4] There are physical boundaries within which the subculture is found, and the individual only spends a certain portion of his life within these boundaries. Outside these limits, many of his behaviour patterns will be different. Moreover, since the individual and his fellow workers all cross these boundaries at about the same time, unless there is a shift system operating, their particular portion of the subculture is suspended until they all return the following morning. Thus, the life of the subculture proceeds in a series of discrete jumps in time.[5]

The stability of the subculture would seem to stem from two sources: firstly, from the extent of the resources controlled within the industrial sector as a whole, which are a considerable help in coping

[3] Burns (1966). The existence of a work culture is also taken for granted by Boguslaw and Bach (1959) in their more psychodynamic approach to industry.

[4] Except for special cases like company towns.

[5] The observations made by Schutz in his essay 'The homecoming' (Schutz, 1967) are applicable to the case of a single individual returning to his organisation after an absence; but they are not applicable when *everyone* has been away, for 'nothing' can have happened in the intervening period with which everyone can be assumed to be familiar.

with the effects of change; and secondly, through the wedding of industry to bureaucracy. Indeed, not only does the industrial subculture appear to be very stable, and becoming more stable, as more mechanisms are developed and deployed to maintain it; it also appears to be establishing outposts in other areas of the societal culture, as industrial techniques, methods and management spread into the public sector.

Neither of these two characteristics, the stability of the industrial subculture, nor its segmented nature in time, space, and in the individual's life, seems to offer any difficulties in the consideration of industry *as* a subculture.[6]

The world of industry can be seen, then, as a series of groups of individuals formed together in a number of ways; into companies, into trade unions, into work groups, into foremen's associations, into management institutes and so on. The social patternings of each of these groups, and the sets of meanings to which these patternings relate, are all different. But they may be linked and considered for some purposes as an ensemble because the members of all of these groups are, to a greater or lesser extent, participating in one world. And this world, the one with which they are familiar, is *not* familiar to those outside the industrial sphere.

The distinctive nature of this world is preserved by processes of socialisation, which encourage newcomers to follow the ways of industry, to behave differently from civil servants and housewives, and to inhabit a context of meaning which is different from that inhabited by academics or by the clergy. The range of official and unofficial sanctions which can be brought to bear against those who do not behave in the appropriate way extends from reprimands to dismissal, and from teasing to ostracism. But by far the most important instrument for establishing control over newcomers is the pre-existence of institutionalised patterns of behaviour to which newcomers naturally tend to conform, unless they have reason not to.[7]

It is possible to obtain a knowledge of the normatively induced values which characterise the subculture by making use of observations of behaviour in industry for this behaviour is the 'manifest representation of the subculture'. But in carrying out exercises of this

[6] Contrast this with the criminal subculture, where Wolfgang and Ferracuti (1967), stating that 'it is in homogeneity that the subculture has strength and durability', suggest that this homogeneity can be removed by breaking up the residential propinquity of those who share it.

[7] '... prior to or apart from any mechanisms of sanctions specifically set up to support an institution ... the primary social control is given in the existence of the institution as such' (Berger and Luckman, 1967, pp. 72–3).

nature, it should be realised that some, or even many, of the individuals who are members of industrial groups will retain different values which are not necessarily shown in behaviour within the subcultural setting. It is not difficult for individual members of the industrial subculture to devote themselves to the active pursuit of values which contrast with those which they may act out at work. For they can make use of the periods of time when their participation in the industrial subculture is suspended, unlike those involved with subcultures in which membership and participation are continuous.

If, then, an industrial sociologist is to study an area of society which forms a distinctive subculture, how should he approach his subject? The discussion so far might suggest that he should begin by asking questions about the values and norms of the industrial subculture, to determine what these values and norms are, and to discover the relation in which they stand to those of the wider culture. But such questions would be premature, for before it is possible to learn much from the answers which might be offered, it is necessary to discover far more about the internal nature of cultures in general, and of the industrial subculture in particular.

A more fruitful starting-point for the industrial sociologist, therefore, would be to look at the way in which the set of shared meanings which constitutes the industrial subculture is sustained. The process of the socialisation of newcomers is one aspect of this, of course, but the communication of the subculture to those newly arrived from outside is not the only thing to be attended to. For one thing, the process of socialisation continues for a long time, until it merges with the day-to-day life of the subculture. And the day-to-day life of industry is the continuing expression of the subculture. If membership of a subculture is the possession of a shared set of meanings which are understood on all sides, these meanings can only be acquired by communicative exchanges, and possession of them can only be demonstrated or utilised in communication, or in acts related to communication.[8] Further, it is only by usage that the set of meanings, and the system of symbols to which they are attached within the subculture, can change, develop and extend.

In other words, since the subculture is not something which is neatly packaged, ready to be handed on from generation to generation, it is not enough for the industrial sociologist to concentrate upon the point of changeover. Instead, he must sensitise himself to the

___

[8] As Duncan phrases it: 'We must show how social order is expressed, for all we can really observe about order is how it is communicated' (Duncan, 1968, p. 3).

existence of the various kinds of meanings which can be encountered in industry, and he must consider the forms of ritual and language which are available for communicating these meanings. Only when he is familiar with these mechanisms can he move on to consider the nature of the meanings which are constantly being conveyed from one member of the industrial subculture to another.

He could begin by noting that as an expression of the naming process which accompanies the acquisition of the language of a subculture, there is also acquired a set of social definitions of all the features which are socially acknowledged within the subculture, but which are not acknowledged in this way in the wider society. Then, he could look at the way in which the social and technical norms of the subculture can be articulated and communicated by the linking of social definitions. Finally, the industrial sociologist could examine the multiplicity of levels of symbolic interpretations of the industrial environment which appear as each individual attempts to attribute meaning to his situation. That is to say, it is necessary to examine the understanding which the individual has of himself, of his colleagues, his bosses, his subordinates, his organisation, and the wider context within which his organisation operates. And included in this understanding the sociologist will find the explanations, the rationales, the anecdotes, the normative views, the myths and the mysteries of that particular section of the industrial subculture within which the individual is located.

All of this, of course, is not as simple as it sounds, for the previous two paragraphs conceal a number of circularities: these circularities exist because there is interaction or potential interaction between almost all of the topics mentioned. The ranges of symbolic interpretations offered not only depend upon the forms of language available and the nature of the prevalent social definitions, but in turn they will influence and shape both of these factors. Although norms may be presented as the linking of social definitions, there are value elements present in certain aspects of the defining of phenomena which are socially agreed to be 'real'. And so on and so on. It is not being maintained that no analysis is possible because all things interact with equal strength, but that any approach to the study of a subculture must recognise that this is an area where the 'interconnectedness of all things' thrusts itself particularly forcibly upon the researcher, and a good deal more work needs to be done before we can identify with confidence the clusters of strong and weak links.

In summary, it is being proposed that there are advantages to be gained by industrial sociologists if they approach their subject as the study of an unfamiliar subculture, with which they need to become intimately familiar, before they can 'step out' of industry, in order to analyse it. Such an approach would be useful at the present time, because it brings certain neglected features of industrial life into prominence. But many of these advantages will be squandered if the analysis is started with a listing of the similarities and differences found in the ranking of values inside and outside the subculture. This kind of procedure encourages the importing into the analysis of assumptions and preconceptions about the nature of the phenomena being studied at too early a stage. Instead, since a culture rests in a commonly held fabric of meanings, these meanings should be sought by analysing the knowledge which individuals possess about the subculture, and about their place in it.[9]

[9] In using this phrasing, we are consciously aligning the present approach with that taken by Berger and Luckman (Berger and Luckman, 1967): '...commonsense "knowledge" rather than "ideas" must be the central focus for the sociology of knowledge. It is precisely this "knowledge" that constitutes the fabric of meanings without which no society could exist' (p. 27).

'If the integration of an institutional order can be understood only in terms of the "knowledge" that its members have of it, it follows that the analysis of such "knowledge" will be essential for an analysis of the institutional order in question' (pp. 82–3).

Although Berger and Luckman's exposition is a recent one, advocacy of this course is not really a novelty. As Burns (1967) has pointed out: 'Weber was concerned with the way in which social values and normative images of social organisation develop as a kind of mental equipment with which men fashion an acceptable or workable framework of institutions. He is constantly reiterating his purpose of establishing the subjective, cognitive structures with which men impart meaning to their social actions' (pp. 142–143).

There are, of course, direct links between Weber, Schutz, and Berger and Luckman.

REFERENCES

BERGER, P. and LUCKMAN, T. (1967) *The Social Construction of Reality*, Allen Lane.

BOGUSLAW, R., and BACH, G. R. (1959) 'Work culture management in industry', *Group Psychotherapy*, **21**, 134–42.

BURNS, T. (1967) 'The comparative study of organizations', in V. H. Vroom, ed., *Methods of Organizational Research*, University of Pittsburgh Press.

BURNS, T., and STALKER, G. M. (1966) *The Management of Innovation*, 2nd edn, Tavistock.

DUNCAN, H. D. (1968) *Communication and Social Order*, Oxford University Press

JAQUES, E. (1951) *The Changing Culture of a Factory*, Tavistock.

SCHUTZ, A. (1967) *Collected Papers*, 2, The Hague, Nizhoff.

SHULL, F., and DEL BÉQUE, A. (1964) 'Norms, a feature of symbolic culture: A major linkage between the individual, small groups and administrative organization', in W. J. Gore and J. W. Dyson, eds., *The Making of Decisions*, New York, Free Press, Glencoe.

WOLFGANG, M. E., and FERRACUTI, E. (1967) *The Subculture of Violence*, Tavistock.

5

Chris Argyris   Peter Blau

Excerpts from Chris Argyris, *The Applicability of Organizational Sociology*, Chapter 1: 'Peter Blau', Cambridge University Press, 1972, pp. 1–19.

Blau, acknowledging the existence of several foci of analysis in organisational research (individual and structure of social relations), has chosen to focus upon the system of interrelated elements that characterise the organisation as a whole (Blau 1965, p. 325). 'The focus . . . is the system of interrelated elements that characterize the organisation as a whole, not its component parts' (Blau 1965, p. 326).

How does one study the whole without its component parts? The answer appears to be to study formal organisation. The whole is therefore equated with the formal, intended aspects of organisations. Is there any research that helps to illuminate the difficulties in equating the whole with the formal organisation? There are several, all of which suggest that the formal organisation, no matter how clearly defined, rarely includes the whole organisation. Arensberg and McGregor (1942), the Ohio State studies (1957), and Simon (1947) have shown that much human behaviour cannot be understood by focusing on the formal organisational structure. More recently Woodward (1965, 1970) and her associates have emphasised the difficulty they found in obtaining organisational charts that were valid (their sample is now over 100 firms). Moreover, they reported that charts did not necessarily depict the important relationships. 'In some firms role relationships prescribed by the chart seemed to be of secondary importance to personal relationships between individuals' (Woodward 1965, p. 24). Petrow reported that he has had difficulties in getting top management to agree on such seemingly easy attributes of formal organisations as the number of levels. He concludes, 'We have been amazed at the nonchalance with which most researchers make their unexplained division of levels and can confidently report that one organisation has five, whereas another has six or four ... All criteria ... charts, formal or informal; salary data ... official level ... designations by the organisations, observations of department heads ... had grave disadvantages' (Perrow 1970, pp. 79–80). Blau himself has questioned the advisability of depending on formal charts and the understanding of formal procedures to understand behaviour in organisations. . . .

Thus we see when researchers, in studying organisations, have collected data depicting actual behaviour, they have concluded that the formal organisations, at best, may represent the whole as it is *intended* but not the whole as it actually exists. If so, then why does Blau state that he is studying the organisation as a whole by focusing on formal organisation? We could find no discussion of this question.

Indeed, the Blau perspective may be even narrower if one asks the question how Blau operationally defines organisational intentions. Again because individual and group behaviour at all levels are excluded, Blau operationally defines intentions as those of a few of the top management. Blau restricts himself 'to those data that can be obtained from the records of organisations and interviews with key informants, without intensive observation or interviewing' (Blau 1965, p. 333). Most of the information about formal structure comes from personnel lists, from elaborate charts specially prepared for the research, all of which were more detailed than the charts kept by the agencies (Blau 1970a, p. 204).

Why develop charts that are more detailed than those used by the organisation in its daily work? One reason may be because, as pointed out above, the formal charts do not describe the organisation as it is; they describe it as it is intended to be. But if one wants to describe the organisation as it is, then is there not some need to show empirically that what exists for the few senior managerial informants actually exists for the remainder of the organisation? Webber has shown that superiors can distort their initiation of actions downward (Webber 1970).

Blau apparently does not believe that it is necessary to obtain empirical data to validate that the few may speak for the many. To do so would take him beyond the boundaries of his interests. The consequence, however, is to question the validity of his results.

An example of the difficulty that Blau creates for himself may be seen in his study of decentralisation. Remaining consistent with his view he operationally measures the decentralisation from the director and his deputy either to middle managers at the state headquarters or to managers of local offices, by obtaining the perceptions of 'several senior managers' (Blau 1970b, pp. 155-66). Blau assumes that several key top managers may speak validly for the remainder of the managerial organisation, but never provides empirical evidence for this assumption. How is it possible to ignore the need for such empirical evidence in the light of ample research that concludes that, in matters such as decentral-isation, superiors may not be valid informants of their subordinates' views? For example, Greiner, Leitch and Barnes (1968) reported that significantly different perceptions existed among managers and tech-nical people in variables that were related to the degree of centralisation or decentralisation participants experience (pp. 205-6).

CAUSAL EXPLANATIONS ARE OFFERED THAT ARE INCOMPLETE OR UNEXPLORED

A stated objective of Blau's work is to refine Weber's theory of bureau-cracy. Blau agrees with Weber that specialisation, administrative apparatus, hierarchy, and impersonal detachment are key characteristics of bureaucracy (Blau 1965, p. 333). He correctly points out that these characteristics exist in matters of degree and therefore can be dimension-alised. This, in turn, leads to quantitative studies where the degree of each characteristic may be correlated with the others or with other criterion variables.

After identifying the key characteristics of bureaucracy Blau also discusses their probable causality. He agrees with Weber that specialisa-tion is caused by the requirement to discharge complex responsibilities; that hierarchy is needed to effect the coordination of tasks and to enable supervisors to guide the performance of subordinates; that impersonal detachment is necessary to preclude the intrusion of such irrational elements (strong emotions and personal bias) as may interfere with rational decision making.

The moment Blau includes these generalisations in his theory, he involves the level of analysis that he has chosen to exclude. For example, why is specialisation necessary or why does hierarchy lead to coordin-ation and guidance? The answer may be found in any book on formal organisation and partially in Blau's writings. Briefly, it goes something like this. According to engineering economics, *given the nature of people*, it is cheaper to specialise work. If people or units are specialised then they should make certain that they do what they are supposed to do. The way to control people and coordinate them is to give that job (a new speciality) to one individual and call him a supervisor. What makes him a supervisor? Among others things his authority to hire, fire, reward and penalise etc. Why give him these powers? Because, given what is known about people, these are ways to induce people to perform what the systems ask them to perform.

The point is that the basic design of the pyramidal structure is based on the properties of human beings. Specialisation, power, hierarchy, follow because people are the basic unit. Thus the explanation for the primary characteristics of bureaucracy and whether they are effective or not does not exist independently of the nature of man. Indeed, it may be more accurate to say that they exist because of the properties of human beings. The formal organisation is a cognitive strategy about how the designers intend that roles be played, given the nature of human beings. Excluding human beings from one's theoretical interest therefore excludes a host of variables that may be the key to under-standing why formal organisations operate as they do, why they change, why they resist change, and how effective they may be.

CERTAIN CONDITIONS ARE IGNORED UNDER WHICH FORMAL
ORGANISATION MAY BE CHANGED BY THE PARTICIPANTS

The moment one includes in this theory statements suggesting that organisational effectiveness is intimately related to the degree of specialisation, hierarchy, and impersonality etc., one's theory is open to examination on what it may say about the effectiveness of organisations. An important question regarding the relationship of effectiveness to specialisation, hierarchy, and impersonality is how does one define when there is too much or too little of each of these variables. Can one derive, *from the theory*, hypotheses about such issues? One response is that specialisation or hierarchy become 'too much' when they are over-constructive and 'too little' when they do not influence the participants' behaviour. But how does one decide when and why a dimension of bureaucracy is over-constrictive or uninfluential? Does not such a study require obtaining the perceptions of the participants, their tolerance toward constraints and structures etc.?

I do not believe that it is possible to derive *a priori* hypotheses about these issues or to make *ad hoc* explanations without including the nature of human beings in one's theory. Blau's human being is narrowly rational and obediently submissive to the organisation. His man is reminiscent of economic man in microeconomics or administra-tive man in traditional scientific management.

Moreover, his conception places the responsibility upon management for the intelligence of the system, for its management, and for its change. Unless the proactive qualities of man are included, how will one be able to derive *a priori* the conditions and operationalise the points where organisational change is created by participants at different levels of the system? Is there not ample research to show that participants will create informal activities to counteract the formal and, in turn, that these informal activities may eventually become a cause of change of the formal structure and/or part of it? If one excludes these individual and group dimensions when one observes empirical variations in hierarchy, specialisation, and impersonality, one may not be able to explain validly the variance; or one may develop generalisations that are invalid.

INVALID GENERALISATIONS AND CONTRADICTORY EXPLANATIONS MAY GO UNNOTICED

To put the problem another way: since Blau excludes individual and group behaviour from his theory, he also excludes it from his empirical research. Consequently the assumption that individual and group behaviour can be ignored (for the problems Blau focuses upon) is never tested. The difficulties that follow from such a position may be illustrated from Blau's work. Blau agrees with Weber that impersonal detachment prevents irrational elements from affecting the decision-making processes. However, if one examines the research of individual and group behaviour on this issue one will find that the way to reduce the irrational component in decision making is to identify the irrational elements in decisions and then rationally eliminate them. How can irrational components of decisions be eliminated unless they are observed and examined? (Argyris 1967, 1968) . . .

. . . Recently Miller concluded that, '. . . contrary to Weber . . . a lack of impersonality may contribute to an organization's functioning. The quality of being well-liked . . . may contribute to the ability to exercise organizational control' (Miller 1970, p. 99).

Another example is related to Blau's operational measure of impersonality, namely the statistical records of the degree to which superior evaluates subordinate (Blau 1968, p. 335). The more frequent the contact the less the impersonality. Again, where individual and group behaviour are actually studied one finds that this assumption is not necessarily valid. For example, Meyer, Kay and French (1965) have presented empirical evidence of what actually goes on during meetings where the superior evaluates the subordinate. They found stronger feelings of mistrust and impersonality after the meeting than before. Thus it was possible for people to feel increased impersonal detachment as a result of increased interactions. However, this was not true in all cases. In some cases, the contact actually did create increased feelings of closeness and loss of detachment. Given Blau's theory and research strategy, the former findings would be unpredictable and the latter impossible to test. However, these findings are crucial to the kinds of predictions Blau is making and the generalisations he is producing.

A similar problem exists for the measurement of hierarchy. Hierarchy, Blau states, is needed to effect coordination of diverse tasks by enabling superiors on successive levels to guide, directly or indirectly, the performance of subordinates (Blau 1965, p. 334). The operational measures used are: (1) the number of levels, (2) the average span of control, and (3) the proportion of personnel in managerial positions. The logic Blau assumes is that the more favourable the span of control etc., the more effective will be the coordination and the direct or indirect guidance. But there are no data presented to illustrate that this, in fact, is the case. Such data are needed, especially since empirical data exist that, in order to study coordination, direction and control accurately, one must also study the manner in which they are actually performed (Likert 1967). Also, how would Blau's measures explain the findings of Argyris (1960) and Goldthorpe *et al*. (1968) that effective supervision existed (for middle and lower level managers and for employees) as long as the former left the latter alone? That is, supervision and coordination were occurring when it was not being done.

The same difficulties arise when Blau asserts that larger units contain a comparatively large number of employees in nearly every occupational speciality, thereby providing a congenial ingroup of colleagues for most employees (often not available in small organisations) and they simultaneously enhance opportunities for stimulating contacts with people whose training and experience are unlike their own (1970b, p. 200). In one study of a large central bank there was little congenial interaction reported within groups and little or no interest evidenced by employees to learn other jobs. In the small branch banks, however, employees developed congenial relationships across occupational specialities and because of group cohesion individuals learned each other's jobs in order to be of help so that all could finish work about the same time (Argyris 1954). The point again is that Blau is assuming a certain conception of man, one who, for example, prefers congenial relations with those with similar occupational interests. Further, he assumes that a heterogeneity of occupational interests leads to interest in widening one's repertoire of skills. One wishes that he would make more explicit this conception of man because it does not fit with the empirical findings available.

Finally, Blau gets into difficulty when he states that his findings may negate Merton's view that formalisation of procedures leads to increased rigidity and eventually less decentralisation (Blau 1970b, p. 160). Blau reports that 'strict adherence to civil service standards in making appointments as well as the elaboration of formalised personnel regulations promotes decentralisation which implies a less rigid structure of decision making' (Blau 1970b, p. 160).

There are at least two reasons to question the assertion that Merton has been disproven. Firstly a methodological reason: if the measures of decentralisation are what a few top people say exist, then all Blau found was that strict adherence to civil service standards and elaboration of formalised personnel regulations led the few senior informants to believe there was greater decentralisation. This generalisation says nothing about what the remainder of the management experience and as such does not necessarily negate Merton's hypothesis which could apply to organisational rigidity as experienced by more than a few key people.

We may also ask why top level informants perceive greater decentralisation with strict adherence to civil service standards and elaboration of formalised personnel regulations. One possibility is that they now feel free to let subordinates do the hiring precisely because strict adherence and elaborate formalised regulations lock the subordinate into what the superior wants. The subordinate can now make a decision because the superior believes he has him programmed to make the decisions as he (superior) would, or, if this is not the case, he can throw the regulations at him.

Is this decentralisation? At one level of analysis it is: subordinates instead of superiors are hiring people. At another level it may not be because the subordinates may not feel they have greater control; they may feel that they are carrying out the orders from the top. The second level asks, if there are formal procedures that give subordinates opportunities to hire, how do the subordinates view these opportunities? Do they experience these opportunities to hire as a sign of decentralisation and flexibility or do they experience it as a sign of pseudo-decentralisation and rigidity? Blau has, by the theory and the empirical measures used, ruled out these kinds of questions in his study of decentralisation.

Blau appears to compound the difficulties by going on to make normative statements, based on his findings, about how people in organisations may be managed more effectively. He begins by asking why the elaboration of formalised personnel procedures into an extensive body of written regulations furthers decentralisation (Blau 1970b, p. 163). He answers that:

the requirement to conform to a simple set of personnel regulations has the disadvantage that these standards become a straitjacket into which must be forced all kinds of different cases in a large variety of situations . . . one way to deal with the many exceptional cases not adequately covered by a simple set of rules is to permit officials to depart from these rules at their discretion, but doing so undermines the important advantages that following personnel standards provides to the organisation. An alternative method for coping with a large variety of cases and situations is to devise appropriate personnel standards for each type, supplemented by additional rules specifying under what conditions which standards are to be applied. This elaborating of the system of personnel regulations preserves the advantage resulting from compliance with merit standards of appointments and simultaneously avoids the disadvantage for personnel-selection resulting from either rigid application of inappropriate standards or idiosyncratic departures from standards.

Blau asserts that giving officials discretion to handle a variety of cases undermines the personnel standards and that elaborate systems of merit standards are more efficient. This may be the case but no empirical data are included that show that 'giving officials discretion . . . undermines personnel standards' or that 'elaborate systems of merit standards are more efficient'. If one has no data and one wishes to make statements like these, then is one not responsible for exploring the relevant behavioural literature?—most of which, by the way, would not support this view. Moreover, if one were to collect data would not one need a concept of efficiency? From what point of view are elaborate systems more efficient? This sounds very much like a statement from a traditional management theorist. Is this the criterion Blau wishes to utilise?

If one examines Blau's statement about decentralisation above, one will find that he argues for such a complete set of rules that individual discretion becomes minimal. How is this an explanation of decentralisation? One way to make the logic consistent is to assume that the act of hiring an individual is more of an index of decentralisation than what behaviour actually is manifested during that act. As a minimum, are we not owed evidence for this assumption?

Blau is, in actuality, making important assumptions about the nature of human beings and what they experience as decentralisation. This concept implies that a man can experience a sense of influence and control in certain decisions (a criterion of decentralisation) when the only choice he has is to behave strictly according to precisely defined regulations. Is it too extreme to ask that if such an individual existed he might not be classified as mildly distorted?

DIFFICULTIES IN FORMALISING ORGANISATIONAL THEORY

Recently, Blau has published a major paper whose objective is the development of a formal theory of formal organisations (Blau 1970a). There are some difficulties with the theory that are relatable to the problem described above.

Let us begin with Blau's statement that he wishes to develop a deductive theory of formal organisations focusing on the process of differentiation within organisations, be it spatial, occupational, hierarchical, or functional. The theory is limited to major antecedents and consequences of structural differentiation. It has been derived from the empirical results of a study of the social forces that govern the interrelations among differentiated elements in the formal structure. It ignores the psychological and group and inter-group forces which govern behaviour (Blau 1970a, p. 210).

How does Blau go about developing such a study? Researchers in the field study fifty-three employment security agencies by obtaining organisation charts, interviewing several key top informants, reading personnel and organisational policy manuals. Next, special formal organisational charts are developed. Then the basic dimensions of bureaucracy are dimensionalised and appropriate correlational analyses made and certain statistical curves are developed. On the basis of these empirical findings, two generalisations are formulated and given the status of axioms from which derivations are made. They are:

1. Increasing size generates structural differentiation in organisations along various dimensions at decelerating rates (Blau 1970a, p. 204).
2. Structural differentiation in organisations enlarges the administrative component (Blau 1970a, p. 212).

In order to explore these generalisations, we should go back to the beginning, namely to the choice of the organisation made. First, the civil service organisations studied operated under conditions that could have affected the forces of differentiation, be they spatial, occupational, hierarchical, or functional. For example:

1. All the organisations existed in a world where budgets had been and continue to be tight. The very tightness of funds may influence the number of people an agency may hire and thus the levels of organisation.

2. The civil service operates under rules that make it increasingly difficult to obtain slots for increasingly higher positions. Thus the higher the position sought, the more pressure against it being created, funded, and filled.

3. The organisations studied have a finite 'marketing' terrain. Each state or local agency is clearly limited to prescribed geographical conditions and to the range of services that can be offered.

4. All the systems have approached or have reached their prescribed limits.

Second, civil service organisations represented a population of organisations that have tended to adhere most rigorously to the traditional formal organisational theory. Consequently, they may not allow the degrees of freedom necessary for testing rival hypotheses. . . .

However, even if this problem were ultimately overcome there is a third problem which is more basic. As mentioned above, civil service organisations are designed directly from such organisational principles as task specialisation, span of control, and unity of command etc. As employees are hired they are, in accordance with unity of command and task specialisation, grouped together into a functional unit. Given the notion of chain of command each unit has to have a boss. Given span of control each boss may supervise a certain number of subordinates. As the organisation grows larger the number of units increases and so does the number of bosses increase, but given the span of control regulations, so does the need to coordinate the bosses. So we have super bosses.

But super bosses are difficult to obtain because they cost more and their slots are centrally managed. Also, given budgetary limitations additional employee help may be obtained if a given superior is willing to squeeze him under his control; or a given superior is willing to squeeze another unit under his control. Both of these forces would act to decrease the forces for expansion as the organisation grew larger.

The point is that the findings Blau reported were *not* generated or caused by size alone. . . . *Size may be correlated with, but may not be said to generate or to cause, structural differentiation.* To put this another way, the results Blau obtained from his study of the organisational charts might have been dramatically different if the basic managerial theory was one of project management and matrix organisations.

.   .   .

Blau's data may be used to illustrate Woodward's point, made in several studies, that size alone was *not* a significant variable to explain

organisational difference (Woodward 1965, pp. 31 and 40). Incidentally, she also reported that 'the size of the management group gave a
better indication of the "bigness" of a firm than the total number of
employees' (Woodward 1965, pp. 41–2). [...]

Perhaps Blau's analysis of his data stems from the need to relate
causality to one variable (size) when many were probably operating,
thereby giving the actual scatter obtained. If this analysis has merit
then Blau's first proposition should be rewritten as follows:

1. Increasing the number of employees is *correlated* with structural
differentiation in organisations along various dimensions *if* the organisation is designed in line with traditional scientific (administrative)
management principles.
2. The prediction of decelerating rates tends to occur when, in addition
to the conditions above, budgets are finite, financial constraints are
strong, position openings become increasingly difficult as one goes up
the hierarchy, and the marketing or service area and functions of the
organisation are limited.

Let us now turn to the second major generalisation. 'Structural
differentiation in organisations enlarges the administrative component.'
First a minor question. Does this mean that any amount of structural
differentiation enlarges the administrative component? I assume the
negative because to do otherwise is to predict that decreasing structural
differentiation . . . enlarges the administrative component. If agreed,
then the generalisation should begin with the word 'increasing'.

Now to the more important points. Let us explore the operational
definitions for structural differentiation and administrative component.
The administrative component is a distinct official status like a supervisor or a subunit like a branch. Structural differentiation is any
criterion on the basis of which members are formally divided into ranks
or subunits. Thus one criterion for structural differentiation is units,
but each unit has a supervisor. But supervisors are an operational
definition of an administrative component. The findings therefore are:
increasing structural differentiation by increasing the number of supervisors or units (each of whom by definition has a supervisor) increases
the number of units that have supervisors. Do we not have a tautology
depending upon what measures are used for administrative components?

Moreover, the second generalisation is stated as an axiom because,
states Blau, as organisations are differentiated, problems of coordination
and communications intensify (Blau 1970a, p. 213). What are the data
Blau presents for this causal explanation? If I read him correctly, he did

not collect data on this issue. Indeed, the variables involved were not measured in the research; they were inferred (Blau 1970a, p. 213). Implicit in the process of inference are, according to Blau, the following assumptions:

1. Differentiation makes an organisation more complex.
2. Complex structures engender problems of communication and co-ordination.
3. These problems, in turn, cause resistance to further differentiation.
4. Line supervisors at all levels have to spend more time dealing with these problems.
5. Line supervisors have less time to review the work of the subordinates, hence more supervisors are needed.

Hence, the more differentiated the formal structure, the more administrative personnel should be found in an organisation of a given size and the narrower the span of control of the supervisors and managers. But Blau defines 'differentiated' by functional units. Since every unit must have a boss (given chain of command), you should find more administrative personnel. Moreover, if you have more bosses and hold size constant, then of course the span of control will be narrowed (Blau 1970a, p. 213). What is Blau's theory telling us that goes beyond the traditional management theory?

Finally, if plans are developed to study the five assumptions above, how will human communication, coordination, resistance, and leadership be studied without including individual and group behavioural variables? What is the nature of the theoretical inheritance that Blau offered those who may choose to follow his work?

INTERRELATIONSHIPS WITH OTHER THEORIES OF FORMAL ORGANISATIONS

There are at least two other theories about why formal organisations arise and develop as they do, which someday will need to be accounted for by Blau's theory of formal organisation. The difficulty is that both theories are based upon the authors' conception of man, the dimensions excluded by Blau.

The first theory is Simon's. He suggests that formal organisational structures arise because they represent the very way man thinks and solves problems. Man's thinking mechanisms naturally lead him to specialisation and hierarchy (Simon 1969). Blau's view that 'Simon's theory is really not one of organization', that Simon 'takes for granted the conditions in the organization' and that Simon ignores the central problem of organisational structure does not seem to be accurate

(Blau 1968, p. 302). Indeed one may argue that Simon has shown as much, if not a more basic, interest in organisational structure because he has attempted to provide a rigorous theory of how and why it arises. Blau may question the theory but why does he apparently choose to rule it out? I suggest because he is committed to ignoring the individual level of analysis.

Blau and his associates will also have to confront another recent view of formal organisations suggested by Jaques. He implies that 'hierarchical pyramidal organizations ... [reflect] the character and distribution of human capacity' (Jaques 1964, p. 8).

Jaques' theory has to be dealt with by Blau because one of its major derivations is that organisational growth may be conceptualised in two different ways. One is growth simply by an increase in numbers of employees, and if necessary, by adding extra managerial commands. If the point is reached where managers become overburdened as a result of having too many subordinates, then additional sections of the same kind may be set up under newly appointed managers (Jaques 1964, p. 14). The other type of growth occurs when the organisation has somehow reached the limit of its existing pattern, and must differentiate itself by taking on new hierarchical state with a significantly different time span. Blau's findings are based on the former concept of growth. If the latter is a valid one, then the two will require eventual integration.

SUMMARY

Our analysis suggests
1. Although Blau states that he is studying organisations as wholes, he does not present a conceptual or operational definition of this view of reality. It may be more accurate to say that he is studying only a part of organisation, or organisations without formal or informal subdivisions.
2. The focus is primarily on formal organisation. This aspect of organisation has been shown to be incomplete and varying in form depending upon whose view one gets. Blau's primary data sources are highly biased toward top management view.
3. Blau's work may be more properly viewed as a quality control check on civil service regulations than as a contribution to new formal organisational theory.
4. The way the data are gathered could lead to contamination by the influence of leadership style, administrative controls, interpersonal relations, group dynamics and intergroup relations. Since none of these is studied, their influence is neither known nor defined.

5. Frequently explanations for correlational findings are developed that utilise or depend upon the variables that have been excluded (e.g. those listed in the previous conclusions).

6. Since the directly observable behaviour of individuals, groups or intergroup is not studied, the measures develop difficulties. For example, what is decentralisation in the eyes of top management can be centralisation for the subordinates. Also the criteria used to define impersonality and its converse are not adequate since impersonality can be created under the conditions that are defined for the converse.

7. There is no apparent way of generating insights about innovation in present organisations or generating new organisational forms that take into account the nature of man and of the group.

8. There are key generalisations that may be tautological.

REFERENCES

ARENSBERG, C., and MCGREGOR, D. (1942) 'Determinaion of morale in an industrial company', *Applied Anthropology*, **1**, 12–34.

ARGYRIS, C. (1968) 'Some unintended consequences of rigorous research', *Psychological Bulletin*, **70**, 185–97.

ARGYRIS, C. (1967) *Some Causes of Organizational Ineffectiveness Within the Department of State*, Center for International Systems Research, Department of State.

ARGYRIS, C. (1960) *Understanding Organizational Behavior*, Homewood, Ill., Dorsey Press.

ARGYRIS, C. (1954) *Organization of a Bank*, Labor and Management Center, Yale University.

BLAU, P. M. (1970a) 'A formal theory of differentiation in organizations', *American Sociological Review*, **35**, no. 2, 201–18.

BLAU, P. M. (1970b) 'Decentralization in bureaucracies', in M. N. Zald, ed., *Power in Organizations*, Vanderbilt University Press.

BLAU, P. M. (1968) 'Theories of organizations', *International Encyclopedia of Social Sciences*, New York, Macmillan, **2**, 297–304.

BLAU, P. M. (1965) 'Comparative study of organizations', *Industrial and Labor Relations Review*, **18**, no. 3, 323–38.

GOLDTHORPE, J. H., LOCKWOOD, D. L., BECHOFER, F., and PLATT, J. (1968) *The Affluent Worker: industrial attitudes and behaviour*, Cambridge University Press.

GREINER, L. E., LEITCH, D. P., and BARNES, L. B. (1968) 'The simple complexity of organizational climate in a government agency'. In R. Taguiri and G. H. Litwin, eds., *Organizational Climate*, Harvard University, Graduate School of Business, pp. 155–221.

JAQUES, E. (1964) 'Two contributions to a general theory of organization and management', *Scientific Business*, August, pp. 1–12.

LIKERT, R. (1967) *The Human Organization: its management and values*, McGraw-Hill.

MEYER, H., KAY, E., and FRENCH, J. (1965) 'Split roles in performance appraisal', *Harvard Business Review*, **43**, 123–9.

MILLER, J. P. (1970) 'Social-psychological implications of Weber's model of bureaucracy: Relations among expertise, control, authority, and legitimacy', *Social Forces*, **49**, no. 1, 91–102.

PERROW, C. (1970) 'Departmental power and perspectives in industrial firms' in M. N. Zald, ed., *Power in Organizations*, Vanderbilt University Press.

SIMON, H. A. (1969) *The Science of the Artificial*, Cambridge, Mass., M.I.T. Press.

SIMON, H. A., (1947) *Administrative Behavior*, New York, Free Press of Glencoe.

WEBBER, R. A. (1970) 'Perceptions of interactions between superiors and subordinates', *Human Relations*, **23**, no. 3, 235–48.

WOODWARD, J., ed. (1970) *Industrial Organization: behaviour and control*, Oxford University Press.

WOODWARD, J. (1965) *Industrial Organization: theory and practice*, Oxford University Press.

6

John Child　　　Organisational structure, environment and performance: the role of strategic choice

Excerpts from John Child, 'Organizational structure, environment and performance: The role of strategic choice', *Sociology*, Vol. 6, no. 1, January 1972, pp. 1–22.

[...] At the present time, some of the most influential models of organisation explicate little more than positively established associations between dimensions of organisational structure and 'contextual' (i.e. situational) factors such as environment, technology or scale of operation. These models proceed to the simplest theoretical solution which is that the contextual factors determine structural variables because of certain, primarily economic, constraints the former are assumed to impose.

It is the purpose of this paper to argue that this simple theory is inadequate, primarily because it fails to give due attention to the agency of choice by whoever have the power to direct the organisation. We shall argue that this 'strategic choice' extends to the context within which the organisation is operating, to the standards of performance against which the pressure of economic constraints has to be evaluated, and to the design of the organisation's structure itself. Incorporation of the process whereby strategic decisions are made directs attention onto the degree of choice which can be exercised in respect of organisational design, whereas many available models direct attention exclusively onto the constraints involved. They imply in this way that organisational behaviour can be understood by reference to functional imperatives rather than to political action.

Our concern will be with work organisations, which are seen as operating within particular environments to certain performance objectives. 'Work organisations' are defined as those within which work is carried out on a regular basis by paid employees, and which have been deliberately established for explicit purposes. The category includes organisations with formal objectives as diverse as business enterprises, hospitals, educational institutions, government departments and the administrative offices of trade unions. An assumption underlying much available research, as well as the present discussion, is that the engagement in systematic work and exchange which characterises all these types, provides a basis for comparison within a common hospital framework. Organisational structure is defined as the formal allocation of work roles and the administrative mechanisms to control and integrate work activities including those which cross formal organisational boundaries. The concept of 'strategic choice' is discussed later in the paper, where its full meaning should emerge.

AVAILABLE THEORETICAL MODELS

There are three particularly influential arguments relevant to an explanation of variation in organisational structure. Each postulates the effects of a major contextual factor. The first argument is from environment, in which environmental conditions are posited as critical constraints upon the choice of effective structural forms. The second and third arguments single out the influence on structure of two physical organisational attributes: technology and size. These three arguments highlight constraints upon structural design because contextual factors are regarded as important determinants of structural patterns. The need to secure a certain level of organisational performance is seen to lend contextual factors an exigent character.

1. *The Argument from Environment*

This argument starts from the observation that the maintenance of organisations depends upon some degree of exchange with outside parties. This dependency upon the environment is seen to impose a degree of constraint upon those directing an organisation. As Sadler and Barry put it (1970: 58) 'an organisation cannot evolve or develop in ways which merely reflect the goals, motives or needs of its members or of its leadership, since it must always bow to the constraints imposed on it by the nature of its relationship with the environment'. Different environmental conditions and different types of relationship with outside parties will, it is argued, require different types of organisational structural accommodation for a high level of performance to be achieved.

Three environmental conditions have been singled out as of particular importance. *Environmental variability* has attracted most attention as the major factor contributing to uncertainty among organisational decision-makers. The concept refers to the degree of change which characterises environmental activities relevant to an organisation's operations. Degree of change may in turn be seen as a function of three variables:

1. the frequency of changes in relevant environmental activities
2. the degree of difference involved at each change
3. the degree of irregularity in the overall pattern of change—in a sense the 'variability of change'.

A number of writers have arrived at the same broad conclusion: that the higher the environmental variability and the uncertainty consequently experienced, the more the prevailing structure of organisation should be adaptive, with roles open to continual redefinition and with coordination being achieved by frequent meetings and considerable lateral communication (cf. Stinchcombe 1959; Burns and Stalker 1961; Hage and Aiken 1967; Lawrence and Lorsch 1967).

Environmental complexity refers to the heterogeneity and range of environmental activities which are relevant to an organisation's operations. The greater the degree of complexity, the more a profusion of relevant environmental information is likely to be experienced by organisational decision-makers. The monitoring of diversified information, it is argued, establishes a requirement for greater role specialisation in areas of the organisation dealing directly with the environment, and problems of coordination between specialists may correspondingly increase (Lawrence and Lorsch 1967). The causal interconnectedness between environmental segments which Emery and Trist (1965) have identified, together with many economists before them, could be regarded as contributing towards complexity. But environmental complexity does not of itself necessarily give rise to uncertainty if little environmental variability is present, and if sufficient organisational resources are devoted to monitoring all the facets of the complex environment. Thus, while Emery and Trist tend to link causal interconnectedness with uncertainty, the latter would not necessarily be high if the nature of environmental sectors is changing slowly and if the order of connectedness between them is not variable.

Thirdly, the concept of *environmental illiberality* refers to the degree of threat that faces organisational decision-makers in the achievement of their goals from external competition, hostility or even indifference. Khandwalla (1970: 12–13) has called this environmental stress, though strictly speaking this is the way in which organisational decision-makers are likely to experience an illiberal environment rather than a feature of the environment *per se*. Khandwalla suggests several consequences of increasing environmental illiberality associated with the reduction of 'organizational slack' which is likely. For instance, the achievement of pluralistic group goals becomes more difficult and an overriding goal for the whole organisation becomes accentuated—that of survival. The associated structural consequence is an attempt to centralise decision-making and to exercise tighter controls, a proposition which Hage (1965) has also discussed.

2. *The Argument from Technology*

There are several distinct variants of the argument from technology. These reflect the different definitions of technology at the organisational level of analysis which theorists and researchers have employed (Hickson, *et al.* 1969: 380). The two most developed approaches are probably found in Woodward's studies of the 'operations technology' of manufacturing organisations (1965; 1970), and in Perrow's more generalisable analysis of 'materials technology' (1967; 1970). Operations technology refers to the equipping and sequencing of activities in an organisation's workflow, while materials technology refers to characteristics of the physical and informational materials used. Both Woodward and Perrow consider that the nature of technological variables presents important implications for the design of effective organisational structure. Woodward has recently concentrated her attention upon problems of production control and administrative rationality which tend to rise with the middle range of complexity in operations technology—large-batch and mass production. Perrow argues that the degree of stability in the nature of materials used and the extent to which routine codifiable techniques ('analysable search') can be applied to them, influence the way in which work roles can effectively be defined. Their arguments, taken together, imply that a high structuring of activities (task specialisation and high role definition by rules and paperwork) is likely to be most effective under conditions of standardised mass production.

3. *The Argument from Size*

The argument from size has a long history within organisational theory. Weber (1947) in his classic analysis of bureaucracy, did not believe that bureaucratic characteristics would be present within small organisations. More recent research evidence appears to lend strong support to this view. For example, Pugh and his colleagues (1969) found larger size to be the most powerful predicator of higher values on their main structural factor which related to the bureaucratic dimensions of specialisation, use of procedures, and reliance on paperwork. Blau (1970) has produced data suggesting that increased size generates structural differentiation within organisations, and that structural differentiation in turn enlarges the absolute (though not the relative) size of an organisation's administrative component.

If we draw together the strands of the argument from size, two main causal processes appear to be suggested, both having similar ultimate implications for effective structural design. The first argues that increasing size offers more opportunities to reap the benefits of increased specialisation. Increased specialisation is likely to manifest itself in the form of greater structural differentiation which exhibits higher heterogeneity among a larger number of organisational subunits, but which may exhibit a greater homogeneity of role within each subunit. This increasing complexity will render the managerial coordination of subunit activities more difficult, especially as strains towards functional autonomy may well appear, and for this reason pressure will be placed upon senior management to impose a system of impersonal controls through the use of formal procedures, the recording of information in writing and the like. The second argument reaches much the same conclusion by pointing out how the problem of directing larger numbers of people makes it impossible to continue employing a personalised, centralised style of management. Instead, a more decentralised system, using impersonal mechanisms of control, has to be adopted. The operation of such a system requires higher numbers of administrative and clerical personnel.

SOURCES OF STRUCTURAL VARIATION

The three preceeding arguments attempt to explain observable patterns of organisational structure by reference to constraints imposed by contextual factors. These constraints are assumed to have force because work organisations must achieve certain levels of performance in order to survive. If organisational structure is not adapted to its context, then opportunities are lost, costs rise, and the maintenance of the organisation is threatened. . . . The environment has normally been regarded as the primary source of constraint upon organisational design, while assumptions about performance requirements underlie the whole notion of constraint itself. It is hoped that a re-examination of these two issues will demonstrate the need for a revised analysis of variation in organisational structure.

Organisation and Environment

The environment of an organisation cannot be satisfactorily defined without reference to what Levine and White have called 'organizational domain' (1961:597). This consists of the specific goals which organisational decision-makers wish to pursue and the functions which they cause an organisation to undertake in order to implement those goals.

With this in mind, writers such as Thompson (1967) and Normann (1969a) have distinguished different segments of the environment in terms of their immediacy for the goals and functions ascribed to an organisation. Organisational decision-makers normally perceive themselves as operating only in certain 'markets' and utilising selected sources of inputs; they regard success in these areas as particularly vital for the organisation's survival. The organisation may also have transactions in other areas, but these are regarded as less central to the main purpose. Finally, there are yet further sectors of the environment with which the organisation normally enters into little or no direct contact.

This distinction of several environmental boundaries proceeding 'outwards' from the organisation implies that organisational decision-makers do take positive steps to define and manipulate their own corners of the environment. Such action is in fact commonly found. Thus trade unions distinguish their own particular environments with respect to categories of membership, as do hospitals regarding types of patient, and business organisations where this takes the familiar form of creating and manipulating product differentiation (Bain 1959). Cyert and March have suggested that the posture towards the environment which those in control of organisations attempt to adopt will reflect their perception of environmental conditions in relation to their desire to attain with some certainty the goals they have set for the organisation (1963: 118–120). In regard to organisational structure, these goals may reflect a preference for an ordered existence and a 'quiet life', or for a distribution of power and status which those in control are determined not to upset. In such circumstances, they may choose either to ignore or restrain certain developments within the environment, a positive response to which would entail a modification to the organisational *status quo*. If the organisation is seen to have a secure grip upon its immediate operating environment, its decision-makers may well attach little economic cost to this policy. Again it is possible to find examples of this hypothetical case in real life. For instance, Normann (1969b) found in thirteen case studies of new product development in Swedish companies that the existing values and power structure of an organisation played a critical role in predicting reaction to new ideas and information.

Similarly, the distinction between environment and the organisation itself (the 'inner' boundary of the environment) is relative to the goals and actions of organisational decision-makers. As Kronenberg points out (1969: Chapter III), traditionally an organisation has been said to comprise all the positions or roles bound together by the same authority system. Yet within its immediate environment, which Normann has called its 'territory' (1969a: 3), those in control of an organisation may in practice be able to exercise a degree of authority (influence that is accepted as legitimate by those over which it is held) over other organisations or individuals which are nominally independent. A similar problem of boundary definition arises in the case of an organisation which forms part of a wider unit, such as the subsidiary of a multi-national firm, where both share the same authority system.

These examples suggest that the relationships between organisation and environment are variable, a notion expressed in the concept of inter-dependence which refers to the closeness of relationships between organisations (Pugh *et al.* 1963: 312). Moreover, the most important aspect of these relationships concerns the degree of influence which the controllers of one organisation can exert over their counterparts in other organisations, and *vice versa*. Thompson and McEwen (1958) have identified the various procedures which may be chosen in order to assert this influence in support of organisational goals. The value of adopting this perspective lies in its rejection of any notion that environmental circumstances determine intra-organisation features directly or indirectly. On the other hand, it still allows that under certain conditions the actions taken by environmental parties may exert considerable pressures for change.

To summarise, we have argued that the analysis of organisation and environment must recognise the exercise of choice by organisational decision-makers. They may well have some power to 'enact' their organisation's environment, as Weick has put it (1969: 63 ff). Thus to an important extent, their decisions as to where the organisation's operations shall be located, the clientele it shall serve, or the types of employees it shall recruit determine the limits to its environment—that is, to the environment significant for the functions which the organisation performs. The boundaries between an organisation and its environment are similarly defined in large degree by the kinds of relationships which its decision-makers choose to enter upon with their equivalents in other organisations, or by the constraints which more dominant counterparts impose upon them. In view of these essentially strategic and political factors, environmental conditions cannot be regarded as a direct source of variation in organisational structure, as open system theorists often imply. The critical link lies in the decision-makers' evaluation of the organisation's position in the environmental areas they regard as important, and in the action they may consequently take about its internal structure.

Organisation and Performance

The available theoretical models reviewed earlier assume at least implicitly that the sanctions which would be invoked against organisational decision-makers in the event of not achieving a certain level of organisational performance act as a severe limitation on the degree of indeterminateness that exists in the relationships between contextual factors and organisational structure.

A theory or organisational structure has, therefore, to take account of performance dimensions. Most research and discussion on organisational performance within the social science has been devoted to a study of the conditions under which organisations achieve different levels of effectiveness (cf. Price 1968). From this perspective structural and other variables have normally been treated as independent, with some measure of effectiveness constituting the dependent variable. Performance has been treated as an outcome. In contrast, a theory of organisational structure would posit structural variables as depending upon decisions which were made with reference to some standard of required performance as well as to some prediction of the effects of structural alternatives upon the performance achieved. Performance is treated as an input to this model, as well as an outcome. Thus two questions which are of some moment for a theory of organisational structure are, first, how performance standards and their degree of achievement may act as a stimulus to structural variation, and, secondly, how far structural variation is likely to affect performance levels. Both questions bear on the issue of how far the choice of organisational structure is subject to economic constraints.

There is little research evidence on the effect that performance standards and their degree of achievement will have upon structural variation. A primary condition here would seem to be that the operation of any particular structural arrangement depends upon a sufficient supply of resources. A declining level of performance, or even a level that fails to meet expectations, may therefore lead to decisions aimed at effecting administrative economies, probably in the direction of simplified procedural and paperwork systems together with a proportionately lower administrative staff component. Allowing for the possibility that alternative structural designs are available and that they represent rather similar overhead costs, then a further condition for performance considerations to influence structural choice must be that those making the choice believe that structural arrangements do have some influence on the level of organisational effectiveness achieved. If they do not believe this, then the level of performance actually reached will only affect structural choice in terms of straight administrative costs.

However, it is likely that in most cases organisational decision-makers do believe that structural design has some consequences for performance. In this event, the level of performance actually achieved will probably influence decisions on structural design, subject to an important proviso. This is that the performance attained does not exceed any target which the decision-makers may have decided is adequate. If performance exceeds this 'satisficing' level (and one is assuming that this level represents a degree of return that is at least sufficient to secure resources required for the fulfilment of present and future plans), then the decision-making group *may* take the view that the margin of surplus permits them to adopt structural arrangements which accord the better with their own preferences, even at some extra administrative cost to the organisation. In such circumstances the dominant organisational power-holders may also permit other interest groups to make or retain their own preferred structural adaptations, a kind of 'organizational slack' (cf. Cyert and March, 1963: 36–8). Given the widespread prevalence of imperfections in the economics of resource allocation and competition, especially for non-business organisations, considerable organisational slack may often be present. The conclusion reached once again is therefore that organisational decision-makers may well perceive that they have a substantial element of choice in the planning of organisational structure. This consideration is of immediate theoretical relevance, even though it represents a speculation that remains eventually to be investigated empirically.

The second question concerns the extent to which structural variation is likely to affect the levels of organisational performance actually achieved. Is there any reason to believe that other strategic choices, such as the choice of environment, of market strategies or of operating scale and technology, could significantly influence performance outcomes quite apart from the structural design which is adopted? The results of economic research into business organisations suggest that other strategic considerations may have considerable influence. For instance, the choice of markets to be served can considerably affect the performance of an enterprise because the return available from different markets and industries varies considerably and because some markets are expanding while others are not—a poor choice here leads to 'market inefficiency'. A business firm may suffer from 'technical inefficiency' if it operates plants that are too small to gain the advantages attainable through economics of scale, and if it utilises an operations technology that does not allow full advantage to be taken of standardisation and long production runs. Thirdly, the failure to seize opportunities for profitable investment either in production facilities or in research and development will cause performance to suffer through a 'lack of progressiveness'. This classification of strategic choices has been utilised by Caves in his review of performance in British industry (Caves 1968), but it is by no means exhaustive. However, it is sufficient to demonstrate that structural design is likely to have only a limited effect upon the level of organisational performance achieved, even though the type of structure utilised may affect the quality of other strategic decisions because of the way it influences the communication of necessary information and so on.

The conclusion that the design of organisational structure may have a restricted influence upon performance levels, and that performance standards may themselves allow for some 'slack', weakens the general proposition that contextual factors will exert a high degree of constraint upon the choice of structural design. In practice, there does appear to be some variation in the structures of otherwise comparable organisations, a variation which is sustained over periods of time without much apparent effect on success or failure. This is frequently remarked upon by the senior personnel within such organisations, and it is not refuted by the fact that multivariate predictions of particular structural dimensions still leave large proportions (40 per cent upwards) of the structural variance unaccounted for (cf. Pugh *et al.* 1969). In addition, a review of research and discussion on business organisations led the present writer to conclude that while there may be limits within which their size, technology and rate of adjustment to the environment should fall if they are to obtain a high level of economic performance, these limits do not as yet seem capable of precise definition (Child 1969: 95–8). In so far as a choice may be exercised in respect of these contextual factors without incurring significant net performance penalties, the possibilities of structural choice would seem to be further strengthened.

Strategic Choice and Organisation Theory

The considerations so far raised direct our attention towards those who possess the power to decide upon an organisation's structural rationale, towards the limits upon that power imposed by the operational context, and towards the process of assessing constraints and opportunities against values in deciding organisational strategies. Up to this point, there has been implicit in our analysis an assumption that in work organisations the actions of all members are not usually of equal weight in identifying the source of variation in major organisation-wide features such as the formal structure of work roles, procedures and communications. The term 'decision-makers' has been employed to refer to the power-holding group on the basis that it is normally possible within work organisations to identify inequalities of power which are reflected in a differential access to decision-making on structural design, and even in a differential ability to raise questions on the subject in the first place. While it has often been suggested that the advancing level of technical expertise required to operate large, sophisticated organisations is in effect taking many decisions out of the hands of senior administrators or officials, there is little evidence to show that the latter do not retain control over policy initiation and implementation (Burns 1966a). This conclusion speaks for the relevance of the 'dominant coalition' concept which was formulated by Cyert and March (1963) and has been employed extensively by Thompson (1967).

The notion of a dominant coalition is advantageous in the way it highlights the immediate source of major structural variation in organisations, but it is an abstraction and could be misleading if not used cautiously. Certain qualifications are therefore apposite. First, the term dominant coalition does not necessarily identify the formally designated holders of authority in an organisation; rather it refers to those who collectively happen to hold most power over a particular period of time. Indeed, one may find situations where there is more than one dominant coalition, where one group is constrained or challenged by another. Some British trade unions illustrate this possibility, in which a degree of polarisation has developed between those elected to national offices and those occupying elected positions at the local or regional level.

Secondly, use of the concept need not imply that other members of an organisation do not have some power to modify plans and decisions which have been formulated; indeed, the modification may be substantial when it is the result of collective action. Information reaching the dominant coalition is open to reinterpretation at the hands of the people who have to pass it on, such as those in boundary roles with respect to information coming in from the environment and those in roles lower down in the hierarchy with respect to information passing up from operating levels. Similarly, the implementation of decisions reached depends on securing the cooperation of other parties to the organisation; this political process accounts for the considerable length of time taken to reach many major organisational decisions (cf. Dubin 1962).

The purpose of employing a concept such as the dominant coalition is primarily to distinguish those who normally have the power to take the initiative on matters such as the design of organisational structure from others who are in a position of having to respond to such decisions. The concept is tenable if one regards the norm within work organisations to be what Mann (1970) in another context has called a 'pragmatic acceptance' by lower level participants of power-holding roles and of the decisions emanating from these. Needless to say, a use of the concept does not imply that the student of organisation should internalise the perspective of organisational power-holders, as has often been the case in the past. However, it does require him to incorporate this perspective and the action to which it gives rise as major variables in his theory.

The dominant coalition concept opens up a view of organisational structures in relation to the distribution of power and the process of strategic decision-making which these reflect. If, as we have argued, there is some freedom of manoeuvre with respect to contextual factors, standards of performance and structural design, then some choice is implied as to how the organisation as an on-going system will be maintained. The dominant coalition concept draws attention to the question of who is making the choice. It thus provides a useful antidote to the sociologically unsatisfactory notion that a given organisational structure can be understood in relation to the functional imperative of 'system needs' which somehow transcend the objectives of any group of organisational members. In this way the analytical contribution of a functional interpretation of organisational behaviour referring to system maintenance in response to contextual constraints, is supplemented by a political interpretation which does not regard such constraints as necessarily acute or immutable, and which highlights the role of choice. In shifting attention towards the role of choice, we are led to account for organisational variation directly through reference to its sources rather than indirectly through reference to its supposed consequences. This shift of emphasis meets one of the major criticisms that Silverman (1970) has raised against much contemporary organisation theory.

In the course of his historical study of American industrial enterprise, Chandler (1962) developed the concept of strategy in referring to the exercise of choice by a dominant coalition as the major source of organisational variation. Chandler's insight lies at the heart of the argument being developed in this paper. 'Strategy', he writes (p. 13), 'can be defined as the determination of the basic long-term goals and objectives of an enterprise, and the adoption of courses of action and the allocation of resources necessary for carrying out these goals. Decisions to expand the volume of activities, to set up distant plants and offices, to move into new economic functions, or become diversified along many lines of business, involve the defining of new basic goals.'

In Chandler's view, the modification of organisational goals is, therefore, a major source of changes in size, technology and location. In regard to structure, his general thesis (which he supports with comparative historical data) is that 'a new strategy required a new or at least refashioned structure if the enlarged enterprise was to be operated efficiently' (p. 15). The process of strategy formulation in this way constitutes a major interface between what Burns (1966b) has called the 'working organization' and the 'political system' within organisations.

Chandler's analysis, and that presented in this paper, leads to the conclusion that strategic choice is the critical variable in a theory of organisations. Other variables which have often been regarded as independent determinants of organisational structures are, within this perspective, seen to be linked together as multiple points of reference for the process of strategic decision-making. Woodward's recent research (1970) has, for example, illustrated how the degree of uncertainty about the environment together with the underlying technological rationale of the product both enter into decisions on the operating plans that are adopted in manufacturing firms. These operating plans in turn were found to possess implications for both formal and informal structures in the organisation. To take another example involving environment and technology, Khandwalla has suggested that if the dominant coalition in a manufacturing firm experiences greater stress from the environment, it is likely to increase the attention it gives to cost reduction (1970: 39–45). The technological manifestation of this will probably be a move towards more standardised and larger batch production. Both the environmental and the technological change are likely to enter as points of reference into any subsequent decisions to standardise working procedures, define work roles more closely, increase centralised decision-making and other structural changes.

In a similar way, it is likely that environmental conditions and organisational size will *together* impinge upon the framework of organisational decision-making. For instance, the extent to which high environmental complexity will be considered by the dominant coalition to establish requirements for greater specialisation in boundary roles will probably depend also on how it assesses the implications of its organisation's size. This helps to explain why small organisations generally have a low degree of specialisation in boundary-spanning activities even though, as in the case of trade union administrations, they face relatively complex environments. The role of size and technology in relation to organisational structure requires a similar theoretical development, as we suggested when reviewing the 'argument from size'.

These simple examples with pairs of contextual referents should not obscure the full complexity of strategic choice in which numerous referents may be involved—the multinational enterprise illustrates this complexity to an extreme degree (Brooke and Remmers 1970). There is also a further important complication to which we have already alluded: that as referents in organisational decision-making, contextual and structural variables may be brought into a reciprocal relationship. Thus if one takes the variable of size, the high value placed by a dominant coalition on the retention or attainment of a given structure may well lead to an attempt to control or change the organisation's scale of operations. We have argued that this action may be economically feasible in some circumstances. Size, many organisation theorists assume, leads to structure; but considered in its relation to other referents of organisational strategic action, such an assumption is naïve, for the reverse could also apply.

In short, when incorporating strategic choice in a theory of organisation, one is recognising the operation of an essentially political process in which constraints and opportunities are functions of the power exercised by decision-makers in the light of ideological values. A consideration of these values has been outside the scope of this paper, but their existence implies that the degree of association which different contextual factors have with structural variables will not conform to any stable mathematical function. Only when these political factors can be adequately measured is greater predictive certainty likely to be achieved.

CONCLUSION

Our contention in this paper has been that many available contributions to a theory of organisational structure do not incorporate the direct source of variation in formal structural arrangements, namely the strategic decisions of those who have the power of structural initiation —the dominant coalition. In this respect, the theoretical models we reviewed attempt to explain organisational structure at one remove. They draw attention to possible constraints upon the choice of effective structures, but fail to consider the process of choice itself in which economic and administrative exigencies are weighed by the actors concerned against the opportunities to operate a structure of their own and/or other organisational members' preferences.

.   .   .

A final comment places our argument in its wider context. We have been concerned with the role of strategic choice as a necessary element in any adequate theory of organisational structure, and have suggested that many available explanations over-emphasise constraints upon that choice. In so doing they draw our attention away from the possibilities first of choosing structural arrangements that will better satisfy the priorities of those in charge of organisations, or indeed of any interested party; and secondly away from the exploration of organisational design as a means of reconciling more successfully economic and social criteria of performance. Until we revise these theoretical perspectives, we shall fail to shake off 'the metaphysical pathos of much of the modern theory of group organisation . . . that of pessimism and fatalism' which Gouldner noted fifteen years ago (1955: 498).

REFERENCES

BAIN, J. S. (1959) *Industrial Organization*, Wiley.
BLAU, P. M. (1970) 'The Formal Theory of Differentiation in Organizations', *American Sociological Review*, **35**, April, 201–18.
BROOKE, M. Z., and REMMERS, H. L. (1970) *The Strategy of Multinational Enterprise*, Longman.
BURNS, T. (1966a) Preface to second edition of Burns and Stalker (1961).
BURNS, T. (1966b) 'On the Plurality of Social Systems', in J. R. Lawrence, ed., *Operational Research and the Social Sciences*, Tavistock, pp. 165–77.
BURNS, T. and STALKER, G. M. (1961) *The Management of Innovation*, Tavistock.
CAVES, R. E. *et al.* (1968) *Britain's Economic Prospects*, Allen and Unwin.
CHANDLER, A. (1962) *Strategy and Structure: Chapters in the History of the Industrial Enterprise*, Cambridge, Mass., M.I.T. Press.
CHILD, J. (1969) *The Business Enterprise in Modern Industrial Society*, Collier-Macmillan.
CYERT, R. M., and MARCH, J. G. (1963) *A Behavioural Theory of the Firm*, Englewood Cliffs, Prentice-Hall.
DUBIN, R. (1962), 'Business Behaviour *Behaviourally* Viewed', in G. B.

Strother, ed., *Social Science Approaches to Business Behaviour*, Tavistock, pp. 11–55.

EMERY, F. E., and TRIST, E. L. (1965) 'The causal texture of organizational environments', *Human Relations*, **18**, 21–32.

GOULDNER, A. W. (1955) 'Metaphysical pathos and the theory of bureaucracy', *American Political Science Review*, **49**, 496–507.

HAGE, J. (1965) 'An axiomatic theory of organizations', *Administrative Science Quarterly*, **10**, 289–320.

HAGE, J., and AIKEN, M. (1967) 'Program change and organizational properties—a comparative analysis', *American Journal of Sociology*, **72**, 503–19.

HICKSON, D. J. *et al.* (1969) 'Operations technology and organization structure: an empirical reappraisal', *Administrative Science Quarterly*, **14**, 378–97.

KHANDWALLA, P. N. (1970) *Environment and the Organization Structure of Firms*, McGill University Faculty of Management Working Paper.

KRONENBERG, P. S. (1969) *Micropolitics and Public Planning*, Chapter 3 on 'Interorganizational Behavior', pre-publication manuscript.

LAWRENCE, P. R., and LORSCH, J. W. (1967) *Organization and Environment*, Harvard Business School.

LEVINE, S., and WHITE, P. E. (1961) 'Exchange as a conceptual framework for the study of interorganizational relationships', *Administrative Science Quarterly*, **5**, 583–601.

MANN, M. (1970) 'The social cohesion of liberal democracy', *American Sociological Review*, **35**, 423–39.

NORMANN, R. (1969a) 'Organization, mediation, and environment', *S.I.A.R. Report*, no. UPM–RN–91, Stockholm.

NORMANN, R. (1969b) 'Some conclusions from 13 case studies of new product development', *S.I.A.R. Report*, no. UPM–RN–100, Stockholm.

PERROW, C. (1967) 'A framework for the comparative analysis of organizations', *American Sociological Review*, **32**, 194–208.

PERROW, C. (1970) *Organizational Analysis: a sociological view*, Tavistock.

PRICE, J. L. (1968) *Organizational Effectiveness: an inventory of propositions*, Homewood, Irwin.

PUGH, D. S. *et al.* (1963) 'A conceptual scheme for organizational analysis', *Administrative Science Quarterly*, **8**, 289–315.

PUGH, D. S. *et al.* (1969) 'The context of organization structures', *Administrative Science Quarterly*, **14**, 91–114.

SADLER, P. J., and BARRY, B. A. (1970) *Organizational Development*, Longman.

SILVERMAN, D. (1970) *The Theory of Organizations*, Heinemann.

STINCHCOMBE, A. L. (1959) 'Bureaucratic and craft administration of production: a comparative study', *Administrative Science Quarterly*, **4**, 168–87.

THOMPSON, J. D. (1967) *Organizations in Action*, McGraw-Hill.

THOMPSON, J. D., and MCEWEN, W. J. (1958) 'Organizational goals and environment: goal-setting as in interaction process', *American Sociological Review*, **23**, 23–31, also no. 10 in this Reader.

WEBER, M. (1947) *The Theory of Social and Economic Organization*, New York, Free Press.

WEICK, K. E. (1969) *The Social Psychology of Organizing*, Addison-Wesley.

WOODWARD, J. (1965) *Industrial Organization: theory and practice*, Oxford University Press.

WOODWARD, J., ed. (1970) *Industrial Organization: behaviour and control*, Oxford University Press.

7

D. *J. Hickson*   A convergence in
organisation theory

D. J. Hickson, 'A convergence in organization theory', *Administrative Science Quarterly*, 1966–7, **11**, 224–37.

In the cycles of investigation and speculation, the plethora of theories sometimes converges, and an underlying similarity in concept emerges from the varied terminologies. It may well be true that in diversity lies innovation. But when diversity is more in jargon than in ideas, research time is wasted before the common base is discovered, and what purports to be a lively range of exploration may disguise a general restriction within the bounds of one limiting perception. Such a convergence can be seen in the approaches of leading students to the structure of organisations.

Theory has converged upon the specificity (or precision) of role prescription and its obverse, the range of legitimate discretion. As Levinson (1959) writes, in his authoritative review of role theory,

It is important also to consider the specificity or narrowness with which the normative requirements are defined. Norms have an 'ought' quality; they confer legitimacy and reward value upon certain modes of action, thought, and emotion, while condemning others. But there are degrees here. Normative evaluations cover a spectrum from 'strongly required', through various degrees of qualitative kinds of 'acceptable', to the more or less stringently tabooed. Organizations differ in the width of the intermediate range on this spectrum. That is, they differ in the number and kinds of adaptation that are normatively acceptable. The wider the range—

the less specific the norms—the greater is the area of personal choice for the individual.

There is nothing remarkable in pinpointing role theory here. Role is often cited as *the* link between social structure and personality, and as such must be central to organisation theory. But to repeat Levinson's crushing comment: 'The concept of role remains one of the most overworked and underdeveloped in the social sciences.'

Of course, to use the very concept of role assumes a minimum prescription of organisational behaviour. Even the untrammelled research fellow who is said to have complete freedom of choice must select *some* pursuits that qualify as academic; even if he can go so far as to set up his own business, he cannot devote himself to it exclusively without some accommodation to his role in the academic organisation. So the specificity dimension runs from such roles, where prescription is in general terms and goes no further than outlining the boundaries of legitimate discretion, to roles where all but a fraction of role behaviour is minutely prescribed. Somewhere near the latter extreme comes the semiskilled assembly-line operator, as well as particular activities in the performance of some roles, for example, the first violin player when on stage. Thus, a role may extend over a range of this dimension.

If roles vary in specificity of prescription, who are the prescribers? The commonly accepted assumption is that structure embodies the prescriptions of the organisation in general and of hierarchical superordinates (bosses) in particular.

CONCEPTS OF PRINCIPAL STUDENTS

The concepts of some principal students of organisation structure can now be examined. Their terminologies for the specificity of role prescription are presented in Table 7.1. In this table the contrast is drawn between high*er* and low*er* specificity, since it is not intended to imply that all the forms of structure discussed are at exactly high or exactly low positions on the continuum. Presumably they range along it, but there is a strong bimodal tendency in what many authors have written.

Structure analysts

Structure analysts from among sociologists and administration theorists have produced a varied list of terms. To begin with Weber's (1947) three ideal types, the structural accompaniments or consequences of the authority source are most elaborated for the rational-legal case. The features of a bureaucratic structure based on rational-legal authority do not need reiteration; this type shows highly specific prescription, as has been accepted by the many researchers and theorists who have used the concept of bureaucracy, and who therefore may be grouped anonymously under Weber's name. The traditionalistic or patriarchal structure can also be routinised to some extent, but a structure based on charisma suggests much lower specificity. Certainly Burns and Stalker (1961) see it that way. They find bureaucratic structure to be 'mechanistic', in that it does not easily adapt to technical and market change because of its 'precise definition of rights and obligations and technical methods attached to each functional role'. They contrast it with the 'organic' form, later called 'organismic' by Burns (1963), in which role definitions are more general and continually change in interaction. Barnes' (1960) study of two engineering groups has produced strikingly similar results. He defines 'open' (as opposed to 'closed') organisational systems by high member autonomy, opportunities for interaction beyond the immediate task, and mutual influence across status levels. This same difference between 'formalised' and 'flexible' structures was noted years before by W. F. Whyte (1948). Hage's (1965, p. 295) synthesis of organisational variables to formulate an axiomatic theory employs Burns and Stalker's terms, 'mechanistic' and 'organic', and contrasts high and low formalisation (standardisation); i.e., 'the proportion of codified jobs and the range of variation that is tolerated within the rules defining the jobs'.

Crozier (1964, p. 192), tracing the patterns of power in organisations and building a 'strategic model' of group behaviour, relates power to the degrees of either structural routinisation or uncertainty; routinization removes power, uncertainty gives scope for power. Hence Crozier attributes the power of the maintenance engineers in the 'industrial monopoly' he studied to their control of machines; i.e., 'Control over the last source of uncertainty remaining in a completely routinised organisational system.' Likewise, Burns and Stalker find political conflict surrounding research and development units, which are relatively organismic, when they are introduced into mechanistic structures. The shift of power within hospitals from physicians to administrators is yet another example, according to Gordon and Becker (1964), who attribute it to modern medical techniques. These enable administrators to specify the procedures and resources to be used in treatment. Specified procedures improve administrative coordination, but mounting conflict may be anticipated as

TABLE 7.1. *The terminologies used by various students of organisation structure for specificity of role prescription*

Students of organisation structure	Terminologies for specificity (or precision) of role prescription	
	Higher specificity	Lower specificity
Structure analysts (Sociologists and administration theorists)		
Weber	Traditionalistic, bureaucratic	Charismatic
Burns and Stalker	Mechanistic	Organic (or organismic)
Barnes	Closed system	Open system
Whyte	Formalised	Flexible
Hage	High formalisation (standardisation)	Low formalisation
Crozier	Routinised	Uncertain
Gordon and Becker	Specified procedures	Unspecified
Thompson	Overspecification	Structural looseness
Litwak	Weberian	Human relations
Janowitz	Domination: manipulation	Fraternal
Frank	Well-defined (and overdefined)	Underdefined
Simon	Programmed	Nonprogrammed
Presthus	Structured perceptual field	Unstructured
Bennis	Habit	Problem-solving
Structure designers (Management writers)		
Taylor	Scientific task determination	Personal rule-of-thumb
Fayol Urwick Brech	Clear statement of responsibilities	Personalities predominant (rather than intended design)
Brown	Explicit authority and accountability	Undefined roles and relationships
Structure critics (Social psychologists)		
Likert	Authoritative	Participative
McGregor	Theory X	Theory Y
Argyris	Rational organisation	Self-actualisation

physicians defend their discretionary prerogatives against the encroaching rules.

Thompson (1965) suspects 'overspecification' of human resources of preventing innovation, whereas 'structural looseness' implies dispersion of power and therefore the forcing of more alternative solutions to those problems in which 'power meets power'. Searching for models of complex organisations that permit such conflict, Litwak (1961) compares three models: the Weberian, the human relations, and the professional, which differ in the extent of '*a priori* specification of job authority' and 'hierarchical authority'. Likewise, Janowitz (1959) contends that under the impact of new weapons, military authority is changing from the 'domination' of explicit instruction to 'manipulation', with a possible further adaptation to a 'fraternal type' system, a trend he sees also in non-military organisations.

Some analysts have used a more psychological frame of reference. Foremost among them is Simon (1960) with his well-known 'programmed-nonprogrammed' continuum. This computer analogy is colourful, but may have obscured the connection with organisation structure. Fortunately, Burns and Stalker forge a link by associating nonprogrammed decision making with what they call organismic systems. Simon also records what has been dubbed 'Gresham's Law of Planning'; i.e., 'that programmed activity tends to drive out nonprogrammed activity' from a job. Here is a second direct link with the sociological point of view, for it complements Crozier's hypothesis about power. To Simon, increasing the routinisation of the area of activity controlled by an executive implies that his attention will be increasingly held by programmed decisions to the neglect of nonprogrammed decisions: to Crozier, increasing routinisation implies a loss of power. Thus, programmed decisions go with a lack of power, and nonprogrammed decisions go with power (as Gordon and Becker's hospital physicians are discovering). Presthus (1958), like Simon, derives his hypotheses from the psychological end of the spectrum. According to Presthus, precise definition of status and role gives clear perceptual cues, i.e., a highly 'structured field'. He uses Sullivan's (1953) formulation of the theory of 'anxiety reduction' as basic social motivation to suggest that the structuring of the perceptual field is inversely related to anxiety. People try to reduce anxiety by more clearly defining the social organisation. This, too, agrees with Burns and Stalker, who, though proposing an organismic structure as suited to present-day dynamic conditions, do not claim that all is bliss in such an organisation; the uncertainty in a flexible structure where a person does not know what he or the other fellow is supposed to be doing brings stress and strain as well as innovation. It is a symptom of what Bennis (1959) calls a 'problem-solving organization' as distinct from a 'habit organisation'.

Structure designers

Specificity of role prescription also preoccupies management writers on the design of organisations. Leading this group is Taylor (1947), advocating detailed task prescription based on 'scientific' investigation instead of rule-of-thumb methods. Fayol (1949) emphasises control and coordination through a clear line of command and specification of responsibility, and this argument is carried forward by Urwick (1947) and his associate Brech (1957). Urwick's 'Principle of definition' states that the responsibilities of each position and its relationships with other positions should be defined in writing and made known to everyone concerned. Similarly, Brown (1960) divides the organisation into an 'Executive system', a 'Representative system', and a 'Legislative system'; and then urges a careful analysis of roles and role relationships so that prescriptions can be clear, and confusion avoided.

Structure-critics

Social psychologists have ranged themselves as critics of rational structure for the narrow limits it puts on group and individual autonomy. They have contended, however, that even with the high specificity of role prescription that it entails, there is sufficient discretion remaining in each superordinate role to allow leaders to ameliorate the effects of this specificity upon subordinate motivation and attitudes. In doing so, leaders may modify the role prescription itself. Impressive evidence has been marshalled by Likert (1961) in favour of increasing subordinate participation; that is, reducing the specificity of role prescription by allowing employees more control of the details of their own tasks. He compares the 'job-organization system of management' developed where repetitive work predominates, which stresses complete prescription of performance and tight control standards, with the 'cooperative-motivation system' intuitively used for more varied work, which leaves much more to the motivation of the employee. This analysis leads Likert to advocate an employee-centred rather than a job-centred style of supervision; and he puts forward a tabulation of the organisational and performance characteristics of 'Authoritative' as against 'Participative' management systems. Very much in the same mould is McGregor's (1960) crystallisation of Theory X and Theory Y as opposing assumptions about motivation, leading respectively to coercion and direction of the employee or to increasing self-control and self-direction.

Argyris (1960) holds that in Western society, individuals need to develop along seven psychological continua toward greater self-actualisation and maturity, a development which the design and management of rational organisation frustrates. He, too (1964, p. 182), notes the convergence of ideas of a number of students upon a mechanistic-organic distinction in organisation.

Curvilinear relationships?

All the writers mentioned appear to accept the hypothesis of a linear relationship between precision of role prescription and whatever other behaviour variables that interest them; as, for example, innovation of ideas, volume of output, job satisfaction, and so on. The curvilinear hypothesis should not be ignored, however. It may be held, for example, that even where output and employee participation are directly related, output will not continue to respond indefinitely to more participation, that is, to decreasing prescription. Perhaps the anxiety brought by participating in responsibility eventually outweighs the motivational benefits. At the other extreme, increasing prescription may go beyond the point where it succeeds in circumscribing behaviour, to a point where so much is explicitly required that it cannot all be done, and individuals must again live on their wits in the resulting confusion. Frank (1963–4) advances this latter hypothesis when he contrasts (1) 'Underdefined' administrative roles, (2) 'Well-defined' administrative roles, and (3) 'Overdefined' roles. *Both* the first and third permit *more* discretion than the second; for in 'Overdefined' roles, expectations are so excessive or so conflicting that people are compelled to innovate in order to 'satisfice' (as Simon puts it).

CONCOMITANTS OF ROLE SPECIFICITY

Although these various students are all concerned with the role specificity of organisation structure, the variables they have chosen to relate to the degree of specificity are several and different, as Table 7.2 shows, and there is no consensus on relationships with organisational and individual performance.

Among the management writers there is comparative unanimity that clear lines of authority and responsibility are desirable, as is clear role definition. Then people can get on with their jobs without confusion, and performance will improve. This is the case for *higher* specificity. In arguing it, Taylor, Fayol, Urwick, Brech, and Brown find themselves an ally in Weber. Almost alone amongst sociologists, Weber regards the calculability of behaviour in organisations with high specificity (bureaucracies) as affording them a superiority in operation that overrides the dysfunctions so often pointed out by subsequent writers.

TABLE 7.2. *Concomitants of specificity of role prescription*

Higher specificity	Lower specificity			
Reduces confusion	More motivating	More innovating	Result: anxiety	Result: power conflict
Taylor	Likert	Burns and	Presthus	Crozier
Favol	McGregor	Stalker	Burns and	Gordon and
Urwick	Argyris	Thompson	Stalker	Becker
Brech	Barnes	Frank		Litwak
Brown	(Bennis)	Bennis		
Weber		Hage		

Likert, McGregor, and Argyris, however, are led by the findings of social psychology to take a critical view of rational structure. Explicitly, or by implication, they prefer *lower* specificity where individual self-realisation, job commitment, and job satisfaction may be raised, and performance too. Barnes agrees; for in his study the 'open system' seemed to show greater personal autonomy and better results than the 'closed system'. Bennis cautiously refrains from evaluation, but contrasts the leadership function in the two settings in a way which accords with the social psychologists. It is a contrast between leadership in enforcing performance criteria and leadership in fostering conditions under which individual and organisational goals become congruent.

Others have hypothesised an inverse relationship between specificity, and technical and structural innovation. This is a severe qualification of the position taken by the management group of writers. Burns and Stalker, Thompson, Frank, Bennis, and Hage, when considering 'adaptiveness', all expect greater innovation when specificity is lower. (Frank also predicts innovation at the other extreme of overdefinition, when role incumbents are forced to use personal initiative in deciding which definitions to fulfil and which to neglect.)

However, lower role specificity can bring anxiety as Presthus, and Burns and Stalker, suggest, because the individual is not able to rely on detailed direction from above. Likewise, though it may bring more power to a role, as Crozier, and Gordon and Becker, hypothesise, it thereby confers the power to engage in conflicts over the distribution of power. So these authors, and Litwak, associate lower specificity with conflict between roles that have differing degrees of specificity, conflict about the extension of rules and procedures, which may increase the power of those making the rules and decrease the power of those subject to the rules.

A developmental trend in organisation structure has been envisaged by several writers, going beyond the contemporary bureaucratic level of specificity to a lower level. Burns and Stalker's 'organic' form is a coming stage more suited to the future rate of innovation, as is Janowitz's 'fraternal type'. Argyris goes so far as to suggest that organisations may be able to arrange that roles have differing levels of specificity for differing areas of decision and activity, so that the structure can be varied according to the type of decision faced. In effect, there will be a different organisation chart for each type of decision. Rather similarly, Whyte notices the possibility of an organisation where relations are flexible when decisions are being discussed, but decisions are made through well-defined channels. Simon looks to electronic data processing to replace such channels and to replace clerical routines as means of gathering information for decisions. Judgment and intuition can then give way to 'heuristic problem-solving techniques', but in a more centralised structure.

Grouping writers by the variables they have associated with role specificity draws attention to other ranges of variables, where little or nothing has been done; for example, small-group formation in organisations, and small-group processes from sociometric choice to tension-release mechanisms. It could be asked whether there are more groups per organisation if specificity is lower: Are they smaller? Are they more cohesive? Do they show more tension? And so on. Nor have possible relationships been tested with personality traits, attitudes, or ways of thinking. For example, does not organisational innovation presuppose individual creativity? If so, then the low specificity associated with innovation must also be related to creativity. But, in addition, it is hypothesised that low specificity is related to anxiety and to power conflict. Drawing these several hypotheses together, if innovation is associated with low specificity, then the underlying individual creativity must not only survive conditions of anxiety and power conflict but even derive stimulation from them. Can this be tested in the field in organisations?

CONCLUSIONS

What is now apparent is the need not only for the integration offered by a concept such as specificity of role prescription, but for means of measuring variations of structure along this common dimension. If theory is so overwhelmingly focused, then measurements of degree of specificity are needed, first to verify the variations discerned by general observation, second to test hypotheses about the kinds of organisation in which differing specificities occur, and third to test hypotheses relating group and individual variables to structure. Measurement may also help to rid us of hypothetical conundrums such as: Which is the more prescribed, a role where the area of discretion is specified precisely, or a role where, although the area of discretion may be less, exactly what it is remains rather vague? Could the idea of a bureaucratic—mechanistic—closed—formalised—routinised—specified—dominant—well-defined—programmed—perceptually structured—habit—'scientific'—authoritative—rational structure be condensed into a prescription-specificity score? This might offer simplicity where, before, the profusion of terminology swamped the student.

The measurers are few, hardly any. Kahn and others (1964, pp. 25, 31) in their major work on organisational stress measure role conflict, and role ambiguity ('the degree to which required information is available'), and this must encourage all who follow them; but they treat 'the prescriptions and proscriptions associated with a particular position' as a given rather than as a variable to be measured. Gross and others (1958) do just touch on specificity with their initiative scale for school superintendents, which assesses how closely superintendents should adhere to the specific prescription of school committee rules. But it is Jaques (1964) who is ahead here. He has long distinguished the 'prescribed' from the 'discretionary' work content of roles, and proposes as a measure the time-span of discretion; i.e., 'the period of time during which marginally substandard discretion could be exercised in a role before information about the accumulating substandard work would become available to the manager in charge of the role'. Successful development of his technique and its widespread use may offer the best chance of profiting from the convergence of theory. A very limited trial of a comparatively crude scale of discretion is reported by Kammerer (1964), who assesses the degree of discretion permitted to American city managers on each of a range of topics.

Also, Pugh, the author, and other researchers (1963)[1] are attempting to devise measures of several dimensions of organisation structure, including standardisation (of procedures), formalisation (amount of paperwork), and centralisation (of decisions). Since a procedure forms part of the specific prescriptions of many roles and may be more highly

[1] *Editors' note:* see also the article by D. S. Pugh and D. J. Hickson, 'The comparative study of organizations' in this Reader, p. 50.

specific if committed to writing, and since it may be unalterable except by higher decision, such measures are likely to be relevant to role specificity. Scales have been tested which, however rudimentary they may seem when published, may provide a starting point for other researchers. Certainly the potential integration demands progress in methods and accompanying operational definitions that will discriminate more subtly than gross characterisations, which tend to obscure convergence in theories.

Finally, it is disconcerting that so much thinking has been and is patterned by the same conceptual dimension, wittingly or unwittingly. There are available, even now, other dimensions of roles in organisation structures which might be used to differentiate organisations. For example, Gross and others (1958), have isolated the direction or sign of expectations (prescriptive or proscriptive) and their particularity (pertaining to a particular role or to many); Kahn and others (1964) have measured role pressures (influence), role ambiguity, and several normative dimensions. Both groups of researchers have studied role conflict. Why should not research distinguish organisations by their degree of role particularity or role pressure, or role conflict, as well as by the customary role specificity? The convergence, if it be such, upon this concept should be recognised, in the hope that fresh ideas will be sought, which are not just the same concept under yet another name.

REFERENCES

ARGYRIS, C. (1960) *Understanding Organizational Behaviour*, Tavistock.
ARGYRIS, C. (1964) *Integrating the Individual and the Organization*, Tavistock.
BARNES, L. B. (1960) *Organizational Systems and Engineering Groups*, Harvard Business School.
BENNIS, WARREN, G. (1959) 'Leadership theory and administrative behaviour: the problem of authority', *Administrative Science Quarterly*, **4**, December, 259–301.
BRECH, E. F. L. (1957) *Organization: the framework of management*, Longmans.
BROWN, W. (1960) *Exploration in Management*, Heinemann.
BURNS, T. (1963) 'Industry in a new age', *New Society*, **18**, January, 17–20.
BURNS, T., and STALKER, G. M. (1961) *The Management of Innovation*, Tavistock.
CROZIER, M. (1964) *The Bureaucratic Phenomenon*, Tavistock.
FAYOL, H. (1949) *General and Industrial Management*, Pitman.
FRANK, A. GUNDER (1963–4) 'Administrative role definition and social change', *Human organization*, **22**, Winter, 238–42.
GORDON, G., and BECKER, S. (1964) 'Changes in medical practice bring shifts in the patterns of power', *The Modern Hospital*, **102**, February, 89–91.

GROSS, N., MASON, W., and MCEACHERN, A. (1958) *Explorations in Role Analysis*, Wiley.

HAGE, J. (1965) 'An axiomatic theory of organizations', *Administrative Science Quarterly*, **10**, December, 289–320.

JANOWITZ, M. (1959) 'Changing patterns of organizational authority: the military establishment', *Administrative Science Quarterly*, **3**, March, 473–93.

JAQUES, E. (1961) *Equitable Payment*, Heinemann.

KHAN, R. L., WOLFE, D. M., QUINN, R. P., SNOEK, J. D., and ROSENTHAL, R. A. (1964) *Organizational Stress: studies in role conflict and ambiguity*, Wiley.

KAMMERER, G. M. (1964) 'Role diversity of city managers', *Administrative Science Quarterly*, **8**, March, 421–42.

LEVINSON, D. J. (1959) 'Role, personality, and social structure in the organizational setting', *Journal of Abnormal and Social Psychology*, **58**, March, 170–81: see also an edited version in this Reader, p. 223.

LIKERT, R. (1961) *New Patterns of Management*, McGraw-Hill.

LITWAK, E. (1961) 'Models of bureaucracy which permit conflict', *American Journal of Sociology*, **67**, 177–84.

MCGREGOR, D. (1960) *The Human Side of Enterprise*, McGraw-Hill.

PRESTHUS, R. V. (1958) 'Toward a theory of organizational behavior', *Administrative Science Quarterly*, **3**, June, 48–72.

PUGH, D. S., HICKSON, D. J., HININGS, C. R., MACDONALD, K. M., TURNER, C., and LUPTON, T. (1963) 'A conceptual scheme for organizational analysis', *Administrative Science Quarterly*, **8**, December, 289–315.

SIMON, H. A. (1960) *The New Science of Management Decisions*, Harper.

SULLIVAN, H. S. (1953) *The Interpersonal Theory of Psychiatry*, Norton.

TAYLOR, F. W. (1947) *Scientific Management*, Harper.

THOMPSON, V. A. (1965) 'Bureaucracy and innovation', *Administrative Science Quarterly*, **10**, June, 1–20.

URWICK, L. F. (1947) *The Elements of Administration*, Pitman.

WEBER, M. (1947) *The Theory of Social and Economic Organization*, trans. A. M. Henderson and T. Parsons, Free Press of Glencoe.

WHYTE, W. FOOTE (1948) 'Incentives for productivity: the Bundy Tubing Company Case', *Applied Anthropology*, **7**, 1–16.

8

Richard H. Hall   Professionalisation and
bureaucratisation

Excerpts from Richard H. Hall, 'Professionalization and bureaucratization',
American Sociological Review, **33**, no. 1, February 1968, 92–104.

Two related but often non-complementary phenomena are affecting the
social structure of Western societies today. The first of these is the
increasing professionalisation of the labour force. . . . At the same
time, work in general is increasingly becoming organisationally based.
This is true among both the established professions and the professionalising occupations. The intent of this paper is to examine the professionalisation process in the context of the organisational structures in
which professional or professionalising workers are found, in order to
determine how these phenomena affect and are affected by each other.
Data from a variety of occupational groups found in a variety of
organisational settings will be used in this analysis.

BACKGROUND

Discussions about the nature of professions typically revolve around the
professional model. The professional model consists of a series of
attributes which are important in distinguishing professions from other
occupations. Movement toward correspondence with the professional
model is the process of professionalisation (cf. Vollmer and Mills,
1966). The attributes of the model are of two basic types. First are
those characteristics which are part of the structure of the occupation,
including such things as formal educational and entrance requirements.
The second aspect is attitudinal, including the sense of calling of the

person to the field and the extent to which he uses colleagues as his major work reference.

The structural side of the professional model has been intensively examined by Wilensky (1964), who noted that occupations pass through a rather consistent sequence of stages on their way to becoming professions. Wilensky includes the following attributes in his discussion:

1. Creation of a full time occupation—this involves the performance of functions which may have been performed previously, as well as new functions, and can be viewed as a reaction to needs in the social structure.

2. The establishment of a training school—this reflects both the knowledge base of a profession and the efforts of early leaders to improve the lot of the occupation. In the more established professions, the move is then followed by affiliation of the training school with established universities. In the newer professions, university affiliation is concurrent with the establishment of training schools.

3. Formation of professional associations—the formation of such associations often is accompanied by a change in the occupational title, attempts to define more clearly the exact nature of the professional tasks, and efforts to eliminate practitioners who are deemed incompetent by the emergent professionals. Local associations unite into national associations after a period of some political manipulations. As stronger associations are formed, political agitation in the form of attempts to secure licensing laws and protection from competing occupations becomes an important function.

4. Formation of a code of ethics—these ethical codes are concerned with both internal (colleague) and external (clients and public) relations. They are designed to be enforced by the professional associations themselves and, ideally, are given legal support.

A professional attribute that is both structural and attitudinal is the presence of professional autonomy. While the structural aspect of autonomy is indirectly subsumed under the efforts of professional associations to exclude the unqualified and to provide for the legal right to practice, autonomy is also part of the work setting wherein the professional is expected to utilise his judgment and will expect that only other professionals will be competent to question this judgment. The autonomy attribute also contains an attitudinal dimension: the belief of the professional that he is free to exercise this type of judgment and decision making.

The attitudinal attributes of professionalism reflect the manner in which the practitioners view their work. The assumption here is that there is some correspondence between attitudes and behaviour. If this assumption is correct, then the attitudes comprise an important part of the work of the professional. If he or his occupation has met the structural prerequisites of professionalism, the approach taken in practice becomes the important consideration. The attitudinal attributes to be considered here are:

1. The use of the professional organisation as a major reference—this involves both the formal organisation and informal colleague groupings as the major source of ideas and judgments for the professional in his work.

2. A belief in service to the public—this component includes the idea of indispensability of the profession and the view that the work performed benefits both the public and the practitioner.

3. Belief in self regulation—this involves the belief that the person best qualified to judge the work of a professional is a fellow professional, and the view that such a practice is desirable and practical. It is a belief in colleague control.

4. A sense of calling to the field—this reflects the dedication of the professional to his work and the feeling that he would probably want to do the work even if fewer extrinsic rewards were available.

5. Autonomy—this involves the feeling that the practitioner ought to be able to make his own decisions without external pressures from clients, those who are not members of his profession, or from his employing organisation.

The combination of the structural and the attitudinal aspects serves as the basis for the professional model. It is generally assumed that both aspects are present to a great degree in highly professionalised occupations, while they are present to lesser degrees in the less professionalised occupations. Whether or not this is the case will be examined in this research. It may be, for example, that occupations which are attempting to become professions may be able to instil in their members strong professional attitudes, while the more established professions may contain less idealistic members.

Variations from the professional model occur in two ways. In the first place, occupations vary in the degree to which they are professionalised. The established professions, such as medicine or law, appear to fit the professional model in most ways, although the attitudinal attributes may or may not adhere to this pattern. The newer emerging professions do not appear to be as professionalised on the various attributes. If each attribute is treated as a separate continuum, multiple variations are possible terms of the degree to which occupations are professionalised.

The second form of variation is intraoccupational. Even among the established professions, members vary in their conformity to the professional model in both the structural and attitudinal attributes. Both inter-occupational and intraoccupational variations appear to be based on three factors. First is the general social structure which, at the abstract level, may or may not need the services performed by the occupation and, at the more pragmatic level, may not give the occupation the legal and behavioural sanctions to perform its functions. The second factor lies within the organisation of the occupation itself. Here, for example, the presence of multiple and competing professional organisations may be divisive and thus inhibit professionalisation through multiple standards for entrance and through varied regulative norms. The third source of variation is the setting in which the occupation is performed. The work situation may have an impact on the degree to which the profession can be self regulative and autonomous.

Professionals work in four distinct types of settings. Many members of established professions are found in individual private practice. This setting for professional work appears to be diminishing in importance as organisationally based professional practice increases, and it will not be considered in this analysis. Lawyers are increasingly found in law firms or in legal departments of larger departments of larger organisations, and medical doctors are increasingly working in group or clinic practices. Among the professionalising groups, almost all are coming from an organisational base such as the social work agency or the business firm.

These organisational bases for professional occupations are of three types. Following Scott's (1965) useful distinction, the first type is the *autonomous* professional organisation exemplified by the medical clinic or the law firm. Here the work of the professional is subject to his own, rather than to external or administrative jurisdiction. The professionals themselves are the major determiners of the organisational structure, since they are the dominant source of authority. The second type is the *heteronomous* professional organisation in which the professional employees are subordinated to an externally derived system. Examples are public schools, libraries, and social work agencies, all of which are affected by externally (often legislatively) based structuring. Scott suggests that the level of professional autonomy is correspondingly lessened in such a setting, a point which will be examined in this research. The third organisational setting is the professional *department* which is part of a larger organisation. Examples of this are the legal or research departments of many organisations. In this kind of situation, the professionals employed are part of a larger organisation and may or may not be able to affect the manner in which their own work is structured. It is this setting which has served as the basis for many discussions of professional-organisational conflict.

One way of analysing these three types of settings is to determine the nature of the organisational structures found in the different organisational bases. In order to do this, the degree of bureaucratisation within each type will be examined with a dimensional approach to the concept of bureaucracy (Udy, 1959 and Hall, 1963). This follows determination of the degree of bureaucratisation of an organisation, or a segment thereof, in terms of the degree of bureaucratisation on *each* dimension.

The dimensions utilised are:

1. The hierarchy of authority—the extent to which the locus of decision making is prestructured by the organisation.
2. Division of labour—the extent to which work tasks are subdivided by functional specialisation decided by the organisation.
3. Presence of rules—the degree to which the behaviour of organisational members is subject to organisational control.
4. Procedural specifications—the extent to which organisational members must follow organisationally defined techniques in dealing with situations which they encounter.
5. Impersonality—the extent to which both organisational members and outsiders are treated without regard to individual qualities.
6. Technical competence—the extent to which organisationally defined 'universalistic' standards are utilised in the personal selection and advancement process.

Each of these dimensions is treated as a separate continuum. Previous research has indicated that these continua do not necessarily vary together (Hall, 1963). It is generally assumed that there is an inverse relationship between professionalisation and bureaucratisation (Blau, Heydebrand, and Stauffer, 1966). In this study the relationship will be examined without making that assumption. Instead, it is anticipated that the empirical findings will show that on some dimensions of bureaucracy, there is a positive relationship with professionalisation. For example, a highly developed division of labour might well be related to a high degree of professionalisation on all attributes, since professionals are specialists. By the same token, a high emphasis on technical competence as the basis for hiring and advancement would also appear to have a logical relationship with professionalisation.

On the other hand, a rigid hierarchy of authority seems incompatible with a high level of professionalism, especially in terms of the attributes of autonomy and colleague control. The presence of extensive organisationally based rules and procedures likewise appears to be negatively associated with a high level of professionalisation. Thus, findings of a mixed nature are anticipated on this basis.

METHODOLOGY

Measurement of the degree of professionalisation is accomplished in two basic ways. The structural attributes of the several occupations included in the study will be examined using the method followed by Wilensky (1964). Personnel managers and stockbrokers, occupations not included in his study, are examined here using the Wilensky format. The use of this approach not only allows comparison with the Wilensky work, but also will permit categorisation of the occupations by length of time the professional attributes have been met by the occupation and the order in which the occupation has proceeded in its attempt to professionalise. According to Wilensky, the closer the occupation follows a given sequence of professionalisation steps, the more likely it is to be more professionalised. In this case, the two additional occupations would fall in the 'doubtful professional' category, since some of the structural criteria are not met. . . .

The attitudinal attributes, including use of the professional organisation as a major reference, a belief in service to the public, belief in self regulation, a sense of calling to the field, and a feeling of autonomy in work are measured by standard attitude scales. The scales were developed by use of the Likert technique. . . .

Each of the bureaucratic dimensions was measured by means of a series of items which form a scale for the dimension (see Hall, 1963). The subjects in each organisation responded to the items according to the degree to which the statement corresponded to their own perception of the organisation. An ordinal scaling of each dimension was thus obtained. For both the professional attitude scales and the bureaucracy scales, the mean score for each set of respondents was utilised as the measure for the group involved.

At the outset of the research, it was decided to try to obtain a wide selection of occupations and employing organisations. The purpose of the research called for inclusion of occupations which are acknowledged professions in addition to those which are aspiring to become professions. At the same time, a variety of organisational settings was desired for the analysis of this variable. With these considerations in mind, organisations were contacted to determine if they were interested in cooperating in the research. The selection of organisations was based on at least some knowledge of their size and functioning. Those selected do not represent a sample of the universe of organisations, but they do appear to be representative of organisations of similar types. After the initial contact was made, personal interviews with officials in each organisation were held and cooperation was solicited. Three organisations declined participation.

. . .

The lawyers in the study represent three medium-sized law firms, two legal departments of private corporations, and part of a department of the federal government. The physicians are members of a medical department in a large government hospital and of a university student health service. The nurses work in a private general hospital and in the same university health service. Both of the Certified Public Accountant groups are part of large national CPA firms, while the accounting departments are part of larger organisations. The teachers are in the same school system at the levels indicated. The social workers represent two private agencies and a social work department of a school system. The stockbrokers are part of large national brokerage firms, while the advertising agencies are both small, regional concerns. The engineering department and the personnel departments are part of large national manufacturing firms. The library is the public library in a large metropolitan area.

FINDINGS

Evidence from the behaviour of the respondents provides strong support for the validity of two of the professionalism scales and also suggests that the attitudes measured are quite strongly associated with behaviour. Background information regarding the frequency of attendance at professional meetings and membership in professional organisations was cross-tabulated with the attitude scale which measures the strength of the professional organisation as a reference group. The behavioural data support the validity of the scales and also suggest that the respondents practise what they verbalise. Similarly, the scale measuring belief in self regulation is strongly associated with the actual presence of licences or certification as reported in the background questions.

The results on the attitude scales reveal some interesting and somewhat surprising patterns. On the belief in service to the public and sense of calling to the field attributes, both of which are related to a sense of dedication to the profession, the teachers, social workers, and nurses emerge as strongly professionalised. This may be related to the relatively low financial compensation which these fields receive since dedication seems necessary if one is to continue in the field. An interesting exception is that the teachers are somewhat weaker on the sense of calling to the field variable. An important factor appears to be the entry of many women into teaching because it is a 'safe' women's occupation rather than because of any real dedication. The established professions are relatively weak on these variables.

Among the lawyers, the results indicate that on all but one attribute a legal department is more professionalised than the law firms. This suggests that professionals working in large organisations are not, by definition, confronted with situations which reduce the level of professionalisation. The variations among the lawyers also suggests that the conditions of employment may play a dominant role in the development of professional attitudes. The lawyers in this study have quite common backgrounds in terms of their legal education and bar organisational memberships. Thus it appears that these attitudinal variations should probably be attributed to the organisational 'climate' in which they work.

... There are rather wide variations in degree of bureaucratisation both among and within occupational groups. There are also rather strong interrelationships among the dimensions, . . . except in the case of the technical competence dimension, where the relationship is reversed. Apparently these organisations, unlike more broadly based samples of organisations, are rather internally consistent in their degree of bureaucratisation. It should be noted that these results represent both the total organisation (in the cases of the autonomous and heteronomous professional organisations) and organisational segments (in the cases of professional departments). Whether or not such internal consistency exists throughout the larger organisations involved in the latter case is subject to further investigation. It seems doubtful in view of the wider variations in task which would be found in the organisations as a whole. . . .

The distribution of the groups into the autonomous, heteronomous, and departmental categories was relatively simple, using Scott's criteria. In the autonomous category are found the physicians (who, even though they are part of larger organisations, autonomously determine their own work structures), the law firms, the CPA firms, and the advertising agencies. . . .

Similarly, the heteronomous organisations were rather easy to classify using Scott's criteria. The social work agencies, the library, and the two schools were placed in this category. Two other occupational groups also were placed in this category on the basis of their degree of self determination of structure and policy. Neither are considered by Scott in his development of this category, but both appear to fit. First are the nurses. As a professional group, nurses are subject to both the administrative and policy practices of the medical staff. Nursing services must, therefore, adjudicate between the policies of the medical staff and their own professional codes. Stockbrokers also were placed in this category. This occupational grouping, which appears to operate quite autonomously within each regional office, nevertheless is subject to rather extensive external policies. The rules of the various stock and commodity exchanges, the Securities and Exchange Commission and the particular company policies themselves, appear to make placement in the heteronomous category most appropriate. Brokers do have individual clients and operate on a fee basis as do members of the autonomous category, but placement in this category appears unwarranted because of the factors noted above. The departmental category is comprised of the three legal departments, the engineering department, the personnel departments, and the accounting departments. . . .

On the hierarchy of authority dimension, the autonomous organisations are significantly less bureaucratic than the other two types of occupational groupings. . . . There is relatively little variation among the ranks in this category, while more variation exists within the heteronomous and departmental categories. This is consistent with Scott's suggestions in this regard. At the same time, the variations within the latter two categories are sufficient to suggest that neither category is inherently more rigid in its hierarchy of authority. With the exception of one legal department . . . the various settings in which lawyers work are essentially the same on this dimension. This suggests that work in the larger organisation does not, by definition, impose a more rigid hierarchy on the practitioner. Nevertheless, the term 'autonomous professional organisation' appears to be relevant since these organisations do, in fact, exhibit less bureaucratisation on this dimension.

On the division of labour dimension, the autonomous organisations are again much less bureaucratic, while the heteronomous organisations and departments are essentially similar. . . . On this dimension, also, the law firms and the legal departments do not vary widely among themselves. While the division of labour is more intense in the other two categories, again there is rather extensive variation in these categories. Obviously, the extent of the division of labour is dependent upon the tasks being performed rather than on the level of professionalisation or the externally imposed administrative structure.

Findings on the presence of rules dimension are somewhat consistent with those already discussed. The autonomous organisations are characterised by much less bureaucratisation on this dimension. In this case, however, the professional departments are less bureaucratic than the heteronomous organisations. This is consistent with Scott's discussion, but at the same time suggests that professional departments in larger organisations are not inherently more bureaucratic than professional organisations. The case of the lawyers in the two settings provides evidence for this position. These results raise an important issue in regard to professional-organisational relationships. The data suggest that the occupational base of an organisation (or an organisational segment) may have a real impact on the structure which the organisation itself takes (Blau, Heydebrand and Stauffer, 1966; Pugh, Hickson *et al.*, 1963). In this case, the professional's self regulatory patterns may reduce the need for and utility of organisational rule systems. It might be hypothesised that the more developed the normative system of the occupations in an organisation, the less need for a highly bureaucraticised organisational system.

Findings on the procedural specifications dimension of bureaucracy are quite similar to those discussed above. The autonomous organisations are characterised by quite a low level of bureaucratisation, while the heteronomous organisations are the most bureaucratic and the professional departments are slightly less bureaucratic.

On the impersonality dimension, the same general pattern emerges, although not to the same degree. Autonomous organisations are the least bureaucratic, while the other two types exhibit more impersonality. The higher level of impersonality found in the latter two categories may be an aspect of the 'bureaucratic personality' which has been discussed as a characteristic of organisations such as social work agencies. The aloofness and detachment which may inhibit the effectiveness of these groups appears to be due partially to the fact that the professions in the heteronomous category must deal with relatively large client populations. Those in the autonomous category have smaller such populations, and professions in the departmental category usually do not have individual clients. While the number of clients may contribute to impersonality, a high level of impersonality may itself inhibit the occupation in its drive toward professionalisation. If public acceptance as a profession is a component of professionalism, then this higher level of impersonality may partially block further professionalisation. The question remains whether or not this higher level of impersonality is a result of organisationally generated norms or of standards imposed upon the organisation by the professions themselves.

The findings in regard to the last dimension, technical competence as the basis for hiring and advancement, are reversed from those previously discussed. On this dimension, the autonomous and heteronomous organisations are relatively bureaucratic, while the professional departments are relatively non-bureaucratic. Here it appears that a higher level of bureaucratisation or more emphasis on technical competence is quite compatible with professional standards in that the practitioner is selected for employment and advancement on the basis of ability. In this case, a real source of conflict for persons employed in a professional department is evident if criteria other than performance are utilised in the personnel policies.

The relationships between professionalisation and bureaucratisation are examined from two perspectives. First is an analysis of the relationships between the attitudinal variables and the bureaucratic dimensions. ... The generally negative relationships indicate that higher levels of professionalisation are related to lower levels of bureaucratisation, and vice versa.

When each of the professional variables is examined, some interesting patterns emerge. First, in the case of the professional organisation as a reference group, there is a relatively small negative relationship between this variable and the presence of a rigid hierarchy of authority. It appears to make little difference if there is extensive reliance upon such a hierarchy in professionalised organisations. This conclusion is supported by the findings of Blau, *et al.* (1966), who suggest that the presence of such a hierarchy may facilitate the work of professionals if they serve coordination and communication functions (Blau, Heydebrand and Stauffer, 1966). This is particularly so when the hierarchy is recognised as legitimate. The professional may thus recognise and essentially approve of the fact that certain decisions must be made by people in the hierarchy.

A stronger negative relationship is found on the division of labour dimension. If a division of labour is very intense, it may force a professional person away from his broader professional ties. This interpretation recognises specialisation within the professions, but the question here is the level of organisationally based division of labour. At the same time, strong professional identification may impede intensive specialisation on the part of organisations. A weaker relationship is found on the presence of rules dimension. Organisationally developed rules governing the behaviour of members appear not to intrude strongly on this or on other professional attitudes.

There is a strong negative relationship between professional attitude and the procedural specifications dimension. This is predictable since strong professional orientations appear to be in basic conflict with organisationally developed techniques of dealing with work situations. As more procedures are developed by the organisation, they may become more burdensome for the professional.

The previously discussed relationship between the level of professionalisation and the degree to which impersonality is stressed is borne out by the findings here in regard to the impersonality dimension. That is, the more professional the atttitude on this variable, the less impersonality is stressed. The more professional groups apparently do not need to utilise impersonality in their organisational arrangements.

The strong positive relationship between this professional variable and the organisational emphasis on technical competence is not unexpected. Since this bureaucratic dimension is so strongly related to most of the professional attitudes, it might serve as an informal indicator of the level of professionalism in organisations if other indicators are not available.

The findings on the belief in service to the public, belief in self-regulation, and sense of calling to the field variables are essentially similar to those just discussed. The areas of congruence and conflict which might emerge also are similar.

Strong negative relationships exist between the autonomy variable and the first five bureaucratic dimensions. This suggests that increased bureaucratisation threatens professional autonomy. It is in these relationships that a potential source of conflict between the professional and the organisation can be found. The strong drive for autonomy on the part of a professional may come into direct conflict with organisationally based job requirements. At the same time, the organisation may be threatened by strong professional desires on the part of at least some of its members. Future research should delineate both the extent of the conflict and its sources and the extent to which it is felt by and threatens both the professional(s) and the organisation.

When the structural aspect of professionalisation is considered, essentially the same findings emerge . . . the more professionalised groups are found in settings which are less bureaucratic. The more professionalised groups, that is, those with more self regulation and longer socialisation in preparation for the field, perhaps do not 'need' the same kinds of organisational controls as less professionalised groups in dealing with problems and decisions. At the same time, the presence of more bureaucratic systems for the less professionalised groups may serve as an inhibitor to their futher professionalisation.

SUMMARY AND CONCLUSIONS

Among the major findings of this research is the fact that the structural and the attitudinal aspects of professionalisation do not necessarily vary together. Some 'established' professions have rather weakly developed professional attitudes, while some of the less professionalised groups have very strong attitudes in this regard. The strength of these attitudes appears to be based on the kind of socialisation which has taken place both in the profession's training programme and in the work itself. An additional factor is the place of the occupation in the wider social structure. If the occupation receives relatively few rewards in a material sense, the level of dedication is likely to be higher. If the occupation is allowed to be self-regulating, it will tend to believe quite strongly in this. Therefore, changes in the social structure may bring about corresponding attitudinal adjustments.

The organisations in which professionals work vary rather widely in their degree of bureaucratisation. The variation is not based on the distinction between professional departments and professional organisations, since some professional departments are less bureaucratic than some professional organisations, and vice versa. There is, however, a general tendency for the autonomous professional organisation to be less bureaucratic than either the heteronomous organisation or the professional department. This suggests that the nature of the occupational groups in an organisation affects the organisational structure. The workers (professionals) *import* standards into the organisation to which the organisation must adjust. In the development of a new organisation, this importation would probably occur without any conflict. In an established organisation, the importation, either by an entire department or by new employees within a professional department, might be a real source of conflict if the professional and organisational standards do not coincide.

With the exception of the technical competence dimension, a generally inverse relationship exists between the levels of bureaucratisation and professionalisation. Autonomy, as an important professional attribute, is most strongly inversely related to bureaucratisation. The other variables are not as inversely related. This suggests that increased bureaucratisation and professionalisation might lead to conflict in either the professional organisation or department, but that this conflict is not inherent, given the relative weakness of most of the relationships found. Conflict occurs within a professional group or within an organisation only to the degree that specific aspects of bureaucratisation or professionalisation vary enough to conflict with other specific aspects.

Stated in another way, the implication is that in some cases an equilibrium may exist between the levels of professionalisation and bureaucratisation in the sense that a particular level of professionalisation may require a certain level of bureaucratisation to maintain social control. Too little bureaucratisation may lead to too many undefined operational areas if the profession itself has not developed operational standards for these areas. By the same token, conflict may ensue if the equilibrium is upset.

An assumption of inherent conflict between the professional or the professional group and the employing organisation appears to be unwarranted. If it is present, the bases of conflict in terms of professional attitudes and/or organisational structure should be made explicit. After this is done, the analysis of conflicts based upon specific issues, such as resistance to non-professional supervision, can proceed. After any particular conflict situation, changes in either the professional orientations or the organisational structure should be noted so that the essentially stable conditions from which conflicts emerge can be established. Since conflicts probably create changes, any conflicts which follow would necessarily emerge from a different setting than that originally noted. These changes must be noted in any longitudinal analyses of professional-organisational relations.

REFERENCES

BLAU, P. M., HEYDEBRAND, W. V., and STAUFFER, R. E. (1966) 'The structure of small bureaucracies', *American Sociological Review*, **31**, April, 179–91.

HALL, R. H. (1963) 'The concept of bureaucracy: an empirical assessment', *American Journal of Sociology*, **69**, July, 32–40.

PUGH, D. S., HICKSON, D. J. *et al.* (1963) 'A scheme for organizational analysis', *Administrative Science Quarterly*, **8**, December, 289–315.

SCOTT, W. R. (1965) 'Reactions to supervision in a heteronomous professional organization', *Administrative Science Quarterly*, **10**, June, 65–81.

UDY, STANLEY H., jr. (1959) 'Bureaucracy and rationality in Weber's theory', *American Sociological Review*, **24**, December, 791–95.

VOLLMER, H. M., and MILLS, D. L., eds., (1966) *Professionalization*, Prentice-Hall.

WILENSKY, H. L. (1964) 'The professionalization of everyone?', *American Journal of Sociology*, **70**, September, 137–58.

9

Walter Buckley   Society as a complex
adaptive system

Excerpts from Walter Buckley, 'Society as a complex adaptive system' in
Walter Buckley, ed., *Modern Systems Research for the Behavioral Scientist*,
Chicago, Aldine Publishing Company, 1968, pp. 490–513.

We have argued at some length in another place (Buckley, 1967) that
the mechanical equilibrium model and the organismic homeostasis
models of society that have underlain most modern sociological theory
have outlived their usefulness. A more viable model, one much more
faithful to the *kind* of system that society is more and more recognised
to be, is in process of developing out of, or is in keeping with, the
modern systems perspective (which we use loosely here to refer to
general systems research, cybernetics, information and communication
theory, and related fields). Society, or the sociocultural system, is not,
then, principally an equilibrium system or a homeostatic system, but
what we shall simply refer to as a complex adaptive system.

To summarise the argument in overly simplified form: Equilibrial
systems are relatively *closed* and *entropic*. In going to equilibrium they
typically *lose structure* and have a *minimum of free energy*; they are
affected only by external 'disturbances' and have *no internal or endo-
genous sources of change;* their component elements are *relatively
simple* and *linked directly via energy exchange* (rather than information
interchange); and since they are relatively closed they have no feedback
or other systematic self-regulating or adaptive capabilities. The homeostatic system (for example, the organism, apart from higher cortical
functioning) is open and negentropic, maintaining a moderate energy
level within controlled limits. But for our purposes here, the system's

main characteristic is its functioning to *maintain the given structure of the system* within pre-established limits. It involves feedback loops with its environment, and possibly information as well as pure energy interchanges, but these are geared principally to *self-regulation* (structure maintenance) rather than adaptation (*change* of system structure). The complex adaptive systems (species, psychological and sociocultural systems) are also open and negentropic. But they are *open 'internally' as well as externally* in that the interchanges among their components may result in *significant changes in the nature of the components themselves* with important consequences for the system as a whole. And the energy level that may be mobilised by the system is subject to relatively wide fluctuation. Internal as well as external interchanges are mediated characteristically by *information flows* (via chemical, cortical, or cultural encoding and decoding), although pure energy interchange occurs also. True feedback control loops make possible not only self-regulation, but self-direction or at least adaptation to a changing environment, such that the system may *change or elaborate its structure* as a condition of survival or viability.

We argue, then, that the sociocultural system is fundamentally of the latter type, and requires for analysis a theoretical model or perspective built on the kinds of characteristics mentioned. . . .

Our argument may be outlined as follows:

• Much of modern sociology has analysed society in terms of largely structural concepts: institutions, culture, norms, roles, groups, etc. These are often reified, and make for a rather static, overly deterministic, and elliptical view of societal workings.

• But for the sociocultural system, 'structure' is only a relative stability of underlying, on-going micro-processes. Only when we focus on these can we begin to get at the selection process whereby certain interactive relationships become relatively and temporarily stabilised into social and cultural structures.

• The unit of dynamic analysis thus becomes the systematic *matrix* of interacting, goal-seeking, deciding individuals and subgroups— whether this matrix is part of a formal organisational or only a loose collectivity. Seen in this light, society becomes a continuous morphogenic process, through which we may come to understand in a unified conceptual manner the development of structures, their maintenance, and their change. And it is important to recognize that out of this matrix is generated, not only *social* structure, but also *personality* structure, and *meaning* structure. All, of course, are intimately interrelated in the morphogenic process, and are only analytically separable.

STRUCTURE, PROCESS, AND DECISION THEORY

Though the problem calls for a lengthy methodological discussion, we shall here simply recall the viewpoint that sees the sociocultural system in comparative perspective against lower-level mechanical, organic and other types of systems. As we proceed upward along such a typology we noted that the ties linking components become less and less rigid and concrete, less direct, simple and stable within themselves. Translation of energy along unchanging and physically continuous links gives way in importance to transmission of information via internally varying, discontinuous components with many more degrees of freedom. Thus for mechanical systems, and parts of organic systems, the 'structure' has a representation that is concrete and directly observable—such that when the system ceases to operate much of the structure remains directly observable for a time. For the sociocultural system, 'structure' becomes a theoretical construct whose referent is only indirectly observable (or only inferable) by way of series of events along a time dimension; when the system ceases to operate, the links maintaining the sociocultural structure are no longer observable. 'Process', then, points to the actions and interactions of the components of an on-going system, in which varying degrees of structuring arise, persist, dissolve, or change. (Thus 'process' should not be made synonymous simply with 'change', as it tended to be for many earlier sociologists.)

More than a half century ago, Albion W. Small argued that, 'The central line in the path of methodological progress in sociology is marked by the gradual shifting of effort from analogical representation of social structures to real analysis of social processes' (Small, 1905, p. ix). This was an important viewpoint for many social thinkers earlier in this century, possibly as part of the trend in physical science and philosophy toward a process view of reality developing from the work of such people as Whitehead, Einstein, Dewey and Bentley. Such views have apparently had little impact on those of recent decades who had developed the more dominant structure-oriented models of current sociology, but it seems clear that—with or without the aid of the essentially process-conscious general systems approach—a more even balance of process with structure in the analysis of sociocultural systems is gradually regaining lost ground . . .

Among sociologists, a perennial critic of the overly-structural conception of the group is Herbert Blumer. Blumer has argued that it is from the process of on-going interaction itself that group life gets its main features, which cannot be adequately analysed in terms of fixed attitudes, 'culture' or social structure—nor can it be conceptualised in terms of mechanical structure, the functioning of an organism, or a system seeking equilibrium, '... in view of the formative and explorative character of interaction as the participants *judge* each other and *guide* their own acts by that judgment'.

> The human being is not swept along as a neutral and indifferent unit by the operation of a system. As an organism capable of self-interaction he forges his actions out of a process of definition involving *choice, appraisal,* and *decision.* . . . Cultural norms, status positions and role relationships are only *frameworks* inside of which that process (of formative transaction) goes on (Blumer, 1953, pp. 199–201).

Highly structured human association is relatively infrequent and cannot be taken as a prototype of a human group life. In sum, institutionalised patterns constitute only one cenceptual aspect of society, and they point to only a part of the ongoing process (and, we might add, they must be seen to include deviant and disfunctional patterns: for conceptual clarity and empirical relevance, 'institutionalisation' cannot be taken to imply only 'legitimacy', 'consent', and ultimately adaptive values).

Finally, it should be noted that Gordon Allport, viewing personality as an open-system, stresses a very similar point concerning the organisation of personality:

> ...the best hope for discovering coherence would seem to lie in approaching personality as a total functioning structure, i.e., as a *system.* To be sure, it is an incomplete system, manifesting varying degrees of order and disorder. It has structure but also unstructure, function but also malfunction. As Murphy says, 'all normal people have many loose ends'. And yet personality is well enough knit to qualify as a system—which is defined merely as *a complex of elements in mutual interaction* (Allport, 1961, p. 567).

In the light of such views, we need only recall the many critiques pointing to the incapacity or awkwardness of the conventional type of framework before the facts of process, 'becoming', and the great range of 'collective behavior' (cf. Gouldner, 1956, pp. 39–40 and Moore, 1955, pp. 111–15).

Statements such as Blumer's, a continuation of the perspective of many neglected earlier sociologists and social psychologists, would seem to constitute a perspective that is now pursued by many under new rubrics such as 'decision theory'. For earlier antecedents it should be enough to mention W. I. Thomas's 'definition of the situation', Znaniecki's 'humanistic coefficient', Weber's 'verstehen', Becker's 'interpretation', and MacIver's 'dynamic assessment'. Much of current structural, consensus theory represents a break from this focus. As Philip Selznick has argued,

> A true theory of social action would say something about goal-oriented or problem-solving behavior, isolating some of its distinctive attributes, stating the likely outcomes of determinate transformations. . . . In Parson's writing there is no true embrace of the idea that structure is being continuously opened up and reconstructed by the problem-solving behavior of individuals responding to concrete situations. This is a point of view we associate with John Dewey and G. H. Mead, for whom, indeed, it had significant intellectual consequences. For them and for their intellectual heirs, social structure is something to be taken account of in action; cognition is not merely an empty category but a natural process involving dynamic assessments of the self and the other (Selznick, 1961, p. 934).

It can be argued, then, that a refocusing is occurring via 'decision theory', whether elaborated in terms of 'role-strain' theory; theories of cognitive dissonance, congruence, balance, or concept formation; exchange, bargaining, or conflict theories, or the mathematical theory of games. The basic problem is the same: How do interacting personalities and groups define, assess, interpret, 'verstehen' and act on the situation? Or, from the broader perspective of our earlier discussion, how do the processes of 'social selection' operate in the 'struggle' for sociocultural structure? Instead of asking how structure affects, determines, channels actions and interactions, we ask how structure is created, maintained and recreated.

Thus we move down from structure to social interrelations and from social relations to social actions and interaction processes—to a matrix of 'dynamic assessments' and intercommunication of meanings, to evaluating, emoting, deciding and choosing. To avoid anthropomorphism and gain the advantages of a broader and more rigorously specified conceptual system, we arrive at the language of modern systems theory.

· · ·

Ralph Turner (1962) has addressed himself to the elaboration of this perspective in that conceptual area fundamental to the analysis of institutions—roles and role-taking. The many valid criticisms of the more static and overdetermining conception of roles is due, he believes, to the dominance of the Linton view of role and the use of an oversimplified model of role functioning. Viewing role-playing and role-taking, however, as a process (as implied in Meadian theory), Turner shows that there is more to it than just 'an extension of normative or cultural deterministic theory' and that a process view of role adds novel elements to the notion of social interaction.

The morphogenic nature of role behaviour is emphasised at the start in the concept of *role-making*. Instead of postulating the initial existence of distinct, identifiable roles, Turner posits 'a tendency to create and modify conceptions of self- and other-roles' as the interactive orienting process. Since actors behave *as if* they were roles, although the latter actually exist only in varying degrees of definitiveness and consistency, the actors attempt to define them and make them explicit—thereby in effect creating and modifying them as they proceed. The key to role-taking, then, is the morphogenic propensity 'to shape the phenomenal world into roles'; formal organisational regulation restricting this process is not to be taken as the prototype, but rather as a 'distorted instance' of the wider class of role-taking phenomena. To the extent that the bureaucratic setting blocks the role-making process, organisation is maximal, 'variety' or alternatives of action minimal, actors are cogs in a rigid machine, and the morphogenic process underlying the viability of complex adaptive systems is frustrated.

Role interaction is a tentative process of reciprocal responding of self and other, challenging or reinforcing one's conception of the role of the other, and consequently stabilising or modifying one's own role as a product of this essentially feedback-testing transaction. The conventional view of role emphasising a prescribed complementarity of expectations thus gives way to a view of role-taking as a process of 'devising a performance on the basis of an imputed other-role', with an important part being played by cognitive processes of inference testing. In a manner consistent with models of the basic interaction process suggested by Goode and by Secord and Backman, Turner (1962) views as a central feature of role-taking 'the process of discovering and creating "consistent" wholes out of behavior', of 'devising a pattern' that will both cope effectively with various types of relevant others and meet some recognisable criteria of consistency. Such a conception generates empirically testable hypotheses of relevance to our concern here with institutional morphogenesis, such as: 'Whenever the social structure is such that many individuals characteristically act from the perspective of two given roles simultaneously, there tends to emerge a single role which encompasses the action' (p. 26).

Turning directly to the implications for formal, institutional role-playing, Turner argues that the formal role is primarily a 'skeleton' of rules which evoke and set into motion the fuller roles built-up and more or less consensually validated in the above ways. Role behaviour becomes relatively fixed only while it provides a perceived consistency and stable framework for interaction, but it undergoes cumulative revision in the role-taking process of accommodation and compromise with the simple conformity demanded by formal prescriptions.

The purposes and sentiments of actors constitute a unifying element in role genesis and maintenance, and hence role-taking must be seen to involve a great deal of selective perception of other-behaviour and relative emphasis in the elaboration of the role pattern. This selection process operates on the great variety of elements in the situation of relevant objects and other-behaviours which could become recognised components in a consistent role pattern. Not all combinations of behaviour and object relations can be classed into a single role; there must be criteria by which actors come to 'verify' or 'validate' the construction of a number of elements into a consistent role. This verification stems from two sources: 'internal validation' of the interaction itself, and 'external validation' deriving from 'the generalised other' of Mead. The former hinges on successful prediction or anticipation of relevant other-behaviour in the total role-set, and hence on the existence of role patterns whereby coherent selection of behaviours judged to constitute a consistent role can be made. But the notion of fixed role prescriptions is not thereby implied, since, first, roles—like norms—often or usually provide a *range of alternative* ways of dealing with any other-role, or, as is most common, the small segment of it activated at any one time, and secondly, the coherence and predictability of a role must be assessed and seen as 'validated', not in terms of any one other-role, but in terms of the Gestalt of all the accommodative and adjusted requirements set by the number of other-roles in the actor's role-set and generated in the on-going role-making process.

An example is provided by the study by Gross *et al.*, of the school superintendent role. It is found that incumbency in this role (1) actually involved a great deal of choice behaviour in selection among the alternative interpretations and behaviours deemed possible and appropriate, and that (2) consistency and coherence of an incumbent's behaviour could be seen only in terms of the total role as an accommodation with correlative other-roles of school board member, teacher, and parent, with which the superintendent was required to interact simultaneously. As Gross puts it, a 'system model' as against a 'position-centric' model involves an important addition by including the interrelations among the counter positions.

A position can be completely described only by describing the total system of positions and relationships of which it is a part. In other words, in a system of interdependent parts, a change in any relationship will have an effect on all other relationships, and the positions can be described only by the relationships (Gross *et al.*, 1958, p. 53).

Thus Turner sees the internal criterion of role validation as ensuring a constant modification, creation, or rejection of the content of specific roles occurring in the interplay between the always somewhat vague and incomplete ideal role conceptions and the experience of their concrete implications by the interpreting, purposive, selectively evaluating and testing self and others.

The basis of 'external validation' of a role is the judgment of the behaviour to constitute a role by others felt to have a claim to correctness or legitimacy. Criteria here include: discovery of a name in common use for the role, support of major norms or values, anchorage in the membership of recognised groups, occupancy of formalised positions, and experience of key individuals as role models acting out customary attitudes, goals and specific actions.

Under the 'normal loose operation of society' these various internal and external criteria of validation are at best only partially conveyant and consistent in identifying the same units and content as roles. The resulting inevitable discrepancies between formal, institutional rules and roles, and the goals, sentiments and selective interpretations arising from the experience of actually trying to play them out, make role conceptions 'creative compromises', and ensure ' that the framework of roles will operate as a hazily conceived ideal framework for behavior rather than as an unequivocal set of formulas ' (Turner, 1962, p. 32).

In sum, 'institutions' may provide a normative framework prescribing roles to be played and thus assuring the required division of labour and minimising the cost of general exploratory role-setting behaviour, but the actual role transactions that occur generate a more or less coherent and stable working compromise between ideal set prescriptions and a flexible role-making process, between the structured demands of others and the requirements of one's own purposes and sentiments. This conception of role relations as 'fully interactive', rather than merely conforming, contributes to the recent trends 'to subordinate normative to functional processes in accounting for societal integration' (Turner, 1962, p. 38) by emphasising the complex adaptive interdependence of actors and actions in what we see as an essentially morphogenic process—as against a merely equilibrial or homeostatic process.

ORGANISATION AS A NEGOTIATED ORDER

Next we shall look at a recently reported empirical study of a formal organisation that concretely illustrates many facets of the above conceptualisation of Turner and contributes further to our thesis. In their study of the hospital and its interactive order, Anselm Strauss and colleagues (1963) develop a model of organisational process that bears directly on the basic sociological problem of 'how a measure of order is maintained in the face of inevitable changes (derivable from sources both external and internal to the organization)' (p. 148). Rejecting an overly structural view, it is assumed that social order is not simply normatively specified and automatically maintained but is something that must be 'worked at', continually reconstituted. Shared agreements, underlying orderliness, are not binding and shared indefinitely but involve a temporal dimension implying eventual review, and consequent renewal or rejection. On the basis of such considerations, Strauss and colleagues develop their conception of organisational order as a 'negotiated order'.

The hospital, like any organisation, can be visualised as a hierarchy of status and power, of rules, role and organisational goals. But it is also a locale for an on-going complex of transactions among differentiated types of actors: professionals such as psychiatrists, residents, nurses and nursing students, psychologists, occupational therapists and social workers; and non-professionals such as various levels of staff, the patients themselves, and their families. The individuals involved are at various stages in their careers, have their own particular goals, sentiments, reference groups, and ideologies, command various degrees of prestige, esteem and power, and invest the hospital situation with differential significance.

The rules supposed to govern the actions of the professionals were found to be far from extensive, clearly stated, or binding; hardly anyone knew all the extant rules or the applicable situations and sanctions. Some rules previously administered would fall into disuse, receive administrative reiteration, or be created anew in a crisis situation. As in any organisation, rules were selectively evoked, broken, and/or ignored to suit the defined needs of personnel. Upper administrative levels especially avoided periodic attempts to have the rules codified and formalised, for fear of restricting the innovation and improvisation believed necessary to the care of patients. Also, the multiplicity of professional ideologies, theories and purposes would never tolerate such rigidification.

In sum, the area of action covered by clearly defined rules was very small, constituting a few general 'house rules' based on long-standing shared understandings. The basis of organisational order was the generalised mandate, the single ambiguous goal, of returning patients to the outside world in better condition. Beyond this, the rules ordering actions to this end were the subject of continual negotiations—being argued, stretched, ignored, or lowered as the occasion seemed to demand. As elsewhere, rules failed to act as universal prescriptions, but required judgment as to their applicability to the specific case.

The ambiguities and disagreements necessitating negotiation are seen by the researchers to be patterned. The various grounds leading to negotiation include: disagreement and tension over the proper ward placement of a patient to maximise his chances of improvement; the mode of treatment selected by the physician, which is closely related to his own psychiatric ideology and training; the multiplicity of purposes and temporal ends of each of the professional groups as they manoeuvre to elicit the required cooperation of their fellow workers; the element of medical uncertainty involved in treating the patient as a unique, 'individual case', and the consequent large area of contingency lying of necessity beyond specific role prescription; and, finally, the inevitable changes forced upon the hospital and its staff by external forces and the unforeseen consequences of internal policies and the round of negotiations themselves. What is concretely observed, then, in researching the organisational order of the hospital, is negotiation between the neurologically trained and the psychothera-peutically oriented physician, between the nurses and the administrative staff, between the nonprofessional floor staff and the physician, between the patient and each of the others.

The negotiation process itself was found to have patterned and temporal features. Thus, different physicians institute their own particular programmes of treatment and patient care and in the process develop fairly stable understandings with certain nurses or other institutional gate-keepers such as to effectuate an efficient order of behaviours with a minimum of communication and special instructions. Such arrangements are not called for by any organisational role prescriptions; nevertheless, they represent a concrete part of the actual organisation generated in the morphogenic process of negotiation (or role-making and -taking, in Turner's terms). Thus, agreements do not occur by chance but are patterned in terms of 'who contracts with whom, about what, as well as when. . . .' (Strauss *et al.*, 1963, p. 162). There is an important temporal aspect, also, such as the specification of a termination period often written into an agreement—as when a physician bargains with a head nurse to leave his patient in the specific ward for 'two more days' to see if things will work themselves out satisfactorily.

In a final section of their paper, Strauss and his colleagues bring out the full implications of their negotiation model in dealing with genuine organisational change. The model presents a picture of the hospital—and perhaps most other institutionalised spheres of social life—as a transactional milieu where numerous agreements are 'continually being established, renewed, reviewed, revoked, revised'. But this raises the question of the relation between this process and the more stable structure of norms, statuses, and the like. The authors see a close systematic relation between the two. The daily negotiations periodically call for a reappraisal and reconstruction of the organisational order into a 'new order, not the re-establishment of an old, as reinstituting of a previous equilibrium'. And, we would add, it contributes nothing to refer to this as a 'moving equilibrium' in the scientifically established sense of the term. The daily negotiative process not only allows the day-by-day work to get done, but feeds back upon the more formalised, stable structure of rules and policies by way of 'a periodic appraisal process' to modify it—sometimes slowly and crescively, sometimes rapidly and convulsively. And, as a reading of history suggests, virtually every formal structure extant can be traced, at least in principle, from its beginnings to its present apparently timeless state through just such a morphogenic process—a process characteristic of what we have called the complex adaptive system.

THE SCHOOL SUPERINTENDENT AND HIS ROLE

We turn to the study by Gross and his associates (1958) of the role system of the school superintendent and his counter-role partners, the school board member, the teacher, and the parent. A major burden of this empirical study is to demonstrate the research sterility of the Lintonian conception of role, and structural theories built on it, due principally to the postulate of consensus on role definition. The study showed a majority of significant differences in the definitions of their own roles by a sample of incumbents of the same social position and by incumbents of different but interrelated counter positions. This fact led Gross and his associates to the demonstration of a number of important theoretical consequences derived from rejection of the postulate of role consensus. It is often assumed, for example, that the socialisation process by which roles are 'acquired' provides for a set of clearly defined and agreed-upon expectations associated with any particular position. But the empirically discovered fact of differential *degrees of consensus* seriously challenged this assumption. From our systems model viewpoint, recognition of degrees of consensus is tantamount to the recognition of a continuous source of 'variety' in the role system, as defined earlier, which leads us to seek the various *selective*, choice processes occurring in the role transactions. At least for the occupational positions studied, it was found that the assumption of socialisation on the basis of prior consensus on role definitions was untenable, and deserved 'to be challenged in most formulations of role acquisition, including even those concerned with the socialization of the child' (Gross *et al.*, 1958, p. 321; cf. Kahn *et al.*, 1964).

Secondly, the research showed that, instead of assuming role consensus and explaining variations of behaviour of incumbents of the same position in terms of personality variables, one would better explain them in terms of the varying role expectations and definitions—which may be unrelated to psychological differences.

The implications are also great for a theory of social control. Instead of a model assuming that the application or threat of negative sanctions leads to conformity to agreed-upon norms, the research pointed to the numerous situations in which, due to variant or ambiguous role definitions, the same behaviour resulted in negative sanctions by some role partners and positive sanctions by others, or failure to apply sanctions because of perceived ambiguity—or nonconformity to perceived expectations of another despite negative sanctions because other expectations were defined as more legitimate.

Another Lintonian postulate challenged by this research is that though an actor may occupy many positions, even simultaneously, he activates each role singly with the others remaining 'latent'. It is found, however, that individuals often perceive and act toward role partners as if simultaneous multiple roles were being activated. For example, one may hold different expectations regarding a teacher who is male, young and unmarried as against one who is female, older and married. In other words, standards and expectations are applied to the whole person as a result, in part, of the complex of positions the person is perceived as occupying at that time. A related consideration involves the time dimension over which two or more individuals interact; other positions they occupy enter progressively into their perception of each other and consequently modify evaluations and expectations. Thus the authors generalise their point to a broader theory of social interaction by suggesting that evaluation standards shift over time from those applied as appropriate to the incumbent of a particular position to those applied to a total person with particular personality features and capacities as the incumbent of multiple positions.

Finally, their rejection of the consensus model led these researchers to find a process of role-strain or role-conflict generation and resolution similar in principle to that conceptualised by others discussed above. Having defined the role set they were studying as a true *complex system* of interrelated components, and having then uncovered and analysed the *variety* continuously introduced into the system by way of variant, ambiguous or changing role definitions, they then focused on the *selection process* whereby this variety was sifted and sorted in the give and take of role transactions. Thus, given the situation in which a role incumbent was faced with incompatible expectations on the part of two of his counter-role partners, a theory was constructed to answer the question of how the actor may choose from among four alternatives in resolving the role conflict. From our present perspective, the theoretical scheme suggested constitutes another important contribution to the forging of a conceptual link between the dynamics of the role transaction and the more stable surrounding social structure— a link that is too often skipped over by the consensus theorist's identification of social structure and consensual role playing.

This linkage is made in terms of the concepts of perceived *legitimacy* of the conflicting expectations, an assessment of the *sanctions* that might be applied, and predispositions to give primacy to a *moral* orientation, an *expedient* orientation, or a balance of the two. We face once again the reciprocal question of how role transactions are conditioned by the surrounding social structure and how that structure is generated and regenerated as a product of the complex of role transactions.

The four alternatives that Gross and colleagues see open to an actor to choose in attempting to resolve a role conflict between incompatible expectations A and B are: (1) conformity to expectation A; (2) conformity to expectation B; (3) compromise in an attempt to conform in part to both expectations; or (4) attempt to avoid conforming to either expectation. The first criterion that the theory postulates to underlie the particular alternative chosen is the actor's definition of the legitimacy of the expectations. Thus the prediction of behaviour on this criterion is that, when only one expectation is perceived as legitimate the actor will conform to that one; when both are defined as legitimate he will compromise; and when neither is seen as legitimate he will engage in avoidance behaviour. The second criterion is the actor's perception of the sanctions that would be applied for nonconformity, which would create pressures to conform if strong negative sanctions are foreseen otherwise. This predicts for three of the four combinations of two sets of expectations, but not for the case of both expectations being perceived as leading to weak or no negative sanctions.

It is assumed that for any role conflict situation an actor would perceive both of these dimensions and make his decision accordingly. Predictions on the basis of the theory so far provide for determinate resolutions of conflict in seven of the sixteen combinations of the four types of legitimacy and the four types of sanctions situations, but the other nine are left indeterminate with only the two criteria. This is because the criteria predispose in different directions, and at least a third criterion is needed to determine the outcome. The authors thus appeal to the actor's predisposition to give primacy to either the legitimacy or to the sanctions dimension, or to balance the two, thus leading to the postulation of three types of predisposing orientations to expectations as listed above—the *moral*, the *expedient*, and the balanced *moral-expedient*. All the combinations of situations now become predictive.

The accuracy of the predictions was tested empirically with the data from the superintendent-role study for four 'incompatible expectation situations', and the evidence supported the theory, though with some incorrect predictions.

The implications of this conceptualisation and empirical analysis are far-reaching, as already suggested, for general sociological theory. The study is concerned with what must be considered 'institutional' organisation and process, and supports a model of that structure and process that is quite different from the more traditional models. As the authors point out, one strong advantage of the theory is its conceptualisation of institutional role behaviour in terms of 'expectations', whether legitimate or illegitimate, rather than in terms of 'obligations' (legitimate expectations) as is assumed in consensus theory. The theory thus allows for the possibility that illegitimate expectations constitute a significant part of institutional role behaviour, and underlie much of the conflict occurring—as we feel intuitively to be the case—within the institutional process. It follows, further, that deviance—nonconformity to expectations—is a more intimate and normal element in institutional behaviour than conformity theory would permit. And it also permits theoretical recognition of the possibility that, as Etzioni (1961) has suggested, a great deal of organisational behaviour is based, not on internalised norms and values, but on an expedient calculation of self-interests and of possible rewards and punishments. This, in turn, leaves open the theoretical possibility that non-legitimised power, as well as legitimised authority, may often be a controlling factor in institutional behaviour.

CONCLUSION

We have argued that a promising general framework for organising these valuable insights of the past and present may be derived from the recent general systems perspective, embracing a holistic conception of complex adaptive systems viewed centrally in terms of information and communication process and the significance of the way these are structured for self-regulation and self-direction. We have clearly arrived at a point in the development of the 'behavioural' sciences at which synthesis or conceptual unification of subdisciplines concerned with social life is challenging simple analysis or categorisation. Not only is there growing demand that the 'cognitive', 'affective' and 'evaluative' be conceptually integrated, but that the free-handed parceling out of aspects of the sociocultural adaptive system among the various disciplines (e.g., 'culture' to anthropology, the 'social system' to sociology, and 'personality' to psychology) be reneged, or at least ignored. The potential of the newer system theory is especially strong in this regard. By way of conclusion we recapitulate the main arguments.

1. The advance of science has driven it away from concern with 'substance' and toward a focus on *relations* between components of whatever kind. Hence the concern with complex organisation or systems, generally defined in terms of the transactions, often mutual and usually intricate, among a number of components such that some kind of more or less stable structure—often tenuous and only statistically delineated—arises (that is, *some* of the relations between components show *some* degree of stability or repetitiveness *some* of the time). Extremely fruitful advances have been taking place, especially since the rapid scientific progress made during World War II, in specifying basic features common to substantively different kinds of complex adaptive systems, as well as delineating their differences. In contrast to some of the general systems theorists themselves as well as their critics, we have argued that this is not simply analogising, but generalising or abstracting as well (although the former is important,

and scientifically legitimate also, when performed with due caution). To say that physiological, psychological, and sociological processes of control all involve the basic cybernetic principles of information flow along feedback loops is no more a mere analogy than to say that the trajectories of a falling apple, an artificial satellite, or a planet all involve the basic principles of gravitational attraction.

2. Complex adaptive systems are open systems in intimate interchange with an environment characterised by a great deal of shifting variety ('booming, buzzing confusion') and its constraints (its structure of causal interrelations). The concept of equilibrium developed for closed physical systems is quite inappropriate and usually inapplicable to such a dynamic situation. Rather, a characteristic resultant is the elaboration of organisation in the direction of the less probable and the less inherently stable.

Features common to substantively different complex adaptive systems can be conceptualised in terms of the perspective of information and control theory. 'Information' in its most general sense is seen, not as a thing that can be transported, but as a selective interrelation or mapping between two or more subsets of constrained variety selected from larger ensembles. Information is thus transmitted or communicated as invariant constraint or structure in some kind of variety, such that subsystems with the appropriate matched internal ensembles, reacting to and acting upon the information, do so in a situation of decreased uncertainty and potentially more effective adaptation to the variety that is mapped. Unless mapping (encoding, decoding, correlating, understanding, etc.) occurs between two or more ensembles we do not have 'information', only raw variety or noise.

In these terms, adaptive systems, by a continuous selective feedback interchange with the variety of the environment, come to make and preserve mappings on various substantive bases, which may be transmitted generationally or contemporaneously to other similar units. By means of such mappings (for example, via genes, instincts, learned events, culture patterns) the adaptive system may, if the mappings are adequate, continue to remain viable before a shifting environment. The transmission and accumulation of such information among contemporaneous adaptive systems (individuals) becomes more and more important at higher levels until it becomes the prime basis of linkage of components for the highest level sociocultural system.

Some of the more important differences between complex adaptive systems include the substantive nature of the components, the types of linkage of the components, the kinds and levels of feedback between system and environment, the degree of internal feedback of a system's own state (for example, 'self-awareness'), the methods of transmission of information between subsystems and along generations, the degree of refinement and fidelity of mapping and information transfer, the degree and rapidity with which the system can restructure itself or the environmental variety, etc.

3. Such a perspective provides a general framework which meets the major criticisms leveled against much of current sociological theory: lack of time and process perspective, over-emphasis on stability and maintenance of given structure, and on consensus and cooperative relations, to the relative neglect—or unsystematic treatment—of deviance, conflict and other dissociative relations underlying system destructuring and restructuring.

4. Thus, the concept of the system itself cannot be identified with the more or less stable structure it may take on at any particular time. As a fundamental principle, it can be stated that a condition for maintenance of a viable adaptive system may be a change in its particular structure. Both stability and change are a function of the same set of variables, which must include both the internal state of the system and the state of its significant environment, along with the nature of the interchange between the two.

5. A time perspective is inherent in this kind of analysis—not merely historical but evolutionary. (It can probably be said that the time was ripe by 1959 for a Darwinian centennial ramifying well beyond the purely biological.) This perspective calls for a balance and integration of structural and processual analysis. As others have pointed out, the Linnean system of classification of structures became alive only after Darwin and others discovered the processes of variation, selection and recombination that gave them theoretical significance, though these discoveries leaned heavily in turn on the classification of systematically varying structures.

And among the important processes for the sociological system are not only cooperation and conformity to norms, but conflict, competition and deviation which may help create (or destroy) the essential variety pool, and which constitute part of the process of selection from it, such that a more or less viable system structure may be created and maintained (or destroyed).

6. In sociological terms, the 'complementarity of expectations' model is an ideal type constituting only one pole of a continuum of equally basic associative and dissociative processes characterising real societies —although the particular 'mix' and intensities of the various types may differ widely with different structural arrangements. Further, the

systematic analysis of a sociocultural system is not exhausted by analysis of its institutionalised patterns. By focusing on process, we are more prepared to include all facets of system operation—from the minimally structured end of the collective behaviour continuum through the various degrees and kinds of structuring to the institutional pole. The particular characteristics of the process, especially the degrees and kinds of mapping and mismatchings of the interacting units, tell us whether we are in fact dealing with certain degrees of structuring and the dynamics underlying this structuring: de facto patterning may be anchored in coercive, normative, or utilitarian compliance, making for very different kinds of system.

7. 'Institutionalised' patterns are not to be construed as thereby 'legitimised' or as embracing only 'conformity' patterns—at least for the sake of conceptual clarity and empirical adequacy. Processes of all degrees and kinds of structuring may be seen in terms of deviant as well as conformity patterns—relative to the point of reference selected by the observer. One may select certain institutional patterns and values (to be clearly specified) as an arbitrary reference point to match against *other* institutional patterns and values, along with less structured behaviours. The concept of *the* institutionalised common value system smuggles in an empirically dubious, or unverified, proposition—at least for complex modern societies.

8. The complex adaptive system's organisation *is* the 'control', the characteristics of which will change as the organisation changes. The problem is complicated by the fact that we are dealing directly with two levels of adaptive system and thus two levels of structure, the higher level (sociocultural) structure being largely a shifting statistical or probability structure (or ensemble of constraints) expressing over time the transactional processes occurring among the lower level (personality) structures. We do not have a sociocultural system *and* personality systems, but only a sociocultural system *of* constrained interactions among personality systems.

We can only speak elliptically of 'ideas' or 'information' or 'meanings' in the head of a particular individual: all we have is an ensemble of constrained variety embodied in a neurological net. 'Meaning' or 'information' is generated only in the process of interaction with other ensembles of similarly mapped or constrained variety (whether embodied in other neurological nets or as the ensemble of causally constrained variety of the physical environment), whereby ensemble is mapped or matched against ensemble via communication links, and action is carried out, the patterning of which is a resultant of the degree of successful mapping that occurred. (Of course, 'meaning' on the symbolic level can be regenerated over a long period by the isolated individual through an internal interchange or 'conversation' of the person with his 'self', made possible by previous socially induced mappings of one's own internal state that we call 'self-awareness'. But in some respects, part of the world literally loses its meaning for such a person.)

If the ensembles of variety of two interacting units, or one unit and its physical environment, have little or no isomorphic structuring, little or no meaning can be generated to channel on-going mutual activity; or in more common terms, there is no 'common ground', no 'meeting of minds' and thus no meaning or information exchange—only raw variety, uncertainty, lack of 'order' or organisation.

Unless 'social control' is taken as simply the more or less intentional techniques for maintaining a given institutional structure by groupings with vested interests, it must refer to the above transactional processes as they operate—now to develop new sociocultural structures, now to reinforce existing ones, now to destructure or restructure older ones. Thus, we cannot hope to develop our understanding much further by speaking of one 'structure' determining, 'affecting', or acting upon another 'structure'. We shall have to get down to the difficult but essential task of (a) specifying much more adequately the distribution of essential features of the component subsystems' internal mappings, including both self-mappings and their mappings of their effective environment, (b) specifying more extensively the structure of the transactions among these units at a given time, the degree and stability of the given structuring seen as varying with the degree and depth of common meanings that are generated in the transaction process, and (c) assessing, with the help of techniques now developing, the on-going process of transitions from a given state of the system to the next in terms of the deviation-reducing and deviation-generating feedback loops relating the tensionful, goal-seeking, decision-making subunits via the communication nets partly specified by (b). Some behaviour patterns will be found to be anchored in a close matching of component psychic structures (for example, legitimised authority or normative compliance); others, in threats of goal-blockage, where there is minimal matching (for example, power or coercive compliance); still others, anchored in a partial matching, primarily in terms of environmental mappings of autonomous subunits and minimally in terms of collective mappings (for example, opportunism or utilitarian compliance). As the distribution of mappings shifts in the system (which normally occurs for a number of reasons), so will the transaction processes and communication nets, and thus will the sociocultural structure tend to shift as gradients of misunderstanding, goal-blockage, and tensions develop.

9. Finally, we have tried to show how this perspective bears on, and may help to integrate conceptually, the currently developing area of 'decision theory' which recognises individual components as creative nodes in an interactive matrix. In the complex process of transactions occurring within a matrix of information flows, the resulting cognitive mappings and mismappings undergo various stresses and strains as component units assess and reassess with varying degrees of fidelity and refinement their internal states and the shifting and partially uncertain, and often goal-blocking environment. Out of this process, as more or less temporary adjustments, arise the more certain, more expected, more codified sequences of events that we call sociocultural structure. In the words of Norbert Wiener (1954), 'By its ability to make decisions' the system 'can produce around it a local zone of organisation in a world whose general tendency is to run down' (p. 34). Whether that structure proves viable or adaptive for the total system is the kind of question that cannot be reliably answered in the present state of our discipline. It most certainly demands the kind of predictive power that comes with the later rather than the earlier stages of development of a science. And later stages can arrive only at some sacrifice of ideas of earlier stages.

REFERENCES

ALLPORT, G. A. (1961) *Pattern and Growth in Personality*, Holt, Rinehart and Winston.

BLUMER, HERBERT (1953) 'Psychological import of the human group', in Muzafer Sherif and M. O. Wilson, eds., *Group Relations at the Crossroads*, Harper.

BUCKLEY, WALTER (1967) *Sociology and Modern Systems Theory*, Prentice-Hall.

ETZIONI, AMITAI (1961) *A Comparative Analysis of Complex Organizations*, New York, Free Press of Glencoe.

GOULDNER, A. W. (1956) 'Some observations on systematic theory, 1945–55', in Hans L. Zetterberg, ed., *Sociology in the United States of America*, Paris, UNESCO.

GROSS, NEAL *et al.* (1958) *Explorations in Role Analysis*, Wiley.

KAHN, R. L. *et al.* (1964) *Organizational Stress: Studies in role conflict and ambiguity*, Wiley.

MOORE, BARRINGTON, jr. (1955) 'Sociological theory and contemporary politics', *American Journal of Sociology*, **61**, September, 111–15.

SELZNICK, PHILIP (1961) 'Review article: The social theories of Talcott Parsons', *American Sociological Review*, **26**, December, 934.

SMALL, ALBION W. (1905) *General Sociology*, University of Chicago Press.

STRAUSS, ANSELM *et al*. (1963) 'The hospital and its negotiated order', in Eliot Freidson, ed., *The Hospital in Modern Society*, New York, Free Press of Glencoe.

TURNER, R. H. (1962) 'Role-taking: process versus conformity', in Arnold M. Rose, ed., *Human Behavior and Social Processes*, Houghton Mifflin, chapter 2.

WEINER, NORBERT (1954) *The Human Use of Human Beings*, 2nd edn, rev., Doubleday Anchor.

IO

James D. Thompson and William J. McEwen Organisational goals and environment: goal-setting as an interaction process

James D. Thompson and William J. McEwen, 'Organizational goals and environment: goal-setting as an interaction process', *American Sociological Review*, **23**, no. 1, 1958, 23–31.

In the analysis of complex organisations the definition of organisational goals is commonly utilised as a standard for appraising organisational performance. In many such analyses the goals of the organisation are often viewed as a constant. Thus a wide variety of data, such as official documents, work activity records, organisational output, or statements by organisational spokesmen, may provide the basis for the definition of goals. Once this definition has been accomplished, interest in goals as a dynamic aspect of organisational activity frequently ends.

It is possible, however, to view the setting of goals (i.e., major organisational purposes) not as a static element but as a necessary and recurring problem facing any organisation, whether it is governmental, military, business, educational, medical, religious, or other type.

This perspective appears appropriate in developing the two major lines of the present analysis. The first of these is to emphasise the interdependence of complex organisations within the larger society and the consequences this has for organisational goal-setting. The second is to emphasise the similarities of goal-setting *processes* in organisations with manifestly different goals. The present analysis is offered to supplement recent studies of organisational operations.

It is postulated that goal-setting behaviour is *purposive* but not necessarily *rational*; we assume that goals may be determined by accident, i.e., by blundering of members of the organisation and, contrariwise, that the most calculated and careful determination of goals may be negated by developments outside the control of organisation members. The goal-setting problem as discussed here is essentially determining a relationship of the organisation to the larger society, which in turn becomes a question of what the society (or elements within it) wants done or can be persuaded to support.

GOALS AS DYNAMIC VARIABLES

Because the setting of goals is essentially a problem of defining desired relationships between an organisation and its environment, change in either requires review and perhaps alteration of goals. Even where the most abstract statement of goals remains constant, application requires redefinition or interpretation as changes occur in the organisation, the environment, or both.

The corporation, for example, faces changing markets and develops staff specialists with responsibility for continuous study and projection of market changes and product appeal. The governmental agency, its legislative mandate notwithstanding, has need to reformulate or reinterpret its goals as other agencies are created and dissolved, as the population changes, or as non-governmental organisations appear to do the same job or to compete. The school and the university may have unchanging abstract goals but the clientele, the needs of pupils or students, and the techniques of teaching change and bring with them redefinition and reinterpretation of those objectives. The hospital has been faced with problems requiring an expansion of goals to include consideration of preventive medicine, public health practices, and the degree to which the hospital should extend its activities out into the community. The mental hospital and the prison are changing their objectives from primary emphasis on custody to a stress on therapy. Even the church alters its pragmatic objectives as changes in the society call for new forms of social ethics, and as government and organised philanthropy take over some of the activities formerly left to organised religion.

Reappraisal of goals thus appears to be a recurrent problem for large organisation, albeit a more constant problem in an unstable environment than in a stable one. Reappraisal of goals likewise appears to be more difficult as the 'product' of the enterprise becomes less tangible and more difficult to measure objectively. The manufacturing firm has a relatively ready index of the acceptability of its product in sales figures; while poor sales may indicate inferior quality rather than public distaste for the commodity itself, sales totals frequently are supplemented by trade association statistics indicating the firm's 'share of the market'. Thus within a matter of weeks, a manufacturing firm may be able to reappraise its decision to enter the 'widget' market and may therefore begin deciding how it can get out of that market with the least cost.

The governmental enterprise may have similar indicators of the acceptability of its goals if it is involved in producing an item such as electricity, but where its activity is oriented to a less tangible purpose such as maintaining favourable relations with foreign nations, the indices of effective operation are likely to be less precise and the vagaries more numerous. The degree to which a government satisfies its clientele may be reflected periodically in elections, but despite the claims of party officials, it seldom is clear just what the mandate of the people is with reference to any particular governmental enterprise. In addition, the public is not always steadfast in its mandate.

The university perhaps has even greater difficulties in evaluating its environmental situation through response to its output. Its range of 'products' is enormous, extending from astronomers to zoologists. The test of a competent specialist is not always standardised and may be changing, and the university's success in turning out 'educated' people is judged by many and often conflicting standards. The university's product is in process for four or more years and when it is placed on the 'market' it can be only imperfectly judged. Vocational placement statistics may give some indication of the university's success in its objectives, but initial placement is no guarantee of performance at a later date. Furthermore, performance in an occupation is only one of several abilities that the university is supposed to produce in its students. Finally, any particular department of the university may find that its reputation lags far behind its performance. A 'good' department may work for years before its reputation becomes 'good' and a downhill department may coast for several years before the fact is realised by the professional world.

In sum, the goals of an organisation, which determine the kinds of goods or services it produces and offers to the environment, often are subject to peculiar difficulties of reappraisal. Where the purpose calls for an easily identified, readily measured product, reappraisal and readjustment of goals may be accomplished rapidly. But as goals call for increasingly intangible, difficult-to-measure products, society finds it more difficult to determine and reflect its acceptability of that product, and the signals that indicate unacceptable goals are less effective and perhaps longer in coming.

ENVIRONMENTAL CONTROLS OVER GOALS

A continuing situation of necessary interaction between an organisation and its environment introduces an element of environmental control into the organisation. While the motives of personnel, including goal-setting officers, may be profits, prestige, votes, or the salvation of souls, their efforts must produce something useful or acceptable to at least a part of the organisational environment to win continued support.

In the simpler society social control over productive activities may be exercised rather informally and directly through such means as gossip and ridicule. As a society becomes more complex and its productive activities more deliberately organised, social controls are increasingly exercised through such formal devices as contracts, legal codes, and governmental regulations. The stability of expectations provided by these devices is arrived at through interaction, and often through the exercise of power in interaction.

It is possible to conceive of a continuum of organisational power in environmental relations, ranging from the organisation that dominates its environmental relations to one completely dominated by its environment. Few organisations approach either extreme. Certain gigantic industrial enterprises, such as the *Zaibatsu* in Japan or the old Standard Oil Trust in America, have approached the dominance-over-environment position at one time, but this position eventually brought about 'countervailing powers'. Perhaps the nearest approximation to the completely powerless organisation is the commuter transit system, which may be unable to cover its costs but nevertheless is regarded as a necessary utility and cannot get permission to quit business. Most complex organisations, falling somewhere between the extremes of the power continuum, must adopt strategies for coming to terms with their environments. This is not to imply that such strategies are necessarily chosen by rational or deliberate processes. An organisation can survive so long as it adjusts to its situation; whether the process of adjustment is awkward or nimble becomes important in determining the organisation's degree of prosperity.

However arrived at, strategies for dealing with the organisational environment may be broadly classified as either *competitive* or *co-operative*. Both appear to be important in a complex society—of the 'free enterprise' type or other. Both provide a measure of environmental control over organisations by providing for 'outsiders' to enter into or limit organisational decision process.

The decision process may be viewed as a series of activities, conscious or not, culminating in a choice among alternatives. For purposes of this paper we view the decision-making process as consisting of the following activities:

1. Recognising an occasion for decision, i.e., a need or an opportunity.
2. Analysis of the existing situation.
3. Identification of alternative courses of action.
4. Assessment of the probable consequences of each alternative.
5. Choice from among alternatives.

The following discussion suggests that the potential power of an outsider increases the earlier he enters into the decision process, and that competition and three sub-types of cooperative strategy—*bargaining*, *cooptation*, and *coalition*—differ in this respect. It is therefore possible to order these forms of interaction in terms of the degree to which they provide for environmental control over organisational goal-setting decisions.

Competition

The term competition implies an element of rivalry. For present purposes competition refers to that form of rivalry between two or more organisations which is mediated by a third party. In the case of the manufacturing firm the third party may be the customer, the supplier, the potential or present member of the labour force, or others. In the case of the governmental bureau, the third party through whom competition takes place may be the legislative committee, the budget bureau, or the chief executive, as well as potential clientele and potential members of the bureau.

The complexity of competition in a heterogeneous society is much greater than customary usage (with economic overtones) often suggests. Society judges the enterprise not only by the finished product but also in terms of the desirability of applying resources to that purpose. Even the organisation that enjoys a product monopoly must compete for society's support. From the society it must obtain resources—personnel, finances, and materials—as well as customers or clientele. In the business sphere of a 'free enterprise' economy this competition for resources and customers usually takes place in the market, but in times of crisis the society may exercise more direct controls, such as rationing or the establishment of priorities during a war. The monopoly competes with enterprises having different purposes or goals but using similar raw materials; it competes with many other enterprises, for human skills and loyalties, and it competes with many other activities for support in the money markets.

The university, customarily a non-profit organisation, competes as eagerly as any business firm, although perhaps more subtly. Virtually every university seeks, if not more students, better-qualified students. Publicly supported universities compete at annual budget sessions with other governmental enterprises for shares in tax revenues. Endowed universities must compete for gifts and bequests, not only with other universities but also with museums, charities, zoos, and similar non-profit enterprises. The American university is only one of many organisations competing for foundation support, and it competes with other universities and with other types of organisations for faculty.

The public school system, perhaps one of our most pervasive forms of near-monopoly, not only competes with other governmental units for funds and with different types of organisations for teachers, but current programmes espoused by professional educators often compete in a very real way with a public conception of the nature of education, e.g., as the three R's, devoid of 'frills'.

The hospital may compete with the midwife, the faith-healer, the 'quack' and the patent-medicine manufacturer, as well as with neighbouring hospitals, despite the fact that general hospitals do not 'advertise' and are not usually recognised as competitive.

Competition is thus a complicated network of relationships. It includes scrambling for resources as well as for customers or clients, and in a complex society it includes rivalry for potential members and their loyalties. In each case a third party makes a choice among alternatives, two or more organisations attempt to influence that choice through some type of 'appeal' or offering, and choice by the third party is a 'vote' of support for one of the competing organisations and a denial of support to the others involved.

Competition, then, is one process whereby the organisation's choice of goals is partially controlled by the environment. It tends to prevent unilateral or arbitrary choice of organisational goals, or to correct such a choice if one is made. Competition for society's support is an important means of eliminating not only inefficient organisations but also those that seek to provide goods or services the environment is not willing to accept.

Bargaining

The term bargaining, as used here, refers to the negotiation of an agreement for the exchange of goods or services between two or more organisations. Even where fairly stable and dependable expectations have been built up with important elements of the organisational environment—with suppliers, distributors, legislators, workers and so on—the organisation cannot assume that these relationships will continue. Periodic review of these relationships must be accomplished, and an important means for this is bargaining, whereby each organisation, through negotiation, arrives at a decision about future behaviour satisfactory to the others involved.

The need for periodic adjustment of relationships is demonstrated most dramatically in collective bargaining between labour and industrial management, in which the bases for continued support by organisation members are reviewed. But bargaining occurs in other important, if less dramatic, areas of organisational endeavour. The business firm must bargain with its agents or distributors, and while this may appear at times to be onesided and hence not much of a bargain, still even a long-standing agency agreement may be severed by competitive offers unless the agent's level of satisfaction is maintained through periodic review. Where suppliers are required to install new equipment to handle the peculiar demands of an organisation, bargaining between the two is not unusual.

The university likewise must bargain. It may compete for free or unrestricted funds, but often it must compromise that ideal by bargaining away the name of a building or of a library collection, or by the conferring of an honorary degree. Graduate students and faculty members may be given financial or other concessions through bargaining, in order to prevent their loss to other institutions.

The governmental organisation may also find bargaining expedient. The police department, for example, may overlook certain violations of statutes in order to gain the support of minor violators who have channels of information not otherwise open to department members. Concessions to those who 'turn state's evidence' are not unusual. Similarly a department of state may forego or postpone recognition of a foreign power in order to gain support for other aspects of its policy, and a governmental agency may reliquish certain activities in order to gain budget bureau approval of more important goals.

While bargaining may focus on resources rather than explicitly on goals, the fact remains that it is improbable that a goal can be effective unless it is at least partially implemented. To the extent that bargaining sets limits on the amount of resources available or the ways they may be employed, it effectively sets limits on choice of goals. Hence bargaining, like competition, results in environmental control over organisational goals and reduces the probability of arbitrary, unilateral goal-setting.

Unlike competition, however, bargaining involves direct interaction with other organisations in the environment, rather than with a third party. Bargaining appears, therefore, to invade the actual decision process. To the extent that the second party's support is necessary he is in a position to exercise a veto over final choice of alternative goals, and hence takes part in the decision.

Cooptation

Cooptation has been defined as the process of absorbing new elements into the leadership or policy-determining structure of an organisation as a means of averting threats to its stability or existence (Selznick, 1949). Cooptation makes still further inroads on the process of deciding goals; not only must the final choice be acceptable to the coopted party or organisation, but to the extent that cooptation is effective it places the representative of an 'outsider' in a position to determine the occasion for a goal decision, to participate in analysing the existing situation, to suggest alternatives, and to take part in the deliberation of consequences.

The term cooptation has only recently been given currency in this country, but the phenomenon it describes is neither new nor unimportant. The acceptance on a corporation's board of directors of representatives of banks or other financial institutions is a time-honoured custom among firms that have large financial obligations or that may in the future want access to financial resources. The state university may find it expedient (if not mandatory) to place legislators on its board of trustees, and the endowed college may find that whereas the honorary degree brings forth a token gift, membership on the board may result in a more substantial bequest. The local medical society often plays a decisive role in hospital goal-setting, since the support of professional medical practitioners is urgently necessary for the hospital.

From the standpoint of society, however, cooptation is more than an expediency. By giving a potential supporter a position of power and often of responsibility in the organisation, the organisation gains his awareness and understanding of the problems it faces. A business advisory council may be an effective educational device for a government, and a White House conference on education may mobilise 'grass roots' support in a thousand localities, both by focusing attention on the problem area and by giving key people a sense of participation in goal deliberation.

Moreover, by providing overlapping memberships, cooptation is an important social device for increasing the likelihood that organisations related to one another in complicated ways will in fact find compatible goals. By thus reducing the possibilities of antithetical actions by two or more organisations, cooptation aids in the integration of the hetero-geneous parts of a complex society. By the same token, cooptation further limits the opportunity for one organisation to choose its goals arbitrarily or unilaterally.

Coalition

As used here, the term coalition refers to a combination of two or more organisations for a common purpose. Coalition appears to be the ultimate or extreme form of environmental conditioning of organisational goals.[1] A coalition may be unstable, but to the extent that it is operative, two or more organisations act as one with respect to certain goals. Coalition is a means widely used when two or more enterprises wish to pursue a goal calling for more support, especially for more resources, than any one of them is able to marshal unaided. American business firms frequently resort to coalition for purposes of research or product promotion and for the construction of such gigantic facilities as dams or atomic reactors.

Coalition is not uncommon among educational organisations. Universities have established joint operations in such areas as nuclear research, archaeological research, and even social science research. Many smaller colleges have banded together for fund-raising purposes. The consolidation of public school districts is another form of coalition (if not merger), and the fact that it does represent a sharing or 'invasion' of goal-setting power is reflected in some of the bitter resistance to consolidation in tradition-oriented localities.

Coalition requires a commitment for joint decision of future activities and thus places limits on unilateral or arbitrary decisions. Furthermore, inability of an organisation to find partners in a coalition venture automatically prevents pursuit of that objective, and is therefore also a form of social control. If the collective judgment is that a proposal is unworkable, a possible disaster may be escaped and unproductive allocation of resources avoided.

DEVELOPMENT OF ENVIRONMENTAL SUPPORT

Environmental control is not a one-way process limited to consequences for the organisation of action in its environment. Those subject to

---

[1] Coalition may involve joint action towards only limited aspects of the goals of each member. It may involve the complete commitment of each member for a specific period of time or indefinitely. In either case the ultimate power to withdraw is retained by the members. We thus distinguish coalition from merger, in which two or more organisations are fused permanently. In merger one or all of the original parts may lose their identity. Goal-setting in such a situation, of course, is no longer subject to inter-organisational constraints among the components.

control are also part of the larger society and hence are also agents of social control. The enterprise that competes is not only influenced in its goal-setting by what the competitor and the third party may do, but also exerts influence over both. Bargaining likewise is a form of mutual, two-way influence; cooptation affects the coopted as well as the coopting party; and coalition clearly sets limits on both parties.

Goals appear to grow out of interaction, both within the organisation and between the organisation and its environment. While every enterprise must find sufficient support for its goals, it may wield initiative in this. The difference between effective and ineffective organisations may well lie in the initiative exercised by those in the organisation who are responsible for goal-setting.

The ability of an administrator to win support for an objective may be as vital as his ability to foresee the utility of a new idea. And his role as a 'seller' of ideas may be as important to society as to his organisation, for as society becomes increasingly specialised and heterogeneous, the importance of new objectives may be more readily seen by specialised segments than by the general society. It was not public clamour that originated revisions in public school curricula and training methods; the impetus came largely from professional specialists in or on the periphery of education. The shift in focus from custody to therapy in mental hospitals derives largely from the urgings of professionals, and the same can be said of our prisons. In both cases the public anger, aroused by crusaders and muck-rakers, might have been soothed by more humane methods of custody. Current attempts to revitalise the liberal arts curricula of our colleges, universities, and technical institutes have developed more in response to the activities of professional specialists than from public urging. Commercial aviation, likewise, was 'sold' the hard way, with support being based on subsidy for a considerable period before the importance of such transportation was apparent to the larger public.

In each of these examples the goal-setters saw their ideas become widely accepted only after strenuous efforts to win support through education of important elements of the environment. Present currents in some medical quarters to shift emphasis from treatment of the sick to maintenance of health through preventive medicine and public health programmes likewise have to be 'sold' to a society schooled in an older concept.

The activities involved in winning support for organisational goals thus are not confined to communication within the organisation, however important this is. The need to justify organisation goals, to explain the social functions of the organisation, is seen daily in all types of 'public relations' activities, ranging from luncheon club speeches to house organs. It is part of an educational requirement in a complicated society where devious interdependence hides many of the functions of organised, specialised activities.

GOAL-SETTING AND STRATEGY

We have suggested that it is improbable that an organisation can continue indefinitely if its goals are formulated arbitrarily, without cognisance of its relations to the environment. One of the requirements for survival appears to be ability to learn about the environment accurately enough and quickly enough to permit organisational adjustments in time to avoid extinction. In a more positive vein, it becomes important for an organisation to judge the amount and sources of support that can be mobilised for a goal, and to arrive at a strategy for their mobilisation.

Competition, bargaining, cooptation, and coalition constitute procedures for gaining support from the organisational environment; the selection of one or more of these is a strategic problem. It is here that the element of rationality appears to become exceedingly important, for in the order treated above, these relational processes represent increasingly 'costly' methods of gaining support in terms of decision-making power. The organisation that adopts a strategy of competition when cooptation is called for may lose all opportunity to realise its goals, or may finally turn to cooptation or coalition at a higher 'cost' than would have been necessary originally. On the other hand, an organisation may lose part of its integrity, and therefore some of its potentiality, if it unnecessarily shares power in exchange for support. Hence the establishment *in the appropriate form* of interaction with the many relevant parts of its environment can be a major organisational consideration in a complex society.

This means, in effect, that the organisation must be able to estimate the position of other relevant organisations and their willingness to enter into or alter relationships. Often, too, these matters must be determined or estimated without revealing one's own weaknesses, or even one's ultimate strength. It is necessary or advantageous, in other words, to have the consent or acquiescence of the other party, if a new relationship is to be established or an existing relationship altered. For this purpose organisational administrators often engage in what might be termed a *sounding out process*.

The sounding out process can be illustrated by the problem of the boss with amorous designs on his secretary in an organisation that taboos such relations. He must find some means of determining her willingness to alter the relationship, but he must do so without risking rebuff, for a showdown might come at the cost of his dignity or his office reputation, at the cost of losing her secretarial services, or in the extreme case at the cost of losing his own position. The 'sophisticated' procedure is to create an ambiguous situation in which the secretary is forced to respond in one of two ways: (1) to ignore or tactfully counter, thereby clearly channelling the relationship back into an already existing pattern, or (2) to respond in a similarly ambiguous vein (if not in a positive one) indicating a receptiveness to further advances. It is important in the sounding out process that the situation be ambiguous for two reasons: (1) the secretary must not be able to 'pin down' the boss with evidence if she rejects the idea, and (2) the situation must be far enough removed from normal to be noticeable to the secretary. The ambiguity of sounding out has the further advantage to the participants that neither party alone is clearly responsible for initiating the change.

The situation described above illustrates a process that seems to explain many organisational as well as personal interaction situations. In moving from one relationship to another between two or more organisations it is often necessary to leave a well-defined situation and proceed through a period of deliberate ambiguity, to arrive at a new clear-cut relationship. In interaction over goal-setting problems, sounding out sometimes is done through a form of double-talk, wherein the parties refer to 'hypothetical' enterprises and 'hypothetical' situations, or in 'diplomatic' language, which often serves the same purpose. In other cases, and perhaps more frequently, sounding out is done through the good offices of a third party. This occurs, apparently, where there has been no relationship in the past, or at the stage of negotiations where the parties have indicated intentions but are not willing to state their positions frankly. Here it becomes useful at times to find a discrete go-between who can be trusted with full information and who will seek an arrangement suitable to both parties.

CONCLUSION

In the complex modern society desired goals often require complex organisations. At the same time the desirability of goals and the appropriate division of labour among large organisations is less self-evident than in simpler, more homogeneous society. Purpose becomes a question to be decided rather than an obvious matter.

To the extent that behaviour of organisation members is oriented to questions of goals or purposes, a science of organisation must attempt to understand and explain that behaviour. We have suggested one classification scheme, based on decision-making, as potentially useful in analysing organisational-environmental interaction with respect to goal-setting and we have attempted to illustrate some aspects of its utility. It is hoped that the suggested scheme encompasses questions of rationality or irrationality without presuming either.

Argument by example, however, is at best only a starting point for scientific understanding and for the collection of evidence. Two factors make organisational goal-setting in a complex society a 'big' research topic: the multiplicity of large organisations of diverse type and the necessity of studying them in diachronic perspective. We hope that our discussion will encourage critical thinking and the sharing of observations about the subject.

REFERENCE

SELZNICK, PHILIP (1949) *TVA and the Grass Roots*, University of California Press.

SECTION 3

Organisational control, rules, roles and power

This section continues the overall concern for and interest in processes of organisational control (or the determination of the behaviour of members of organisations) with reference to analyses of actual events and interactions within organisations and to the ways in which persons' behaviour is influenced by their membership of the organisation. Adopting this focus of interest leads inevitably to a consideration of the two concepts that have been used by sociologists and organisational members alike to theorise about and explain the processes whereby individual members of organisations have their behaviour controlled: role and rule. These concepts are critically considered in the light of their application within studies of organisation.

It will be clear that throughout the Reader an attempt has been made to move from general, abstract, formalistic arguments to more specific, empirical analyses of organisational situations and circumstances. And while this should not be taken as suggesting that a concern for organisational structure is in any way unnecessary or unimportant, it can be seen as arguing for the importance of considering organisational structure and the actions and interactions of organisational members as a result of decisions, choices and strategies of those with organisational power and of negotiations and bargains of all who belong to the organisation. The importance and necessity of attending to actors' perceptions, evaluations, priorities and choices in understanding their actions is insisted upon in this and the following sections.

A view of organisations as arenas of conflicting or competing groups and ideologies underlies Hickson *et al*.'s analysis of intra-organisational power (11). Deviating from the traditional treatment of organisational power the authors explain 'differential sub-unit power' in terms of 'contingencies ensuing from varying combinations of coping with uncertainty, substitutability, and centrality'. In rejecting a conception of organisational power as a given, an independent, variable, they consider it as a consequence of organisational negotiations and relationships. This view of power differs markedly from that which sees it as a means of coordinating and organising the interdependent activities, responsibilities and activities of organisational members.

Katz's article (12) too is concerned with processes of organisational control, and, like Hickson *et al*., he focuses on the negotiations and compromises that underlie the apparent orderliness of organisational structure. Katz focuses on 'actual behaviour of people rather than abstract rules, on collaboration on the local level among the interacting people rather than collaboration with the total organization'. And he argues convincingly that the autonomy displayed by informal work groups is an inevitable aspect of organisational structure (a point later developed by ethnomethodologists) and can be seen as a mechanism whereby workers are allowed to develop or transplant a form of interaction and culture which serves to integrate them into the work organisation. It might be felt that such an integration would depend on the nature and content of this informal work group culture, which presumably might be markedly antipathetic to the organisation, or which might contain definitions and expectations that are incompatible with new, developing, organisational forms and methods.

Katz notes that organisational roles vary with respect to what may be termed their autonomy allowance. While executive roles contain directly specified areas of autonomy and discretion, but refer to a wide range of activities, blue-collar roles contain very little autonomy, but because they refer to just a narrow range of activities, they allow opportunities for non-work interactions and cultures (as described by Roy, see reading 13).

Roy's description of 'Banana Time', of the social interactions that occurred in a work group of which Roy was a member and the ways in which the working day was divided and made meaningful in terms of the traditional patterns and themes of the interactants, is a classic in its field. This article must surely strike the reader as meaningful and sensible in relation to his organisational experiences, in a way that most organisational research and discussion will not. But apart from its status and importance as a descriptive account of actual organisational activities, this article is also relevant for the way in which it draws attention to what is called 'a social structure of statuses and roles'. Roy says of this structure, that it 'may be discerned in the carrying out of the various informal activities which provide the content of the sub-culture of the group. The times and themes were performed with a system of roles which formed a sort of pecking hierarchy.' In short, like many others, Roy suggests that the behaviour of members of organisations may be the result of their commitment to what could be called 'unofficial' roles.

But whether role is seen only in its 'official' capacity, or whether it is modified to allow for the possibility of other demands and constraints, does not remove certain difficulties and confusions that often attend the utilisation of this concept. Some of these difficulties are considered by Levinson (14) (and by Hickson in his article in section 2, reading 7), and are further elaborated by Pugh (15). It is necessary to consider critically the concept role since it is typically given a great deal of explanatory weight in analyses of organisations, and their structure. Levinson describes the mechanistic image of organisational roles which defines them in terms of an interlocking system of coordinated demands and expectations known and acted upon by organisational members. He argues convincingly that such a view confuses three different uses (or assumes that the three uses are highly congruent), and ignores the possibility that roles may vary with respect to their coherence, consensus and capacity for individual choice. Pugh continues the critique, again with reference to organisations, by arguing that not only may roles involve conflicting demands and expectations, but that these conflicts may be of more than one sort: namely role-legitimation conflict and role activation conflict.

Zimmerman's analysis of rule (16) use follows the main theme of this section (and the Reader as a whole) in that it investigates the actual application and utilisation of rules within organisations: in particular Zimmerman considers the work that members of organisations (in this case reception personnel in a public assistance bureau) do in employing the organisational rules. But Zimmerman's study (like others in this section and in section 4), although ostensibly concerned with similar questions and issues as the other readings, stems from a distinctly different theoretical stance, one that disregards commitments to what is described as a natural attitude view of phenomena,[1] i.e. one that considers the existence of the 'real' world as a fact, unproblematically. Instead, ethnomethodology attends to the way in which people fashion what is accepted (to those considered as competent members of the society, organisation or group) as a sensible, relevant and meaningful account or explanation of what happened. Thus the point for Zimmerman is not simply that rules are broken, but that *they cannot be obeyed*, since rules are inevitably vague and general and unable to describe exactly and to prescribe actual situational applications. For this reason Zimmerman is interested in, as he puts it: 'what rules, policies and goals mean for the bureaucratic actor upon the concrete occasion of their use (for example, to guide, to account for, or to justify action).'

A similar theoretical position underlies Bittner's article (17). This constitutes a new and provocative view of the concept of organisation. Like Zimmerman, Bittner is interested in the notion of organisational structure not as a description of activities, but as a plan that members of the organisation use and refer to in the course of their attempts to communicate to each other about their or others', organisational activities. So Bittner argues that the concept of organisation is a common-sense one, i.e. one that is used by those in organisations. Furthermore, he suggests that the sociological usages of the concept rely, implicitly, on the common-sense uses, and that this has caused considerable confusion. (A similar argument concerning the concept of role has been put forward by Cicourel, 1970.) In other words, both Bittner and Zimmerman are arguing that the important and interesting questions to ask of organisational structure or organisational rules are: How is knowledge of these concepts employed by those who work in organisations, how do members apply these concepts to actual behaviour and events, and recognise activities as being subsumed by them? Unfortunately, however, they claim, sociologists have tended typically to use these concepts without realising that they are common-sense concepts and that any sociological utilisation of them rests upon members of the organisation interpreting them. Consequently, these key questions are largely ignored. It will be seen that these suggestions and considerations are directly relevant to the obvious difficulty sociologists have experienced in uncovering, measuring and describing the organisational structure which they refer to.

[1] This is not the occasion to offer a statement of what-ethnomethodology-is-really-about. Readers interested in this fascinating theoretical development should consult Douglas (1971), or Filmer *et al.* (1972), or Sudnow, ed. (1972).

REFERENCES

CICOUREL, AARON (1970) 'Basic and normative rules in the negotiation of status and role', in DREITZEL, HANS PETER, ed., *Recent Sociology No. 2*, New York, Macmillan, pp. 4–48.

DOUGLAS, JACK D., ed. (1971) *Understanding Everyday Life*, Routledge and Kegan Paul.

FILMER, P., PHILLIPSON, M., SILVERMAN, D., and WALSH, D. (1972) *New Directions in Sociological Theory*, Collier-MacMillan.

SUNDOW, DAVID, ed. (1972) *Studies in Social Interaction*, New York, The Free Press.

I I

D. J. *Hickson,*
C. R. *Hinings,*
C. A. *Lee,*
R. E. *Schneck and*
J. M. *Pennings*

A strategic contingencies' theory of intra organisational power

Excerpts from D. J. Hickson *et al.* 'A strategic contingencies' theory of intraorganizational power', *Administrative Science Quarterly*, **16**, no. 2, June 1971, 216–29.

Typically, research designs have treated power as the independent variable. Power has been used in community studies to explain decisions on community programmes, on resource allocation, and on voting behaviour: in small groups it has been used to explain decision making; and it has been used in studies of work organisations to explain morale and alienation. But within work organisations, power itself has not been explained. This paper sets forth a theoretical explanation of power as the dependent variable with the aim of developing empirically testable hypotheses that will explain differential power among subunits in complex work organisations.

The problems of studying power are well known from the cogent reviews by March (1955, 1966) and Wrong (1968). These problems led March (1966, p. 70) to ask if power was just a term used to mask our ignorance, and to conclude pessimistically that the power of the concept of power 'depends on the kind of system we are confronting'.

Part of March's (1966) pessimism can be attributed to the problems inherent in community studies. When the unit of analysis is the community, the governmental, political, economic, recreational, and other units which make up the community do not necessarily interact and may even be oriented outside the supposed boundaries of the community. However, the subunits of a work organisation are mutually related in the interdependent activities of a single identifiable social system. The perspective of the present paper is due in particular to the encouraging studies of subunits by Lawrence and Lorsch (1967a, 1967b), and begins with their (1967a, p. 3) definition of an organisation as 'a system of interrelated behaviours of people who are performing a task that has been differentiated into several distinct subsystems'.

Previous studies of power in work organisations have tended to focus on the individual and to neglect subunit or departmental power. This neglect led Perrow (1970, p. 84) to state:

> Part of the problem, I suspect, stems from the persistent attempt to define power in terms of individuals and as a social psychological phenomenon.... Even sociological studies tend to measure power by asking about an individual.... I am not at all clear about the matter, but I think the term takes on different meanings when the unit, or power-holder, is a *formal group* in an *open system* with *multiple goals*, and the system is assumed to reflect a political-domination model of organization, rather than only a cooperative model. . . . The fact that after a cursory search I can find only a single study that asks survey questions regarding the power of functional *groups* strikes me as odd. Have we conceptualized power in such a way as to exclude this well-known phenomenon?

The concept of power used here follows Emerson (1962) and takes power as a property of the social relationship, not of the actor. Since the context of the relationship is a formal organisation, this approach moves away from an overpersonalised conceptualisation and operationalisation of power toward structural sources. Such an approach has been taken only briefly by Dubin (1963) in his discussion of power, and incidentally by Lawrence and Lorsch (1967b) when reporting power data. Most research has focused on the vertical superior-subordinate relationship, as in a multitude of leadership studies. This approach is exemplified by the extensive work of Tannenbaum (1968) and his colleagues, in which the distribution of perceived power was displayed on control graphs. The focus was on the vertical differentiation of perceived power, that is the exercise of power by managers who by changing their behaviour could vary the distribution and the total amount of perceived power.

By contrast, when organisations are conceived as interdepartmental systems, the division of labour becomes the ultimate source of intraorganisational power, and power is explained by variables that are elements of each subunit's task, its functioning, and its links with the activities of other subunits. Insofar as this approach differs from previous studies by treating power as the dependent variable, by taking subunits of work organisations as the subjects of analysis, and by attempting a multivariate explanation, it may avoid some of the previous pitfalls.

ELEMENTS OF A THEORY

Thompson (1967, p. 13) took from Cyert and March (1963) a viewpoint which he hailed as a newer tradition:

> A newer tradition enables us to conceive of the organization as an open system, indeterminate and faced with uncertainty, but subject to criteria of rationality and hence needing certainty . . . we suggest that organizations cope with uncertainty by creating certain parts specifically to deal with it, specializing others parts in operating under conditions of certainty, or near certainty.

Thus organisations are conceived of as interdepartmental systems in which a major task element is coping with uncertainty. The task is divided and allotted to the subsystems, the division of labour creating an interdependency among them. Imbalance of this reciprocal inter-dependence (Thompson, 1967) among the parts gives rise to power relations. The essence of an organisation is limitation of the autonomy of all its members or parts, since all are subject to power from the others; for subunits, unlike individuals, are not free to make a decision to participate, as March and Simson (1958) put it, nor to decide whether or not to come together in political relationships. They must. They exist to do so. Crozier (1964, p. 47) stressed in his discussion of power the necessity for the members of the different groups to live together; the fact that each group's privileges depend to quite a large extent on the existence of other groups' privileges'. The groups use differential power to function within the system rather than to destroy it.

If dependency in a social relation is the reverse of power (Emerson, 1962), then the crucial unanswered question in organisations is: what factors function to vary dependency, and so to vary power? Emerson (1962, p. 32) proposed that 'the dependence of actor A upon actor B is (1) directly proportional to A's motivational investment in goals mediated by B, and (2) inversely proportional to the availability of those goals to A outside of the A–B relation'. In organisations, subunit B will have more power than other subunits to the extent that (1) B has the capacity to fulfil the requirements of the other subunits and (2) B monopolises this ability. If a central problem facing modern organisa-tions is uncertainty, then B's power in the organisation will be partially determined by the extent to which B copes with uncertainties for other subunits, and by the extent to which B's coping activities are available elsewhere.

Thus, intraorganisational dependency can be associated with two contributing variables: (1) the degree to which a subunit copes with uncertainty for other subunits, and (2) the extent to which a subunit's coping activities are substitutable. But if coping with uncertainty, and substitutability, are to be in some way related to power, there is a necessary assumption of some degree of task interconnection among subunits. By definition, organisation requires a minimum link. Therefore, a third variable, centrality, refers to the varying degree above such a minimum with which the activities of a subunit are linked with those of other subunits.

Before these three variables can be combined in a theory of power, it is necessary to examine their definition and possible operationalisation, and to define power in this context.

Power

Hinings *et al.* (1967, p. 62) compared power to concepts such as bureaucracy or alienation or social class, which are difficult to understand because they tend to be treated as 'large-scale unitary concepts'. Their many meanings need disentangling. With the concept of power, this has not yet been accomplished (Cartwright, 1965), but two conceptualisations are commonly employed: (1) power as coercion, and (2) power as determination of behaviour.

Power as coercive force was a comparatively early conceptualisation among sociologists (Weber, 1947; Bierstedt, 1950). Later, Blau (1964) emphasised the imposition of will despite resistance.

However, coercion is only one among the several bases of power listed by French and Raven (1959) and applied across organisations by Etzioni (1961); that is, coercion is a means of power, but is not an adequate definition of power. If the direction of dependence in a relationship is determined by an imbalance of power bases, power itself has to be defined separately from these bases. Adopting Dahl's (1957) concept of power, as many others have done (March, 1955; Bennis *et al.*, 1958; Emerson, 1962; Harsanyi, 1962; Van Doorn, 1962; Dahlstrom, 1966; Wrong, 1968; Tannenbaum, 1968; Luhmann, 1969), power is defined as the determination of the behaviour of one social unit by another.

If power is the determination of A's behaviour by B, irrespective of whether one, any, or all the types of bases are involved, then authority will here be regarded as that part of power which is legitimate or normatively expected by some selection of role definers. Authority may be either more or less than power. For subunits it might be represented by the formally specified range of activities they are officially required to undertake and, therefore, to decide upon.

Discrepancies between authority and power may reflect time lag. Perrow (1970) explored the discrepancy between respondent's perceptions of power and of what power should be. Perhaps views on a preferred power distribution precede changes in the exercise of power, which in turn precede changes in expectations of power, that is in its legitimate authority content. Perhaps today's authority hierarchy is partly a fossilised impression of yesterday's power ranking. However this may be, it is certainly desirable to include in any research not only data on perceived power and on preferred power, but also on positional power, or authority, and on participation, or exercised power (Clark [ed.], 1968).

Kaplan (1964) succinctly described three dimensions of power. The weight of power is defined in terms of the degree to which B affects the probability of A behaving in a certain way, that is, determination of behaviour in the sense adopted here. The other dimensions are domain and scope. Domain is the number of A's, persons or collectivities, whose behaviour is determined; scope is the range of behaviour of each A that are determined. For subunit power within an organisation, domain might be the number of other subunits affected by the issues, scope the range of decision issues affected, and weight the degree to which a given subunit affects the decision process on the issues. In published research such distinctions are rarely made. Power consists of the sweeping undifferentiated perceptions of respondents when asked to rank individuals or classes of persons, such as supervisors, on influence. Yet at the same time the complexity of power in organisations is recognised. If it is taken for granted that, say, marketing has most to do with sales matters, that accounting has most to do with finance matters, supervisors with supervisory matters, and so on, then the validity of forcing respondents to generalise single opinions across an unstated range of possibilities is questionable.

To avoid these generalised opinions, data collected over a range of decision topics or issues are desirable. Such issues should in principle include all recognised problem areas in the organisation, in each of which more than one subunit is involved. Examples might be marketing strategies, obtaining equipment, personnel training, and capital budgeting.

Some suggested subvariables and indicators of power and of the independent variables are summarised in Table 11.1. These are intended to include both individual perceptions of power in the form of questionnaire responses and data of a somewhat less subjective kind on participation in decision processes and on formal position in the organisation.

TABLE 11.1. *Variables and operationalisable subvariables*

Power (weight, domain, scope)
Positional power (authority)
Participation power
Perceived power
Preferred power

Uncertainty
Variability of organisational inputs
Feedback on subunit performance;
  Speed
  Specificity
Structuring of subunit activities

Coping with uncertainty, classified as:
By prevention (forestalling uncertainty)
By information (forecasting)
By absorption (action after the event)

Substitutability
Availability of alternatives
Replaceability of personnel

Centrality
Pervasiveness of workflows
Immediacy of workflows

It is now possible to examine coping with uncertainty, substitutability and centrality.

Uncertainty and coping with uncertainty

Uncertainty may be defined as a lack of information about future events, so that alternatives and their outcomes are unpredictable. Organisations deal with environmentally derived uncertainties in the sources and composition of inputs, with uncertainties in the processing of throughputs, and again with environmental uncertainties in the disposal of outputs. They must have means to deal with these uncertainties for adequate task performance. Such ability is here called coping.

In his study of the French tobacco manufacturing industry, Crozier (1964, p. 164) suggested that power is related to 'the kind of uncertainty upon which depends the life of the organization'. March and Simon (1958) had earlier made the same point, and Perrow (1961) had discussed the shifting domination of different groups in organisations following the shifting uncertainties of resources and the routinisation of skills. From studies of industrial firms, Perrow (1970) tentatively thought that power might be due to uncertainty absorption, as March and Simon (1958) call it. Lawrence and Lorsch (1967b) found that marketing had more influence than production in both container-manufacturing and food-processing firms, apparently because of its involvement in (uncertain) innovation and with customers.

Crozier (1964) proposed a strategic model of organisations as systems in which groups strive for power, but his discussion did not clarify how uncertainty could relate positively to power. Uncertainty itself does not give power: coping gives power. If organisations allocate to their various subunits task areas that vary in uncertainty, then those subunits that cope most effectively with the most uncertainty should have most power within the organisation, since coping by a subunit reduces the impact of uncertainty on other activities in the organisation, a shock absorber function. Coping may be by prevention, for example, a subunit prevents sales fluctuations by securing firm orders: or by information, for example, a subunit forecasts sales fluctuations; or by absorption, for example, a drop in sales is swiftly countered by novel selling methods (Table 11.1). By coping, the subunit provides pseudo certainty for the other subunits by controlling what are otherwise contingencies for other activities. This coping confers power through the dependencies created.

Thus organisations do not necessarily aim to avoid uncertainty nor to reduce its absolute level, as Cyert and March (1963) appear to have assumed, but to cope with it. If a subunit can cope, the level of uncertainty encountered can be increased by moving into fresh sectors of the environment, attempting fresh outputs, or utilising fresh technologies.

Operationally, raw uncertainty and coping will be difficult to disentangle, though theoretically the distinctions are clear. For all units, uncertainty is in the raw situation which would exist without the activities of the other relevant subunits, for example, the uncertainty that would face production units if the sales subunit were not there to forecast and/or to obtain a smooth flow of orders. Uncertainty might be indicated by the variability of those inputs to the organisation which are taken by the subunit. For instance, a production subunit may face variability in raw materials and engineering may face variability in equipment performance. Lawrence and Lorsch (1967a) attempted categorisations of this kind. In addition, they (1967a, p. 14) gave a lead with 'the time span of definitive feedback from the environment'. This time span might be treated as a secondary indicator of uncertainty, making the assumption that the less the feedback to a subunit on the results of what it is doing, and the less specific the feedback, the more likely the subunit is to be working in a vague, unknown, unpredictable task area. Both speed and specificity of feedback are suggested variables in Table 11.1.

Furthermore, the copious literature on bureaucratic or mechanistic structures versus more organic and less defined structures could be taken to imply that routinised or highly structured subunits, for example, as conceptualised and measured by Pugh *et al.* (1968), will have stable homogeneous activities and be less likely to face uncertainty. This assumption would require empirical testing before structuring of activities could be used as an indicator of uncertainty, but it is tentatively included in Table 11.1.

In principle, coping with uncertainty might be directly measured by the difference between the uncertainty of those inputs taken by a subunit and the certainty with which it performs its activities nonetheless. This would indicate the degree of shock absorption.

The relation of coping with uncertainty to power can be expressed by the following hypothesis:

Hypothesis 1. The more a subunit copes with uncertainty, the greater its power within the organisation.

The hypothesis is in a form which ignores any effects of centrality and substitutability.

Substitutability

Concepts relating to the availability of alternatives pervade the literature on power. In economics theory the degree of competition is taken as a measure of the extent to which alternatives are available from other organisations, it being implied that the power of an organisation over other organisations and customers is a function of the amount of competition present. The same point was the second part of Emerson's (1962) power-dependency scheme in social relations, and the second requirement or determinant in Blau's (1964) model of a power relationship.

Yet only Mechanic (1962) and Dubin (1957, 1963), have discussed such concepts as explanations of organisational power. Mechanic's (1962, p. 358) hypothesis 4 stated: 'Other factors remaining constant, a person difficult to replace will have greater power than a person easily replaceable.' Dubin (1957) stressed the very similar notion of exclusiveness, which as developed later (Dubin, 1963, p. 21), means that: 'For any given level of functional importance in an organisation, the power residing in a functionary is inversely proportional to the number of other functionaries in the organisation capable of performing the function.' Supporting this empirically, Lipset *et al.* (1956) suggested that oligarchy may occur in trade unions because of the official's monopoly of political and negotiating skills.

The concept being used is represented here by the term substitutability, which can, for subunits, be defined as the ability of the organisation to obtain alternative performance for the activities of a subunit, and can be stated as a hypothesis for predicting the power of a subunit as follows:

Hypothesis 2. The lower the substitutability of the activities of a subunit, the greater its power within the organisation.

Thus a purchasing department would have its power reduced if all of its activities could be done by hired materials agents, as would a personnel department if it were partially substituted by selection consultants or by line managers finding their staff themselves. Similarly, a department may hold on to power by retaining information the release of which would enable others to do what it does.

The obvious problem in operationalisation is establishing that alternative means of performing activities exist and if they do, whether they could feasibly be used. Even if agents or consultants exist locally, or if corporation headquarters could provide services, would it really be practicable for the organisation to dispense with its own subunit? Much easier to obtain are data on replaceability of subunit personnel such as length of training required for new recruits and ease of hiring, which can be regarded as secondary indicators of the substitutability of a subunit, as indicated in Table 1.

Centrality

Given a view of organisations as systems of interdependent roles and activities, then the centrality of a subunit is the degree to which its activities are interlinked into the system. By definition, no subunit of an organisation can score zero centrality. Without a minimum of centrality, coping with uncertainty and substitutability cannot affect power; above the minimum, additional increments of centrality further differentiate subunit power. It is the degree to which the subunit is an interdependent component, as Thompson (1967, p. 54) put it, distinguishing between pooled, sequential, and reciprocal interdependence patterns. Blau and Scott (1962) made an analogous distinction between parallel and interdependent specialisation. Woodward (1965, p. 126) also introduced a concept of this kind into her discussion of the critical function in each of unit, large batch and mass, and process production: 'there seemed to be one function that was central and critical in that it had the greatest effect on success and survival'.

Within the overall concept of centrality, there are inconsistencies which indicate that more than one constitutive concept is being used. At the present stage of conceptualisation their identification must be very tentative. First, there is the idea that the activities of a subunit are central if they are connected with many other activities in the organisation. This workflow pervasiveness may be defined as the degree to which the workflows of a subunit connect with the workflows of other subunits. It describes the extent of task interactions between subunits, and for all subunits in an organisation it would be operationalised as the flow-chart of a complete systems analysis. For example, the integrative subsystems studied by Lawrence and Lorsch (1967a, p. 30), 'whose members had the function of integrating the sales-research and the production-research subsystems' and which had structural and cultural characteristics intermediate between them, were presumably high on workflow pervasiveness because everything they did connected with the workflows of these several other subsystems. Research subsystems, however, may have been low on this variable if they fed work only to a single integrative, or production, subsystem.

Secondly, the activities of a subunit are central if they are essential in the sense that their cessation would quickly and substantially impede the primary workflow of the organisation. This workflow immediacy is defined as the speed and severity with which the workflows of a subunit affect the final outputs of the organisation. Zald (1962) and Clark (1956) used a similar idea when they explained differential power among institution staff and education faculty by the close relation of their activities to organisation goals.

The pervasiveness and immediacy of the workflows of a subunit are not necessarily closely related, and may empirically show a low correlation. A finance department may well have pervasive connections with all other subunits through the budgeting system, but if its activities ceased it would be some time before the effects were felt in, say, the production output of a factory; a production department controlling a stage midway in the sequence of an automated process, however, could have high workflow immediacy though not high pervasiveness.

The two main centrality hypotheses can, therefore, be stated as follows:

Hypothesis 3a. The higher the pervasiveness of the workflows of a sub-unit, the greater its power within the organisation.

Hypothesis 3b. The higher the immediacy of the workflows of a sub-unit, the greater its power within the organisation.

CONTROL OF CONTINGENCIES

Hypotheses relating power to coping with uncertainty, substitutability, and the subvariables of centrality have been stated in a simple single-variable form. Yet it follows from the view of subunits as interdependent parts of organisational systems that the hypotheses in this form are misleading. While each hypothesis may be empirically upheld, it is also hypothesised that this cannot be so without some values of both the other main independent variables. For example, when a marketing department copes with a volatile market by forecasting and by switching sales staff around to ensure stable orders, it acquires power only because the forecast and the orders are linked to the workflow of production, which depends on them. But even then power would be limited by the availability of a successful local marketing agency which could be hired by the organisation, and the fact that salesmen were low skilled and easily replaceable.

To explain this interrelationship, the concept of control of contingencies is introduced. It represents organisational interdependence; subunits control contingencies for one another's activities and draw power from the dependencies thereby created. As a hypothesis:

Hypothesis 4. The more contingencies are controlled by a subunit, the greater its power within the organisation.

A contingency is a requirement of the activities of one subunit which is affected by the activities of another subunit. What makes such a contingency strategic, in the sense that it is related to power, can be deduced from the preceding hypotheses. The independent variables are each necessary but not sufficient conditions for control of strategic contingencies, but together they determine the variation in interdependence between subunits. Thus contingencies controlled by a subunit as a consequence of its coping with uncertainty do not become strategic, that is, affect power, in the organisation without some (unknown) values of substitutability and centrality. A strategic contingencies theory of power is therefore proposed and is illustrated by the diagram in Fig. 11.1.

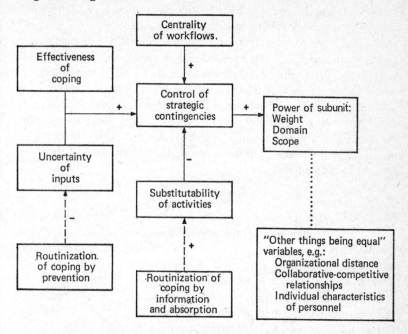

———▶Direct relationship with power; ———— indirect relationship with power; ••••••
relationship with power other than by control of contingencies.

FIG. 11.1.   *The strategic contingencies theory and routinisation*

In terms of exchange theory, as developed by Blau (1964), subunits can be seen to be exchanging control of strategic contingencies one for the other under the normative regulation of an encompassing social system, and acquiring power in the system through the exchange. The research task is to elucidate what combinations of values of the independent variables summarised in hypotheses 1–3 allow hypothesis 4 to hold. Ultimately and ideally the aim would be to discover not merely the weightings of each in the total effect upon power, but how these variables should be operationally interrelated to obtain the best predictions. More of one and less of another may leave the resulting power unchanged. Suppose an engineering subunit has power because it quickly absorbs uncertainty by repairing breakdowns which interfere with the different workflows for each of several organisation outputs. It is moderately central and non-substitutable. A change in organisation policy bringing in a new technology with a single workflow leading to a single output would raise engineering's centrality, since a single break-down would immediately stop everything, but simultaneously the un-certainty might be reduced by a maintenance programme which all but eliminates the possibility of such an occurrence.

Though three main factors are hypothesised, which must change if power is to change, it is not assumed that all subunits will act in accord with the theory to increase their power. This has to be demonstrated. There is the obvious possibility of a cumulative reaction in which a subunit's power is used to preserve or increase the uncertainty it can cope with, or its centrality, or to prevent substitution, thereby in-creasing its power, and so on. Nor is it argued that power or authority are intentionally allocated in terms of the theory, although the theory is open to such an inference.

Routinisation

Most studies that refer to uncertainty contrast it with routinisation, the prior prescription of recurrent task activities. Crozier (1964) held that the power of the maintenance personnel in the tobacco plants was due to all other tasks being routinised. A relative decline in the power of general medical personnel in hospitals during this century is thought to be due to the routinisation of some tasks, which previously presented uncertainties which could be coped with only by a physician, and the transfer of these tasks to relatively routinised subunits, such as inocula-tion programmes, mass X-ray facilities, and so on (Perrow, 1965); Gordon and Becker, 1964). Crozier (1964, p. 165) crystallised the presumed effects of routinisation; 'But the expert's success is constantly self-defeating. The rationalization process gives him power, but the end results of rationalization curtail his power. As soon as a field is well covered, as soon as the first intuitions and innovations can be translated into rules and programmes, the expert's power disappears.'

The strategic contingencies' theory as developed in Fig. 11.1 clarifies this. It suggests that research has been hampered by a confusion of two kinds of routinisation, both of which are negatively related to power but in different ways. Routinisation may be (*a*) of coping by prevention, which prevents the occurrence of uncertainty; and (*b*) of coping by information or absorption which define how the uncertainty which does occur shall be coped with.

Preventive routinisation reduces or removes the uncertainty itself, for example, planned maintenance, which maintenance in Crozier's (1964) tobacco factories would have resisted; inoculation or X-ray pro-grammes; and long-term supply contracts, so that the sales staff no longer have to contend with unstable demand. Such routinisation removes the opportunity for power, and it is this which is self-defeating (Crozier, 1964, p. 165) if the expert takes his techniques to a point when they begin not only to cope but to routinely diminish the uncertainty coped with. Thus reducing the uncertainty is not the same as reducing the impact of uncertainty. According to the hypothesis, a sales department which transmits steady orders despite a volatile market has high power; a sales department which reduces the uncertainty itself by long-term tied contracts has low power.

Routinisation of coping by information and absorption is embodied in job descriptions and task instructions prescribing how to obtain information and to respond to uncertainty. For maintenance personnel, it lays down how to repair the machine; for physicians, it lays down a standard procedure for examining patients and sequences of remedies for each diagnosis. How does this affect power, since it does not eliminate the uncertainty itself, as preventive routinisation does? What it does is increase substitutability. The means of coping become more visible and possible substitutes more obvious, even if those substitutes are unskilled personnel from another subunit who can follow a standard procedure but could not have acquired the previously unexpressed skills.

There is probably some link between the two kinds of routinisation. Once preventive routinisation is accomplished, other coping routinisation more easily follows, as indeed it follows any reduction of uncertainty.

CONCLUSION

The concept of work organisations as interdepartmental systems leads to a strategic contingencies theory explaining differential subunit power by dependence on contingencies ensuing from varying combinations of coping with uncertainty, substitutability, and centrality. It should be stressed that the theory is not in any sense static. As the goals, outputs, technologies, and markets of organisations change so, for each subunit, the values of the independent variables change, and patterns of power change.

Many problems are unresolved. For example, does the theory implicitly assume perfect knowledge by each subunit of the contingencies inherent for it in the activities of the others? Does a workflow of information affect power differently to a workflow of things? But with the encouragement of the improved analysis given of the few existing studies, data can be collected and analysed, hopefully in ways which will afford a direct test.

REFERENCES

BENNIS, WARREN G., BERKOWITZ, N., AFFINITO, M., and MALONE, M. (1958) 'Authority, power and the ability to influence', *Human Relations*, **11**, 143–56.

BIERSTEDT, ROBERT (1950) 'An analysis of social power', *American Sociological Review*, **15**, 730–6.

BLAU, PETER (1964) *Exchange and Power in Social Life*, Wiley.

BLAU, PETER, and RICHARD, SCOTT, W. (1962) *Formal Organizations: a comparative approach*, Routledge & Kegan Paul.

CARTWRIGHT, DARWIN (1965) 'Influence, leadership, control', in James G. March, ed., *Handbook of Organizations*, Rand McNally, pp. 1–47.

CLARK, BURTON, R. (1956) 'Organizational adaptation and precarious values: a case study', *American Sociological Review*, **21**, 327–36.

CLARK, TERRY N., ed. (1968) *Community Structure and Decision-Making: comparative analyses*, San Francisco, Chandler.

CROZIER, MICHAEL (1964) *The Bureaucratic Phenomenon*, Tavistock.

CYERT, R. M., and MARCH, J. G. (1963) *A Behavioral Theory of the Firm*, Prentice-Hall.

DAHL, R. A. (1957) 'The concept of power', *Behavioral Science*, **2**, 201–15.

DAHLSTROM, E. (1966) 'Exchange, influence, and power', *Acta Sociologica*, **9**, 237–84.

DUBIN, ROBERT (1957) 'Power and union management relations', *Administrative Science Quarterly*, **2**, 60–81.

DUBIN, ROBERT (1963) 'Power, function, and organization', *Pacific Sociological Review*, **6**, 16–24.

EMERSON, R. E. (1962) 'Power-dependence relations', *American Sociological Review*, **27**, 31–41.

ETZIONI, AMITAI (1961) *A Comparative Analysis of Complex Organizations*, New York, Free Press of Glencoe.

FRENCH, J. R. P., and RAVEN, B. (1959) 'The bases of social power', in D. Cartwright, ed., *Studies in Social Power*, University of Michigan Press, pp. 150–67.

GORDON, GERALD, and SELWYN BECKER (1961) 'Changes in medical practice bring shifts in the patterns of power', *The Modern Hospital*, February, pp. 89–91, 154–6.

HARSANYI, J. C. (1962) 'Measurement of social power, opportunity costs, and the theory of two-person bargaining games', *Behavioral Science*, **7**, 67–80.

HININGS, C. R., PUGH, D. S., HICKSON, D. J., and TURNER, C. (1967) 'An approach to the study of bureaucracy', *Sociology*, **1**, 61–72.

KAPLAN, ABRAHAM (1964) 'Power in perspective', in Robert L. Khan and Elise Boulding, eds., *Power and Conflict in Organizations*, Tavistock, pp. 11–32.

LAWRENCE, P. R., and LORSCH, J. W. (1967a) 'Differentiation and integration in complex organizations', *Administrative Science Quarterly*, **12**, 1–17.

LAWRENCE, P. R., and LORSCH, J. W. (1967b) *Organization and Environment*, Division of Research, Graduate School of Business Administration, Harvard University.

LIPSET, S. M., TROW, M. A., and COLEMAN, J. A. (1956) *Union Democracy*, New York, Free Press of Glencoe.

LUHMANN, NIKLAUS (1969) 'Klassische Theorie der Macht', *Zeitschrift für Politik*, **16**, 149–70.

MARCH, J. G. (1955) 'An introduction to the theory and measurement of influence', *American Political Science Review*, **49**, 431–50.

MARCH, J. G. (1966) 'The power of power', in David Easton, ed., *Varieties of Political Theory*, Prentice-Hall, pp. 39–70.

MARCH, J. G., and SIMON, H. A. (1958) *Organizations*, Wiley.

MECHANIC, DAVID (1962) 'Sources of power of lower participants in complex organizations', *Administrative Science Quarterly*, **7**, 349–64.

PERROW, CHARLES (1961) 'The analysis of goals in complex organizations', *American Sociological Review*, **26**, 854–66.

PERROW, CHARLES (1965) 'Hospitals: technology, structure, and goals', in James G. Marsh, ed., *Handbook of Organizations*, Rand McNally, pp. 910–71.

PERROW, CHARLES (1970) 'Departmental power and perspectives in industrial firms', in Mayer N. Zald, ed., *Power in Organizations*, Vanderbilt University Press, pp. 59–89.

PUGH, D. S., HICKSON, D. J., HININGS, C. R., and TURNER, C. (1968) 'Dimensions of organization structure', *Administrative Science Quarterly*, **13**, 65–105.

TANNENBAUM, A. S. (1968) *Control in Organizations*, McGraw-Hill.

THOMPSON, J. D. (1967) *Organizations in Action*, McGraw-Hill.

VAN DOORN, J. A. A. (1962) 'Sociology and the problem of power', *Sociologica Neerlandica*, **1**, 3–47.

WEBER, MAX (1947) *The Theory of Social and Economic Organization*, New York, Free Press of Glencoe.

WOODWARD, JOAN (1965) *Industrial Organization: theory and practice*, Oxford University Press.

WRONG, DENNIS (1968) 'Some problems in defining social power', *American Journal of Sociology*, **73**, 673–81.

ZALD, MAYER, N. (1962) 'Organizational control structures in five correctional institutions', *American Journal of Sociology*, **68**, 335–45.

12

Fred E. Katz

Integrative and adaptive uses of autonomy: worker autonomy in factories

Excerpts from Fred E. Katz, 'Integrative and adaptive uses of autonomy: worker autonomy in factories', in *Autonomy and Organization: the limits of social control*, New York, Random House, 1968, chapter 2.

A generation after the well-known Hawthorne studies (Roethlisberger and Dickson, 1939), no one questions the existence of informal groups in complex organisations. Numerous studies have documented their existence, especially among employees in the lowest ranks. But the task remains of developing an adequate *conceptual* explanation of how persons in the lowest ranks, having limited career prospects in their work and slight opportunity for advancement, are incorporated into work organisations on a relatively permanent basis. In other words, how can we account for the integration of organisations that include a large number of persons who are largely disenfranchised from the organisation's reward system? How can we account for the apparent collaboration, if not loyalty, of persons, who, since the time of Marx, have been described as being alienated from their work? (Cf. Blauner, 1964.) A brief, though oversimplified, answer is that workers need work and factories need workers. We can hardly argue with this statement. Yet the economic interdependence of workers and factories does not clarify the nature of the structural arrangement under which the interdependence is worked out.

The proposed answer to the question of how workers are incorporated into complex organisations has two aspects. First, workers have considerable autonomy within the confines of the organisation. Even when their work is prescribed in exact detail, the work role tends to be defined narrowly. This situation leaves a considerable portion of the worker's life within the work organisation *undefined*. Second, workers tend to use this autonomy to bring their working-class culture into the organisation, even though it is alien to the bureaucratic ethos of the higher echelons of the organisation. This practice produces continuity between the workman's outside life and his participation in the work setting—a setting to which he has very limited allegiance (cf. Argyris, 1964; Dubin, 1963). This continuity in turn promotes workers' integration into work organisations.

The guiding perspective of our study is that the culture of informal work groups is a manifestation of autonomy within the confines of the organisation and that autonomy is an aspect of organisational structure even as it was in the schools. Autonomy, defined as independence from external control, means in this case that the activities of workers within the organisation are not fully controlled by the organisation. There is, therefore, scope for the development of various informal patterns: some patterns lessen the boredom of workers and in other ways help get work done; others are contrary to the goals of the organisation. Autonomy can be considered as an aspect of the very structure of the organisation, which materialises as spheres of independence delegated directly or indirectly by the organisation. Directly delegated autonomy refers to specific rules that delimit an area of independence; for example, a rule specifying that the foreman can decide who will work the night shift indicates a sphere in which the foreman has autonomy, one in which he exercises discretion. By contrast, indirect delegation of autonomy results from the absence of rules; in a sphere where no clear rules exist, autonomy exists by default. Both direct and indirect delegation of autonomy promote spheres of activity that are not closely controlled by the organisation. Our thesis is that the resulting autonomous behaviour must be considered as an aspect of organisational structure, not merely as deviance from it. In the main, this chapter will examine autonomy based on indirect delegation, since this aspect seems to characterise informal patterns among workers.

Worker autonomy can be regarded as part of the barter arrangement between workers and the organisation, in which limited affiliation with the organisation is exchanged for a degree of autonomy. The arrangement has important adaptive functions for both parties. For the organisation it is a way of promoting the affiliation of some of its employees with the organisation, while at the same time excluding them from certain vital spheres of organisational activity. For workers it permits continuation of the working-class style of life and provides ties of sociability in a context that in many ways is alien to the workman's culture. In short, the autonomy appears to have adaptive and pattern-maintenance functions for the workers and adaptive and goal-attainment functions for the organisation. It must be noted that worker autonomy, although enacted *in* the work organisation, is essentially *external* to his work role. Worker autonomy thus contrasts with the autonomy pattern for white-collar workers, that is, for all those who, from the lowliest clerk to the president, make up the administrative hierarchy. They have greater autonomy *within* their work role, but their role is more broadly defined than that of the worker. . . .

In the case of the white-collar worker it means taking his work role *outside* the organisation; for the blue-collar worker, it means bringing his nonwork role *into* the organisation.

The term 'autonomy' here covers much of the same ground that is now covered by the term 'informal organisation'. However, the present way of looking at autonomy tries to eliminate some of the ambiguities in the distinction between informal organisation and formal organisation. Herbert A. Simon and his colleagues (1962) summarise the existing distinction. Formal organisation is defined as 'a planned system of cooperative effort in which each participant has a recognized role to play and duties or tasks to perform' (p. 5). Informal organisation is defined as 'the whole pattern of actual behavior—the way members of the organization really do behave—insofar as these actual behaviors do not coincide with the formal plan' (p. 87). Research findings support the idea that the formal organisation is made up of a planned system and informal organisation of actual behaviour that deviates from the formal plans. But the research procedures themselves seem to lay the groundwork for producing these findings. The very nature of the research strategies promotes the search for deviance where informal patterns are concerned and the assumption of legitimacy where the formal patterns are concerned.

The explicit rules of formal organisation do not prescribe informal behaviour patterns; therefore, informal behaviour must be discovered through direct, detailed investigation and observation. This kind of research is likely to dwell on actual behaviour of people rather than abstract rules, on collaboration on the local level among the interacting people rather than collaboration with the total organisation. All this is likely to show innovation and departure from rules rather than compliance with rules. The findings resulting from this emphasis in the research process tend to perpetuate the initial contention that informal patterns deviate from the planned system, thereby creating a self-fulfilling prophecy. As a result, despite evidence that informal patterns may be very firmly established within an organisation

(Roethlisberger and Dickson, 1939; see also Blau, 1960 and 1955), the view persists that informal patterns lack legitimacy and permanence. If the behaviour patterns that are relevant to formal structure were subjected to similarly detailed observational scrutiny, a picture might emerge that is far closer to so-called informal patterns than we now have.[1] It is noteworthy that when studying 'planned' patterns, researchers usually omit the behaviour involved in the *planning* of these patterns!

To define the difference between formal organisation and informal organisation as that between a planned system and actual behaviour is theoretically weak. Actual behaviour is undoubtedly relevant to planned systems; and system characteristics, even planned ones, are relevant to actual behaviour. The distinction seems to need refocusing to enable orderly analysis of structure and behaviour. The following formulation should help to clarify the situation: *Organisational structure includes relatively controlled and relatively autonomous spheres*. The controlled sphere can include both direct and indirect specification of behaviour; similarly, the autonomous sphere can include directly and indirectly specified behaviour. Table 12.1 offers an application of this approach by giving an idealised comparison of the way the roles of executive and blue-collar workers are structured. Each role contains spheres of autonomy and spheres of controlled behaviour. The executive's role contains autonomy within his organisational tasks. His role is defined by broad lines that serve as guidelines to his behaviour but do not define closely which particular acts he must perform. The rules specify the areas in which he has flexibility. On the other hand, this is an indirect way of specifying control over him: he *must* comply with the guidelines, but his compliance can be assessed only by judging how he uses his flexibility. The blue-collar worker, on the other hand, has very little autonomy in his work, since his tasks tend to be specified in detail. But this leaves him with opportunity to engage in nonwork behaviour, which is not specified by his organisational task responsibilities.

The traditional conception of formal patterns parallels the 'controlled' spheres (cells 3 and 4 in Table 12.1). In the present approach both 'formal' and 'informal' are subsumed under analytical categories that conceptualise both in comparable terms. No longer are informal patterns merely stubbornly recurring residual patterns within a formalised scheme of organisational structure.

The writings of Chester I. Barnard illustrate that autonomous and

[1] Indeed, Blau's work comes close to providing just such a picture; see Blau (1955).

controlled behaviour coexist within organisations and that the executive must fuse them. Barnard (1938) notes that autonomy among personnel is not necessarily detrimental to executive control but may, in fact, be an asset to administrative processes. He suggests that the executive must rely on the 'willingness to serve' (pp. 83ff) of those under his command; he must recognise that there is a 'zone of indifference' (pp. 167ff) in which persons are prepared to accept orders

TABLE 12.1. *Structural components of the roles of executives and blue-collar workers*

	Directly specified behaviour	Indirectly specified behaviour
Spheres of autonomous behaviour	*Executive role:* Rules act as broad guidelines to behaviour, specify areas of autonomy within organisational tasks. <div align="right">1</div>	*Blue-collar worker role:* Narrowly defined tasks permit autonomy to exist externally to work tasks, yet enacted *in* the organisation. 2
Spheres of controlled behaviour	<div align="right">4</div>*Blue-collar worker role:* Tasks are governed by detailed specifications.	3 *Executive role:* Rules set *limits* to autonomy; adherence to the limits is judged by executive's use of autonomy.

but beyond which they are apt to oppose orders. Informal patterns, in Barnard's view of the executive, are not divisive forces but 'expansions of the means of communication with reduction in the necessity for formal decisions, the minimising of undesirable influences, and the promotion of desirable influences concordant with the scheme of formal responsibilities' (p. 227). From Barnard's perspective both formal and informal patterns can be harnessed in the service of a 'co-operating system'. It seems, however, that the real point is not the blending of formally and informally organised behaviours, but the blending of controlled and autonomous behaviours that exist within organisations. Barnard's model of the organisation is filled with autonomy patterns that can serve the whole organisation; some of these patterns proceed from direct official specification of behaviour and some come from indirect specification.

THE WORKER'S PLACE IN THE ORGANISATION

Workers are viewed here as being permitted to develop relatively autonomous subcultures and subsystems of social interaction in their day-to-day routines. The autonomous patterns diverge from the officially prescribed patterns but are very much in line with the workman's style of life and culture outside the organisation. The culture of the working-class man is in many ways alien to the decorum and demeanour expected of white-collar members of the organisation. In the routinised work of the white-collar worker there is no room for the sudden display of anger of the working-class male; for the white-collar worker who meets the public there is little scope for the pervasive sexual allusions of the working-class male. Yet within the working clique inside the organisation, the workman can enact the culture patterns of his life outside the organisation. He can, for example, indulge freely in what is perhaps one of the workman's major forms of creative mental activity: the verbal play, imaginative exploits, and romanticism on the theme of sex. This does not mean that middle and upper-class males do not engage in this form of mental sport, but merely that for the working-class male it seems to be a *major* creative outlet, and much less so for the middle and upper classes. The workman's pattern is made possible by the fact that he has a large sphere of verbal freedom, since much of what he says 'doesn't count', as far as his work is concerned. Unlike the white-collar worker, whose work consists of a world of words, written and spoken, the worker is basically measured by the contributions of his hands. Therefore, his verbal jostlings, such as the razzing of the lowest person on the prestige totem pole, are not considered part of his job. As will be shown in the review of Donald F. Roy's study, the content of the workman's verbal banter is related to his niche in the social order and the conditions of his social existence.[2] The same relationship is also reflected in patterns of practical jokes and prankish physical contact, which are characteristic of the workman's culture but taboo in the culture of the white-collar worker. Participating in physical contact—be it fighting, prankish shoving, or contact sports—is chiefly characteristic of male pre-adult culture. Presumably it is only at the low socio-economic levels that this pattern continues into adulthood.

By contrast, the white-collar workers, whether senior executives or junior administrators, have a broad affinity for the organisational style of behaviour. They are likely to be members of the middle or upper class, where they have learned the demeanour and proprieties of manner they will be expected to exercise in their position in the

---

[2] S. M. Miller and Frank Riesman (1964, pp. 24–35) suggest that the 'factory "horseplay"', the 'ritualistic kidding', are partly an expression of the working-class theme of person centredness.

organisation. There is little discrepancy, for instance, between the style of dress and speech of their social class and that associated with the bureaucratic style of behaviour. White-collar workers can apply elements of their external life to their job in the organisation without having to make fundamental adjustments in their general style of behaviour, although this does not mean that they have nothing to learn in their work. The thesis of the organisation man makes the same point in converse terms: The work habits and interests of the white-collar worker spill over into his family and community life. For the white-collar worker, the organisation is less clearly differentiated from the culture of his private world than it is for the worker; the organisation is not the enemy camp. The blue-collar worker, on the other hand, is eager to leave his work behind him as he leaves the gates of the factory (Blauner, 1964).

In sum, white-collar workers have greater autonomy *in their task-related* activities than do the blue-collar workers. The time clock, the regimentation involved in feeding a machine and gearing one's work to the pace of a machine, the necessity of doing one's work exclusively at the location of a particular machine apply to the blue-collar worker to a far larger extent than to the white-collar worker. For the latter, work is defined more broadly than it is for the blue-collar worker, requiring a more diffuse commitment. Thus, for the white-collar worker, a broad range of activities and personal attributes, from personal grooming to getting along with others, are defined as relevant to work. A good organisation man's allegiance to the organisation and its style of action include taking part in such activities as organising a Little League baseball team, helping with the local community chest drive, and participating in college alumni affairs after working hours. And he must communicate his outside interests to his work peers. It is difficult to assess which activities are regarded as clearly *external* to his work role. On the other hand, the worker's tasks are defined more narrowly, leaving scope for activity that is defined as *external* to his work to be enacted while he is at his place of work.

The limited bases for the worker's *allegiance* to the work organisation are tacitly recognised not only by the exclusion of the worker from administrative decision making but also by his being allowed to bring into the work setting working-class culture patterns and to fashion them into relatively autonomous subcultures. In short, the worker's external affiliations with the working-class style of life are permitted to intrude into the organisation that employs him. This can be viewed as part of the exchange (in addition to monetary pay) for the limited forms of reward and participation that the worker is given by the employing organisation. In view of the differentiation between worker subculture and bureaucratic culture, the worker's immersion in working-class patterns may serve to perpetuate his disenfranchisement from the administrative sphere, resulting in a vicious cycle.

The pattern pictured thus far, of workers in relation to factory, is chiefly characteristic of the modern Western world. A contrasting example exists in the Japanese pattern, where the worker is expected to make a lifetime commitment to one firm.[3] The worker does not expect to leave his initial place of employment—the idea of moving to a better job seems highly incongruous. The firm does not intend to dismiss employees, no matter how uneconomical it may be to keep them. In this arrangement the worker's affiliation with the firm is a relatively complete one, and there appears to be little external autonomy.

ENACTMENT OF WORKER AUTONOMY: AN EXAMPLE

The empirical study of workers in factories has been a favourite of sociologists and social psychologists. Among the most eloquently descriptive studies of the culture and interaction patterns of workers are those by Roy. In ' "Banana Time" . . .' Roy (1960) describes a small work group of men engaged in the exceedingly simple manual work of operating a punch press. It took about fifteen minutes to learn this work. Roy himself participated, and his description shows his intimate immersion in the field situation as well as his keen observational skills. Roy describes how he attempted, during the early days of work, to meet the problems of great boredom by inventing little games. He partly succeeded. After a while he noticed that the bantering and 'kidding' by the workers around him were not purely haphazard, but actually served a similar function as his games; they too, reduced boredom. Following this insight he made systematic studies and discovered *patterns* in the bantering and joking.

.   .   .

Roy discovered that the day's routine was broken by activities other than those formally instituted by the company or those which were 'idiosyncratically developed disjunctions'. There were also an 'ordered

[3] James C. Abegglen (1960). Opinion differs as to whether Abegglen's formulation about lifelong commitment applies to blue-collar workers in large factories.

series of informal interactions'. Roy describes many forms of interruption that took place and the patterning involved in them. One of these was 'peach time', when one worker, Sammy, provided a peach and shared it. His beneficiaries greeted his contribution with disgruntlement and complaints about the quality of the peach. 'Banana time' followed. . . .

In addition to peach time and banana time there were coffee time, fish time, coke time, lunch time, and window-opening time. Each of them was marked by a distinctive pattern of interaction. In addition to these patterned times, Roy notes themes in verbal interplay. . . . In this verbal interplay exaggeration was a common feature. For instance, one of the men had received one hundred dollars from his son: from that day he was seen as a man ready to retire with a sizeable, steady income. Roy, after having admitted that he owned two acres of land, became a large landowner, and his farm became populated with horses, cows, pigs, and chicken. Sexuality also came in for a large share of regular and inventive verbal play.

Roy's article is perhaps a culmination in a series of research findings that, since the days of the Hawthorne studies, have pointed to the demise of the economic man without, however, completing the task of making social organisation the focus of analysis. The early studies opposed the economic-man thesis by pointing out that the individual was not guided only by his own monetary self-interest. Indeed, he could be guided against his own self-interest by his worker peer group; the individual worker might actually lose income by following the output control patterns of his peers. It was emphasised that there was a 'group factor' in work situations; but still an individualistic, social psychological focus was retained for this group factor. In the Hawthorne studies there was much concern with changes in attitude toward work. The meaning of work was considered a basic factor in individuals' performance, and work groups were considered in moulding the meaning and attitudes for members of the group. (Roethlisberger and Dickson, 1939; Gross, 1958, chap. 14.) Roy's interpretation of his findings is similarly social-psychological. To him, the informal patterns serve primarily to provide job satisfaction by relieving boredom. Along with many students of industrial relations in the last thirty years, he notes the existence of relatively distinct subgroups that are separate from the formal structure in the factory and have relatively distinct culture and interaction patterns. Yet his basic interpretation is in individualistic, psychological terminology—it relieves boredom. Even if one accepts the psychological perspective, one must question whether routine, repetitive work is necessarily conducive to boredom. For example, Ely Chinoy's (1955) study of automobile assembly-line workers suggests the workers' response to routine, repetitive work is perhaps better characterised by irritation at their lack of control over their work than by boredom. To understand this feature, it is not necessary to conclude that repetitive activity necessarily leads to boredom; rather, one must allow for the influence of culture. The researcher may exaggerate the activistic theme of Western societies. The Jicarilla Apache, for example, 'have an infinite capacity for not being bored. They can sit for hours on end and apparently do nothing; they certainly don't intellectualize about doing nothing.'

On the basis of Roy's evidence that *considerable structuring of the work situation is done by the workers themselves*, attention will be directed to the autonomy that is enjoyed by the work group and that seems to be a basic feature in the social organisation of the work situation. Concentrating on autonomy structure does not completely avoid the danger of over-emphasising one set of structures and one set of functions, just as social-psychological studies have done. But it should help to broaden the existing perspective. As Roy describes it, the work situation in the autonomous group culture includes a great variety of behaviours that are not directly connected with their work. Many of these types of behaviour fit Georg Simmel's (1950, pp. 43ff) description of play forms of social reality. Subjects that are of serious concern, such as economic security, sexual virility, health and death, submission to the authority of other men, family loyalty, and status aspirations are examined in a context where they are stripped of their serious content. Flitting from one topic to another—from the deeply serious to the comic, from the immediately practical to the remotely romantic—implies an irrelevance of the practical, concrete reality in which each of the subjects is, in fact, embedded. Perhaps it is because members are simultaneously engaged in serious work that they feel free to treat other concerns in such a detached manner. Roy's group appears to be a veritable haven for the enactment of play forms. Elements of life that are largely beyond the control of the individual are exposed and, in a fashion, dealt with. The verbal themes are the clearest evidence of this area of enactment. In addition to play forms, it may well be that the various social interaction patterns— the 'razzing' of Sammy, the paternalism of George—are reiterations of serious realities in the larger social context in which the men find themselves. Notice that it is Sammy, the newest immigrant (all three men are immigrants) who is the scapegoat; it is George, the only Gentile, who quietly occupies the superior status; it is the Negro handyman who is the object of stereotypical banter about uncontrolled sexuality.

These elements, whether they are fairly explicit reiterations or play forms of the workman's life outside the factory, are continuities between life outside the factory and life inside the factory and, therefore, are important for understanding the nature of the bond between the worker and the organisation in which he is employed. Work peers participate in a common culture that relies heavily on their common fate both within and outside the organisation. By means of their commonality they retain a fundamental alienation from the white-collar ranks in the organisation. This condition is demonstrated in Chinoy's (1955, Chap. 5) findings of workers' widespread lack of interest in becoming foremen or white-collar workers. It is also supported by Charles R. Walker and Robert H. Guest's study of assembly-line workers. Walker and Guest (1952, pp. 139–40) found that workers were favourably disposed toward their immediate job but intensely dissatisfied with the factory as a whole. Although there is a lack of affiliation with the white-collar ranks of the organisation, the worker does form bonds within the organisation with his own peers. For the organisation, this division of workers into two cultural groups permits an uneasy truce but also assures the continuity of the fundamental internal antithesis between the two. The dichotomy manifests itself in problems of morale and communications.

Roy points out that the group had developed a 'full-blown sociocultural systems. The group was to a considerable extent a separate and distinct system in which the members had active, at times even creative, participation contrasting sharply with their minimal participation in the larger organisation. *Work was not at all a major focus in this sociocultural system*. Recognition of this point gives a new perspective to the dilemma as to whether factory workers are strongly alienated from their work. It appears that work was *one of a variety* of topics around which Roy's group had developed behavioural patterns, but work was by no means the central point of attention of this 'full-blown sociocultural system'.

The contention that work was not a central feature of Roy's work group differs considerably from traditional explanations of informal groups. It must be understood that the kind of data Roy presented have traditionally been interpreted largely in terms of their relevance to work. Typical statements would be to the effect that informal activities give meaning to dull, routine factory work (Gross, 1958) and that 'work output is a function of the degree of work satisfaction, which in turn depends upon the informal social patterns of the work group' (Bendix and Fisher, 1961, p. 119). These statements provide a social-psychological explanation of the groups' mediating effect between the individual and his work, but they do not provide an adequate structural explanation of the place of informal groups in a complex organisation.

In addition to the social-psychological interpretations, there are well-documented studies by Roy and others (1952 and 1961) that show production control and worker collusion by informal groups of workers against management. In these cases there can be no doubt that informal patterns are relevant to work. But it is not certain, even here, that informal groups exist primarily for the worker's control over work or whether the explanation should not be reversed; that is, that control over work exists because of the presence of informal groups, which, in turn, exist because of the worker's relative autonomy.

In summary, it is suggested that Roy's work group exhibits a rich sociocultural system that is made possible by substantial worker autonomy. The autonomy exists by default; a worker's role is so narrowly defined that there remains a considerable sphere of undefined action within the confines of the organisation. The content of the sociocultural system to which a worker belongs is made up of a variety of elements from the culture and social context of workers outside the factory. These elements manifest themselves as direct reiterations as well as play forms of the reality. They provide continuity between the workman's life outside the factory and his participation within the factory.

In using the Roy study to illustrate autonomy patterns among factory workers, certain cautionary statements must be made. The group Roy studied may be atypical in its small amount of managerial supervision and in its degree of isolation from the rest of the factory, so that it might be allowed a disproportionately high degree of autonomy compared with other work groups. Further investigation would be required to demonstrate whether the Roy group is typical or atypical. However, worker-autonomy structure is evident from many other studies. For instance, Alvin W. Gouldner's (1954) discovery of a managerial 'indulgency pattern' toward workers and Joseph Bensman and Israel Gerver's (1963) finding of 'deviancy in maintaining the social system' in a factory all point to distinctly structured worker autonomy.

THEORTICAL CONSIDERATIONS ABOUT INTEGRATION
WITHIN COMPLEX ORGANISATIONS

Complex organisations must have ways of procuring and integrating the services of a variety of participants. The process of procurement and integration can obviously be accomplished most readily in organisations that have coercive means at their disposal. Prisons can force inmates to peel potatoes. But organisations that do not have coercion at their disposal are of particular interest, for there can be little doubt that most noncoercive complex organisations do, in fact, solve the problem.

The concern of this paper has been the integration of a particular segment of the membership of complex organisations, namely, blue-collar workers in factories. It specifically faced up to the vital question of how these persons are integrated into an organisation that offers them so few of the rewards that it can bestow. The answer lies in a kind of federalism that governs the situation. Workers are permitted ample separation from the total organisation, and to a considerable extent their integration into the larger system is left up to themselves. Informal work-group cultures are the concrete structures that make up the solution.

The separation of workers from the employing organisation permits workers flexibility and options as to the degree of alienation from the whole organisation. At the same time, the separation gives the organisation freedom to adopt means and goals that are different from, if not alien to, those of the workers. The federalistic balance between the autonomy of the blue-collar workers and the autonomy of the white-collar staff allows flexibility to both sides. This dualism is also a potential source of divergence and conflict, which finds nurture in the separate subcultures.

In contrast to the form of integration suggested here, other writings have been concerned with developing models of organisation that stress lessening internal differentiation. It is felt that the perceived divergence of interest between workers and the white-collar staff can and *needs to be* lessened if the organisation is to operate effectively (Argyris, 1964; see also Whyte, 1951, 1955). These writings differ from the present discussion both in theoretical and practical focuses. On the theoretical side, the above exposition is based on the view that autonomy can be viewed as a structural principle of organisations, which can have positive or negative consequences for their operation. Structured autonomy manifests itself in internal divergences, but these are not necessarily disruptive and maladaptive for the whole organisation or any part of it. As to practical goals, many writers, notably W. F. Whyte (1951 and 1955) and Chris Argyris (1964) are concerned with the problem of improving human relations in industrial concerns. In contrast, the practical focus here is not on improving social relationships in complex organisations; it is on the problem of improving the analytic theory of complex organisations. This is not necessarily a more worthy or pressing problem than that of improving human relationships in complex organisations; but it, too, is a problem.

In the present perspective, then, so-called informal patterns are facilitated by the existence of structurally guaranteed autonomy. That this is so does not make tension and strain inevitable. To be sure, informal patterns may give rise to hostile coalitions toward the organisation, such as restriction of output; but they may also give rise to workers developing, on their own, forms of integration with the organisation that are acceptable to that organisation as well as to the workers themselves. The real point is that many adaptive functions of the total organisation are delegated to the individual members of the organisation by the mechanism of *not* being officially promulgated in a set of official rules.

REFERENCES

ABBEGGLEN, J. C. (1960) *The Japanese Factory: aspects of its social organiza-tion*, New York, Free Press of Glencoe.

ARGYRIS, CHRIS (1964) *Integrating the Individual and the Organization*, John Wiley.

BARNARD, CHESTER I. (1938) *The Functions of the Executive*, Harvard University Press.

BENDIX, R., and FISHER L. H. (1961) 'The perspectives of Elton Mayo', in Amitai Etzioni, ed., *Complex Organizations: a sociological reader*, Holt, Rinehart and Winston.

BENSMAN, J., and GERVER, I. (1963) 'Crime and punishment in the factory: the function of deviancy in maintaining the social system', *American Sociological Review*, **28**, August, 588-98.

BLAU, P. M. (1955) *Th Dynamics of Bureaucracy*, 2nd edn, University of Chicago Press.

BLAU, P. M. (1960) 'Structural effects', *American Sociological Review*, **25**, 178-93.

BLAUNER, ROBERT (1964) *Alienation and Freedom: the factory worker and his industry*, University of Chicago Press.

CHINOY, ELY (1955) *Automobile Workers and the American Dream*, Random House.

DUBIN, ROBERT (1963) 'Industrial workers' world: a study of the *'central life interests'* of industrial workers', in Erwin O. Smigel, ed., *Work and Leisure*, New Haven, College and University Press, pp. 53-72.

GOULDNER, A. W. (1954) *Wildcat Strike*, Yellow Springs, Ohio, Antioch Press.

GROSS, EDWARD (1958) *Work and Society*, Crowell.

MILLER, S. M., and RIESMAN, FRANK (1964) 'The working-class subculture', in A. B. Shostak and W. Gamberg, eds., *Blue Collar World*, Prentice-Hall, pp. 24-35.

ROETHLISBERGER, F. J., and DICKSON, W. J. (1939) Management and the *Worker*, Harvard University Press.

ROY, D. F. (1952) 'Quota restriction and goldbricking in a machine shop', *American Journal of Sociology*, **57**, March, 427-42.

ROY, D. F. (1960) 'Banana time: job satisfaction and informal interaction', *Human Organization*, **18**, 156-68 (also excerpts in *This Reader*, no. 13).

ROY, D. F. (1961) 'Efficiency and "the fix": informal intergroup relations in a piecework machine shop', in S. M. Lipset and N. J. Smelser, eds., *Sociology: the progress of a decade*, Prentice-Hall, pp. 378-90.

SIMMEL, GEORG (1950) *The Sociology of Georg Simmel*, ed. and trans. K. H. Wolff, New York, Free Press of Glencoe.

SIMON, H. A., SMITHBURG, D. W., and THOMPSON, V. (1962) *Public Administration*, Knopf.

WALKER, C. R., and GUEST, R. H. (1952) *The Man on the Assembly Line*, Harvard University Press.

WHYTE, W. F. (1951) *Patterns of Industrial Peace*, Harper & Row.

WHYTE, W. F. (1955) *Money and Motivation*, Harper & Row.

13

D. F. Roy   Banana time: job satisfaction and informal interaction

Excerpts from D. F. Roy, 'Banana time: job satisfaction and informal interaction', *Human organization*, **18**, 156–68, 1960.

This paper undertakes description and exploratory analysis of the social interaction which took place within a small work group of factory machine operatives during a two-month period of participant observation. The factual and ideational materials which it presents lie at an intersection of two lines of research interest and should, in their dual bearing, contribute to both. Since the operatives were engaged in work which involved repetition of very simple operations over an extra-long workday, six days a week, they were faced with the problem of dealing with a formidable 'beast of monotony'. Revelation of how the group utilised its resources to combat that 'beast' should merit the attention of those who are seeking solution to the practical problem of job satisfaction, or employee morale. It should also provide insights for those who are trying to penetrate the mysteries of the small group.

Convergence of these two lines of interest is, of course, no new thing. Among the host of writers and researchers who have suggested connection between 'group' and 'joy in work' are Walker and Guest (1952), observers of social interaction on the automobile assembly line. They quote assembly-line workers as saying, 'We have a lot of fun and talk all the time' (p. 77), and, 'If it weren't for the talking and fooling, you'd go nuts' (p. 68).

My account of how one group of machine operators kept from 'going nuts' in a situation of monotonous work activity attempts to lay bare the tissues of interaction which made up the content of their adjustment. The talking, fun, and fooling which provided solution to the elemental problem of 'psychological survival' will be described according to their embodiment in intra-group relations. In addition, an unusual opportunity for close observation of behaviour involved in the maintenance of group equilibrium was afforded by the fortuitous introduction of a 'natural experiment'. My unwitting injection of explosive materials into the stream of interaction resulted in sudden, but temporary, loss of group interaction.

My fellow operatives and I spent our long days of simple, repetitive work in relative isolation from other employees of the factory. Our line of machines was sealed off from other work areas of the plant by the four walls of the clicking room. . . . There were occasional contacts with 'outside' employees, usually on matters connected with the work; but, with the exception of the daily calls of one fellow who came to pick up finished materials for the next step in processing, such visits were sporadic and infrequent.

Moreover, face-to-face contact with members of the managerial hierarchy were few and far between. No one bearing the title of foreman ever came around. The only company official who showed himself more than once during the two-month observation period was the plant superintendent. . . .

As far as our work group was concerned, this was truly a situation of laissez-faire management. There was no interference from staff experts, no hounding by time-study engineers or personnel men hot on the scent of efficiency or good human relations. Nor were there any signs of industrial democracy in the form of safety, recreational, or production committees. . . .

Our work group was thus not only abandoned to its own resources for creating job satisfaction, but left without that basic reservoir of ill-will toward management which can sometimes be counted on to stimulate the development of interesting activities to occupy hand and brain. Lacking was the challenge of intergroup conflict, that perennial source of creative experience to fill the otherwise empty hours of meaningless work routine (cf. Roy, 1953).

The clicking machines were housed in a room approximately thirty by twenty-four feet. They were four in number, set in a row, and so arranged along one wall that the busy operator could, merely by raising his head from his work, freshen his reveries with a glance through one of three large barred windows. . . . At the opposite end of the line sat another table which was intermittently the work station of a female employee who performed sundry scissors operations of a more intricate nature on raincoat parts. Boxed in on all sides by shelves and stocks of materials, this latter locus of work appeared a cell within a cell. . . .

THE WORK GROUP

Absorbed at first in three related goals of improving my clicking skill, increasing my rate of output, and keeping my left hand unclicked, I paid little attention to my fellow operatives save to observe that they were friendly, middle-aged, foreign-born, full of advice, and very talkative. Their names, according to the way they addressed each other, were George, Ike, and Sammy.[1] George, a stocky fellow in his late fifties, operated the machine at the opposite end of the line; he, I discovered, had emigrated in early youth from a country in south-eastern Europe. Ike, stationed at George's left, was tall, slender, in his early fifties, and Jewish; he had come from eastern Europe in his youth. Sammy, number three man in the line, and my neighbour, was heavy set, in his late fifties, and Jewish; he had escaped from a country in eastern Europe just before Hitler's legions had moved in. All three men had been downwardly mobile as to occupation in recent years. . . .

I discovered also that the clicker line represented a ranking system in descending order from George to myself. George not only had top seniority for the group, but functioned as a sort of leadman. His superior status was marked by the fact that he received five cents more per hour than the other clickermen, put in the longest workday, made daily contact, outside the workroom, with the superintendent on work matters which concerned the entire line, and communicated to the rest of us the directives which he received. . . .

Ike was next to George in seniority, then Sammy. I was, of course, low man on the totem pole. Other indices to status differentiation lay in informal interaction, to be described later. . . .

The female who worked at the secluded table behind George's machine put in a regular plant-wide eight-hour shift from 8 to 4.30. Two women held this job during the period of my employment; Mable was succeeded by Baby. Both were Negroes, and in their late twenties.

A fifth clicker operator, an Arabian *emigré* called Boo, worked a night shift by himself. He usually arrived about 7 p.m. to take over Ike's machine.

---

[1] All names used are fictitious.

THE WORK

It was evident to me, before my first workday drew to a weary close, that my clicking career was going to be a grim process of fighting the clock, the particular timepiece in this situation being an old-fashioned alarm clock which ticked away on a shelf near George's machine. I had struggled through many dreary rounds with the minutes and hours during the various phases of my industrial experience, but never had I been confronted with such a dismal combination of working conditions as the extra-long workday, the infinitesimal cerebral excitation, and the extreme limitation of physical movement. . . . This job was standing all day in one spot beside three old codgers in a dingy room looking out through barred windows at the bare walls of a brick warehouse, leg movements largely restricted to the shifting of body weight from one foot to the other, hand and arm movements confined, for the most part, to a simple repetitive sequence of place the die, —— punch the clicker, —— place the die, —— punch the clicker, and intellectual activity reduced to computing the hours to quitting time.

Before the end of the first day, Monotony was joined by his twin brother, Fatigue. I got tired. My legs ached, and my feet hurt. . . .

My reverie toyed with the idea of quitting the job and looking for other work.

The next day was the same: the monotony of the work, the tired legs and sore feet and thoughts of quitting.

THE GAME OF WORK

In discussing the factory operative's struggle to 'cling to the remnants of joy in work', Henri de Man (1927) makes the general observation that 'it is psychologically impossible to deprive any kind of work of all its positive emotional elements', that the worker will find *some* meaning in any activity assigned to him . . .

So did I search for *some* meaning in my continuous mincing of plastic sheets into small ovals, fingers, and trapezoids. . . . I did find a 'certain scope for initiative', and out of this slight freedom to vary activity, developed a game of work.

The game developed was quite simple. . . . Fundamentally involved were: (*a*) variation in colour of the materials cut, (*b*) variation in shapes of the dies used, and (*c*) a process called 'scraping the block'. The basic procedure which ordered the particular combination of components employed could be stated in the form: 'As soon as I do so many of these, I'll get to do those' . . . Or the . . . goal might involve switching dies.

Scraping the block made the game more interesting by adding to the number of possible variations in its playing; and, what was perhaps more important, provided the only substantial reward, ... on days when work with one die and one colour of material was scheduled. As a physical operation, scraping the block was fairly simple; it involved application of a coarse file to the upper surface of the block to remove roughness and unevenness resulting from the wear and tear of die penetration. But, as part of the intellectual and emotional content of the game of work, it could be in itself a source of variation in activity. The upper left-hand corner of the block could be chewed up in the clicking of 1,000 white trapezoid pieces, then scraped. Next, the upper right-hand corner, and so on. . . .

Thus the game of work might be described as a continuous sequence of short-range production goals with achievement rewards in the form of activity change. . . .

But a hasty conclusion that I was having lots of fun playing my clicking game should be avoided. . . .

Henri de Man speaks of 'clinging to the remnants of joy in work', and this situation represented just that. How tenacious the clinging was, how long I could have 'stuck it out' with my remnants, was never determined. Before the first week was out this adjustment to the work situation was complicated by other developments. The game of work continued, but in a different context. Its influence became decidedly subordinated to, if not completely overshadowed by, another source of job satisfaction.

INFORMAL SOCIAL ACTIVITY OF THE WORK GROUP: TIMES AND THEMES

The change came about when I began to take serious note of the social activity going on around me; my attentiveness to this activity came with growing involvement in it. What I heard at first, before I started to listen, was a stream of disconnected bits of communication which did not make much sense. Foreign accents were strong and referents were not joined to coherent contexts of meaning. It was just 'jabbering'. What I saw at first, before I began to observe, was occasional flurries of horseplay so simple and unvarying in pattern and so childish in quality that they made no strong bid for attention. For example, Ike would regularly switch off the power at Sammy's machine whenever Sammy made a trip to the lavatory or the drinking fountain. Correlatively, Sammy invariably fell victim to the plot by making an attempt to operate his clicking hammer after returning to the shop. And, as the simple pattern went, this blind stumbling into the trap was always followed by indignation and reproach from Sammy, smirking satisfaction from Ike, and mild paternal scolding from George. My interest in this procedure was at first confined to wondering when Ike would weary of his tedious joke or when Sammy would learn to check his power switch before trying the hammer.

But, as I began to pay closer attention, as I began to develop familiarity with the communication system, the disconnected became connected, the nonsense made sense, the obscure became clear, and the silly actually funny. And, as the content of the interaction took on more and more meaning, the interaction began to reveal structure. There were 'times' and 'themes', and roles to serve their enaction. The interaction had subtleties, and I began to savour and appreciate them. I started to record what hitherto had seemed unimportant.

Times

This emerging awareness of structure and meaning included recognition that the long day's grind was broken by interruptions of a kind other than the formally instituted or idiosyncratically developed disjunctions in work routine previously described. These additional interruptions appeared in daily repetition in an ordered series of informal interactions. They were, in part, but only in part and in very rough comparison, similar to those common fractures of the production process known as the coffee break, the coke break, and the cigarette break. Their distinction lay in frequency of occurrence and in brevity. As phases of the daily series, they occurred almost hourly, and so short were they in duration that they disrupted work activity only slightly. Their significance lay not so much in their function as rest pauses, although it cannot be denied that physical refreshment was involved. Nor did their chief importance lie in the accentuation of progress points in the passage of time, although they could perform that function far more strikingly than the hour hand on the dull face of George's alarm clock. . . . The major significance of the interactional interruptions lay in . . . a carryover of interest. The physical interplay which momentarily halted work activity would initiate verbal exchanges and thought processes to occupy group members until the next interruption. The group interactions thus not only marked off the time; they gave it content and hurried it along.

Most of the breaks in the daily series were designated as 'times' in the parlance of the clicker operators, and they featured the consumption of food or drink of one sort or another. . . .

My attention was first drawn to this times business during my first week of employment when I was encouraged to join in the sharing of two peaches. It was Sammy who provided the peaches; he drew them

from his lunch box after making the announcement, 'Peach time!'
On this first occasion I refused the proffered fruit, but thereafter
regularly consumed my half peach. Sammy continued to provide the
peaches and to make the 'Peach time!' announcement, although there
were days when Ike would remind him that it was peach time, urging
him to hurry up with the mid-morning snack. Ike invariably com-
plained about the quality of the fruit, and his complaints fed the fires of
continued banter between peach donor and critical recipient. I did find
the fruit a bit on the scrubby side but felt, before I achieved insight into
the function of peach time, that Ike was showing poor manners by
looking a gift horse in the mouth. I wondered why Sammy continued
to share his peaches with such an ingrate.

Banana time followed peach time by approximately an hour. Sammy
again provided the refreshments, namely, one banana. There was,
however, no four-way sharing of Sammy's banana. Ike would gulp it
down by himself after surreptitiously extracting it from Sammy's lunch
box, kept on a shelf behind Sammy's work station. Each morning, after
making the snatch, Ike would call out, 'Banana time!' and proceed to
down his prize while Sammy made futile protests and denunciations.
George would join in with mild remonstrances, sometimes scolding
Sammy for making so much fuss. The banana was one which Sammy
brought for his own consumption at lunch time; he never did get to
eat his banana, but kept bringing one for his lunch. At first this daily
theft startled and amazed me. Then I grew to look forward to the
daily seizure and the verbal interaction which followed.

Window time came next. It followed banana time as a regular consequence of Ike's castigation by the indignant Sammy. After 'taking'
repeated references to himself as a person badly lacking in morality and
character, Ike would 'finally' retaliate by opening the window which
faced Sammy's machine, to let the 'cold air' blow in on Sammy. The
slandering which would, in its echolalic repetition, wear down Ike's
patience and forbearance usually took the form of the invidious comparison: 'George is a good daddy! Ike is a bad man! A very bad
man!' ...

Pickup time, fish time, and coke time came in the afternoon. I name
it pickup time to represent the official visit of the man who made daily
calls to cart away boxes of clicked materials. The arrival of the pickup
man, a Negro, was always a noisy one, like the arrival of a daily
passenger train in an isolated small town. Interaction attained a quick
peak of intensity to crowd into a few minutes all communications,
necessary and otherwise. Exchanges invariably included loud depreciations by the pickup man of the amount of work accomplished in the

clicking department during the preceding twenty-four hours. Such scoffing would be of the order of 'Is that all you've got done? What do you boys do all day?' These devaluations would be countered with allusions to the 'soft job' enjoyed by the pickup man. During the course of the exchanges news items would be dropped, some of serious import, such as reports of accomplished or impending layoffs in the various plants of the company, or of gains or losses in orders for company products. . . .

An invariable part of the interactional content of pickup time was Ike's introduction of the pickup man to George. 'Meet Mr. Papeatis!' Ike would say in mock solemnity and dignity. Each day the pickup man 'met' Mr Papeatis, to the obvious irritation of the latter. Another pickup time invariably would bring Baby (or Mable) into the inter-action. George would always issue the loud warning to the pickup man: 'Now I want you to stay away from Baby! She's Henry's girl!' Henry was a burly Negro with a booming bass voice who made in-frequent trips to the clicking room with lift-truck loads of materials. . . . Baby's only part in this was to laugh at the horseplay.

About mid-afternoon came fish time. George and Ike would stop work for a few minutes to consume some sort of pickled fish which Ike provided. Neither Sammy nor I partook of this nourishment, nor were we invited. For this omission I was grateful; the fish, brought in a newspaper and with head and tail intact, produced a reverse effect on my appetite. . . .

Coke time came late in the afternoon, and was an occasion for total participation. The four of us took turns in buying the drinks and in making the trip for them to a fourth floor vending machine. Through George's manipulation of the situation, it eventually became my daily chore to go after the cokes; the straw boss had noted that I made a much faster trip to the fourth floor and back than Sammy or Ike. . . .

Themes

To put flesh, so to speak, on this interactional frame of 'times', my work group had developed various 'themes' of verbal interplay which had become standardised in their repetition. These topics of conversa-tion ranged in quality from an extreme of nonsensical chatter to another extreme of serious discourse. Unlike the times, these themes flowed one into the other in no particular sequence of predictability. Serious conversation could suddenly melt into horseplay, and vice versa. In the middle of a serious discussion on the high cost of living, Ike might drop a weight behind the easily startled Sammy, or hit him over the head with a dusty paper sack. Interaction would immediately drop to a low comedy exchange of slaps, threats, guffaws, and disapprobations which would invariably include a ten-minute echolalia of 'Ike is a bad man, a very bad man! George is a good daddy, a very fine man!' . . .

'Kidding themes' were usually started by George or Ike, and Sammy was usually the butt of the joke. Sometimes Ike would have to 'take it', seldom George. . . .

Sammy received occasional calls from his wife, and his claim that these calls were requests to shop for groceries on the way home were greeted with feigned disbelief. Sammy was ribbed for being closely watched, bossed, and henpecked by his wife, and the expression 'Are you man or mouse?' became an echolalic utterance, used both in and out of the original context.

Ike, who shared his machine and the work scheduled for it with Boo, the night operator, came in for constant invidious comparison on the subject of output. The socially isolated Boo, who chose work rather than sleep on his lonely night shift, kept up a high level of performance, and George never tired of pointing this out to Ike. It so happened that Boo, an Arabian Moslem from Palestine, had no use for Jews in general; and Ike, who was Jewish, had no use for Boo in particular. Whenever George would extol Boo's previous nights production, Ike would try to turn the conversation into a general discussion on the need for educating the Arabs. George, never permitting the development of serious discussion on this topic, would repeat a smirking warning, 'You watch out for Boo! He's got a long knife!'

[Another] kidding theme [was that] which developed from some personal information contributed during a serious conversation on property ownership and high taxes. I dropped a few remarks about two acres of land which I owned in one of the western states, and from then on I had to listen to questions, advice, and general nonsensical comment in regard to 'Danelly's farm'.[2] This 'farm' soon became stocked with horses, cows, pigs, chickens [and] ducks. . . .

Serious themes included the relating of major misfortunes suffered in the past by group members. George referred again and again to the loss, by fire, of his business establishment. Ike's chief complaints centered around a chronically ill wife who had undergone various operations and periods of hospital care. . . . Sammy's reminiscences centered on the loss of a flourishing business when he had to flee Europe ahead of Nazi invasion.

But all serious topics were not tales of woe. One favourite serious theme which was optimistic in tone could be called either 'Danelly's

[2] This spelling is the closest I can come to the appellation given me in George's broken English and adopted by other members of the group.

future' or 'getting Danelly a better job'. It was known that I had been attending 'college', the magic door to opportunity, although my specific course of study remained somewhat obscure. Suggestions poured forth on good lines of work to get into, and these suggestions were backed with accounts of friends, and friends of friends, who had made good via the academic route. My answer to the expected question, 'Why are you working here?' always stressed the 'lots of overtime' feature, and this explanation seemed to suffice for short-range goals.

There was one theme of especially solemn import, the 'professor theme'. This theme might also be termed 'George's daughter's marriage theme'; for the recent marriage of George's only child was inextricably bound up with George's connection with higher learning. The daughter had married the son of a professor who instructed in one of the local colleges. This professor theme was not in the strictest sense a conversation piece; when the subject came up, George did all the talking. The two Jewish operatives remained silent as they listened with deep respect, if not actual awe, to George's accounts of the Big Wedding which, including the wedding pictures, entailed an expense of $1,000. It was monologue, but there was listening, there was communication, the sacred communication of a temple, when George told of going for Sunday afternoon walks on the Midway with the professor, or of joining the professor for a Sunday dinner. . . . I came to the conclusion that it was the professor connection, not the straw-boss-ship or the extra nickel an hour, which provided the fount of George's superior status in the group.

If the professor theme may be regarded as the cream of verbal interaction, the 'chatter themes' should be classed as the dregs. The chatter themes were hardly themes at all; perhaps they should be labelled 'verbal states', or 'oral autisms'. Some were of doubtful status as communication; they were like the howl or cry of an animal responding to its own physiological state. They were exclamations, ejaculations, snatches of song or doggerel, talkings-to-oneself, mutterings. Their classification as themes would rest on their repetitive character. They were echolalic utterances, repeated over and over. An already mentioned example would be Sammy's repetition of 'George is a good daddy, a very fine man! Ike is a bad man, a very bad man!' Also, Sammy's repetition of 'Don't bother me! Can't you see I'm busy? I'm a very busy man!' for ten minutes after Ike had dropped a weight behind him would fit the classification. . . .

So initial discouragement with the meagreness of social interaction I now recognised as due to lack of observation. The interaction was there, in constant flow. It captured attention and held interest to make the long day pass. The twelve hours of 'click,——move die,——click, ——move die' became as easy to endure as eight hours of varied activity in the oil fields or eight hours of playing the piece-work game in a machine shop. The 'beast of boredom' was gentled to the harmlessness of a kitten.

BLACK FRIDAY: DISINTEGRATION OF THE GROUP

But all this was before 'Black Friday'. Events of that dark day shattered the edifice of interaction, its framework of times and mosaic of themes, and reduced the work situation to a state of social atomisation and machine-tending drudgery. The explosive element was introduced deliberately, but without prevision of its consequences.

On Black Friday, Sammy was not present; he was on vacation. There was no peach time that morning, of course, and no banana time. But . . . a steady flow of themes was filling the morning quite adequately. It seemed like a normal day in the making, at least one which was going to meet the somewhat reduced expectations created by Sammy's absence.

Suddenly I was possessed of an inspiration for modification of the professor theme. When the idea struck, I was working at Sammy's machine, clicking out leather parts for billfolds. It was not difficult to get the attention of close neighbour Ike to suggest *sotto voce*, 'Why don't you tell him you saw the professor teaching in a barber college on Madison Street? . . . Make it near Halstead Street.'

Ike thought this one over for a few minutes, and caught the vision of its possibilities. After an interval of steady application to his clicking, he informed the unsuspecting George of his near West Side discovery; he had seen the professor busy at his instructing in a barber college in the lower reaches of Hobohemia.

George reacted to this announcement with stony silence. The burden of questioning Ike for further details on his discovery fell upon me. Ike had not elaborated his story very much before we realised that the show was not going over. George kept getting redder in the face, and more tight-lipped; he slammed into his clicking with increased vigour. I made one last weak attempt to keep the play on the road by remarking that barber colleges paid pretty well. George turned to hiss at me, 'You'll have to go to Kankakee with Ike!' I dropped the subject. Ike whispered to me, 'George is sore!'

George was indeed sore. He didn't say another word the rest of the morning. There was no conversation at lunchtime, nor was there any after lunch. A pall of silence had fallen over the clicker room. Fish time was a casualty. George did not touch the coke I brought for him. A very long, very dreary afternoon dragged on. . . .

Then came a succession of dismal workdays devoid of times and barren of themes. Ike did not sing, nor did he recite bawdy verse. The shop songbird was caught in the grip of icy winter. What meagre communication there was took a sequence of patterns which proved interesting only in retrospect.

On the third day George advised me of his new communication policy, designed for dealing with Ike, and for Sammy, too, when the latter returned to work. Interaction was now on a 'strictly business' basis, with emphasis to be placed on raising the level of shop output. The effect of this new policy on production remained indeterminate. Before the fourth day had ended, George got carried away by his narrowed interests to the point of making sarcastic remarks about the poor work performances of the absent Sammy. Although addressed to me, these caustic depreciations were obviously for the benefit of Ike. Later in the day Ike spoke to me, for George's benefit, of Sammy's outstanding ability to turn out billfold parts. For the next four days, the prevailing silence of the shop was occasionally broken by either harsh criticism or fulsome praise of Sammy's outstanding workmanship. I did not risk replying to either impeachment or panegyric for fear of involvement in further situational deteriorations.

Twelve-hour days were creeping again at snail's pace. The strictly business communications were of no help, and the sporadic bursts of distaste or enthusiasm for Sammy's clicking ability helped very little. With the return of boredom, came a return of fatigue. . . .

In desperation, I fell back on my game of work, my blues and greens and whites, my ovals and trapezoids, and my scraping the block. I came to surpass Boo, the energetic night worker, in volume of output. George referred to me as a 'day Boo' (day-shift Boo) and suggested that I 'keep' Sammy's machine. I managed to avoid this promotion, and consequent estrangement with Sammy, by pleading attachment to my own machine.

When Sammy returned to work, discovery of the cleavage between George and Ike left him stunned. 'They were the best of friends!' he said to me in bewilderment.

George now offered Sammy direct, savage criticisms of his work. For several days the good-natured Sammy endured these verbal aggressions without losing his temper; but when George shouted at him 'You work like a preacher!' Sammy became very angry, indeed. I had a few anxious moments when I thought that the two old friends were going to come to blows.

Then, thirteen days after Black Friday, came an abrupt change in the pattern of interaction. George and Ike spoke to each other again, in friendly conversation. . . .

That afternoon Ike and Sammy started to play again, and Ike burst once more into song. Old themes reappeared as suddenly as the desert flowers in spring. At first, George managed to maintain some show of the dignity of superordination. When Ike started to sing snatches of 'You Are My Sunshine', George suggested that he get 'more production'. Then Ike backed up George in pressuring Sammy for more production. Sammy turned this exhortation into low comedy by calling Ike a 'slave driver' and by shouting over and over again, 'Don't bother me! I'm a busy man!' . . .

I knew that George was definitely back into the spirit of the thing when he called to Sammy, 'Are you man or mouse?' He kept up the 'man or mouse' chatter for some time.

George was for a time reluctant to accept fruit when it was offered to him, and he did not make a final capitulation to coke time until five days after renewal of the fun and fooling. . . .

Of course, George's demand for greater production was metamorphised into horseplay. His shout of 'Production please!' became a chatter theme to accompany the varied antics of Ike and Sammy.

The professor theme was dropped completely. George never again mentioned his Sunday walks on the Midway with the professor.

CONCLUSIONS

Speculative assessment of the possible significance of my observations on information interaction in the clicking room may be set forth in a series of general statements.

Practical application

First, in regard to possible practical application to problems of industrial management, these observations seem to support the generally accepted notion that one key source of job satisfaction lies in the informal interaction shared by members of a work group. In the clicking-room situation the spontaneous development of a patterned combination of horseplay, serious conversation, and frequent sharing of food and drink reduced the monotony of simple, repetitive operations to the point where a regular schedule of long work days became liveable. This kind of group interplay may be termed 'consumatory' in the sense indicated by Dewey (1925, pp. 202–6), when he makes a basic distinction between 'instrumental' and 'consumatory' communication. The enjoyment of communication 'for its own sake' as 'mere sociabilities', as 'free, aimless social intercourse', brings job satisfaction, at least job endurance, to work situations largely bereft of creative experience.

In regard to another managerial concern, employee productivity, any appraisal of the influence of group interaction upon clicking-room output could be no more than roughly impressionistic. I obtained no evidence to warrant a claim that banana time, or any of its accompaniments in consumatory interaction, boosted production. . . . However, I did not obtain sufficient evidence to indicate that, under the prevailing conditions of laissez-faire management, the output of our group would have been more impressive if the playful cavorting of three middle-aged gentlemen about the barred windows had never been. As far as achievement of managerial goals is concerned, the most that could be suggested is that leavening the deadly boredom of individualised work routines with a concurrent flow of group festivities had a negative effect on turnover. . . .

Theoretical considerations

Secondly, possible contribution to ongoing sociological inquiry into the behaviour of small groups, in general, and factory work groups, in particular, may lie in one or more of the following ideational products of my clicking-room experience:

1. In their day-long confinement together in a small room spatially and socially isolated from other work areas of the factory the Clicking Department employees found themselves ecologically situated for development of a 'natural' group. Such a development did take place; from worker inter-communications did emerge the full-blown socio-cultural system of consumatory interactions which I came to share, observe, and record in the process of my socialisation.

2. These interactions had a content which could be abstracted from the total existential flow of observable doings and sayings for labelling and objective consideration. That is, they represented a distinctive sub-culture, with its recurring patterns of reciprocal influencings which I have described as times and themes.

3. From these interactions may also be abstracted a social structure of statuses and roles. This structure may be discerned in the carrying out of the various informal activities which provide the content of the sub-culture of the group. The times and themes were performed with a system of roles which formed a sort of pecking hierarchy. . . .

. . . The fun went on with the participation of all, but within the controlling frame of status, a matter of who can say or do what to whom and get away with it.

4. In both the cultural content and the social structure of clicker group interaction could be seen the permeation of influences which flowed from the various multiple group memberships of the participants. Past and present 'other-group' experiences or anticipated 'outside' social connections provided significant materials for the building of themes and for the establishment and maintenance of status and role relationships. The impact of reference group affiliations on clicking-room interaction was notably revealed in the sacred, status-conferring expression of the professor theme. This impact was brought into very sharp focus in developments which followed my attempt to degrade the topic, and correlatively, to demote George.

5. Stability of the clicking-room social system was never threatened by immediate outside pressures. Ours was not an instrumental group, subject to disintegration in a losing struggle against environmental obstacles or oppositions. It was not striving for corporate goals; nor was it faced with the enmity of other groups. It was strictly a consumatory group, devoted to the maintenance of patterns of self-entertainment. Under existing conditions, disruption of unity could come only from within.

Potentials for breakdown were endemic in the interpersonal interactions involved in conducting the group's activities. Patterns of fun and fooling had developed within a matrix of frustration. Tensions born of long hours of relatively meaningless work were released in the mock aggressions of horseplay. In the recurrent attack, defence, and counter-attack there continually lurked the possibility that words or gestures harmless in conscious intent might cross the subtle boundary of accepted, playful aggression to be perceived as real assault. While such an occurrence might incur displeasure no more lasting than necessary for the quick clarification or creation of kidding norms, it might also spark a charge of hostility sufficient to disorganise the group.

A contributory potential for breakdown from within lay in the dissimilar 'other group' experiences of the operators. These other-group affiliations and identifications could provide differences in tastes and sensitivities, including appreciation of humour, differences which could make maintenance of consensus in regard to kidding norms a hazardous process of trial and error adjustments.

6. The risk involved in this trial and error determination of consensus on fun and fooling in a touchy situation of frustration—mock aggression —was made evident when I attempted to introduce alterations in the professor theme. The group disintegrated, *instanter*. That is, there was an abrupt cessation of the interactions which constituted our groupness. Although both George and I were solidly linked in other-group affiliations with the higher learning, there was not enough agreement in our

attitudes toward university professors to prevent the interactional development which shattered our factory play group. George perceived my offered alterations as a real attack, and he responded with strong hostility directed against Ike, the perceived assailant, and Sammy, a fellow traveller.

My innovations, if accepted, would have lowered the tone of the sacred professor theme, if not to 'Stay Away From Baby' ribaldry, then at least to the verbal slapstick level of 'finding Danelly an apartment'. Such a downgrading of George's reference group would, in turn, have downgraded George. His status in the shop group hinged largely upon his claimed relations with the professor.

7. Integration of our group was fully restored after a series of changes in the patterning and quality of clicking-room interaction. It might be said that reintegration took place *in* these changes, that the series was a progressive one of step-by-step improvement in relations, that re-equilibration was in process during the three weeks that passed between initial communication collapse and complete return to 'normal' interaction.

The cycle of loss and recovery of equilibrium may be crudely charted according to the following sequence of phases: (*a*) the stony silence of 'not speaking'; (*b*) the confining of communication to formal matters connected with work routines; (*c*) the return of informal give-and-take in the form of harshly sarcastic kidding, mainly on the subject of work performance, addressed to a neutral go-between for the 'benefit' of the object of aggression; (*d*) highly emotional direct attack, and counter-attack, in the form of criticism and defence of work performance; (*e*) a sudden rapprochement expressed in serious, dignified, but friendly conversation; (*f*) return to informal interaction in the form of mutually enjoyed mock aggression; (*g*) return to informal interaction in the form of regular patterns of sharing food and drink.

The group had disintegrated when George withdrew from participation; and, since the rest of us were at all times ready for rapprochement, reintegration was dependent upon his 'return'. Therefore, each change of phase in interaction on the road to recovery could be said to represent an increment of return on George's part. Or, conversely, each phase could represent an increment of reacceptance of punisher deviants. Perhaps more generally applicable to description of a variety of reunion situations would be conceptualisation of the phase changes as increments of reassociation without an atomistic differentiation of the 'movements' of individuals.

8. To point out that George played a key role in this particular case of re-equilibration is not to suggest that the homeostatic controls of a social system may be located in a type of role or in a patterning of role relation-

ships. Such controls could be but partially described in terms of human interaction; they would be functional to the total configuration of conditions within the field of influence. The automatic controls of a mechanical system operate as such only under certain achieved and controlled conditions. The human body recovers from disease when conditions for such homeostasis are 'right'. The clicking-room group regained equilibrium under certain undetermined conditions. One of a number of other possible outcomes could have developed had conditions not been favourable for recovery.

For purposes of illustration, and from reflection on the case, I would consider the following as possibly necessary conditions for reintegration of our group: (*a*) Continued monotony of work operations; (*b*) Continued lack of a comparatively adequate substitute for the fun and fooling release from work tensions; (*c*) Inability of the operatives to escape from the work situation or from each other, within the work situation. George could not fire Ike or Sammy to remove them from his presence, and it would have been difficult for the three middle-aged men to find other jobs if they were to quit the shop. Shop space was small, and the machines close together. Like a submarine crew, they had to 'live together'; (*d*) Lack of conflicting definitions of the situation after Ike's perception of George's reaction to the 'barber college' attack. George's anger and his punishment of the offenders was perceived as justified; (*e*) Lack of introduction of new issues or causes which might have carried justification for new attacks and counter-attacks, thus leading interaction into a spiral of conflict and crystallisation of conflict norms. For instance, had George reported his offenders to the superintendent for their poor work performance; had he, in his anger, committed some offence which would have led to reporting of a grievance to local union officials; had he made his anti-Semitic remarks in the presence of Ike or Sammy, or had I relayed these remarks to them; had I tried to 'take over' Sammy's machine, as George had urged; then the interactional outcome might have been permanent disintegration of the group.

9. Whether or not the particular patterning of interactional change previously noted is somehow typical of a 're-equilibration process' is not a major question here. My purpose in discriminating the seven changes is primarily to suggest that re-equilibration, when it does occur, may be described in observable phases and that the emergence of each succeeding phase should be dependent upon the configuration of conditions of the preceding one. Alternative eventual outcomes may change in their probabilities, as the phases succeed each other, just as prognosis for recovery in sickness may change as the disease situation changes.

10. Finally, discrimination of phase changes in social process may have practical as well as scientific value. Trained and skilful administrators might follow the practice in medicine of introducing aids to re-equilibration when diagnosis shows that they are needed.

REFERENCES

DE MAN, HENRI (1927) *The Psychology of Socialism*, Holt.
DEWEY, JOHN (1925) *Experience and Nature*, Chicago, Open Court Publishing Co.
ROY, D. F. (1953) 'Work satisfaction and social reward in quota achievement: an analysis of piecework incentive', *American Sociological Review*, **18**, October, 507–14.
WALKER, C. R., and GUEST, R. H. (1952) *The Man on the Assembly Line*, Harvard University Press.

14

Daniel Levinson   ## Role, personality and social structure in the organisational setting

Excerpts from Daniel Levinson, 'Role, personality and social structure in the organizational setting', *Journal of Abnormal and Social Psychology*, 58, 1959, 170–81.

During the past twenty years the concept of role has achieved wide currency in social psychology, sociology, and anthropology. From a socio-psychological point of view, one of its most alluring qualities is its double reference to the individual and to the collective matrix. The concept of role concerns the thoughts and actions of individuals, and, at the same time, it points up the influence upon the individual of socially patterned demands and standardising forces. Partly for this reason, 'role' has been seen by numerous writers . . . as a crucial concept for the linking of psychology, sociology, and anthropology. However, while the promise has seemed great, the fulfilment has thus far been relatively small. The concept of role remains one of the most overworked and underdeveloped in the social sciences.

My purpose here is to examine role theory primarily as it is used in the analysis of organisations. . . . The organisation provides a singularly useful arena for the development and application of role theory. It is small enough to be amenable to empirical study. Its structure is complex enough to provide a wide variety of social positions and role-standardising forces. It offers an almost limitless opportunity to observe the individual personality *in vivo* (rather than in the psychologist's usual *vitro* of laboratory, survey questionnaire, or clinical office), selectively utilising and modifying the demands and opportunities given in the social environment. . . .

Organisational theory and research has traditionally been the province of sociology and related disciplines that focus most directly upon the collective unit. Chief emphasis has accordingly been given to such aspects of the organisation as formal and informal structure, administrative policy, allocation of resources, level of output, and the like. . . . The prevailing image of the organisation has been that of a mechanical apparatus operating impersonally once it is set in motion by administrative edict. The prevailing conception of social role is consonant with this image: the individual member is regarded as a cog in the apparatus, what he thinks and does being determined by requirements in the organisational structure.

This paper has the following aims:

1. To examine the traditional conception of organisational structure and role and to assess its limitations from a socio-psychological point of view.
2. To examine the conception of social role that derives from this approach to social structure and that tends, by definition, to exclude consideration of personality.
3. To provide a formulation of several, analytically distinct, role concepts to be used in place of the global term 'role'.
4. To suggest a theoretical approach to the analysis of relationships among role, personality, and social structure.

TRADITIONAL VIEWS OF BUREAUCRATIC STRUCTURE AND ROLE

Human personality has been virtually excluded from traditional organisation theory. Its absence is perhaps most clearly reflected in Weber's (1946, 1947) theory of bureaucracy, which has become a major source of current thought regarding social organisation and social role. . . . In Weber's writings, the bureaucratic organisation is portrayed as a monolithic edifice. Norms are clearly defined and consistently applied, the agencies of role socialisation succeed in inducing acceptance of organisational requirements, and the sanctions system provides the constraints and incentives needed to maintain behavioural conformity. Every individual is given a clearly defined role and readily 'fills' it. There is little room in this tightly bound universe for more complex choice, for individual creativity, or for social change. . . .

For Weber, bureaucracy as an ideal type is administered by 'experts' in a spirit of impersonal rationality and is operated on a principle of discipline according to which each member performs his required duties as efficiently as possible. Rationality in decision-making and obedience in performance are the pivots on which the entire system operates.

In this scheme of things, emotion is regarded merely as a hindrance to efficiency, as something to be excluded from the bureaucratic process.

The antipathy to emotion and motivation in Weber's thinking is reflected as well in his formulation of three types of authority: traditional, charismatic, and rational-legal. The rational-legal administrator is the pillar of bureaucracy. He receives his legitimation impersonally, from 'the system', by virtue of his *technical* competence. His personal characteristics, his conception of the organisation and its component groupings, his modes of relating to other persons (except that he be fair and impartial)—these and other psychological characteristics are not taken into theoretical consideration. There is no place in Weber's ideal type for the ties of affection, the competitive strivings, the subtle forms of support or of intimidation, so commonly found in even the most 'rationalized' organisations. It is only the 'charismatic' leader who becomes emotionally important to his followers and who must personally validate his right to lead.

While Weber has little to say about the problem of motivation, two motives implicitly become universal instincts in his conception of 'bureaucratic man'. These are *conformity* (the motive for automatic acceptance of structural norms), and *status-seeking* (the desire to advance oneself by the acquisition and exercise of technical competence). More complex motivations and feelings are ignored.

There has been widespread acknowledgment of both the merits and limitations of Weber's protean thought. However, the relevance of personality for organisational structure and role-definition remains a largely neglected problem in contemporary theory and research. Our inadequacies are exemplified in the excellent *Reader in Bureaucracy*, edited by Merton, Gray, Hockey, and Selvin (1952). Although this book contains some of the most distinguished contributions to the field, it has almost nothing on the relation between organisational structure and personality. The editors suggest two lines of interrelation: first, that personality may be one determinant of occupational choice; and second, that a given type of structure may in time modify the personalities of its members. These are valuable hypotheses. However, they do not acknowledge the possibility that personality may have an impact on social structure. 'The organization' is projected as an organism that either selects congenial personalities or makes over the recalcitrant ones to suit its own needs. . . . In other words, when social structure and personality fail to mesh, it is assumed to be personality alone that gives. Structure is the prime, uncaused, cause.

The impact of organisational structure on personality is indeed a significant problem for study. There is, however, a converse to this.

When a member is critical of the organisational structure, he *may* maintain his personal values and traits, and work toward structural change. The manifold impact of personality on organisational structure and role remains to be investigated. To provide a theoretical basis for this type of investigation we need, I believe, to re-examine the concept of role.

'SOCIAL ROLE' AS A UNITARY CONCEPT

The concept of role is related to, and must be distinguished from, the concept of social position. A position is an element of organisational autonomy, a location in social space, a category of organisational membership. A role is, so to say, an aspect of organisational physiology; it involves function, adaptation, process. It is meaningful to say that a person 'occupies' a social position; but it is inappropriate to say, as many do, that one occupies a role.

There are at least three specific senses in which the term 'role' has been used, explicitly or implicitly, by different writers or by the same writer on different occasions.

(*a*) Role may be defined as the *structurally given demands* (norms, expectations, taboos, responsibilities, and the like) associated with a given social position. . . .

(*b*) Role may be defined as the member's *orientation* or *conception* of the part he is to play in the organisation. It is, so to say, his inner definition of what someone in his social position is supposed to think and do about it. . . .

(c) Role is commonly defined as the *actions* of the individual members—actions seen in terms of their relevance for the social structure (that is, seen in relation to the prevailing norms). . . .

Many writers use a definition that embraces all of the above meanings without systematic distinction, and then shift, explicitly or implicitly, from one meaning to another (Cf. Parsons, 1945 and 1951; Parsons and Shils, 1951). . . .

More often, the term is used in a way that includes all three meanings at once. In this *unitary*, all-embracing conception of role, there is, by assumption, a close fit between behaviour and disposition (attitude, value), between societal prescription and individual adaptation. This point of view has its primary source in the writings of Linton, whose formulations of culture, status, and role have had enormous influence. According to Linton (1945), a role 'includes the attitudes, values and behaviour ascribed by the society to any and all persons occupying this status'. In other words, society provides for each status or position a single mould that shapes the beliefs and actions of all its occupants.

Perhaps the most extensive formulation of this approach along socio-psychological lines is given by Newcomb (1950). Following Linton, Newcomb asserts, 'Roles thus represent ways of carrying out the functions for which positions exist—ways which are generally agreed upon within (the) group' (p. 281). And, 'Role is strictly a sociological concept; it purposely ignores individual, psychological facts' (p. 329). Having made this initial commitment to the 'sociological' view that individual role-activity is a simple mirroring of group norms, Newcomb later attempts to find room for his 'psychological' concerns with motivation, meaning, and individual differences. He does this by partly giving up the 'unitary' concept of role, and introducing a distinction between 'prescribed role' and 'role behaviour'. He avers that prescribed role is a sociological concept, 'referring to common factors in the behaviours required' (p. 459), whereas role behaviour is a psychological concept that refers to the activities of a single individual. The implications of this distinction for his earlier general definition of role are left unstated.

Whatever the merits or faults of Newcomb's reformulation, it at least gives conceptual recognition to the possibility that social prescription and individual adaptation may not match. This possibility is virtually excluded in the definition of social role forwarded by Linton and used by so many social scientists. In this respect, though certainly not in all respects, Linton's view is like Weber's: both see individual behaviour as predominantly determined by the collective matrix. The matrix is, in the former case, culture, and in the latter, bureaucracy.

In short, the 'unitary' conception of role assumes that there is a 1:1 relationship, or at least a *high degree of congruence*, among the three role aspects noted above. In the theory of bureaucratic organisation, the rationale for this assumption is somewhat as follows. The organisation-ally given requirements will be internalised by the members and will thus be mirrored in their role-conceptions. People will know, and will want to do, what is expected of them. The agencies of role socialisation will succeed except with a deviant minority—who constitute a separate problem for study. Individual action will in turn reflect the structural norms, since the appropriate role-conceptions will have been internalised and since the sanctions system rewards normative behaviour and punishes deviant behaviour. Thus, it is assumed that structural norms, individual role-conceptions and individual role-performance are three isomorphic reflections of a single entity: 'the' role appropriate to a given organisational position.

It is, no doubt, reasonable to expect some degree of congruence among these aspects of a social role. Certainly, every organisation contains numerous mechanisms designed to further such congruence. At the same time, it is a matter of common observation that organisations vary in the degree of their integration; structural demands are often contradictory, lines of authority may be defective, disagreements occur and reverberate at and below the surface of daily operations. To assume that what the organisation requires, and what its members actually think and do, comprise a single, unified whole is severely to restrict our comprehension of organisational dynamics and change.

... We should, I believe, eliminate the single term 'role' except in the most general sense, i.e., of 'role theory' as an over-all frame of analysis. Let us, rather, give independent conceptual and empirical status to the above three concepts and others. Let us investigate the relationships of each concept with the others, making no assumptions about the degree of congruence among them. Further, let us investigate their relationships with various other characteristics of the organisation and of its individual members. I would suggest that the role concepts be named and defined as follows.

ORGANISATIONALLY GIVEN ROLE-DEMANDS

The role-demands are external to the individual whose role is being examined. They are the situational pressures that confront him as the occupant of a given structural position. They have manifold sources: in the official charter and policies of the organisation; in the traditions and ideology, explicit as well as implicit, that help to define the organisation's purposes and modes of operation; in the views about this position which are held by members of the position (who influence any single member) and by members of the various positions impinging upon this one; and so on.

It is a common assumption that the structural requirements for any position are as a rule defined with a *high degree of explicitness, clarity, and consensus* among all the parties involved. ...

In attempting to characterise the role-requirements for a given position, one must therefore guard against the assumption that they are unified and logically coherent. There may be major differences and even contradictions between official norms, as defined by charter or by administrative authority, and the 'informal' norms held by various groupings within the organisation. Moreover, within a given-status group, such as the top administrators, there may be several conflicting viewpoints concerning long-range goals, current policies, and specific role-requirements. In short, the structural demands themselves are often multiple and disunified. . . .

It is important also to consider the specificity or *narrowness* with which the normative requirements are defined. Norms have an 'ought' quality; they confer legitimacy and reward-value upon certain modes of action, thought and emotion, while condemning others. But there are degrees here. Normative evaluations cover a spectrum from 'strongly required', through various degrees of qualitative kinds of 'acceptable', to more or less stringently tabooed. Organisations differ in the width of the intermediate range on this spectrum. That is, they differ in the number and kinds of adaptation that are normatively acceptable. The wider this range—the less specific the norms—the greater is the area of personal choice for the individual. . . .

There are various other normative complexities to be reckoned with. A single set of role-norms may be internally contradictory. In the case of the mental hospital nurse, for example, the norm of maintaining an 'orderly ward' often conflicts with the form of encouraging self-expression in patients. The individual nurse then has a range of choice, which may be narrow or wide, in balancing these conflicting requirements. . . .

The degree of *coherence* among the structurally defined role-requirements, the degree of *consensus* with which they are held, and the degree of *individual choice* they allow (the range of acceptable alternatives) are among the most significant properties of any organisation. In some organisations, there is very great coherence of role-requirements and a minimum of individual choice. In most cases, however, the degree of integration within roles and among sets of roles appears to be more moderate. This structural pattern is of especial interest from a socio-psychological point of view. To the extent that the requirements for a given position are ambiguous, contradictory, or otherwise 'open', the individual members have greater opportunity for selection among existing norms and for creation of new norms. In this process, personality plays an important part. I shall return to this issue shortly.

While the normative requirements (assigned tasks, rules governing authority-subordinate relationships, demands for work output, and the like) are of great importance, there are other aspects of the organisation that have an impact on the individual member. I shall mention two that are sometimes neglected.

Role-facilities

In addition to the demands and obligations imposed upon the individual, we must also take into account the techniques, resources, and conditions of work—the means made available to him for fulfilling his organisational functions. The introduction of tranquillising drugs in the mental hospital, or of automation in industry, has provided tremendous leverage for change in organisational structure and role-definition. The teacher-student ratio, an ecological characteristic of every school, grossly affects the probability that a given teacher will work creatively with individual students. In other words, technological and ecological facilities are not merely 'tools' by which norms are met; they are often a crucial basis for the maintenance or change of an organisational form.

Role-dilemmas or problematic issues

In describing the tasks and rules governing a given organisational position, and the facilities provided for their realisation, we are, as it were, looking at that position from the viewpoint of a higher administrative authority whose chief concern is 'getting the job done'. Bureaucracy is often analysed from this (usually implicit) viewpoint. What is equally necessary, though less often done, is to look at the situation of the position-members from their own point of view: the meaning it has for them, the feelings it evokes, the ways in which it is stressful or supporting. From this socio-psychological perspective, new dimensions of role analysis emerge. The concept of role-dilemma is an example. The usefulness of this concept stems from the fact that every human situation has its contradictions and its problematic features. Where such dilemmas exist, there is no 'optimal' mode of adaptation; each mode has its advantages and its costs. . . .

Role-dilemmas have their sources both in organisational structure and in individual personality. Similarly, both structure and personality influence the varied forms of adaptation that are achieved. The point to be emphasised here is that every social structure confronts its members with adaptive dilemmas. If we are to comprehend this aspect of organisational life, we must conceive of social structure as having intrinsically *psychological* properties, as making complex psychological demands that affect, and are affected by, the personalities of its members.

PERSONAL ROLE-DEFINITION

In the foregoing we have considered the patterning of the environment for an organisational position—the kind of socio-psychological world with which members of the position must deal. Let us turn now to the individual members themselves. Confronted with a complex system of requirements, facilities, and conditions of work, the individual effects his modes of adaptation. I shall use the term 'personal role-definition' to encompass the individual's adaptation within the organisation. This may involve passive 'adjustment', active furthering of current role-demands, apparent conformity combined with indirect 'sabotage', attempts at constructive innovation (revision of own role or of broader structural arrangements), and the like. The personal role-definition may thus have varying degrees of fit with the role-requirements. It may serve in various ways to maintain or to change the social structure. It may involve a high or a low degree of self-commitment and personal involvement on the part of the individual (Selznick, 1957).

For certain purposes, it is helpful to make a sharp distinction between two levels of adaptation: at a more *ideational* level, we may speak of a role-conception; at a more *behavioural* level, there is a pattern of role-performance. Each of these has an effective component. Role-conception and role-performance are independent though related variables; let us consider them in turn.

Individual (and modal) role-conceptions

The nature of a role-conception may perhaps be clarified by placing it in relation to an ideology. The boundary between the two is certainly not a sharp one. However, ideology refers, most directly to an orientation regarding the entire organisational (or other) structure—its purposes, its modes of operation, the prevailing forms of individual and group relationships, and so on. A role-conception offers a definition and rationale for one position within the structure. If ideology portrays and rationalises the organisational world, then role-conception delineates the specific functions, values, and manner of functioning appropriate to one position within it.

The degree of uniformity or variability in individual role-conceptions within a given position will presumably vary from one organisation to another. When one or more types of role-conception are commonly held (consensual), we may speak of modal types. The maintenance of structural stability requires that there be at least moderate consensus and that modal role-conceptions be reasonably congruent with role-requirements. At the same time, the presence of incongruent modal role-conceptions may, under certain conditions, provide an ideational basis for major organisational change.

Starting with the primary assumption that each member 'takes over' a structurally defined role, many social scientists tend to assume that there is great uniformity in role-conception among the members of a given social position. They hold, in other words, that for every position there is a *dominant, modal role-conception corresponding to the structural demands*, and that there is relatively little individual deviation from the modal pattern. Although this state of affairs may at times obtain, we know that the members of a given social position often have quite diverse conceptions of their proper roles (Greenblatt, Levinson and Williams, 1957; Gross, Mason, and McEachern, 1958; Reissman and Rohrer, 1957; Bendix, 1956). After all, individual role-conceptions are formed only partially within the present organisational setting. The individual's ideas about his occupational role are influenced by childhood experiences, by his values and other personality characteristics, by formal education and apprenticeship, and the like. . . . There is reason to expect, then, that the role-conceptions of individuals in a given organisational position will vary and will not always conform to official role-requirements. Both the diversities and the modal patterns must be considered in organisational analysis.

Individual (and modal) role-performance

This term refers to the overt behavioural aspect of role-definition—to the more or less characteristic ways in which the individual acts as the occupant of a social position. Because role-performance involves immediately observable behaviour, its description would seem to present few systematic problems. However, the formulation of adequate variables for the analysis of role-performance is in fact a major theoretical problem and one of the great stumbling blocks in empirical research.

Everyone would agree, I suppose, that role-performance concerns only those aspects of the total stream of behaviour that are structurally relevant. But which aspects of behaviour are the important ones? And where shall the boundary be drawn between that which is structurally relevant and that which is incidental or idiosyncratic?

One's answer to these questions probably depends, above all, upon his conception of social structure. Those who conceive of social structure rather narrowly in terms of concrete work tasks and normative requirements, are inclined to take a similarly narrow view of role. In this view, role-performance is simply the fulfilment of formal role-norms, and anything else the person does is extraneous to role-performance as such. . . .

A more complex and inclusive conception of social structure requires correspondingly multi-dimensional delineation of role-performance. An organisation has, from this viewpoint, 'latent' as well as 'manifest' structure; it has a many-faceted emotional climate; it tends to 'demand' varied forms of interpersonal allegiance, friendship, deference, intimidation, ingratiation, rivalry, and the like. If characteristics such as these are considered intrinsic properties of social structure, they they must be included in the characterisation of role-performance. My own preference is for the more inclusive view. . . . Ultimately, we must learn to characterise organisational behaviour in a way that takes into account, and helps to illuminate, its functions for the individual, for the others with whom he interacts, and for the organisation.

It is commonly assumed that there is great uniformity in role-performance among the members of a given position. . . . The rationale here parallels that given above for role-conceptions. However, where individual variations in patterns of role-performance have been investigated, several modal types rather than a single dominant pattern were found (Argyris, 1957; Greenblatt *et al.*, 1957).

. . . Role-performance, like any form of human behaviour, is the resultant of many forces. Some of these forces derive from the organisational matrix; for example, from role-demands and the pressures of authority, from informal group influences, and from impending sanctions. Other determinants lie within the person, as for example his role-conceptions and role-relevant personality characteristics. Except in unusual cases where all forces operate to channel behaviour in the same direction, role-performance will reflect the individual's attempts at choice and compromise among diverse external and internal forces.

The relative contributions of various forms of influence to individual or modal role-performance can be determined only *if each set of variables is defined and measured independently of the others*. That is, indeed, one of the major reasons for emphasising and sharpening the distinctions among role-performance, role-conception, and role-demands. Where these distinctions are not sharply drawn, there is a tendency to study one element and to assume that the others are in close fit. . . .

More careful distinction among these aspects of social structure and role will also, I believe, permit greater use of personality theory in organisational analysis. Let us turn briefly to this question.

ROLE-DEFINITION, PERSONALITY, AND SOCIAL STRUCTURE

Just as social structure presents massive forces which influence the individual from without toward certain forms of adaptation, so does personality present massive forces from within which lead him to select, create, and synthesise certain forms of adaptation rather than others. Role-definition may be seen from one perspective as an aspect of personality. It represents the individual's attempt to structure his social reality, to define his place within it, and to guide his search for meaning and gratification. Role-definition is, in this sense, an *ego achievement*—a reflection of the person's capacity to resolve conflicting demands, to utilise existing opportunities and create new ones, to find some balance between stability and change, conformity and autonomy, the ideal and the feasible, in a complex environment.

The formation of a role-definition is, from a dynamic psychological point of view, an 'external function' of the ego. Like the other external (reality-oriented) ego functions, it is influenced by the ways in which the ego carries out its 'internal functions' of coping with, and attempting to synthesise, the demands of id, superego, and ego. . . .

In viewing role-definition as an aspect of personality, I am suggesting that it is, *to varying degrees*, related to and imbedded within other aspects of personality. An individual's conception of his role in a particular organisation is to be seen within a series of wider psychological contexts: his conception of his occupational role generally (occupational identity), his basic values, life-goals, and conception of self (ego identity), and so on. . . .

There are variations in the degree to which personal role-definition is imbedded in, and influenced by, deeper-lying personality characteristics. The importance of individual or modal personality for role-definition is a matter for empirical study and cannot be settled by casual assumption. Traditional sociological theory can be criticised for assuming that individual role-definition is determined almost entirely by social structure. Similarly, dynamic personality theory will not take its rightful place as a crucial element of social psychology until it views the individual within his sociocultural environment. , . .

Clearly, individual role-conception and role-performance do not emanate, fully formed, from the depths of personality. Nor are they simply mirror images of a mould established by social structure. Elsewhere (Levinson, 1954), I have used the term 'mirage' theory for the view, frequently held or implied in the psycho-analytic literature, that ideologies, role-conceptions, and behaviour are mere epiphenomena or by-products of unconscious fantasies and defences. Similarly, the term 'sponge' theory characterises the view, commonly forwarded in the sociological literature, in which man is merely a passive mechanical absorber of the prevailing structural demands.

Our understanding of personal role-definition will remain seriously impaired as long as we fail to place it, analytically, in *both intra-personal and structural-environmental contexts*. That is to say, we must be concerned with the meaning of role-definition both for the individual personality and for the social system. . . .

Theory and research on organisational roles must consider relationships among at least the following sets of characteristics: structurally given role-demands and role-opportunities, personal role-definition (including conceptions and performance), and personality in its role-related aspects. Many forms of relationship may exist among them. I shall mention only a few hypothetical possibilities.

In one type case, the role-requirements are so narrowly defined, and the mechanisms of social control so powerful, that only one form of role-performance can be sustained for any given position. An organisation of this type may be able selectively to recruit and retain only individuals who, by virtue of personality, find this system meaningful and gratifying. If a congruent modal personality is achieved, a highly integrated and stable structure may well emerge. I would hypothesise that a structurally congruent modal personality is one condition, though by no means the only one, for the stability of a rigidly integrated system. . . .

However, an organisation of this kind may acquire members who are not initially receptive to the structural order, that is, who are *incongruent* in role-conception or in personality. Here, several alternative developments are possible.

1. The 'incongruent' members may change so that their role-conceptions and personalities come better to fit the structural requirements.
2. The incongruent ones may leave the organisation, by choice or by expulsion. . . .
3. The incongruent ones may remain, but in a state of apathetic conformity. In this case, the person meets at least the minimal requirements of role-performance but his role-conceptions continue relatively unchanged, he gets little satisfaction from work, and he engages in repeated 'sabotage' of organisational aims. . . .
4. The incongruent members may gain sufficient social power to change the organisational structure. This phenomenon is well known, though not well enough understood. For example, in certain of our mental hospitals, schools and prisons over the past 20–30 years, individuals with new ideas and personal characteristics have entered in large enough numbers, and in sufficiently strategic positions, to effect major structural changes. . . .

The foregoing are a few of many possible developments in a relatively monolithic structure. A somewhat looser organisational pattern is perhaps more commonly found. In this setting, structural change becomes a valued aim and innovation is seen as a legitimate function of members at various levels in the organisation. . . .

In summary, I have suggested that a primary distinction be made between the structurally given role-demands and the forms of role-definition achieved by the individual members of an organisation.

Personal role-definition then becomes a linking concept between personality and social structure. It can be seen as a reflection of those aspects of individual personality that are activated and sustained in a given structural-ecological environment. This view is opposed both to the 'sociologising' of individual behaviour and to the 'psychologising' of organisational structure. At the same time, it is concerned with both the psychological properties of social structure and the structural properties of individual adaptation.

Finally, we should keep in mind that both personality structure and social structure inevitably have their internal contradictions. No individual is sufficiently all of a piece that he will for long find any form of adaptation, occupational or otherwise, totally satisfying. . . .

The organisation has equivalent limitations. Its multiple purposes cannot all be optimally achieved. It faces recurrent dilemmas over conflicting requirements. . . . And perpetual changes in technology, in scientific understanding, in material resources, in the demands and capacities of its members and the surrounding community, present new issues and require continuing organisational readjustment.

In short, every individual and every socio-cultural form contains within itself the seeds of its own destruction—or its own reconstruction. To grasp both the sources of stability and the seeds of change in human affairs is one of the great challenges to contemporary social science.

REFERENCES

ARGYRIS, C. (1957) *Personality and Organization*, Harper.

BENDIX, R. (1956) *Work and Authority in Industry*, Wiley.

GREENBLATT, M., LEVINSON, D. J., and WILLIAMS, R. H., eds (1957) *The Patient and the Mental Hospital*, New York, Free Press of Glencoe.

GROSS, N., MASON, W. S., and MCEACHERN, A. W. (1958) *Explorations in Role Analysis*, Wiley.

LEVINSON, D. J. (1954) 'Idea systems in the individual and society', paper presented at Boston University, Founder's Day Institute. Mimeographed: Center for Sociopsychological Research, Massachusetts Mental Health Center.

LINTON, R. (1954) *The Cultural Background of Personality*, Appleton-Century.

MERTON, R. K., GRAY, A. P., HOCKLEY, BARBARA, and SELVIN, H. C. (1957) *Reader in Bureaucracy*, New York, Free Press of Glencoe.

NEWCOMB, T. M. (1950) *Social Psychology*, Dryden.

PARSONS, T. (1945) *Essays in Sociological Theory*, rev. edn, New York, Free Press of Glencoe.

PARSONS, T. (1951) *The Social System*, New York, Free Press of Glencoe.

PARSONS, T., and SHILLS, E. A., eds (1951) *Toward a General Theory of Action*, Harvard University Press.

REISSMAN, L., *and* ROHRER, J. J., eds. (1957) *Change and Dilemma in the Nursing Profession*, Putnam.

SELZNICK, P. (1957) *Leadership in Administration*, Row, Peterson.

WEBER, M. (1946) *Essays in Sociology*, ed. H. H. Gerth and C. W. Mills, Oxford University Press.

WEBER, M. (1947) *The Theory of Social and Economic Organization*, ed. T. Parsons, Oxford University Press.

15

Derek Pugh

Role activation conflict: a study of industrial inspection

Derek Pugh, 'Role activation conflict: a study of industrial inspection', *American Sociological Review*, **31**, 1966, 835–42.

In their seminal book *Explorations in Role Analysis*, Gross, Mason and McEachern (1968) maintain that role theory has been relatively sterile in its generation of insightful hypotheses for empirical investigation, although it has been useful in drawing attention to particular phenomena. They suggest that one possible reason for this paucity of empirical hypotheses is the holistic manner in which the concept 'role' has been defined and used. The term refers to a family of concepts which need to be distinguished from one another and studied empirically. Not enough attention has been given to the distinction between expectation and behaviour, and between legitimate and illegitimate expectations: role consensus among groups of role-definers and even in society-at-large has been assumed and thus not subjected to investigation, and so on. Operational definitions are required, and these and other distinctions must be studied, if role theory is to become heuristically useful. This paper is offered as a contribution to this process.

Role theory has developed a considerable and sometimes confusing array of terms which makes it necessary for us to start with basic definitions. A role is a set of expectations and behaviours associated with a given position in a social system. We shall follow Levinson (1959) in using this as a blanket term, and distinguish within it, where necessary, three more specifically defined elements: (1) role expectations are the set of structurally given normative demands and responsibilities associated with a position; (2) a role conception is an individual's definition of what someone in his position is supposed to think and do; (3) role performance is an individual's actual behaviour in respect of his position. There is, of course, no necessarily direct one-to-one relationship between these three elements, since an individual's role conception and role performance are a function not only of the role expectations put upon him, but also of his personality, abilities and attitudes. A further distinction between types of role expectation, crucial for our discussion, is made by Gross *et al.* (1958). An actor may consider that a member of his role-set has a right to hold certain expectations of him, but no right to hold certain others. A legitimate expectation will be called a perceived obligation, an illegitimate expectation, a perceived pressure.

Role conflict occurs when an individual is subjected to incompatible role expectations. Two main sources have been identified in the literature. The terminology varies, but the concepts are well established. In multiple role conflict (Krech *et al.*, 1962) there is a conflict of expectations due to an individual holding a position in each of two or more different social systems. This has also been called intrapersonal role conflict (Thibaut and Kelly, 1961), inter-role conflict (Gross *et al.*, 1958; Kahn *et al.*, 1964), role incompatibility (Simmel, 1955), and so forth. The classic example here is the conflict between a man's roles at work and at home. There may also be incompatibility between a man's work role and his trade union role, his religious affiliations and his social activities, and so on.

In single role conflict, which will be our main concern here, there is a conflict of expectations concerning a single position due to the differing expectations of members of the social system with whom the individual interacts, i.e., due to differences between the members of his role-set. This has been called role incompatibility (Krech *et al.*, 1962), role confusion (Hare, 1962), interpersonal role conflict (Thibaut and Kelly, 1961), intra-role conflict (Gross *et al.*, 1958), and inter-sender conflict (Kahn *et al.*, 1964). Standard here are the studies of the conflicting expectations of management and workers of the foreman as 'the man in the middle'. Similar studies of conflicting expectations of School Boards and teachers on School Superintendents (Seeman, 1953), and of bureaucratic and professional expectations of scientists in research organizations (Brown, 1953–54), may be noted. The conflict is exacerbated where the social system is a formal organisation which concurrently legitimises two incompatible expectations, as in Grusky's study of the conflict between treatment and custodial expectations among prison camp officials (Grusky, 1958–59).

This type of role conflict, conflicting expectations of members (usually groups or categories) of an individual's role-set owing to their location in a formal organisation and consequent structural perspective, has been the most frequent subject of investigation, but other variants of single role conflict have also been noted. Hare (1962) uses the term 'role collision' to indicate the situation occurring if two individuals hold roles which overlap in some respect, for example, two doctors who are called to treat the same patient. Seeman (1953) has examined the situation in which there is significant disagreement *within* the criterion group (i.e. one category of members of the role-set) on the role expectations of a particular position. He found a 60–40 split in opinion among teachers on a question such as whether a school superintendent should invite them to his home for social occasions. Gross *et al.* (1958) also challenge very strongly the *assumption* of consensus of role definition in *any* situation. Seeman (1953) describes a variant in which there is agreement within the role-set, but on expectations which are mutually difficult to achieve under the given institutional conditions. Frank (1963–4) labels this an 'over-defined' role. We shall return to this type of situation in greater detail after a description of the empirical study of inspectors.

THE INSPECTION FUNCTION

This study is concerned with the relationship between the inspection and production departments of an engineering firm and the role conflicts which derive therefrom. The firm, which will be referred to as Messrs Aye Ltd, manufacture electrical appliances by the usual mass production methods. The firm has three main plants making different electrical products, but organised on comparable lines. During the investigation the writer interviewed every member of the production and inspection hierarchies from foreman to chief executive (51 interviews). The interviews were unstructured and took the form of a discussion of the inspection-production relationship and its conflicts.[1]

The functions of an inspection department in an engineering firm are well established in the management literature (cf. Juran, 1962; Brech, 1963). They may be regarded as threefold:

1. *Inspection as an assurance of quality.* The first function of inspection is that of comparing the articles produced with the standard laid down.

[1] The empirical study described here was part of a project directed by R. M. McKenzie on 'Human Aspects of Inspection in Industry' carried out at the Social Sciences Research Centre of the University of Edinburgh during 1956.

2. *Inspection as a production auxiliary.* The second function of inspection is to provide information on the quality of manufacture during the actual production process. The aim of immediate and continuous 'feed-back' of quality information to the production operator is not only to detect faulty work, but to prevent it from occurring.

3. *Inspection as a management control.* The third function of inspection is as part of the control system of management. It is from inspection department reports that top management obtains its information on the efficiency of the plants as regards quality.

The Inspection departments at Aye's conform to this pattern. They have the usual tasks of goods inwards, standards room, process and final inspection. In addition they prepare rejection and scrap reports. The departments also have the responsibility for the issue of re-operation tickets for work where this is necessary. It is their prerogative to allocate the charge for this and for scrap costs to the section responsible. Originally decisions on this matter were made by discussion among the various departments, but so much argument ensued that this was discontinued and the responsibility given entirely to inspection.

In this situation it is not surprising that role conflict concerning the inspection function exists at Aye's. This can easily be identified by reference to the management interviews and also by reference to a further 61 structured interviews which were held with the 'patrol inspectors'—the front-line members of the inspection department, whose job it is to check the quality of the work produced. In every case except one, their replies showed an awareness of the inherent role conflict. In the stressful inspection situation the need for inspectors to be tactful, to be able to get along with people and to have integrity, is continually emphasised both in these interviews and in the literature on the subject (Juran, 1962; Brech, 1963). It is this very emphasis on 'Human Relations' skills which demonstrates the existence of sources of role conflict.

THE CAUSES OF ROLE CONFLICT BETWEEN INSPECTION AND PRODUCTION

What are the causes of this role conflict? Let us consider first the obvious hypothesis that the role conception of inspection (that its primary function is quality assurance) comes into conflict with the production expectation of inspection (as primarily a production auxiliary) and that role conflict therefore ensues. There is evidence in favour of this analysis. The Inspection departments certainly feel that their basic job is to carry out their assurance function. One chief inspector put it: 'After all, in the end we are here as policemen.'

The inspection departments feel that their other functions have come upon them rather more fortuitously, because they happen to be in a good position to do them rather than because they are a basic part of inspection's work. Their reasons for having these functions in addition to quality assurance show this. For example, they are responsible for the allocation of scrap and re-operation charges because they do have the figures available and are a department not usually involved. (A number of their other non-assurance functions are defended in these same *ad hoc* ways.)

A result of this is that functions other than assurance are regarded as far more expendable since they are of necessity less clearly defined. They are much more easily abrogated when a 'crisis' occurs in favour of the assurance function. From the point of view of role-conflicts the difficulty is that it is precisely in a crisis that production expects the auxiliary function to take precedence over the assurance one.

The production department's basic expectation of inspection is that it should function as a 'production auxiliary'. For example: 'Inspection is an adjunct and an assistance' (a production manager). Coupled with this stress on the auxiliary function, there is the insistence that there should be no division of responsibility—the responsibility for quality rests with production in the same way as the responsibility for quantity and cost. A common remark by production men is: 'Quality cannot be inspected into the product.'

On this analysis, using Gross, Mason and McEachern's (1958) terms, the role conflicts of inspectors are due to their perceived obligation to be a quality assurance becoming incompatible with their perceived pressure to be a production auxiliary. This view has some plausibility, but it is, in fact, too simple and too stark to account for the facts of the situation. It implies that each side presses its own expectations to the exclusion of the other's (whose legitimacy it questions). 'Inspection is here to ensure that only good products go out of the factory gate; it is not our concern how this is achieved', and 'Inspection is here to help us make a good product, not to sit in judgment on us', would be the extreme typical reactions if this stark situation held good. In fact, it will be demonstrated that neither side questions the legitimacy of the other's expectations in this way.

STANDARDS OF ACCEPTABILITY

The question of acceptable standards in modern industrial production is a very thorny one. In theory the procedure is straightforward. The standards are set by the engineering department; they specify the dimensions and tolerance of all parts to be made. The production department produces work to these standards, and it is the responsibility of the inspection department to reject any work which does not come up to them.

In practice the position is not so simple. As one general manager of Aye's put it: 'At least three-quarters of what we produce here is not to drawing.' The basic inspection decision thus becomes not whether the job is up to the standard laid down or not, but whether there is a sufficiently large error on a sufficiently critical dimension to warrant rejection. This is a more nebulous and subjective matter than the specifications and tolerance of an engineering drawing. It also requires two judgments, on the degree of error and on the 'criticalness' of the dimension concerned. An inspection decision can be challenged on both these grounds. Whether a dimension is critical or not is not marked on the drawings, so that a non-critical dimension that could be anything from say 1 to 2 inches, will still be marked one inch plus or minus five-thousandths. From the point of view of inspection, the result is that decisions on acceptability are not the simple straightforward ones that they should be in theory, but complex and less clearly definable ones, subjected to a variety of 'obligations' which inspectors accept as legitimate.

The first of these is cost. For example, a chief inspector said: 'We could insist that every part is made exactly to drawing, but that would shoot the cost up sky-high.' Then there is the schedule pressure. For example, a foreman inspector said: 'We must give production people a reasonable chance to produce the target.' There is also the direct sales pressure. When there is an expanding market, the demand for products ensures that production comes to the fore. In a contracting market, the standards of the sales force go up, and they are willing to make complaints about faults which they would earlier have passed over. In the face of such sales pressure, inspection combines with production to maintain that the standards are high enough.

Standards of acceptability are thus the end result of a social process and it is clear that inspection accepts the need to adjust these standards to the obligations of the situation, and that the production auxiliary expectations laid on them in this respect, are legitimate.

THE PRESSURES ON THE PRODUCTION DEPARTMENT

Production's expectations of the inspection function must be considered in the light of the forces to which the production supervision is exposed. The three major controls are on the quantity, cost and quality of the product, and are exercised by the Planning, Cost and Inspection Departments respectively. The Planning Department issues the schedules, the Cost Department produces the budgets, and the Inspection Department sets the standard of acceptable work. The interviews reveal that the control exercised by the Planning and Cost Departments is felt by production to be considerably greater than that exerted by inspection.

In this situation, production supervision does not contest the legitimacy of the Inspection Department acting as an *independent* quality assurance. For example a production manager was asked: 'If inspection is a production assistance, what do you think of the idea that it should report to production?' He replied: 'I wouldn't want to have inspection at the moment. The problems of production have such ramifications of material control, progress control and so on that I wouldn't want to take on inspection as well. And you would be trying to push things over the borderline at times.' All production supervisors, when asked the same question, felt that there must be an independent final inspection, not responsible in any way to production.

We have now seen that there is basic agreement upon the inspection functions of quality assurance and production auxiliary among *both* inspection and production. These two sets of expectations are accepted as legitimate, yet they are often incompatible, and role conflict certainly occurs. We must therefore examine more closely what form this conflict takes.

CONFLICT SITUATIONS AND THEIR RESOLUTION

The typical situation which gives rise to conflict between inspection and production occurs when an inspector has rejected a certain product or part as not being up to the necessary quality standards. This affects a production supervisor's ability to achieve his schedule and keep within his budgeted costs. The conflicts arise because Production questions not the legitimacy of the quality assurance function, but only the relevance and priority of the particular judgment involved. The question is asked: 'Surely this product is good enough, considering it is half past three on a Friday afternoon and we have a consignment to get away before the weekend—and there has been so much trouble making it that we are already overspent on our budgeted allowance?' And these are obligations which, as we have seen, Inspection, too, recognises as legitimate. With engineering drawings of necessity having limits to their complete specification of the product, the translation of 'a good product' into 'a good enough product' is accepted by Inspection. So the conflict in these situations is always restricted to a particular decision, and is not generalised to the whole function. This, of course, scales it down considerably and keeps it within manageable bounds. The argument is over which facet of the inspection function should be *activated* at this particular time—quality assurance or production auxiliary.

The outcome of this conflict can be considered in terms of a scale from greatest to least conflict. Since both sides accept the legitimacy of both facets of the inspection function, conflict is most marked when only one of these aspects is activated at the expense of the other. This is the case when there is an appeal to a higher authority—as is always possible in a hierarchical organisation like a factory. The line authority (the higher management of the factory), or the technical authority (the engineering department), may be brought in. This form of outcome involves, either specifically or at least by implication, a re-definition or clarification of the standards. In effect it has now been added to the drawings that this degree of departure from them is, or is not, acceptable.

At the other extreme, since both sides accept the legitimacy of both facets of the inspection function, conflict is least marked when both of these aspects are activated at the same time. This is the case when the inspection department demonstrates that it is at the same time *both* a quality assurance *and* a production auxiliary. It can do this most elegantly by issuing a 'temporary concession'—which it has discretion to do. This permits a specific limited departure from standard in a particular case. Thus, by insisting that the bad work is a departure from standard the inspection department is fulfilling its quality assurance function, while by allowing a temporary concession it is acting as a production auxiliary. This involves no change in standards which would have implications for the future; it affects only the resolution of the particular conflict. It will be seen that the pressures for change in standards are directly related to the degree of conflict.

Between these two extremes, situations occur in which the inspection department attempts to reduce the conflict by showing that, while it must activate its quality assurance function by rejecting the product, it is also prepared to activate its production auxiliary function at the same time (although perhaps not to the same degree). A common way of doing this, if a mixed batch of good and bad parts is under dispute, is to offer to sort them out on behalf of Production. Inspection can show some degree of involvement by discussing with Production the causes and possible remedies of high re-operation or scrap charges.

ROLE ACTIVATION CONFLICT

The foregoing discussion suggests that it would be useful to make a distinction between two types in the analysis of 'single role conflict'. In the first type, the legitimacy of some of the incompatible expectations is called into question and they are regarded as pressures. What is being challenged is the content of the particular role and what should in principle be included in it and what left out. This may be called *role-legitimation conflict*. In the second type of conflict, *all* expectations are perceived as legitimate obligations, but their relevancies and priorities in a particular situation are challenged. The conflict is over which expectations should be activated, and in what way, in relation to the particular problem situation. This may be called *role-activation conflict*. In this form of conflict, a common resolution involves the simultaneous activation of multiple expectations—a resolution not available in role-legitimation conflict.

Seeman's (1953) situation of role conflict characterised by agreement within the criterion group on behaviours which are mutually difficult to achieve, would appear to be another example of role-activation conflict. Teachers require of school superintendents both that they should be non-separatist and that they should obtain salary increases. There is objective evidence which links (with a correlation of 0.40) such separatism, i.e., lack of informal interaction, and amount of salary increases obtained for the teaching staff over a three-year period. There is clearly role conflict here, as Seeman admits—and as indicated by the fact that the correlation is not higher than 0.40—some superintendents do succeed in achieving both salary increases and low separatism. That is, a simultaneous activation is a possible resolution in this situation.

Role-activation conflict would appear to be at the other extreme from the situation described by Grusky (1958–9). In his study of role conflict among prison warders, each side challenged the legitimacy of the other, and received its own legitimation from conflicting superordinate authorities. Grusky describes how the succession of a 'custodially-oriented' chief official altered the balance of power between the conflicting expectations. This exacerbated the role conflict of those warders who were 'treatment-oriented', and who drew their legitimation from the appropriate source. This is typical of a role legitimation conflict, which is characteristically a win-or-lose situation. It may be contrasted with a comparable change in the balance of power in one of the plants of Aye's, which happened just before the present study took place.

The change involved making the chief inspector responsible directly to the general manager (the chief executive) but leaving the production manager responsible only to the works manager. The general manager had made this change because he thought that both the works manager and the chief inspector were too 'production-minded', and he wanted to give more emphasis to the quality assurance function of inspection, and less to the production auxiliary one. A nice demonstration that we are here concerned with role activation conflict, in which the legitimacies of the opposing expectations are not questioned, is that, with the single exception of the production manager, it was the opinion of all production supervision (including the works manager from whose jurisdiction inspection was taken) that the new form of organisation was the correct one, and should continue if the quality assurance function of inspection was to have its proper place at that time.

The discussion so far has been in terms of single role conflict. But role-activation conflict can also be distinguished in multiple-role conflict. Most wives do not question the legitimacy of a husband doing a job well and being successful, in the way that most wives in our culture question the legitimacy of a husband's taking a mistress. What they do question are the relevance and priorities at six o'clock in the evening of a lecturer discussing role theory with his students, as against a father taking his evening meal with the family. This is role-activation conflict, and the resolution can be in terms of simultaneous activation of multiple expectations, e.g., by inviting the students home. If, however, the legitimacy of certain expectations is challenged, then the resolution of this role-legitimation conflict will bring into play such mechanisms as compartmentalisation (Goode, 1960) and abridgment of the role set (Merton, 1957).

SUMMARY AND CONCLUSION

This paper reviews some of the literature on role conflict, and then examines in detail one example of such role conflict—that of inspectors in manufacturing industry. Expectations are held that inspectors be both a quality assurance and a production auxiliary, but these expectations are often incompatible, and role conflict ensues. The particular form the conflict takes is the questioning of the relevance and priorities of these expectations in relation to a particular problem situation. The legitimacy of any of the expectations is not challenged, since both inspection and production men specifically legitimise each others' expectations in general terms. It is suggested that this type of role conflict be called role-activation conflict, because the dispute is over which facet of the role function should be activated in a particular situation. This type of conflict may be distinguished from role-legitimation conflict, in which the occupant of focal role and the members of the role set challenge the legitimacy of each others' expectations. A most important difference between the two types is that in role-activation conflict a common form of resolution involves the simultaneous activation of multiple expectations—a resolution not available in role-legitimation conflict.

Parsons (1951), as Gross *et al.* (1958) point out, restricts the concept of role conflict to situations with incompatible legitimised role expectations (and so do Getzels and Guba (1954), and Stouffer (1949)). In our terminology this would reduce all role conflict to role-activation conflict. But there is a difference in orientation here, since our concept of role-activation conflict is a limited and empirically oriented one. We would follow Gross *et al.* (1958), Kahn *et al.* (1964) and others in not assuming consensus on the legitimacy of incompatible expectations, but would restrict the term 'role-activation conflict' to those situations where this consensus has been demonstrated. In the many situations where the legitimacy is challenged by the actors, we would use the term 'role-legitimation conflict'.

REFERENCES

BRECH, E. F. L. (1963) *The Principles and Practices of Management*, 2nd edn, Longmans.

BROWN, PAULA (1953–4) 'Bureaucracy in a government laboratory', *Social Forces*, **32**, 259–68.

FRANK, A. G. (1963–4) 'Administrative role definition and social changes', *Human Organization*, **23**, 238–42.

GETZELS, J. W., and GUBA, E. G. (1954) 'Role, role conflict, and effectiveness', *American Sociological Review*, **19**, April, 164–75.

GOODE, W. J. (1960) 'A theory of role strain', *American Sociological Review*, **25**, August, 483–96.

GROSS, N., MASON, W. S., and MCEACHERN, A. W. (1958) *Explorations in Role Analysis*, Wiley.

GRUSKY, OSCAR (1958–9) 'Role conflict in organization', *Administrative Science Quarterly*, **3**, 452–72.

HARE, A. P. (1962) *Handbook of Small Group Research*, New York, Free Press of Glencoe.

JURAN, J. M. (1962) *Quality Control Handbook*, 2nd edn, McGraw-Hill.

KAHN, R. L., WOLFE, D. M., QUINN, R. P., SNOEK, J. D., and ROSENTHAL, R. A. (1964) *Organizational Stress*, Wiley.

KRECH, D., CRUTCHFIELD, R. S., and BALLACHEY, E. L. (1962) *Individual in Society*, McGraw-Hill.

LEVINSON, D. J. (1959) 'Role, personality, and social structure in the organizational setting', *Journal of Abnormal and Social Psychology*, **58**, 170–80 (also in no. 14 this Reader).

MERTON, R. K. (1957) *Social Theory and Social Structure*, New York, Free Press of Glencoe.

PARSONS, TALCOTT (1951) *The Social System*, New York, Free Press of Glencoe.

SEEMAN, MELVIN (1953) 'Role conflict and ambivalence in leadership', *American Sociological Review*, **18**, August, 373–80.

SIMMEL, GEORG (1955) *Conflict and the Web of Group Affiliations*, New York, Free Press of Glencoe.

STOUFFER, S. A. (1949) 'An analysis of conflicting social norms', *American Sociological Review*, **14**, December, 707–17.

THIBAUT, J. W., and KELLEY, H. H. (1961), *The Social Psychology of Groups*, Wiley.

16

Don Zimmerman | The practicalities of rule use

Excerpts from Don Zimmerman, 'The practicalities of rule use' in Jack Douglas, ed., *Understanding Everyday Life*, Routledge & Kegan Paul, 1971, pp. 221–38.

Introduction

Research interests in formal organisations traditionally have been guided by the basic conception of the employee as a specialised bureaucratic actor. The bureaucratic actor is seen as responsible for the systematic manipulation of an organisationally predefined environment of objects and events by the use of explicitly stated policies and procedures designed to advance formally defined goals. A key element of this traditional perspective—however modified to handle intrusive 'non-bureaucratic' elements in organisational life—is the view that the process and product of organisational activities is 'administratively rational' to the degree that personnel comply with the intent (if not the letter) of formally instituted policies and procedures and commit themselves to the attainment of organisational goals.

This paper examines certain aspects of the work activities of such bureaucratic actors in a public assistance organisation. Drawing on observational materials collected in the setting, it describes in detail the work of reception personnel in inducting applicants for public assistance into the organisational routine. The analysis is concerned particularly with the judgmental work of receptionists in employing a procedure for assigning applicants to intake caseworkers.

The study reported here, however, is not concerned with how adequately the formal programme of the organisation and the structural arrangements whereby it is implemented provide for 'rational' goal accomplishment (Bittner, 1965). Nor is it directed to the specification of the conditions under which personnel comply with or depart from their prescribed duties as set forth in the formal programme, or come to be more or less partisan to organisational objectives. Its primary concern is to investigate the variety of practices and mundane considerations involved in determinations of the operational meaning and situational relevance of policies and procedures for ongoing, everyday organisational activities. The ways in which this concern contrasts with the traditional viewpoint may be clarified by reference to the considerations below.

Numerous studies of formal organisations have found that some significant portion of the observed practices of bureaucrats are not easily reconciled with the investigator's understanding of what the formally instituted rules and policies dictate. Bureaucrats, in conducting their ordinary everyday affairs in organisations, have been seen in study after study to honour a range of formally, extraneous considerations in making decisions and concerting actions. The asserted contrasts between theory and practice reported by organisational studies are so commonplace that documentation seems hardly necessary.

It is important to note how such contrasts are obtained (Bittner, 1965, p. 240). The basic conception referred to above warrants the investigator's use of the formal plan of the given organisation as a device for deciding the theoretical status of observed activities (as planned or unplanned, formal or informal). Such a procedure would seem to require, first of all, that the investigator 'map out' the alternative possible behavioural dispositions called for by the rules. However, such decisions are typically made on an *ad hoc* basis. The investigator determines the deviant or conforming status of some activity or event upon encountering it without reference to a set of unambiguous criteria that specify the defining features of situations and the behaviours appropriate to such situations.

By whatever means the investigator accomplishes these crucial decisions, it is typically the case that the issue of what such rules mean to, and how they are used by, personnel on *actual occasions* of bureaucratic work is ignored as an empirical issue. For the investigator to make decisions about rules without clarifying the basis of such decisions—particularly without reference to how personnel make such decisions—invites the treatment of rules as idealisations, possessing stable operational meanings invariant to the exigencies of actual situations of use, and distinct from the practical interests, perspective, and interpretative practices of the rule user. The practices employed by bureaucrats to render such idealisations relevant as prescriptions, justifications, descriptions, or accounts of their activities is lost to analysis by the investigator's unclarified interpretive work in turning the formal plan of the organisation into the methodological purpose outlined above.

It is sometimes argued by students of organisation that rules and policies are to some degree abstract and general, and hence by their very nature incapable of completely encompassing the perversely contingent features of manifold and changing organisational situations. This conception would seem to speak to the concerns of this chapter.

However, this 'defect' of rules is typically dealt with by proposing that informal rules and policies develop in response to this lacuna that warrant modification, redefinition, or circumvention of the formal rule by personnel in light of operating conditions. Invoking one set of rules to account for the interpretation of another set dodges the issue.

In addition, this line of reasoning would propose that whatsoever patterned conduct is observed, it is formulable as conduct in accord with *some* rule. This view slights the question of *what it takes* to warrant the application of any rule—formal or informal—in concrete situations, thus failing to address as a crucial problem the judgmental processes that members must use to employ rules on relevant occasions.

A related issue of interest here is the way in which 'departures' from the formal organisational plan are dealt with. It has been consistently found that bureaucrats ('governed by' rules and procedures designed to effect rational goal accomplishment) are keenly attuned to a number of practical matters at hand as these are grasped as constraints or facilities, justifications or contra-indications, resources or troubles in the course of pursuing bureaucratic work. Indeed, these practical matters often seem to be critical elements informing the bureaucrats' use of the rules, resources, and formal arrangements of the organisation.

Investigators typically invoke such features of the bureaucrats' circumstances, and their situationally enforced interests in coming to terms with them, in order to account for the asserted discrepancy between the formally ordained and observed 'actual' state of organisation affairs. These circumstances are often conceived to be obstacles —or problems to be solved—on the way to rational goal accomplishment. Organisation members' ways of dealing with these states of affairs are examined in the interest of deciding whether or not they constitute 'functional' or 'disfunctional' detours en route to the ideal of administrative rationality presumably embodied to some degree in the formal plan of the organisation.

In contrast, the problem that concerns this chapter is how the formal plan of an organisation (or some aspect of it) is used by the organisation's members to deal with everyday work activities. What are the features of the sanctioned courses of common-sense judgment that members use to recognise, to interpret, and to instruct others about the operational intent and behavioural implications of such a plan? Thus conceived, the problem dictates, first of all, that the relationship of the formal plan to actual conduct be investigated with specific reference to how members of the organisation reconcile the two on a day-to-day basis. This approach also leads to a revision of the theoretical treatment of the range of practical circumstances typically confronted by the bureaucrat. This revision consists in entertaining the possibility that these circumstances may in fact be consulted by bureaucrats in order to decide what the formal plan might reasonably be taken to mean and 'what it would take' to implement it in the first instance.

This argument is not to be taken to mean that rule violations do not occur, or that bureaucrats might not respect alternative informal rules in doing their work—although the latter distinction as it is usually drawn would require modification. The point is that the issue of what rules, policies, and goals mean for the bureaucratic actor upon the concrete occasion of their use (for example, to guide, to account for, or to justify action) must be treated as problematic. In accordance with this view, the major assumption guiding the present endeavour is that the relationship of such idealisations to conduct may be found only by investigating the features of the circumstances in which they are deemed relevant and used by members.[1]

Following a brief discussion of the setting of the study, receptionists' use of an intake assignment procedure will be described in detail. This procedure is examined within its organisational context, with close attention paid to the features of actual occasions of its use and the contingencies encountered upon these occasions. Analysis will suggest that

---

[1] Behind this tack is the assumption that *the* problematic topic of sociological inquiry is the member-of-society's 'socially organized common practices' for detecting, describing, warranting, and accounting for the sensible features of everyday activities. Any socially organised setting, precisely in the way it organises itself, provides an occasion for the study of these practices. The description of the phenomena subsumed under the rubrics of social organisation, formal organisation, informal organisation, and the like is then a description of these practices. Hence, the present study is not a sociology of organisations *per se*, but an inquiry into the practices members employ in sustaining the 'sense' that their own and others' conduct is orderly, understandable, and reasonable—'given the circumstances'. See Garfinkel (1967: especially chapter 1) for the original statement of this view.

the operational import of formal rules and organisational policy (of which the assignment procedure is an instance) is decided by personnel on a case-by-case basis and warranted on 'reasonable grounds'.

It will be argued that the 'reasonableness' of such decisions, from the point of view of personnel, relies upon a taken-for-granted grasp of, and implicit reference to, the situated practical features of task activity (actual task structure). The chapter will suggest an alternative to the compliance model of rule use typically employed in sociological studies of rule-governed behaviour: a notion of competent rule use.

THE SETTING

The study was conducted in one district office of the Metropolitan County Bureau of Public Assistance, located in a large western state. In broad terms, the Bureau—like other public assistance organisations in the country—administers the several programmes of federal-state financed assistance (Aid to Families with Dependent Children or AFDC, etc.) as well as a county financed 'residual' programme (GA, or General Assistance), which provides for those persons not meeting the eligibility criteria of the categoric aids.[2]

Administration of these programmes requires an investigation of the applicant's circumstances in order to provide a 'factual' basis for determining need and entitlement to assistance under the provisions of the several categories. In the Metropolitan County Bureau this responsibility is discharged by the intake division.

Once certified as eligible, the applicant comes under the supervision of the 'approved' division. The routine administration of the case, including periodic reinvestigation of the applicant's eligibility for assistance, is the responsibility of this division.

Within the 'Lakeside Office' of the Bureau (one of several district offices in the county) the inquiry was focused upon the day-to-day operation of the intake function. Concentration on the work activities of intake personnel led as a matter of course to observation of the work done by reception. Just as the approved worker's caseload is assembled by virtue of the work of the intake worker in certifying eligibility, so the intake worker's investigation is preceded by the work of receptionists in preprocessing new applications for assistance. A discussion of the reception function follows.

[2] Other categories of assistance include OAA (Old Age Assistance), ATD (Aid to the Total Disabled), and MAA (Medical Assistance to the Aged).

THE RECEPTION FUNCTION

A major responsibility of reception (and a prominent concern of receptionists) is to provide for the orderly and appropriately paced preprocessing of applicants for public assistance and their assignment to an intake caseworker, who investigates their claim and decides its merit. As accomplished work, preprocessing and assignment appear to be contingent upon receptionists' performance of a series of related tasks that may be referred to as the 'steps' in the reception process.

These steps involve, but are not exhausted by, screening persons entering the office (determining the business bringing the person 'in'), categorising those persons discovered to be new applicants for public assistance as one or another type of application (as AFDC or GA, etc.), collecting preliminary information relevant to the subsequent processing of the application (name, age, residence data, etc.), generating and updating records (providing for the initiation of or search for a previous dossier on the applicant),[3] and, at the terminus of these activities, assigning the applicant to an intake worker, accomplished by use of a procedure operationalising the maxim, 'first come, first served'.

Assignment by this procedure is effected by the use of an intake book, a looseleaf binder the pages of which are ruled to form a matrix. One axis of the matrix represents the order in which the panel of intake workers on duty on a given day are to receive assignments; the other axis represents the order of assignments for a given worker (typically six in total). By use of the rule, top to bottom, left to right, in that order

[3] While perhaps obvious, it is worth observing that record-keeping activities such as these are crucial to the maintenance of an organisational 'routine', that is, in the present case, facilitating the matter-of-course processing of applications. Given what records of various sorts may be construed to *possibly* report, the generation of records of various sorts permits, first of all, the identification of the person reported on as one who has been 'run through' the usual procedures, and hence as one to whom the typical organisational constraints and opportunities may pertain. Such records may be used to 'reconstruct' the person's career in the organisational process in order to argue, according to the circumstances and interests of the reviewer, that the organisation has or has not done its job. A much longer list of the uses of records within organisations could undoubtedly be specified. The point to be stressed here is that, whatever the uses to which records may be put, it appears crucial that records of some sort be produced. For however in fact they are generated, the use of records to chronicle (or more likely reconstruct) a given person's fate at the hands of some organisational process seems indispensable for the typical claim of organisations that (at least most of the time) they handle their affairs in a routinised, rational, and responsible fashion.

(that is, the 'next available cell'), applicants are assigned to the cells in the order in which their processing was initiated. The execution of this procedure as described above, invariant to any situational exigencies, may be termed a literal (as opposed to judgmental or interpretive) application of the procedure (cf. Bittner, 1965, pp. 241–2; Wilson, 1970). This terminal step will be discussed at length later in the chapter.

From the vantage point of observer not involved in the work process of reception, the execution of these steps has the appearance of a busy but nonetheless orderly round of activities. Applicants (and others) coming into the office appear to be integrated into the reception process in a matter-of-course way.

The routine character of the process will be seen to be one of its most salient features, one to which receptionists orient and, by their management of work activities, seek to preserve. That is, receptionists (and other personnel as well) orient to the management of the day's work so as to provide for the defensible claim that it was accomplished in sufficient-for-all-practical-purposes accord with rule and policy 'Sufficient for all practical purposes' may be taken to mean the judgment by competent and entitled persons in the setting that the work was acceptably done, forgiving what may be forgiven, ignoring what may be ignored, allowing for what may be allowed based on both tacit and explicit understandings of such matters *in light of* 'what anyone knows' about the practical circumstances of work in general and on particular occasions.

The practical circumstances of work may be encountered in such things as the receptionists' fond hope that applicants *will* conduct themselves properly, their sure knowledge that *some* will not, and the often demanding task of dealing with the 'oddballs' and 'troublemakers' in the context of an ongoing work routine.

That the process is to be kept ongoing is itself a practical feature of the work. To keep things moving requires continual attention to such matters as scheduling and coordinating the activities of applicants, receptionists, and caseworkers. The receptionist must avoid, insofar as possible, marked disruptions or 'hitches' in the flow of work and at the same time be able to defend if necessary the sanctionable relationship of her practices on achieving the above to the rules and policies of the organisation to which these practices are accountable.

In order to examine how the receptionist, as an everyday accomplishment, achieves the reasonable reconciliation of the formal programme of the organisation with the practical features of doing work *in* the organisation, it is necessary to examine in more detail what will be called the 'actual task structure' of reception. This term refers to the variety of problematic features generated by the attempt to put into practice a programmatically specified task such as that of receptionists outlined above.

Actual task structure in reception

Temporal features. The temporal-coordinative contingencies of the reception process are inadequately depicted by speaking of the task as a series of steps, or a 'first this and then that' matter. From the perspective of a given applicant, the process may perhaps have this appearance (first, the initial contact, then the collection of preliminary information, and so on). For the receptionists, however, these steps are discontinuous with respect to each applicant. That is, step one of the process may take place for one applicant at a given time, step two somewhat later, and so on, with the various steps in the processing of other applicants intervening.

The steps in the process for receptionists are thus interspersed over an aggregate of applicants. Reception activities consist in multiple dealings with a set of applicants, imbedded in sequence of varying maturity, in constant motion, fitted together according to present circumstances and future prospects, and paced with respect to the ebb and flow of applicants in and out of the doors.

Viewed in this light, the appearance of the activities (to an observer or to organisation personnel themselves) as a timely and orderly steplike execution of the various phases of the preprocessing and assignment routines is provided for by the work of receptionists in attending to and managing such problems as matching the pace of work to the current demand (the number of applicants—and others—requesting service at a given time) in terms of their practical interests in moving applicants through the process with reasonable speed and a minimum of difficulty.

Troubles and consequences. Receptionists' practical interests in the trouble-free development of the workday reflect their knowledge that things sometimes go awry and that they are accountable to others in the setting for their efforts to manage the course of work to minimise disruptions and control departures from routines. As indicated above, close attention to timing and scheduling are critical features of the receptionists' task of making the workday 'come out right'.

Receptionists were seen to monitor the flow of work with the explicit concern that it be done by a certain time. Accomplishment of the latter required management of such matters as the timely 'closing' of intake, that is, cutting off the processing of new applications so that no excess of applicants awaiting interviews over caseworkers available to do interviews occurs at the end of the day.

A consideration adding urgency to concerns about timing and co-ordination is the proper utilisation of the caseworker as a resource. It is the caseworker's expeditious completion of the intake interview that moves the applicant out of the office completing the process. On the part of the receptionists, 'proper' utilisation requires prompt preparation of each new applicant for assignment, the promptness gain-ing its particular temporal specification by reference to the press of demands and available resources at the time. The dispatch with which caseworkers complete assigned interviews is a factor over which recep-tionists apparently have little direct control. The occurrence of an in-ordinately lengthy interview may be potentially troublesome for recep-tionists, as will be seen in the following section.

ACTUAL TASK STRUCTURE AND COMPETENT RULE USE

The intake assignment procedure

The 'literal' application of the intake assignment procedure was defined above as the employment of the 'next available cell' rule invariant to any exigencies of the actual situation of use. However, as might be expected, this literal usage was not maintained in every instance of an assignment of an application to an intake worker. If the literal-use model is posited as the 'proper' use of the rule, other alternatives would have to be designated as deviations. As was indicated in the introduc-tion, use of such a model would put out of account any exercise of judgment by the rule user, and leave as unproblematic the empirical issue of what the rule intends and how its operational sense is discovered by attempts to employ it in actual situations.

The task taken here will be to examine such 'deviations' (detectable by reference to the literal-use model) as possibly competent 'uses' of the rule by personnel employing judgments based upon their understanding of the features of the actual situation of use and the practicalities of action in the setting. Two instances of 'deviation' will be analysed.

Case 1. A third intake was about to be assigned to worker Jones. At this time, Jones was engaged in conducting an interview with her *first* assigned applicant. From the point of view of receptionists, this inter-view was presumed to have posed unusual problems since it had not been completed at the time a third assignment was contemplated.[4]

----

[4] The 'unusual' character of the interview thus appears to be formulated by reference to the stacking up of assignments. A prevailing concern of

A receptionist commented, in connection with the present case:

The biggest problem is keeping these people moving. Jones had her first assignment, well, shortly after 8:00 a.m. [It was 10:30 a.m. at this time.] She hasn't picked up her second and here is a third.

At 11:20 a.m., almost an hour after its assignment, the third intake had yet to be picked up. A receptionist called Jones's unit clerk and informed her that 'there's a woman out here who has been waiting a long time'. She was told that Jones was conducting an interview (the second assignment). This call had been occasioned by the third applicant's expressed anxiety that she was going to miss a 12:30 doctor's appointment. The receptionist who made the call remarked, 'If she has a doctor's appointment at 12:30 she's not going to make it at the rate Jones is going.'

The senior receptionist then decided that the third applicant would be switched to another worker. The switch entailed a discussion among receptionists concerning which worker to assign her to, as well as taking the next assignment of the worker receiving Jones's case and assigning it to her. The change also required alternation in the intake book and changes in certain other records. The potential third intake of Jones was in fact assigned to another worker, thereby 'suspending' the rule. That the suspension was observable as such may be seen in a receptionist's comment at that time that the 'skipped turn' was not 'fair'.

It is proposed here that this suspension be understood in terms of the actual task structure of the reception function. Reception, as depicted above, is a temporally complex system of activities. The prevailing emphasis is placed upon the rapid accomplishment of the preprocessing on a given case. The concern, aptly expressed by a receptionist, is to 'keep people moving'.

The case reported here posed a dilemma, since it represented a 'snag' upon which several cases were caught. The snag was in part structured into the situation by the intake assignment rule itself, which provided that each case was taken in order under a literal application. The smoothness with which this literal application effects the movement of applicants out of the office is contingent on the dispatch with which

receptionists is to move applicants through the process in a rapid and orderly manner. Effecting this state of affairs assumes the ready availability of the chief resource: the caseworkers. From the point of view of caseworkers, the chief concern is the assembly of information sufficient to ensure the rapid processing of the case. Caseworkers were not observed to express or to indicate by their method of conducting an interview any concern that assignments might backlog.

intake workers could accomplish the initial interview. Hence, the rule's capacity (literally applied) to achieve the objective of orderly and rapid processing is contingent upon the intake worker's system of relevances in conducting an interview, which are not necessarily congruent with that of reception, hence, disjuncture is guaranteed for *some* portion of the cases, which may lead to situations of the sort documented above.

One solution to such situations of course, is to maintain the priority of the next available cell rule. Apparently, from the point of view of the receptionist who made the decision, the rule could be suspended and the suspension deemed a 'reasonable' solution to the minor dilemma the situation presented.

The critical consideration here is the fact that the literal application of the assignment rule is apparently deemed adequate most of the time to deal with the typical applicant. Processing, from the point of view of receptionists, proceeds in a routine fashion most of the time. This *sense* of routineness provides receptionists a way to recognise the exceptional character of a given event and, thereby, the good grounds for suspending or otherwise modifying the rule as normally applied. That the use of the rule 'typically' effects the expected outcome, that, 'typically', applicants do not 'stack up' in this fashion, and that for most situations only the most commonplace and regular considerations need be entertained, constitutes the receptionists' sense of an organisationally normal state of affairs.

By suspending the rule in light of the exceptional character of the situation, the intent of the rule might be said to be honoured—its intent being formulable on a particular occasion by situationally relevant reference to the 'usual' course of affairs its routine or precedented use typically reproduces. Through the situated judgmental modification of the routine application of the rule, the 'same' business as usual course of affairs may be—for all intents and purposes—reliably reproduced.

In other words, what the rule is intended to provide for is discovered in the course of employing it over a series of actual situations. The use of a procedure, in the way that it is used, generates the state of affairs that, when things go wrong, may be referred to as the end in view 'all along'. For example, the attempt to use a procedure in a given situation may produce an array of troubles that motivate alterations in the manner in which the rules are put into practice, in turn affecting the state of affairs generated. The modification established, the resultant outcomes (if less troublesome) might then be invoked or assumed to argue what the rule intended 'all along' if an issue subsequently arose around what the rule 'really' calls for by way of action.

It may then be argued that the above *kinds* of considerations provide for the receptionist *a* reasonable solution for the dilemma confronted. The present argument, however, is not intended to argue the receptionist's case for her, thereby 'justifying' her decisions. The point is rather that receptionists appear to employ such considerations as justifications for the reasonableness of the action. By deciding to suspend the rule in *this* instance of its potential application, the intent of the rule was apparently not seen to be violated. Furthermore, in finding such modifications to be 'reasonable', receptionists appear to provide for ways to ensure that the continuing accomplishment of the normal pacing and flow of work may be reconciled with their view of these task activities *as governed by rules*, in this instance, the intake assignment procedure.

If this is generally the case, then it would seem that the notion of action-in-accord-with-a-rule is a matter not of compliance or noncompliance *per se* but of the various ways in which persons *satisfy* themselves and others concerning what is or is not 'reasonable' compliance in particular situations. Reference to rules might then be seen as a common-sense method of accounting for or making available for talk the orderly features of everyday activities, thereby *making out* these activities as orderly in some fashion. Receptionists, in accomplishing a for all practical purposes ordering of their task activities by undertaking the 'reasonable' reconciliation of particular actions with 'governing rules' may thus sustain their sense of 'doing good work' and warrant their further actions on such grounds.

Case 2. The following incident appears anomalous in terms of the preceding discussion. Here, contrary to the implications of the analysis thus far, a suspension of the rule of assignment was apparently allowed for reasons of 'personal preference' rather than for practical work considerations.

A GA case was prepared by 10:10 a.m. of the same day as the incident reported above. It was assigned to worker Hall at 10:16 a.m. At the same time an OAA case was assigned to worker Kuhn. Several minutes after this, the investigator noted that Hall had taken the OAA case and Kuhn the GA assignment. What had transpired was the intervention of the OAA applicant who specifically requested that Hall process her case.

Here again the rule was suspended. The same senior receptionist who had permitted the previous suspension on the grounds of exigent circumstances connected with the routine processing of cases allowed the 'switch' even though, strictly speaking, a disruption of the normal pacing of work was not immediately at issue. She was considerably more circumspect in permitting the suspension, commenting 'We don't do this very often. They're not supposed to get a case just because they want it.'

It may first be noted that this suspension has an illegitimate character to it. By this is meant that it was so treated by the receptionist, even though allowed. If this is the case, why did the receptionist not stand by the rule?

In answer to this problem, it is proposed here that single instances of illegitimate suspension *may* be allowed simply in order to avoid confrontation of the issue of procedural correctness, particularly when 'making an issue of it' might involve a dispute between the receptionists, the worker, *and* the applicant. Note that in allowing the impropriety it was cast in terms of a 'one time only' exception. Further, the switch was occasioned by an applicant's specific request: to deny it 'might' have required confrontation of both the applicant and the worker. What is more, the switch was arranged between the two workers, with consent given by both to the change. It is suggested that what is entailed in a circumstance of this sort is a permissiveness in the interest of avoiding difficulties and getting on with the work.

The burden of the preceding argument has been that receptionists orient to a normal course of affairs and seek by their action to guarantee its continuing reproduction. Such an orientation requires judgmental work on the part of receptionists in the use of procedures to effect such results, since contingent circumstance may sometimes render the literal use of such rules inappropriate, that is, the actions that could ordinarily be reconciled with the literal use would lead to 'trouble'—potential or actual. One such circumstance is 'occasional deviance'. By this is meant those instances wherein something recognised as illegitimate in the situations is proposed or encountered, and where such deviance may be permitted to stand by virtue of the explicit provision for its non-precedential character—simply to sidestep possible resistance (and the troubles it might bring) to enforcement of the 'proper' procedure.

It is a moot point whether or not the receptionist's insistence on adherence to the procedure would have generated a serious dispute. The fact remains that she did not so insist, even though she gave clear indication of disapproval. At least two alternative accounts are available. The first would be to assign the instance to a defect in the motivation of the receptionist to enforce the 'legitimate' ordering of events. The second is to refer the permissiveness to the receptionists' interests in preserving the routine flow of work in the setting. Allowance for occasional deviance would appear to be consistent with this latter interest. . . . From the point of view of receptionists, the steps of the reception process, including the use of intake assignment procedure typically achieve the desired outcomes. That is, for all practical purposes, and for most of the time, receptionists are able to coordinate applicants (who typically cooperate) and bring off the day's work with respect to the constraints of timing, pacing, and scheduling represented by the described 'actual task structure'. For receptionists, these outcomes are typically effected in an acceptable fashion by actions that are describable by them as in accordance with rules. This provides for the receptionists' sense of, and way of accounting for, normal everyday routine affairs in the setting. Further, these routine affairs are looked to by receptionists to decide what the rule or procedure is 'up to' after all.

On a more general level, it appears that the 'competent use' of a given rule or a set of rules is founded upon members' practical grasp of what particular actions are necessary on a given occasion to provide for the regular reproduction of a 'normal' state of affairs. A feature of the member's grasp of his everyday affairs is his knowledge, gained by experience, of the typical but unpredictable occurrence of situational exigencies that threaten the production of desired outcomes. Often, troubles develop over which little control is possible, save to restore the situation as well as possible. Certain exigencies may be dealt with on an *ad hoc* basis and others may be provided for systematically.

The use of formally prescribed procedures viewed from the perspective of the notion of their 'competent use' thus becomes a matter not of compliance or deviance but of judgmental work providing for the reasonableness of viewing particular actions as *essentially* satisfying the provisions of the rule, even though the action may contrast with invocable precedent, with members' idealised versions of what kinds of acts are called for by the rule, or with the sociologists' ideas concerning the behavioural acts prescribed or proscribed by the rule.

REFERENCES

BITTNER, EGON (1965) 'The concept of organization', *Social Research*, **32**, 239–55 (also no. 17 in this Reader).
GARFINKEL, HAROLD (1967) *Studies in Ethnomethodology*, Prentice-Hall.
WILSON, T. P. (1970) 'Conceptions of interaction and forms of sociological explanation', *American Sociological Review*, **35**.

17

Egon Bittner   The concept of organisation

Egon Bittner, 'The concept of organization', *Social Research*, **32**, no. 3, Autumn 1965, pp. 239–55.

In recent years a good deal of the very best sociological work has been devoted to the study of organisation. Although the term, organisation, belongs to the category of expressions about which there is maintained an air of informed vagueness, certain special conventions exist that focus its use, with qualifications, on a delimited set of phenomena. In accordance with these conventions, the term applies correctly to stable associations of persons engaged in concerted activities directed to the attainment of specific objectives. It is thought to be a decisive characteristic of such organisations that they are deliberately instituted relative to these objectives. Because organisations, in this sense, are implementing and implemented programmes of action that involve a substantial dose of comprehensive and rational planning, they are identified as instances of formal or rational organisation in order to differentiate them from other forms.[1]

---

[1] These characteristics are generally noted when the task is to identify real instances of 'formal organization', cf. Talcott Parsons (1960, pp. 16–96); Amitai Etzioni (1961); P. M. Blau and W. R. Scott (1962). Various authors have studied such organisations in ways that seem to disregard the identifying characteristics, or to subordinate them to other interests. To study a phenomenon while suspending the relevance of that feature by which it is recognised is not an unusual procedure, though it produces peculiar problems. G. E. Moore and Edmund Husserl have explored these problems from substantially different perspectives.

It has been one of the most abiding points of interest of modern organisational research to study how well the programmatically intended formal structures of organisations describe what is going on within them, and what unintended, unprogrammed, and thus informal structures tend to accompany them.

How do sociologists go about distinguishing the facts of formal organisation from the facts of informal organisation? There seem to be two things that matter in the ways this distinction is drawn. There is, in the first place, a certain scholarly tradition in which the distinction is rooted. It dates back to Pareto's definition of rationality, Tönnies' typology, Cooley's concept of primary-group, and—tracing through the seminal achievement of the Hawthorn studies—the tradition is very much alive today. Being steeped in this line of scholarship allows a sociologist to claim his colleagues' consent to the decisions he makes. In this way the distinction is a fact of life in sociological inquiry, and perceiving it correctly is a trademark of professional competence. Although this is undoubtedly a potent factor in many decisions, it does not furnish a clear-cut rule for the distinction.

The rule, which is the second consideration, can be stated as follows: In certain presumptively identified fields of action, the observed stable patterns of conduct and relations can be accounted for by invoking some *programmatic constructions* that define them prospectively. Insofar as the observed stable patterns match the dispositions contained in the programme they are instances of formal organisational structure. Whereas, if it can be shown that the programme did not provide for the occurrence of some other observed patterns which seem to have grown spontaneously, these latter belong to the domain of the informal structures.

Despite its apparent cogency, the rule is insufficient. The programmatic construction is itself a part of the presumptively identified field of action, and thus the sociologist finds himself in the position of having borrowed a concept from those he seeks to study in order to describe what he observes about them.

In general, there is nothing wrong with borrowing a common-sense concept for the purposes of sociological inquiry. Up to a certain point it is, indeed, unavoidable. The warrant for this procedure is the sociologists's interest in exploring the common-sense perspective. The point at which the use of common-sense concepts becomes a transgression is where such concepts are expected to do the analytical work of theoretical concepts. When the actor is treated as a permanent auxiliary to the enterprise of sociological inquiry at the same time that he is the object of its inquiry, there arise ambiguities that defy clarification. Now, if the idea of formal structure is basically a common-sense notion, what role can it have in sociological inquiry?

I. THE THEORETICAL SENSE OF FORMAL STRUCTURES OF ORGANISATION

In an influential essay, Philip Selznick (1948) explicitly addressed the problem of the theoretical significance of formal constructions by relating them, as facts of life, to functional imperatives of organisations conceived as cooperative-adaptive systems. Arguing along the lines of structural-functional analysis, he showed convincingly why 'formal administrative design can never adequately or fully reflect the concrete organisation to which it refers', but is nevertheless a relevant element in the sociological study of organisations. In his view, the design represents that particular conception of organisation which management technicians seek to explicate. Even though there may attach to these explications some descriptive or analytic intent, they are primarily active elements of the concrete phenomenon of organisation rather than disinterested statements about it. As such, the presence of rational organisational design in social systems of action is a source of tension and dilemma. These consequences arise out of the 'recalcitrance of the tools of action', relative to the 'freedom of technical or ideal choice' reflected in plans and programmes.

It is important to note that in this new and rich context the old conception of formal organisation, which is traceable to Max Weber, remained intact. Together with Weber, Selznick assumes that the formal structures represent an ideally possible, but practically unattainable state of affairs. While Weber outlined the contents of the normative idealisation in general terms, Selznick pointed out that the normative idealisation, to be an effective source of restraint, must be constantly adapted to the impact of functional imperatives of social systems. Thus he furnished the necessary theoretical argument for an entire field of sociological investigations by directing attention to a sphere of adaptive and cooperative manipulations, and to the tensions typically found in it.

Despite the gain, the argument retains a certain theoretical short circuit. While Selznick quite clearly assigns the formal schemes to the domain of sociological data, he does not explore the full range of consequences arising out of this decision. By retaining Weber's conception of them as normative idealisations, Selznick avoids having to consider what the constructions of rational conduct mean to, and how they are used by, persons who have to live with them from day to day. It could be, however, that the rational schemes appear as unrealistic normative idealisations only when one considers them literally, i.e., without considering some tacit background assumptions that bureaucrats take for granted.

In the following we shall endeavour to show that the literal interpretation of formal schemes is not only inappropriate but, strictly speaking, impossible. We shall further show that the tacit assumptions are not simply unspecified, but instead come to the fore only on occasions of actual reference to the formal scheme. Finally, we shall argue that the meaning and import of the formal schemes must remain undetermined unless the circumstances and procedures of its actual use by actors is fully investigated.

2. CRITIQUE OF WEBER'S THEORY OF BUREAUCRACY

We shall introduce our argument by considering Weber's work critically because the short circuit in theorising occurred first in his work and because most of contemporary research in formal organisation claims to stand in some sort of relationship to the definitions formulated by him. We shall be discussing the theory of bureacracy as the most general case of many possible, more specific, rational schemes. But what we say about general form is applicable to such specific instances as manuals of operations, tables of organisation or programmes of procedure.

Weber used the concept of organisation to refer to a network of authority distribution. As is well known, he asserted that such a network may be said to exist when and insofar as there prevails a high degree of correspondence between the substance of commands and conditions favouring compliance with them. Confining our interest to bureaucracy, we note that the condition favouring compliance with its authority structure lies in its acceptance as being efficient (Gerth and Mills, 1948, pp. 214–16). From this premise, pure bureaucracy obtains when the principle of technical efficiency is given overriding priority above all other considerations. The ideal type of bureaucracy is, consequently, the product of ostensibly free conceptual play with this principle.

To say, however, that the resulting scheme is a meaningful conceptualisation indicates that the ideal of efficiency is exercised over a domain of objects and events that are known to exist and that are known to possess independent qualities of their own. The efficiency principle merely selects, identifies, and orders those existing elements of a scene of action that are perceived as related to it. The relevance of the known qualities of things becomes very apparent when one considers that it must be at least possible for them to be related in ways that the idealisation stipulates. What sorts of things are taken for granted may vary, but it is not possible to have any rational construction of reality that does not rest on some tacit assumptions.

It could be said that this is not an unusual state of affairs. In scientific inquiry it is always the case that in order to assert anything one must leave some things unsaid. Such unsaid things stand under the protection of the *ceteris paribus* clause. The use of this clause is, however, restricted and its contents are always open to scrutiny.

When one lifts the mantle of protection from the unstated presupposition surrounding the terms of Weber's theory of bureaucracy one is confronted with facts of a particular sort. These facts are not sociological data, or even theoretically defensible hypotheses. Instead, one is confronted with a rich and ambiguous body of background information that normally competent members of society take for granted as commonly known. In its normal functioning this information furnishes the tacit foundation for all that is explicitly known, and provides the matrix for all deliberate considerations without being itself deliberately considered. While its content can be raised to the level of analysis, this typically does not occur. Rather, the information enters into that commonplace and practical orientation to reality which members of society regard as 'natural' when attending to their daily affairs. Since the explicit terms of the theory are embedded in this common-sense orientation, they cannot be understood without tacit reference to it. If, however, the theorist must be persuaded about the meaning of the terms in some prior and unexplicated way, there then exists collusion between him and those about whom he theorises. We call this unexplicated understanding collusive because it is a hidden resource, the use of which cannot be controlled adequately.

Some examples will help to clarify this point. Consider the term 'employee'. There is little doubt that Weber presupposed, rather than neglected, a whole realm of background information in using it. Certainly employees must be human beings of either the male or female sex, normally competent adults rather than children, and in many ways familiar types of persons whose responsiveness, interests, inclinations, capacities and foibles are in a basic sense known as a matter of course. All this information is obvious, of course, but does not by any means coincide with the scientifically demonstrable or even scientifically tenable. Rather, the full meaning of the term 'employee', as it is used in the theory of bureaucracy, refers to that understanding of it which fully franchised persons in society expect from one another when they converse on matters of practical import. That is, insofar as the term refers meaningfully to some determinate object, it does so only in the context of actors making common sense of it in consequential situations.

Let us consider the ideal of efficiency itself. While Weber is quite clear in stating that the sole justification of bureaucracy is its efficiency, he provides us with no clear-cut guide on how this standard of judgment is to be used. Indeed, the inventory of features of bureaucracy contains not one single item that is not arguable relative to its efficiency function. Long-range goals cannot be used definitively for calculating it because the impact of contingent factors multiplies with time and makes it increasingly difficult to assign a determinate value to the efficiency of a stably controlled segment of action. On the other hand, the use of short-term goals in judging efficiency may be in conflict with the ideal of economy itself. Not only do short-term goals change with time and compete with one another in determinate ways, but short-term results are of notoriously deceptive value because they can be easily manipulated to show whatever one wishes them to show (cf. Haire, 1962, pp. 8–10). Clearly, what Weber had in mind when speaking about efficiency was not a formally independent criterion of judgment but an ideal that is fully attuned to practical interests as these emerge and are pursued in the context of everyday life. The standard itself and the correct way to use it are, therefore, a part of the selfsame order of action that they purport to control. The power and right to judge some procedure as more or less efficient require the same kind of sensitivity, responsiveness and competence that using the procedure presupposes in the first place. Only those who have serious business in doing what must be done are also franchised to judge it.

Weber, of course, intended to achieve an idealised reconstruction of organisation from the perspective of the actor. He fell short of attaining this objective precisely to the extent that he failed to explore the underlying common-sense presuppositions of his theory. He failed to grasp that the meaning and warrant of the inventory of the properties of bureaucracy are inextricably embedded in what Alfred Schutz (1953) called the attitudes of everyday life and in socially sanctioned common-sense typifications.

Thus, if the theory of bureaucracy is a theory at all, it is a refined and purified version of the actors' theorising. To the extent that it is a refinement and purification of it, it is by the same token, a corrupt and incomplete version of it; for it is certainly not warranted to reduce the terms of common-sense discourse to a lexicon of culturally coded significances to satisfy the requirements of theoretical postulation. This is the theoretical shortcut we mentioned at the beginning of our remarks.

3. THE STUDY OF THE CONCEPT OF ORGANISATION AS A COMMON-SENSE CONSTRUCT

Plucked from its native ground, i.e., the world of common sense, the concept of rational organisation, and the schematic determinations that are subsumed under it, are devoid of information on how its terms relate to facts. Without knowing the structure of this relationship of reference, the meaning of the concept and its terms cannot be determined.

In this situation an investigator may use one of three research procedures. He can, for one thing, proceed to investigate formal organisation while assuming that the unexplicated common-sense meanings of the terms are adequate definitions for the purposes of his investigation. In this case, he must use that which he proposes to study as a resource for studying it.

He can, in the second instance, attach to the terms a more or less arbitrary meaning by defining them operationally. In this case, the relationship of reference between the term and the facts to which it refers will be defined by the operations of inquiry. Interest in the actor's perspective is either deliberately abandoned, or some fictitious version of it is adopted.

The investigator can, in the last instance, decide that the meaning of the concept, and of all the terms and determinations that are subsumed under it, must be discovered by studying their use in real scenes of action by persons whose competence to use them is socially sanctioned.

It is on'y the last case which yields entirely to the rule specifying the relevance of the perspective of the actor in sociological inquiry. This is so because in order to understand the meaning of the actor's thought and action, which Weber sought, one must study *how* the terms of his discourse are assigned to real objects and events by normally competent persons in ordinary situations.

Insofar as the procedures and considerations actors invoke in relating terms of rational common-sense construction to things in the world exhibit some stable properties, they may be called a method. It is, of course, not proper to assume that this method is identical with, or even similar to, the method of scientific inquiry. Garfinkel proposed that in order to differentiate the study of this method from the study of the methods of scientific inquiry it be called ethnomethodology.

In the following we shall propose in brief outline a programme of inquiry which takes as its object of interest the study of the methodical use of the rational constructions subsumed under the concept of organisation. We shall also present examples of this programme. The concept itself and its methodical use are, of course, defined as belonging entirely to the domain of facts.

We must emphasise that our interest is in outlining a programme of inquiry, not in producing a theory of organisation. It is to be this way because the inquiry cannot get under way without first employing the very sensibilities that it seeks to study, i.e., the common-sense outlook. At the outset the phenomenon of organisation comes to our attention in just the way it comes to the attention of any normal member of our linguistic community. Even as we turn to the investigation of the common-sense presuppositions in which it is embedded, and from which it derives its socially sanctioned sense, other common-sense presuppositions will continue to insinuate themselves into our thinking and observation. The important point in the proposed study is that we must be prepared to treat every substantive determination we shall formulate as a case for exploring the background information on which it in turn rests.

By way of defining our task we propose that *the study of the methodical use of the concept of organisation seeks to describe the mechanisms of sustained and sanctional relevance of the rational constructions to a variety of objects, events and occasions relative to which they are invoked.*

In order to free ourselves progressively from the encumbrance of presumptive understanding we shall take two preliminary measures. First, the author of the rational scheme, typically the managerial technician who deals with organisation in the 'technical sense', will not be treated as having some sort of privileged position for understanding its meaning. By denying him the status of the authoritative interpreter we do not propose to tamper with the results of his work in the least. From our point of view he is merely the toolsmith. It seems reasonable that if one were to investigate the meaning and typical use of some tool, one would not want to be confined to what the toolmaker has in mind.

Second, we will not look to the obvious or conspicuous meaning of the expressions used in the scheme to direct us to objects and events which they identify. Rather, we will look for the way the scheme is brought to bear on whatever happens within the scope of its jurisdiction. The consequence of this step is that the question of what the scheme selects and neglects is approached by asking how certain objects and events meet, or are made to meet, the specifications contained in the scheme.

After denying the technician and his scheme the authority to organise the field of observation for the sociologist, the question of how they, nevertheless, organise it in some other sense is open for investigation.

If one suspends the presumptive notion that a rational organisational scheme is a normative idealisation with a simple import, i.e., demanding literally what it says it demands; and if one views a rational organisational scheme without information about what it is ostensibly meant to be, then it emerges as a *generalised formula to which all sorts of problems can be brought for solution*. In this sense there is no telling what determinations a formal organisational scheme contains prior to the time that questions are actually and seriously addressed to it.

More important than the open capacity and applicability of the formula is, however, the fact that *problems referred to the scheme for solution acquire through this reference a distinctive meaning that they would not otherwise have.* Thus the formal organisational designs are schemes of interpretation that competent and entitled users can invoke in yet unknown ways whenever it suits their purposes. The varieties of ways in which the scheme can be invoked for information, direction, justification, and so on, without incurring the risk of sanction, constitute the scheme's methodical use. In the following we propose to discuss some examples of possible variations in the methodical use of organisational rationalities.

4. EXAMPLES OF VARIATION IN THE METHODICAL USE OF THE CONCEPT OF ORGANISATION

(a) *The gambit of compliance*[2]

As we have noted earlier, the concept of rational organisation is often regarded by sociologists and management technicians as a normative idealisation. Even though one finds only '*is*' and '*is not*' in the substantive determination, there attaches the sense of '*ought*' to the entire scheme.

Conceived as a rule of conduct, the concept of organisation is defined as having some determining power over action that takes place under the scope of its jurisdiction. This power to produce an intended result is uncertain and depends for its effectiveness on complex structural conditions. Hence, research informed by the conception of organisation as a rule of conduct will seek to procure estimates of its effectiveness, and will relate the findings

---

[2] We should like to point out that this example corresponds to what Selznick (1948) suggests when he urges the study of the 'manipulation of the formal processes and structures in terms of informal goals', p. 32.

to factors that favour or mitigate against compliance. All such research is necessarily based on the assumption that the relationship of correspondence between the rule and the behaviours that are related to it is clear. A cursory consideration of the significance of rules as social facts reveals, however, that their meaning is not exhausted by their prospective sense. Aside from determining the *occurrence* of certain responses under suitable conditions, rules are also invoked to clarify the *meaning* of actions retrospectively. For example, one knows what a driver of an automobile signalling intent to make a left turn is doing in the middle of an intersection because one knows the rule governing such procedures. Indeed, it is a readily demonstrable fact that a good deal of the sense we make of things happening in our presence depends on our ability to *assign them* to the phenomenal sphere of influence of some rule. Not only do we do this but we count on this happening. That this is so is richly documented in the work of Goffman who has shown how persons conduct themselves in such a way as to enable observers to relate performances to some normative expectation.

When we consider the set of highly schematic rules subsumed under the concept of rational organisation, we can readily see an open realm of free play for relating an infinite variety of performances to rules as responses to these rules. In this field of games of representation and interpretation, the rule may have the significance of informing the competent person about the proper occasion and form for doing things that could probably never be divined from considering the rule in its verbal form. Extending to the rule the respect of compliance, while finding in the rule the means for doing whatever need be done, is the gambit that characterises organisational acumen.

We propose that we must proceed from the theoretical clarification of the essential limitation of formal rules achieved by Selznick to the investigation of the limits of manœuverability within them, to the study of the skill and craftsmanship involved in their use, and to a reconsideration of the meaning of strict obedience in the context of varied and ambiguous representations of it. This recommendation is, however, not in the interest of accumulating more materials documenting the discrepancy between the lexical meaning of the rule and events occurring under its jurisdiction, but in order to attain a grasp of the meaning of the rules as common-sense constructs from the perspective of those persons who promulgate and live with them.

(b) The concept of formal organisation as a model of stylistic unity

It is often noted that the formal organisation meets exigencies arising out of the complexity and large scope of an enterprise. The rationally conceived form orders affiliations between persons and performances that are too remote for contingent arrangement, by linking them into coherent maps or schedules. The integration transcends what might result from negotiated agreements between contiguous elements, and lends to elements that are not within the sphere of one another's manipulative influence the character of a concerted action. As a consequence of this, however, each link derives its meaning not so much from the specific rule that determines it, but from the entire order of which the rule itself is a part. Each link is intrinsically a member of a chain or fabric of links which conducts a reproducible theme. In this context, many specific instances or elements can be compared with each other as variations of a single pattern. For example, a simple polarisation of authority pervades the whole order of an organisation and can be found as a redundant thematic focus in many segments of it. A rational principle of justice may prevail in the entire structure while governing differentially correct associations between particular performances and rewards. The varieties of demeanours that are appropriate to a particular status within the system may be perceived as variations of a more general pattern.

We are suggesting the possibility of a principle of discipline that derives from the formal style of the rational scheme and which works against centrifugal tendencies and heterogeneity. The resulting coherence will be in evidence as outwardly proper conduct and appearance. One would then ask how the sensibility of esthetic appreciation is summoned for direction, information and control in various concrete situations. The dominant consideration underlying this construction would not be found in the field of means-ends relations but in allpervading sense of piety, i.e., in accordance with Burke's (1954) definition of the term, a sure-footed conviction of 'what properly goes with what' (pp. 74ff.).

The question whether the syntactic composition of the formal scheme is the leading metaphor for the interpretation of the composition of actual performances and relations is obviously difficult to investigate. A tentative approach may be in the investigation of ties and performances that appeal to bureaucrats as incongruous or in bad taste, and the study of those observed proprieties and tolerated licenses that are restricted to 'on the job' circumstances. In further development the problem could lead to experimental studies. For example, the features of the stylistically normal could be studied by having subjects perform tasks that are not related or even contrary to their routine activities. The subjects would be induced to perform these tasks under the gaze of their work associates, and would be penalised for attracting attention and rewarded for remaining unnoticed.

(c) The concept of organisation as corroborative reference

There is another problem which is related to the problem of stylistic unity. A large-scale and complex organisation is often composed of fragmented tasks and relations that are not capable of acquiring a phenomenal identity of their own or, at least, it is thought to be extremely difficult to value them for their intrinsic merits. Whether it is enough to relate these tasks to work obligations, and whether work requires any corroboration of worth beyond pointing to its market price is an open question. If it does, however, the formal scheme could be invoked to attest to it.

When from the perspective of a fragmentary involvement the actual contingent outcome of one's work cannot be appraised, or appears senseless, then it can be understood and judged in terms of its over-all functional significance by invoking the formal scheme. For example, mismanagement and waste could be defined as merely accidental or perhaps even justified, relative to the total economy of the enterprise. This consideration of the formal scheme not only persuades the participants of some correct or corrected value of their duties, but can also be used as a potent resource for enforcing prohibitions when interest dictates that such prohibitions should be justified.

In this construction, the formal scheme is used as a resource for bringing anything that happens within an organisation under the criterion of success or failure when real results are not visible, or must be discredited. This is not a simple matter, of course, because the scheme does not promote a single ideal of economy but specifies a field of economy in which various aspects of an operation may compete for priority. For example, in an industrial enterprise certain ways of doing things may have one value relative to interest in production and an altogether different value relative to interest in maintenance. The problem that requires investigation is how various evaluations can be used as credits, and what sorts of credits have the consequence of assimilating some partial performance closer to the larger enterprise. The investigation of this problem would reveal the negotiable relationship between policy and politics.

CONCLUSION

We have cited the gambit of compliance, stylistic unity, and corroborative reference merely as examples of the possible methodical use of the concept of organisation by competent users. The examples are based on reflections about ethnographic materials depicting life in large-scale and formally programmed organisations. We have indicated earlier that such formulations must be regarded as preliminary at best. Whether what we have tentatively called the reference through the sensibility of esthetic appreciation exists effectively or not, is a matter to be decided by empirical research. Without doubt, these suggestions will have to be revised and amplified, but they must suffice to illustrate the ethno-methodological study of rational organisation.

In conclusion, we should like to mention that there remains for this inquiry one more problem that we have mentioned in passing but have not discussed adequately. We have noted that the methodical use of the concept of organisation must be studied by observing *competent* users. We mean, of course, socially recognised competence. Consequently it is not within the prerogative of the researcher to define competence. Instead, while he looks for the right way to use the rationalities subsumed under the concept of organisation, he must also be looking for the rules governing the right to use the concept.

REFERENCES

BLAU, P. M., and SCOTT, W. R. (1962) *Formal Organizations,* San Francisco, Chandler Publications, Inc.

BURKE, KENNETH (1954) *Permanence and Change,* 2nd edn, rev. Los Altos, Calif.: Hermes Publications.

ETZIONI, AMITAI (1961) *Complex Organizations,* New York, Free Press of Glencoe.

GERTH, H. H., and MILLS, C. W., eds. and trans. (1948) *From Max Weber: essays in sociology,* Routledge & Kegan Paul.

HAIRE, MASON (1962) 'What is organized in an organization?', in Mason Haire, ed., *Organization Theory in Industrial Practice,* Wiley.

PARSONS, TALCOTT (1960) *Structure and Process in Modern Societies,* New York, Free Press of Glencoe.

SCHUTZ, ALFRED (1953) 'Common sense and scientific interpretation of action', *Philosophy and Phenomenological Research,* **14,** 1–38.

SELZNICK, PHILIP (1948) 'Foundations of the theory of organization', *American Sociological Review,* **13,** 25–35.

Knowledge and information

It will be clear from the readings contained in earlier sections that the behaviour of members of organisations does not follow their obedience and commitment to unambiguous and clearly applicable rules or goals. Rather, organisations have been seen as consisting of interacting individuals and groups, negotiating and bargaining with each other in terms of their definitions, evaluations and priorities. Of course, in these interactions some groups have considerably more power than others; and it has been noted that the most significant (and previously overlooked) form of organisational power is the ability to initiate organisational structure—rules, procedures, the organisation of work and so on. But it has also been argued that official statements and intentions concerning the way things should be, are not only intrinsically inadequate as guides to situational decision-making—except in very extreme cases— but are also themselves the subject of alteration, avoidance and interpretation in the actual occasions of their use. Finally, that even in a context of highly specific rules and procedures, organisational members typically develop or transplant their own subcultural definitions and knowledge.

This section is concerned with organisations as constructors of social reality, as phenomena that consist of, develop, transmit and impose definitions of the nature of the world, the organisation, its members, their membership and those persons who are routinely processed or dealt with by the organisational members in their work. It has been suggested, and it is argued in these readings, that an understanding of what are variously termed organisational values and ideas, the 'multiplicity of purposes' found in an organisation, the symbols and notions of rationality current within an organisation, or what members of an organisation consider as 'typical' of normal persons, clients and cases, is crucially important in any effort to understand the behaviour of members of organisations.

The excerpt from Perrow (18) on decision-making nicely summarises some salient issues that underlie considerations of rationality in decision-making. This reading is especially relevant to the considerations of the Reader as a whole, since not only is it addressed to a discussion of the variety of meanings and applications of the concept of rationality in models of organisational decision-making, but it also argues forcibly for the salience of what are termed the premises underlying decisions —the ways in which the issues to be decided and the sanctioned procedures to follow and the established repertoire of available choices are limited and controlled. As Perrow notes, most decisions and choices within the organisation are not overtly controlled and supervised, yet regularity is apparent. The reason for this is that control is achieved by mechanisms listed in the reading which are unobtrusive in their constraining influence. (This is clearly related to what Blau and Schoenherr call insidious forms of control: see reading 1.)

Thompson (19) continues this interest in the values and preferences underlying organisational behaviour by considering the case of religious organisations. Once again this reading is closely related to earlier contributions which argued for the importance of considering organisational structure as an outcome of values and priorities held by powerful, interacting organisational groups attempting to attain their conceptions of an efficient, or satisfactory organisation. Thompson notes that in the case of religious organisations—which are considered to be largely concerned with the 'promulgation and propagation of certain values'—it is possible to discern a relationship between the religious symbols and theology of the group and the models of organisational structure that members prefer and consider appropriate. So it is argued that members of religious bodies consider certain symbols, doctrines and images as goals (or, at least, constraints) which have normative implications for organisational structure, as they see it.

The contribution by Strauss *et al.* (20) is relevant to the main themes of this Reader in a number of ways. For one thing it is a classic description of the ways in which organisations are made up of constantly ongoing negotiations and adjustments (although it should be noted that organisations vary with respect to the degree to which this sort of activity is possible: Strauss *et al.* suggest it is particularly probable when an organisation is made up of people with different occupational trainings and philosophies; such processes of negotiation will be less marked within industrial enterprises).

This reading is also relevant for its attention to rules and rule use within the psychiatric hospital. It is noted that rules were relevant to only a small 'area of action', dependent on judgment and discretion, and by no means the determinants of actual behaviour, which stemmed more from the interplay of ideologies, definitions and priorities of the various occupational/professional groupings. It is also noted (and this is highly pertinent to the sorts of analyses described by Sudnow, Bittner and Emerson) that the rules, far from determining behaviour, were used by organisational personnel in their attempts to 'obtain what they themselves wished'.

Considerations of industrial organisations in terms of the sorts of knowledge their members share have usually been restricted to the question of legitimacy, since this is an issue that has obvious theoretical and practical significance. Fox (21) discusses managerial legitimation in terms of the relationship between workers' experience of their employing organisation and its power structure and their own values and expectations of 'proper' managerial behaviour. It might be argued that legitimation too—when it is achieved—is a result of negotiation between workers and management. But in this case management attempts to define the nature of the organisation and its personnel are inherently unstable, as Fox (21) shows, and are consequently reinforced by numerous sanctions. Finally, Fox notes how not only is it normal for some attempt to be made to legitimise the hierarchy and inequalities within organisations, in terms of ideas concerning the nature of the relationships between managers and workers, but also, that members of industrial organisations, as well as professional ones, bring into the organisation with them already formed conceptions and expectations of the industrial enterprise.

The three readings by Bittner (22), Sudnow (23) and Emerson (24) consist of detailed investigations of what might be called the interface between organisations and their publics. All three articles describe the behaviour of members of organisations with respect to their clients. All three articles reveal the ways in which the behaviour of the practitioner rests upon and reveals, a knowledge of normal, typical, clients. And how such knowledge is used in the classification—and consequent treatment—of the client. The studies by Bittner and Sudnow show how the problems of policemen in skid row, and of public defenders, are not derived from the official rhetoric of the organisation or the available and relevant statutes and rules, but stem from situational demands and exigencies which involve practitioners achieving what they take to be their main tasks in the light of what they know about their clients. The outstanding conclusion from these two studies is that it is neither possible nor legitimate to assume that the application of categories (whether bureaucratic or academic) to events and persons is an un-problematic exercise involving reference to a body of precedents and principles. What these studies show is that in both cases the practitioners use their available powers and influence in bargaining with their clients so as to achieve what the practitioners, with their knowledge of the clients, see as necessary and useful outcomes.

Emerson's article differs slightly from the other two ethnographical studies in that while Bittner and Sudnow are interested in the knowledge shared by bureaucratic practitioners and how it influences their utilisation of bureaucratic procedures and bureaucratic rules, Emerson is concerned with the ways in which definition (knowledge) of a situation is constructed for those involved. She argues that a 'successful' gynaecological examination is one where 'normal' definitions of what's going on are discarded, or at least overwhelmed, by medical consider-ations. But it is pointed out that such a definition of reality is extremely precarious and vulnerable, requiring constant guidance and support from the doctor.

18

Charles Perrow — The neo-Weberian model: decision making, conflict, and technology

Charles Perrow, 'The neo-Weberian model: decision making, conflict, and technology' in *Complex Organizations: A Critical Essay*, Glenview, Ill., Scott, Foreman & Co., 1972, pp. 145–76.

DECISION MAKING

The human relations theorists sought to restore the individual, with his needs and drives, to a central place in organisational theory, a place denied to him by the classical management theory or by Weberian bureaucratic theory. While the human relations theorists focused upon the individual to an extent that Barnard would not approve, they joined with Barnard by taking for granted what he found necessary to insist upon, the moral and cooperative nature of organisations. We have argued that their model is deficient in many respects: It lacks empirical support and conceptual clarity, and it fails to grapple with the realities of authoritarian control in organisations and the true status of the subordinate. But even if our critique is valid, the question still remains: What do we do about the individual in organisations? Do we have to more or less ignore him, as Weber did, because the alternative is to become mired in all his complexities and contingencies? There is, obviously, cooperation in organisations, and it is individuals who cooperate. There are such things as good and bad leadership exercised by individuals and identification with the goals of the organisation on the part of individuals. Organisations are something more than the structural categories of the Weberian model—the skeleton of hierarchy, rules, offices, roles, careers, and so on. If we cannot accept the human relations propositions as being adequate or plausible, must we ignore individuals?

Herbert Simon and James March have provided, somewhat un-wittingly, the muscle and flesh for the Weberian skeleton, giving it more substance, complexity, and believability without reducing organisational theory to propositions about individual behaviour. Or, to be more accurate, part of the work of March and Simon does this. Roughly half of their work, as laid out in two extremely important volumes, Simon's *Administrative Behavior* (1957) and *Organizations* by March and Simon (1958),[1] is concerned with the organisation as a problem of social psychology. The other half uses a structural perspec-tive; it speaks to *organisational* rather than to *individual* decision making.

MODELS OF MAN

Two different 'models of man' are involved, and a discussion of them will serve to introduce the decision-making view of organisations. When individual decision making is under discussion, man is seen as able to make rational computations and rational decisions once he has decided upon his goals. 'Two persons, given the same skills, the same objectives and values, the same knowledge and inclination, can ration-ally decide only upon the same course of action.'[2] Goals depend in part upon group influences, but these can be mapped out. This is done extensively in Chapters Three and Four of *Organizations*, involving about 120 propositions with literally dozens of influences impinging upon, for example, the decision to stay with or leave the organisation. Man also internalises the goals of the organisation and seeks affiliation with his group. He has a number of needs that require satisfaction. His social characteristics—age, sex, status, etc.—influence his decision. Finally, he has aspirations: if his aspirations are satisfied, his effort is relaxed, and if they are not, it is increased.

This portrait of man is, if anything, even more complex than the highly contingent human relations models, such as Fiedler's. Yet it is

[1] It will be impossible in this section to separate out the respective contri-butions of March and Simon when discussing this important book. Since the positions we are concerned with are also at least implicit in Simon's *Administrative Behavior* we will generally speak only of Simon, rather than of March and Simon.

[2] Simon, *Administrative Behavior*, pp. 13, 39. 'Once the system of values which is to govern an administrative choice has been specified, there is one and only one "best decision"....', *ibid.*, p. 204.

supposed to be the key to understanding organisations. Simon argues, first, organisations are made up of individuals. 'An organization is, after all, a collection of people, and what the organization does is done by people' (p. 110). Therefore, understanding them is 'a problem in social psychology' (pp. 1–2). Or, as March and Simon put it more decisively in a later volume, 'propositions about organizations are statements about human behavior. . . .'[3]

There is another model of the individual in the writings of Simon and March, however. In the second model the complexity of individual wants, desires, and values and the multitude of the influences on his decisions are ignored. Instead, this model makes simplifying assumptions about the individual, so that we can get on with studying the organisation rather than the individual. It assumes that the individual is not all that rational and that his behaviour, within limits, can be deliberately controlled.

In this model, man is only 'intendedly rational'. He attempts to be rational but his limited capacities and the limited capacities of the organisation prevent anything near complete rationality. For one thing, he does not have complete knowledge of the consequences of his act. There will be both unanticipated and unintended consequences of action. Second, he either does not have complete knowledge of the alternative courses of action available to him or he cannot afford to attain that knowledge. That is, he does not sit down and prepare an exhaustive list of alternatives before making every decision, and even if he tried to do so, the list could not be exhaustive. Therefore, he grossly simplifies the alternatives that are available and selects the first acceptable one. Third, even when he has several alternatives, he cannot accurately rank them in terms of their preference; he cannot be sure which is the most desirable and which is the least desirable (March and Simon, 1958, p. 138; Simon, 1957, p. 81). These limitations on man conflict sharply with statements by Simon regarding rationality, efficiency, and the 'one best decision'.

It is important, before we go any further, to note the implications of this view and to distinguish it from Barnard's view of nonrational man and rational organisation. In Barnard's model, man by himself is nonrational, but he achieves rationality through organisations. Simon's man is intendedly rational, but participation in the organisation does not produce a more rational or superior man, nor does it produce an

---

[3] March and Simon, *Organizations*, p. 26. This, presumably, would rule out of court a proposition such as 'the higher the degree of specialization, the higher the centralization'.

organisationally induced increment of rationality in the individual. Instead, the individual has his decisons made 'subject to the influences of the organization group in which he participates'.[4] This is done, Simon says, through the division of labour, standard practices, the authority system, channels of communication, and training and indoctrination. (He might have noted that these are the building blocks of the Weberian model, but March and Simon [1958, pp. 36–7] dismiss the Weberian model in a couple of paragraphs as too mechanical.) The result is that members are made to 'adapt their decisions to the organization's objectives' and they are provided with the information needed to make correct organisational decisions (Simon, 1957, p. 79). The organisation gains, not the individual. It is organisational rationality that is enhanced through such devices as the division of labour. Simon, in his model of organisational decision making, is concerned with the organisation as a tool, or with individuals as tools of the organisation.[5] Barnard could not admit to this possibility, because organisations in his view are cooperative systems where the organisational and the individual objective must coincide. For Simon this is not the case; the individual satisfies his needs (for income, for example) through the organisation, but his personal ends are not necessarily the ends of the organisation.

Given the limits on rationality, what does the individual in fact do when confronted with a choice situation? He constructs a simplified model of the real situation. This 'definition of the situation', as sociologists call it, is built out of past experience (it includes prejudices and stereotypes) and highly particularised, selective views of present stimuli. Most of his responses are 'routine'; he invokes solutions he has used before. Sometimes he must engage in problem solving. When he does so, he conducts a *limited* search for alternatives along familiar and well-worn paths, selecting the first satisfactory one that comes along. He does not examine all possible alternatives nor does he keep searching for the optimum one. He 'satisfices' instead of 'optimizes'. That is, he selects the first satisfactory solution rather than search for the optimum. His very standards for satisfactory solutions are a part of the definition of the situation. They go up and down with positive and negative experience. As solutions are easier to find, the standards are raised; as they are harder to find, the standards fall. *The organisation can control*

---

[4] Simon, *Administrative Behavior*, p. 102. Simon veers more strongly to the view that man becomes rational only through organisations in his *Models of Man* (1956).

[5] 'The behavior of individuals is the tool with which organization achieves its purposes' (Simon, p. 108).

these standards and it defines the situation; only to a limited extent are they up to the individual.[6]

The importance of this assumption about human beings is that it gives to organisational variables (division of labour, communications system, etc.) the predominant control over individual behaviour. This control is so extensive that we can neglect individual behaviour (supposedly the real stuff of organisational life) in all its multiplicity and variability and deal with group or subunit behaviour. It calls for simplifying models of *individual* behaviour in order to capture the complexities of *organisational* behaviour.

THE MODEL OF ORGANISATIONS

What does the Simon model of organisations look like? First, we learn that goals are set by the leaders and then broken down into subgoals at each level of the organisation. Each lower-order goal becomes a means to a higher-order goal. People do not accept these goals because they necessarily share them or believe in them, in contrast to the cooperative model, but because the organisation has mechanisms to ensure that working toward them meets the individual's own* personal values. (These personal values, of course, influence the organisational goal to some extent.) In commercial, governmental, and voluntary organisations, the controlling group of top administrators identifies closely with the objectives of the organisation (Simon, 1957, pp. 120–1); the rest

[6] This is one of the additional reasons . . . that the equilibrium model of inducements and contributions, utilised in both *Administrative Behavior* and *Organizations* is so suspect—the organisation sets the terms of the expectations and thus can manufacture the ratio of inducements to contributions in its own interests. This is noted by Storing (1962), p. 106.

In an effort to defend the rational, economic man view, some critics have pointed out that satisficing behaviour is really maximising behaviour when one takes into account the costs of search. That is, the person who selects the first acceptable alternative is saying, 'there may be a better one, but it will not be so much better as to make up for the cost of additional search'. March and Simon illustrate their satisficing model with the example of looking for a needle in a haystack—you do not search for the sharpest needle, only one sharp enough to sew with. But the example is not apt; no economist (who is supposed to deal only with completely rational man) would argue that you search for the sharpest needle. The real reason why the Simon formulation is so useful is that the costs of search are usually unknown to the individual. He does not know if there is a sharper needle or how long it would take to find it. Therefore, he cannot take into account the cost of search in many cases. At any rate, Simon does not say that all behaviour ignores cost of search, or does not seek maximum solutions, but only that it is impossible to do so all or most of the time.

need not. Once established, the goals remain quite stable because of such things as the high cost of innovative activity, 'sunk cost', and 'sunk assets'. These refer to capital investments which cannot easily be changed (e.g., single purpose machinery in a plant) and to the know-how or knowledge and the goodwill. Regardless of 'wants, motives, and desires' or the dynamics of decision making in individuals, these non-personal aspects stabilise objectives and activities.[7]

Other sources of stability in the organisation stem from the routinisation of activity through the establishment of programmes and standard operating procedures. Changes are introduced only when objectives are clearly not met, and even then the search for new programmes follows well-worn paths, minimising the disruption; the satisficing solution is to select the least disruptive alternatives. Even planning is difficult, for 'daily routine drives out planning' (March and Simon, 1958, p. 185). To plan—and thus change—routines, resources have to be allocated to units which have as their tasks innovation and planning. Another source of change is the deadlines that provoke crises in which programmed activity must be abandoned. March and Simon devote a chapter to planning and innovation, but it is clear that these are only adaptive responses of an organisation, not ends in themselves. Innovation is designed to stabilise the organisation and allow routine to be reestablished or to reappear.

The key to the Simon model of organisations is the concept of organisational structures. March and Simon define this as 'those aspects of the pattern of behavior in the organization that are relatively stable and that change only slowly' (p. 170). Clinging to their psychological predisposition, they argue that the basic features of the structure 'derive from the characteristics of human problem-solving processes and rational human choice' (p. 169). But once we have established that humans do not maximise, but only satisfice, can attend to only a few things at a time, and tend to factor problems into established and familiar dimensions, the attention to the characteristics of human behaviour is not necessary. Because of these limits upon human capacities and the complexity of organisational problems, 'rational behavior calls for simplified models that capture the main features of a problem without capturing all its complexities' (p. 169).

The simplified model can be described as follows, drawing from the two volumes: it calls for satisficing behaviour; sequential and limited search processes that are only mildly innovative; specialisation of activities and roles so that attention is directed to 'a particular restricted set

---

[7] Simon, pp. 66, 95, 120. Simon treats sunk costs at one point as 'mechanisms of behavior-persistence', thus retaining a psychological perspective (p. 95).

of values'; 'attention-directors that channelize behavior'; rules, programmes, and repertories of action that limit choice in recurring situations and prevent an agonising process of optimal decision making at each turn; a restricted range of stimuli and situations that narrow perception; training and indoctrination enabling the individual to 'make decisions, by himself, as the organisation would like him to decide'; and the factoring of goals and tasks into programmes that are semi-independent of each other so as to reduce interdependencies. Most organisational activity takes most of the conditions as given; 'only a few elements of the system are adaptive at any one time'.[8]

The view of authority in this model departs from that of Barnard (cf. Barnard, 1938 (eds)). In March and Simon's view, authority is not bottom-up, emphasising the power of the subordinate to grant authority to the superior or emphasising participation as in the human relations school. Instead, the superior has the power or tools to structure the environment and perceptions of the subordinate in such a way that he sees the proper things and in the proper light. The superior actually appears to give few orders (confirming my own observations in organisations). Instead, he sets priorities ('we had better take care of this first'; 'this is getting out of hand and creating problems, so let's give it more attention until the problems are cleared up') and alters the flow of inputs and stimuli. The image of the order-barking boss is not there, but neither is the image of participative management or of Barnard's soldier deciding whether or not to move forward into battle after receiving the command.

The term 'communication' looms large in this model, but it is not the term that is associated with the platitudes regarding clarity of orders or the authoritativeness of the source or even mechanical discussions of 'information overload' and 'flow charts'. Instead, communication strategies centre around check-points in the channels, the specialisation of channels, the widening and deepening of favoured

[8] For the quoted passages, see Simon, *Administrative Behavior*, pp. 98–103, and March and Simon, *Organizations*, p. 169. One of the most widely cited sections of *Organizations* concerns the authors' models of the theories of Robert Merton, Philip Selznick, and Alvin Gouldner. I find that these models violate the originals in several respects. But more important, most of the factors that are supposed to be 'pathological' processes contributing to the 'dysfunctions' supposedly described by Merton, Gouldner, and Selznick reappear in the second part of the book as functional. The pathologies of limited perspectives and subgroup goals and identification turn out to be necessary for the division of labour and provide means of control. Inattention to the complexities of human actors and their wants and needs proves to be necessary. The surveillance and control features of rules and programmes are no longer self-defeating, but functional and essential.

channels which may bypass key stations inadvertently, the development of organisational vocabularies which screen out some parts of reality and magnify other parts, and the attention-directing, cue-establishing nature of communication techniques.

For example, let us explore March and Simon's concept of 'uncertainty absorption'. An organisation develops a set of concepts influenced by the technical vocabulary and classification schemes; this permits easy communication. Anything that does not fit into these concepts is not easily communicated. For the organisation, 'the particular categories and schemes of classification it employs are reified, and become, for members of the organisation, attributes of the world rather than mere conventions' March and Simon, 1958, p. 165). This is especially apparent when a body of information must be edited and summarised in order to make it fit into the conceptual scheme—to make it understandable. The references from the material rather than the material itself are transmitted. The recipient can disbelieve the 'facts' that are transmitted to him, but he can rarely check their accuracy unless he himself undertakes the summarisation and assessment. This gives personnel who are in direct contact with the information considerable discretion and influence. They 'absorb' quantities of 'uncertainty'.

The most significant examples of uncertainty absorption occur at the boundaries of organisations, where information about the environment is obtained. The selective perception, distortions, omissions, and so on that can occur in a marketing unit are numerous, and there is little that can be done to check this tendency for it is impossible to obtain complete and accurate information. Even the information obtained still leaves much uncertainty because consumer preferences, competitor's actions, disposable income, or the weather may change rapidly. The tendency to tell the boss only what he wants to hear, so well noted in the literature, is probably not as important as the tendency to see things only in terms of the concepts reflected in the organisation's vocabulary. In this way, we can translate an explanation regarding personal predispositions (the subordinate fears to tell the truth) into an organisational explanation ('truth' is an organisationally established frame of reference, independent of courageous or timid members).

Information sources and uncertainty absorption also have a good deal to do with the amount of consensus in organisations, according to the March and Simon model (1958, p. 127). Consensus depends in part upon the number of sources of information that are utilised and the degree to which uncertainty absorption can be centralised into one unit. If there are few sources of information, or if there is only one processing unit, the possibility for divergent subgroup perspectives to develop is reduced. An industrial organisation with only a few customers and a few products would be such an organisation, as would a prison or a mental hospital with a steady supply of inmates and patients and little concern about what happens to them after discharge. But if the mental hospital began to develop extensive links with the environment through social workers, public relations personnel, legislative lobbying activities, and contacts with courts of law enforcement agencies—all in an attempt to improve its services and responsiveness to the community—it could expect divergent views to develop regarding the kind of services needed, the techniques to be used, and the goals to be pursued. Similarly, an industrial organisation with active links to the environment of technological developments, multiple consumer demands, varied suppliers, and personnel sources—all developed to broaden its product base and keep up with changing markets, products, and competitors—could expect internal consensus to decline. This explanation has little to do with the process of choice in individuals, nor, we might add, with the typical explanations of the human relations school. With the decline in consensus, there may well be increased conflict or a decline in the quality of interpersonal relations and organisational goal identification. But poor interpersonal relations and goal identification are not the causes of a decline in consensus or increased conflict; they are the result of multiple sources of communication and an increase in uncertainty absorption, which in turn reduces the chance for consensus.

One important implication of the March and Simon model is that to change individual behaviour you do not have to change individuals, in the sense of altering their personalities or teaching them human relations skills. Instead, you change the premises of their decisions. March and Simon give few examples in their book of concrete problems or instances of organisational behaviour, so it is necessary to fabricate one to illustrate this point. (Although the example is fabricated, the idea was suggested in a conversation with James March.) A common problem in organisation is how does one make a basic change in the perspectives and values of the organisational leaders. To change the perspectives of the individual leaders themselves, is, we know, very difficult. In large organisations it is often difficult to merely replace them since those with sufficient experience and knowledge of the organisation at the next level are likely to share the very perspectives one wishes to change. Going outside the organisation for top management personnel also has its difficulties.

One way, though a slow one, is to change the kind of experiences that will be had by people who will have access to top management

positions. Typically, we might find that the perspectives of top management were shaped by the experiences they had while in the lower
echelons of the organisation and that these experiences were embedded
in conventional career lines. Promotion may have typically been from
line rather than staff positions, sales rather than production, home office
experience rather than field or overseas experience, combat unit assignments rather than political assignments, custodial rather than clinical
experience, large rather than small chapters of a voluntary association.
We should then start promoting rapidly people who have had deviant
rather than conventional career lines. (This is the burden of a percep-
tive analysis of modern military careers by Morris Janowitz, 1960.)

There are costs involved in this strategy, because, up to the time of
the change, those with the most ambition and ability have probably
been following conventional career lines, since that has been the quick-
est way to the top. Therefore, in the short run, some competence
must be sacrificed in order to secure altered perspectives. Those with
experiences that promote the proper perspective must be rapidly, and
quite visibly, promoted, even though they are not the most competent.
In time, the ambitious people with high competence and willingness to
adopt organisational goals as their own will seek these kinds of assignments. In the long run, both proper values and competence will be
found in top management.

Note that this kind of analysis is foreign to the view of leadership
held by Barnard and by the human relations school, and it would find
no place in Weber's theory of bureaucracy or that of the classical school
of management. It is based upon the idea that to shape behaviour, you
have to shape the premises of decision making—in this case through the
use of rewards and sanctions.

Thus, from Simon (1957) we learn that it is the premises of decisions
that are important, rather than the decision-making capabilities of
individuals—once it is established that they are not superhuman. The
organisation does not control the 'process of decision making', as he
says at several points, but the premises for decision making, as he says
only occasionally (pp. xii, 79). These premises are to be found in the
'vocabulary' of the organisation, the structure of communication, rules
and regulations and standard programmes, selection criteria for personnel, and so on—in short, in the structural aspects.

UNOBTRUSIVE CONTROL

But March and Simon are not merely 'structuralists'; their view of
organisations is superior to most sociological views in two respects.

First, in the second part of their book, they strew about insights that have not often been surpassed in organisational theory. Second, by providing a vocabulary or conceptual scheme for discussing control in organisations without relying upon simple-minded views of control, they have enriched analysis. This second point will take some elaboration.

The conventional, structural viewpoint says that rules direct or control behaviour. You tell a man what the rule is and he follows it or is punished. Or, we say that authority is vested in the office, and the commands that issue forth tell people what to do. Coordination is achieved by having one person or group find out what two other groups are doing and direct them to do it in such a way as to make their efforts fit together. Yet, the vast proportion of the activity in organisations goes on without personal directives and supervision—and even without written rules—and sometimes in permitted violation of the rules. We tend to pass over this 'residue', which constitutes perhaps 80 per cent of the behaviour, by invoking general concepts such as habit, training, socialisation, or routine.

March and Simon, however, fill in a good part of that residue by pointing to mechanisms that do not seem to be activated by directives or rules and by describing what these mechanisms do. Involved are such things as uncertainty absorption, organisational vocabularies, programmed tasks, procedural and substantive programmes, standardisation of raw materials, frequency of communication channel usage, interdependencies of units and programmes. Such mechanisms affect organisational behaviour in the following ways: they limit information content and flow, thus controlling the premises available for decisions; they set up expectations so as to highlight some aspects of the situation and play down others; they limit the search for alternatives when problems are confronted, thus ensuring more predictable and consistent solutions; they indicate the threshold levels as to when a danger signal is being emitted (thus reducing the occasions for decision making and promoting satisficing rather than optimising behaviour): they achieve coordination of effort by selecting certain kinds of work techniques and schedules.

Note the extent to which behaviour is shaped, or controlled, without reference to conventional items of rules and commands. In most organisational theory, the discussion of such 'latent' or unobtrusive means of control of behaviour applies primarily to professional roles and their reliance upon professional training, standards, and expectations and to informal group pressures. March and Simon make it very clear that the informal group and the characteristics of professionals are not the only sources of unobtrusive control in organisations. Most of us have neglected to locate and describe these unobtrusive controls, either taking them for granted or relying instead upon very general concepts, such as the division of labour or socialisation, or unobtrusive devices, such as rules or job specifications. By moving back from the actual process of decision making to the premises of decision making, March and Simon have begun to fill in a significant gap surrounding organisational behaviour. I suspect that their social-psychological preoccupation enabled them to do this more easily, but the level of analysis remains a sociological, or structural, one.

Thus, March and Simon join the mainstream of the classical theorists, especially Weber, and augment that stream significantly. The problem with humans in organisations is not just that they may go their own, selfish way, and thus need to be kept in line through such devices as hierarchical control, division of labour, job specifications, impartial and impersonal rules and standards, and so on: the problem is also that there are real limits to human rationality, and thus the premises of decisions and the flow of information upon which decisions are based must be controlled. As a result, organisations need not only the familiar appurtenances of bureaucracy, but also the more subtle and unobtrusive controls of communication channels, organisational vocabulary, and so on. The prospects for spontaneous cooperative activity are dim in this view; what 'cooperation' there is, in Barnard's sense, is engineered. The prospects for participative management are also dim; they are reduced to minor innovations within a complex network of established premises for action. The organisation is not static, by any means, but change is incremental, partial, hit-or-miss, and channelled in the well-worn grooves of established adaptations.

REFERENCES

BARNARD, C. (1938) *The Functions of the Executive*, Harvard University Press.
JANOWITZ, MORRIS (1960) *The Professional Soldier*, New York, Free Press of Glencoe.
MARCH, J. G., and SIMON, H. A. (1958) *Organizations*, Wiley.
SIMON, H. A. (1957) *Administrative Behavior*, 2nd edn, Collier-Macmillan.
SIMON, H. A. (1956) *Models of Man*, Wiley.
STORING, H. J. (1962) 'The science of administration: Herbert A. Simon', in H. J. Storing, ed., *Essays on the Scientific Study of Politics*, Holt, Rinehart & Winston.

19

Kenneth A.
Thompson

Religious organisations:
the cultural perspective

Excerpt from Kenneth A. Thompson, 'The religious organization', in J. McKinlay, ed., *Processing People: case studies in organizational behaviour*, Holt, Rinehart & Winston, 1973.

What is here loosely termed the cultural perspective includes within its purview the symbols and the types of rationality employed by religious bodies in evaluating their organisations. Obviously these factors are important in any organisation, and organisational theory neglects them at its peril, but they are of particular importance in the case of religious organisations for three reasons. Firstly, they are important because religious bodies have a strong ideological character in that they are concerned with the promulgation and propagation of certain values. Secondly, a religious group is always fundamentally a cultural organisation in the sense that the end is achieved, at least in part, in the *process* of meeting with others, while in a utilitarian or instrumental association it is the *product* that is directly significant (Page, 1951). Thirdly, religious groups are probably unique in the extent to which their basic character causes them to favour the rationality of symbolic-appropriateness over one of a logico-experimental type. This last point requires some further elucidation before we go on to examine some examples of sociology of religion research that have explored the relationship and correspondence between religious symbols and models of organisation.

Talcott Parsons' discussion of different criteria of logical action provides some indication as to why religious groups tend to favour the criterion of symbolic-appropriateness over logico-experimental criteria. He points out that the ultimate ends of intrinsic means–end chains of reasoning must have an empirical location, because if the end is transcendental it cannot be said that the means employed are ineffective, but only that there is no criterion for determining logico-experimentally, whether the means are effective or not (Parsons, 1949, p. 256). Logico-experimental criteria can only be applied on the intermediate, temporal level below that of any point of transcendental reference. In religious organisations, however, especially in those of the *ecclesia* and denomination types, extensive accommodation of such intermediate goals and values is always occurring and inviting the charge of 'compromising' with the secular, from dissatisfied groups appealing to transcendental goals and values.

In examining the correspondences between religious symbols and the models of organisation favoured by different religious groups, it is useful to bear in mind this discussion of the relation of transcendental ends to means, and especially to the means–end chain of reasoning. As Parsons (1949) explains:

> There seem to be two logical possibilities. First, a given transcendental end, like eternal salvation, may be held by the actor to imply one or more ultimate empirical ends as a necessary means to it . . . [But] the 'theory' cannot be entirely logico-experimental, since one element at least, the transcendental end itself, is not observable even after the action. Hence not only, as in the case of an ultimate empirical end, is the end itself given, but the link between the last empirical link in the means–end chain and the ultimate transcendental end is nonlogical, since a scientifically verifiable theory can establish an intrinsic relation only between entities both of which are observable (pp. 257–8).

Thus the setting of a compromise, temporal and empirical goal by church executives facilitates the adoption of formally rational organisation, and can be tested by logico-experimental criteria.[1] But the empirical goal itself cannot be evaluated in its relation to the transcendental goals by a similar means-end chain of reasoning. However, Parsons does suggest a second logical possibility for relating transcendental ends to means:

> 'Secondly, a transcendental end may be pursued directly without the intervention of an empirical end and an intrinsic means–end

---

[1] An example of such an interposed empirical goal would be that of the Ecclesiastical Commissioners in the nineteenth century Church of England, who had the express purpose of strengthening the parochial unit as an agent of social control and stability. *Cf.* Thompson (1970), chapter 3.

chain leading up to it. In so far the means–end relation cannot by definition be intrinsically rational. The question then arises whether it is merely arbitrary or there is a selective standard of the choice of means involved . . . there is at least one alternative selective standard, what has been called the symbolic. The term the 'symbolic means – end relationship' will be used whenever the relation of means and ends can conveniently be interpreted by the observer as involving a standard of selection of means according to 'symbolic appropriateness' that is, a standard of the order of the relation of symbol and meaning, not of cause and effect (*ibid.*).

There are two possibilities, therefore, for logically evaluating the relation between transcendental ends and the means employed in a religious organisation. They are illustrated in the criticisms which church members often level at their religious organisations for becoming 'bureaucratic' (in the derogatory sense). On the one hand, they are often criticisms of the empirical goals that have been adopted, and on the other hand they can be a sweeping condemnation of the symbolic-inappropriateness of the organisational form as judged by particular theological ideals about organisation.

An example of these two sources of evaluation—the interposed empirical goal and symbolic-appropriateness—can be found in a discussion by F. W. Dillistone (1951) of the reasons for the preference that many modern Christians have for the 'organic' model of organisation:

'Thus at a time when there is much dissatisfaction with over-specialisation it is natural for men to turn back nostalgically to the middle ages when society seems to have been remarkably integrated and when every section seems to have found its own particular function to fulfil within the life of the unified whole. To these two attractions of a general kind must be added the particular fascination which this view holds for the Christian because of its relation to the New Testament conception of the Body, Divinely originated and sustained, then organic structures and categories must be of peculiar importance to Christian theologians and sociologists (p. 169).[2]

There has been little empirical research in the sociology of religion that has dealt explicitly with the correspondences between certain religious symbols and the models of organisation favoured by religious

[2] The interposed empirical goals here are social integration and cooperation, and symbolic appropriateness lies in the congruence between the organic model of organisation and the New Testament conception of the Body.

groups. However, it is possible to make some theoretical connections between the two sets of data that do exist—that on religious symbols and theology, and that on models and theories of organisation. Two typologies of a symbolic type have been offered by Paul S. Minear and H. Richard Niebuhr. Minear (1961) has provided a selection of the main images of the Church in the New Testament, each of which emphasise a particular dimension that has been favoured by a religious group at some time. They are: (1) the People of God (stressing the historical dimension); (2) the New Creation (stress on the cosmic dimension); (3) the Fellowship in the Faith (emphasising the personal factor); (4) the Body of Christ (which favours the corporate dimension, as we have seen). A second typology can be derived from Niebuhr's (1952) discussion of different perceptions of the mission of Christ in the World. These are: (a) Christ against culture; (b) Christ the fulfilment of culture; (c) Christ above culture; (d) Christ and culture co-exist; (e) Christ the transformer of culture.

Peter F. Rudge, an Australian priest and student of ecclesiastical administration, is one of the few practitioners in the field of the sociology of religious organisations to attempt to systematically relate such typologies to a corresponding set of theories and models of organisation. Rudge (1968) maintains that it is possible to transpose some of the main points of sociological theories and models of organisation into their theological counterparts. For example: conception of the organisation would correspond to theology of the church, function of the leader to theology of the ministry, estimate of man to theology of man, and relation of the organisation to the environment corresponds to theology of the church in society.

A typology of five major theories of leadership and organisation can be constructed from current literature on the subject. They are: the Traditional, Charismatic, Classical (bureaucratic or mechanistic), Human Relations, and Systemic (or organic). The typology is a conflation of two sets of theories. The traditional, charismatic and classical positions are basically those developed by Max Weber in his discussion of the typical forms of administration that accompany the three main types of legitimate authority—traditional, charismatic, and rational–legal. The human relations and systemic theories have been largely developed in industrial management theory (which has also further developed Weber's classical bureaucratic theory).[3]

[3] There are obviously certain objections that can be levelled at a typology that is derived from such divergent sources, especially as Weber's categories were ideal types drawn from a wide range of social institutions, whereas management theory has a practical basis and has centred mainly on profit-

The traditional theory rests on Weber's (1947, p. 341) definition, according to which a system of imperative authority is called 'traditional' if legitimacy is claimed for it and believed in on the basis of the sanctity of the order and the attendant powers of control as they have been handed down from the past, and have always existed. He distinguished three sub-types of administration: gerontocracy, patriarchalism and patrimonialism. The characteristics of this type of organisation that have significance for organisation studies are its methods of recruitment—loyalty to a chief, favouritism and depotism; and its methods of remuneration—maintenance within the household, allowance in kind, the right to use resources in return for services, appropriation of specific incomes or fees and the granting of benefices.

The charismatic type of authority derives from 'a certain quality of an individual personality by virtue of which he is set apart from ordinary men and treated as endowed with supernatural, superhuman, or at least specifically exceptional powers or qualities' (Weber, 1947, pp. 358–9). The form of organisation that attaches to such an authority is best typified by the band of disciples. The charismatic leader seems to be engaged in pursuing an intuition, and operates independently of any constituted office. There is a certain degree of randomness and unpredictability compared with the stability of traditional organisation.

The classical theory of organisation derives from Weber's description of the process by which charismatic and traditional sources of authority were steadily giving way to rational–legal authority in the modern world. He believed that modern, Western organisation could be characterised as possessing legal authority with a bureaucratic administration; it involved the exercise of control by the occupants of legally sanctioned offices on the basis of factual knowledge, which gave it the dual nature of rational-legal authority. An organisation administered on such lines is committed to striving for technical efficiency, precision of operation, control of experts, speed, continuity of policy, and an optimal return for the labour and money expended.

Human relations theory emphasises the personal element in organisations over against the rather mechanistic picture of organisations suggested by classical theory. It also focuses on informal relations rather than the formal structure of organisation. Its founder was Elton Mayo

making firms. A more fundamental criticism, as we will see (and Rudge admits this), is that the typology might mask quite different or alternative approaches to the study of organisations, such as that which considers power to be the main focus for understanding an organisation, in contrast to a concern with personal relationships, or the interrelation of task and environment.

and the Hawthorne Experiments of the 1930s (Roethlisberger and Dickson, 1939). It directed attention to small group relationships, informal norms and sanctions, participative decision-making, and group dynamics in general. In some aspects it represents the influence of democratic theory on administration.

In terms of relationships between superior and subordinate, the classical and human relations theories may be regarded either as dichotomous, or simply as representing opposite ends of a continuum.[4] Warren G. Bennis (1959, pp. 259–301) has characterised the two extremes as 'organizations without people' and 'people without organizations'. As far as proponents of systemic theory are concerned, both classical and human relations theories go astray in focusing their attention on the internal relationship between superior and subordinate as the major determinant of organisational health. The systemic theory concentrates on adaptation of an organisation to a fast-changing environment. Whereas classical theory produces a model of organisation designed for mass, homogeneous, and stable conditions, systemic theory lies at the other end of the continuum, favouring complete flexibility and innovation.[5]

Despite its original derivation from the organic analogy, systemic theory owes its present popularity to the influence of cybernetics on modern thought. In the computer system there is a built-in self-regulating device (a 'homeostat') by means of which the appropriate interaction with the environment is achieved in relation to the goals that are set. The computer makes the decision; but it cannot itself provide the goals nor acquire the information about the outside world. Transposed into managerial terms, the system within which the decisions are made is the organisation; the task of management is to interpret the environment to the organisation and to set its goals, and then to facilitate the decision-making process within the whole system so that there is a continuing and instantaneous rapport with the external world and a consistent focus on the purpose of the organisation (Beer, 1959).

Rudge suggests that correspondences can be found between these theories and models of organisation and the symbols and models of theology. Thus, Minear's selection of images of the Church in the New Testament seems to correspond at some points with at least four of the

[4] For an analysis of the two theories in terms of a dichotomy, see McGregor (1960), pp. 33–7. Rensis Lickert sees them as part of a continuum that can be further subdivided, e.g. exploitive/authoritative type—benevolent/authoritative—consultative—participative (Lickert, 1961, pp. 223–33).

[5] *Cf.* Burns and Stalker (1961) for a detailed analysis of the two ideal types of organisation at opposite ends of the flexibility dimension.

theories of organisation. The image of the People of God corresponds to the traditional theory of organisation; the image of the New Creation corresponds to the charismatic theory; the image of the Fellowship in the Faith corresponds to human relations theory; the image of the Body of Christ corresponds to the systemic theory. It is interesting to note that no New Testament image corresponds to the classical theory with its emphasis on formal rationality, specialised division of labour, and relationships based on observance of written rules.[6] We will see later that this has important repercussions on clergy attitudes towards certain developments in denominational organisation, especially where a bureaucratic definition of their role fails to correspond to any theology of ministry that is symbolically-appropriate by reason of its congruence with one of these images of the Church.

These suggestions for a systematic analysis of the different modes of perceiving and evaluating religious organisations (the cultural perspective) could eventually be combined with insights gained from the developmental perspective and the political dimension to provide a general theory of religious organisation. Thus developmental sequences along the church-sect continuum might correspond to changes in the mode of perceiving and evaluating the organisation in some determinate way. A likely hypothesis that could be deduced is that the charismatic type of organisation would fit most closely the cult. Some sects would also fit this type of organisation, although 'established' sects,[7] especially, might begin to combine elements of the human relations model (particularly those with a largely middle-class membership).

The denomination increasingly takes on the characteristics found in the classical bureaucratic type of organisation, although the sect-

[6] A similar correspondence can be found between Niebuhr's list of the different perceptions of the mission of Christ in relation to culture and the theories of organisation. Christ against culture corresponds to Charismatic theory; Christ the fulfilment of culture corresponds to human relations theory; the Christ of culture, or above culture (Christ enters in from above and culture then enshrines and is enriched by the supernatural) corresponds to traditional theory; Christ the transformer of culture corresponds to systemic theory (the Church adapts in order to transform society). In this case, however, there is an image that corresponds to classical theory, and that is Christ and culture co-existing—a duality in effect. Holders of this last position would tend to exclude the criterion of symbolic appropriateness in evaluating the functioning of some branches of ecclesiastical administration.

[7] An established or institutionalised sect is one which has come to terms with its societal setting—it is organised on a wider and continuing basis, and has achieved some respectability and power—but it still maintains a conflict with some of the prevailing attitudes.

originated, and the denomination with a more democratic (or congregationalist) ecclesiology, are more likely to include elements of the theory and practice of the human relations type. The *ecclesia* will tend to exhibit a traditional type of organisation. The systemic, or organic, type of organisation is largely a theoretical ideal in that it seeks to transcend such dichotomies as arise between the human relations approach to organisation (maximum involvement of all members in decision-making) and the other three approaches (which represent different attempts to specialise decision-making), and the theological dichotomies between parity of all believers and specialised ministries. Despite its idealist nature, however, it plays an important role in many religious reform movements.[8]

Most sociologists who have studied religious organisations have concentrated on tracing developments along a simplified version of this typology. They have used Ferdinand Tönnies distinction between *Gemeinschaft* and *Gesellschaft* types of organisation (Tönnies, 1953). These correspond roughly to the traditional and classical bureaucratic types respectively. The former refers to the natural community based on personal and diffuse ties; the latter is a rationally constructed organisation based on contractual relationships. E. K. Francis (1950, pp. 437–449) has examined the development of religious orders in terms of this typology and showed that the familial, *Gemeinschaft* character of early monosticism had gradually given way to highly rationalised orders of a *Gesellschaft* type. A Catholic sociologist, Andrew M. Greeley (1966), has summarised recent development in that Church as a movement from *Gemeinschaft* to *Gesellschaft*, and contends that just as the Catholic Church is getting something of a late start in its transition into the modern world, it will travel the road much more quickly than most other institutions. According to Greeley, it will tend to evolve much more quickly the post-*Gesellschaft* forms which modern man seeks in order to maintain some of the advantages and supports of

---

[8] The attraction of the systemic or organic model, as we have seen in the statement by Dillistone, lies in the fact that it seems to achieve a successful combination of the otherwise divergent sets of criteria—calculable efficiency in attaining empirical goals, and symbolic appropriateness. Unfortunately it ignores one of the main sources of conflict in religious organisation, which is the fact that religious symbols cannot in practice be broken down very easily into specifiable, empirical conditions without generating controversy. The reason for this has been given by Paul Tillich (1966): 'Religious symbols are distinguished from others by the fact that they are a representation of that which is unconditionally beyond the conceptual sphere; they point to the ultimate reality implied in the religious act, to that which concerns us ultimately' (p. 17).

Gemeinschaft society in a *Gesellschaft* world. Greeley seems to be predicting that the modern Church will quickly move beyond the rigidities of the classical bureaucratic type of organisation so typical of other modern organisations, and eventually combine the best of both the human relations and systemic models. It is his belief that modern man looks to the Church to provide the advantages of both *Gemeinschaft* and *Gesellschaft*:

> He wishes to enjoy warm, intimate support of *Gemeinschaft* at the same time as he enjoys the freedom, and rationality, and the technological flexibility of a *Gesellschaft* world. Modern man wishes to put aside irrelevant myths and the obsolescent sacred symbols of the past but only so he might devise relevant and exciting new sacred symbols. Modern man wishes to put aside the primary groups in which his grandfathers were imprisoned and replace them with primary groups which enable him to enjoy even greater personal development and freedom. Modern man wants Community in the midst of his Associations (p. 125).

Although this statement comes from a sociologist, nothing could better illustrate our earlier observation that symbols are formative and determinative forces no less powerful than the operational forces in religious organisations. Although we need more studies of the structure and functioning of religious organisations along the lines laid down by the various organisation theories, we should also pay more attention to the fact that organisations are judged not only for their efficiency, but also for their symbolic appropriateness. Such considerations are essential for making sense of the bitter conflict that often seems to accompany attempts to change even quite minor parts of a religious organisation. To take one example, the century of bitter party strife that ensued when the Church of England began reforming its organisation in the 1830s is only explicable when it is shown that reforms were evaluated not just in efficiency terms, but also for their symbolic appropriateness. It soon becomes clear that the symbols employed by the different church parties reflected their concern for different system problems (such as co-existence with the State to preserve the Establishment, or restoration of autonomous theological principles), and so it was not surprising that their evaluations of the reforms differed so widely.[9]

[9] *Cf.* Thompson (1970) chapter 2, for a discussion of the symbols favoured by the different church parties, and the correspondences between the symbols and the main system problems with which the various parties were concerned.

REFERENCES

BENNIS, W. G. (1959) 'Leadership theory and administrative behaviour: the problem of authority', *Administrative Science Quarterly*, **4**, no. 3, December, 259–301.

BEER, STAFFORD (1959) *Cybernetics and Management*, English Universities Press.

BURNS, T., and STALKER, G. M. (1961) *The Management of Innovation*, Tavistock.

DILLISTONE, F. W. (1951) *The Structure of the Divine Society*, Lutterworth Press.

FRANCIS, E. K. (1950) 'Toward a typology of religious orders', *American Journal of Sociology*, **55**, no. 5, March, 437–49.

GREELEY, A. M. (1966) 'After secularity: the neo-Gemeinschaft society: a post-Christian postscript', in *Sociological Analysis*, **27**, no. 3, 119–27.

LIKERT, R. (1961) *New Patterns of Management*, McGraw-Hill.

MCGREGOR, DOUGLAS (1960) *The Human Side of Enterprise*, McGraw-Hill.

MINEAR, P. S. (1961) *Images of the Church in the New Testament*, Lutterworth Press.

NIEBUHR, H. R. (1952) *Christ and Culture*, Faber.

PAGE, C. H. (1951) 'Bureaucracy and the Liberal Church', *The Review of Religion*, **16**, nos. 3–4, 137–50.

PARSONS, TALCOTT (1949) *The Structure of Social Action*, New York, Free Press of Glencoe.

ROETHLISBERGER, F. J., and DICKSON, W. J. (1939) *Management and the Worker*, Harvard University Press.

RUDGE, P. F. (1968) *Ministry and Management*, Tavistock.

THOMPSON, K. A. (1970) *Bureaucracy and Church Reform*, Oxford, The Clarendon Press.

TILLICH, PAUL (1966) 'The religious symbol', in F. W. Dillistone, ed., *Myth and Symbol*, London, S.P.C.K.

TÖNNIES, FERDINAND (1955) *Community and Association: Gemeinschaft und Gesellschaft*, trans. and supplemented by C. P. Loomis, Routledge & Kegan Paul.

WEBER, MAX (1947) *Theory of Social and Economic Organization*, trans. Talcott Parsons and A. M. Henderson, Oxford University Press.

20

**A. Strauss,
L. Schatzman,
D. Ehrlich,
R. Bucher and
M. Sabshin**

The hospital and its negotiated order

Excerpts from A. Strauss *et al.*, 'The hospital and its negotiated order', in E. Friedson, ed., *The Hospital in Modern Society*, New York, Macmillan, 1963, pp. 147–69.

INTRODUCTION

In the pages to follow, a model for studying hospitals will be sketched, along with some suggested virtues of the model. It grew out of the authors' research, which was done on the premises of two psychiatric hospitals. The reader must judge for himself whether a model possibly suited to studying psychiatric hospitals might equally well guide the study of other kinds of hospitals. We believe that it can, and shall indicate why at the close of our presentation; indeed, we shall argue its usefulness for investigating other organisations besides hospitals.

Our model bears upon that most central of sociological problems, namely, how a measure of order is maintained in the face of inevitable changes (derivable from sources both external and internal to the organisation). Students of formal organisation tend to underplay the processes of internal change as well as overestimate the more stable features of organisations—including its rules and its hierarchical statuses. We ourselves take our cue from Mead (1936), who some years ago, when arguing for orderly and directed social change, remarked that the task turns about relationships between change and order:

> How can you bring those changes about in an orderly fashion and yet preserve order? To bring about change is seemingly to destroy the given order, and yet society does and must change. That is the problem, to incorporate the method of change into the order of society itself.

Without Mead's melioristic concerns, one can yet assume that order is something at which members of any society, any organisation must work. For the shared agreements, the binding contracts—which constitute the grounds for an expectable, non-surprising, taken-for-granted, even ruled orderliness—are not binding and shared for all time. Contracts, understandings, agreements, rules—all have appended to them a temporal clause. That clause may or may not be explicitly discussed by the contracting parties, and the terminal date of the agreement may or may not be made specific, but none can be binding forever—even if the parties believe it so, unforeseen consequences of acting on the agreements would force eventual confrontation. Review is called for, whether the outcome of review be rejection or renewal or revision, or what not. In short, the bases of concerted action (social order) must be reconstituted continually; or, as remarked above, 'worked at'.

Such considerations have led us to emphasise the importance of negotiation—the processes of give-and-take, of diplomacy, of bargaining —which characterises organisational life. In the pages to follow, we shall note first the relationship of rules to negotiation, then discuss the grounds for negotiation. Then, since both the clients and much of the personnel of hospitals are laymen, we wish also to underscore the participation of those laymen in the hospital's negotiative processes. Thereafter we shall note certain patterned and temporal features of negotiation; then we shall draw together some implications for viewing social order. A general summary of the argument and its implications will round out the paper.

A PSYCHIATRIC HOSPITAL

Before discussing negotiation in hospitals, it will help to indicate two things: first, what was engaging our attention when research was initiated; and, second, the general characteristics of the hospital that was studied.[1] At the outset of our investigation, three foci were especially pertinent. The first was an explicit concern with the professional careers of the personnel: Who was there? Where did they come from? Where did they think they were going in work and career? What were they doing at this particular hospital? What was happening to them at this place? A second concern was with psychiatric ideology: Were different ideologies represented on the floors of this hospital? What were these ideologies? Did people clearly recognise their existence as well as did their more articulate advocates? And anyway, what difference did these

[1] Two psychiatric hospitals were studied, but only one will be discussed here, namely the psychiatric wing of Michael Reese Hospital in Chicago.

philosophies make in the lives and work of various personnel? A third focus consisted of the realisation that a hospital is par excellence an institution captained and maintained principally by professionals. This fact implied that the nonprofessionals who worked there, as well as those nonprofessionals there as patients, must manage to make their respective ways within this professionalised establishment. How, then, do they do this—and vice versa, how do the professionals incorporate the nonprofessionals into their own schemes of work and aspiration? These directions of interest, and the questions raised in consequence, quickly led us to perceive hospitals in terms to be depicted below.

A PROFESSIONALISED LOCALE

A hospital can be visualised as a professionalised locale—a geographical site where persons drawn from different professions come together to carry out their respective purposes. At our specific hospital, the professionals consisted of numerous practising psychiatrists and psychiatric residents, nurses and nursing students, psychologists, occupational therapists, and one lone social worker. Each professional echelon has received noticeably different kinds of training and, speaking conventionally, each occupies some differential hierarchical position at the hospital while playing a different part in its total division of labour.

But that last sentence requires elaboration and emendation. The persons within each professional group may be, and probably are, at different stages in their respective careers. Furthermore, the career lines of some may be quite different from those of their colleagues: thus some of our psychiatrists were just entering upon psychoanalytic training, but some had entered the medical speciality by way of neurology, and had dual neurological-psychiatric practices. Implicit in the preceding statement is that those who belong to the same profession also may differ quite measurably in the training they have received, as well as in the theoretical (or ideological) positions they take toward important issues like etiology and treatment. Finally, the hospital itself may possess differential significance for colleagues: for instance, some psychiatrists were engaged in hospital practice only until such time as their office practices had been sufficiently well established; while other, usually older, psychiatrists were committed wholeheartedly to working with hospitalised patients.

Looking next at the division of labour shared by the professionals: never do all persons of each echelon work closely with all others from other echelons. At our hospital it was notable that considerable variability characterised who worked closely with whom—and how—

depending upon such matters as ideological and hierarchical position. Thus the services of the social worker were used not at all by some psychiatrists, while each man who utilised her services did so somewhat differently. Similarly some men utilised 'psychologicals' more than did others. Similarly, some psychiatrists were successful in housing their patients almost exclusively in certain wards, which meant that, wittingly or not, they worked only with certain nurses. As in other institutions, the various echelons possessed differential status and power, but again there were marked internal differences concerning status and power, as well as knowledgeability about 'getting things done'. Nor must it be overlooked that not only did the different professions hold measurably different views—derived both from professional and status positions— about the proper division of labour; but different views also obtained within each echelon. (The views were most discrepant among the psychiatrists.) All in all, the division of labour is a complex concept, and at hospitals must be seen in relation to the professionalised milieu.

RULED AND UNRULED BEHAVIOUR

The rules that govern the actions of various professionals, as they perform their tasks, are far from extensive, or clearly stated or clearly binding. This fact leads to necessary and continual negotiation. It will be worth deferring discussions of negotiation *per se* until we have explored some relationships between rules and negotiation, at least as found in our hospital; for the topic of rules is a complicated one.

In Michael Reese, as unquestionably in most sizeable establishments, hardly anyone knows all the extant rules, much less exactly what situations they apply to, for whom, and with what sanctions. If this would not otherwise be so in our hospital, it would be true anyway because of the considerable turnover of nursing staff. Also noticeable—to us as observers—was that some rules once promulgated would fall into disuse, or would periodically receive administrative reiteration after the staff had either ignored those rules or forgotten them. As one head nurse said, 'I wish they would write them all down sometimes'—but said so smilingly. The plain fact is that staff kept forgetting not only the rules received from above but also some rules that they themselves had agreed upon 'for this ward'. Hence we would observe that periodically the same informal ward rules would be agreed upon, enforced for a short time, and then be forgotten until another ward crisis would elicit their innovation all over again.

As in other establishments, personnel called upon certain rules to obtain what they themselves wished. Thus the nurses frequently acted as virtual guardians of the hospital against some demands of certain attending physicians, calling upon the resources of 'the rules of the hospital' in countering the physicians' demands. As in other hospital settings, the physicians were only too aware of this game, and accused the nurses from time to time of more interest in their own welfare than in that of the patients. (The only difference, we suspect, between the accusatory language of psychiatrists and that of internists or surgeons is that the psychiatrists have a trained capacity to utilise specialised terms like 'rigid' and 'overcompulsive'.) In so dredging up the rules at convenient moments, the staff of course is acting identically with personnel in other kinds of institutions.

As elsewhere, too, all categories of personnel are adept at breaking the rules when it suits convenience or when warrantable exigencies arise. Stretching the rules is only a further variant of this tactic, which itself is less attributable to human nature than to an honest desire to get things accomplished as they ought, properly, to get done.[2] Of course, respective parties must strike bargains for these actions to occur.

In addition, at the very top of the administrative structure, a tolerant stance is taken both toward extensiveness of rules and laxity of rules. The point can be illustrated by a conversation with the administrative head, who recounted with amusement how some members of his original house staff wished to have all rules set down in a house rule book, but he had staved off this codification. As will be noted more fully later, the administrative attitude is affected also by a profound belief that care of patients calls for a minimum of hard and fast rules and a maximum of innovation and improvisation. In addition, in this hospital, as certainly in most others, the multiplicity of medical purpose and theory, as well as of personal investment, are openly recognised: too rigid a set of rules would only cause turmoil and affect the hospital's over-all efficiency.

Finally, it is notable that the hospital must confront the realities of the attending negotiations with patients and their families—negotiations carried out beyond the physical confines of the hospital itself. Too many or too rigid rules would restrict the medical entrepreneurs' negotiation. To some degree any hospital with attending men has to give this kind of leeway (indeed, the precise degree is a source of tension in these kinds of hospitals).

Hence, the area of action covered directly by clearly enunciated rules is really very small. As observers, we began to become aware of this when, within a few days, we discovered that only a few very general

[2] Dalton's book (1959) is crammed with such instances. See especially pp. 104-7.

rules obtained for the placement of new patients within the hospital. Those rules, which are clearly enunciated and generally followed, can, for our purposes, be regarded as long-standing shared understandings among the personnel. Except for a few legal rules, which stem from state and professional prescription, and for some rulings pertaining to all of Michael Reese Hospital, almost all these house rules are much less like commands, and much more like general understandings: not even their punishments are spelled out; and mostly they can be stretched, negotiated, argued, as well as ignored or applied at convenient moments. Hospital rules seem to us frequently less explicit than tacit, probably as much breached and stretched as honoured, and administrative effort is made to keep their number small. In addition, rules here as elsewhere fail to be universal prescriptions: they always require judgment concerning their applicability to the specific case. Does it apply here? To whom? In what degree? For how long? With what sanctions? The personnel cannot give universal answers; they can only point to past analogous instances when confronted with situations or give 'for instance' answers, when queried about a rule's future application.

THE GROUNDS FOR NEGOTIATION

Negotiation and the division of labour are rendered all the more complex because personnel in our hospital—we assume that the generalisation, with some modification, holds elsewhere—share only a single, vaguely ambiguous goal. The goal is to return patients to the outside world in better shape. This goal is the symbolic cement that, metaphorically speaking, holds the organisation together: the symbol to which all personnel can comfortably and frequently point—with the assurance that *at least* about this matter everyone can agree! Although this symbol, as will be seen later, masks a considerable measure of disagreement and discrepant purpose, it represents a generalised mandate under which the hospital can be run—the public flag under which all may work in concert. Let us term it the institution's constitutional grounds or basic compact. These grounds, this compact, are never openly challenged; nor are any other goals given explicit verbal precedence. (This is so when a hospital, such as ours, also is a training institution.) In addition, these constitutional grounds can be used by any and all personnel as a justificatory rationale for actions that are under attack. In short, although personnel may disagree to the point of apoplexy about how to implement patients' getting better, they do share the common institutional value.

The problem, of course, is that when the personnel confront a specific patient and attempt to make him recover, then the disagreements flare up—the generalised mandate helps not at all to handle the specific issues—and a complicated process of negotiation, of bargaining, of give-and-take necessarily begins. The disagreements that necessitate negotiation do not occur by chance, but are patterned. Here are several illustrations of the grounds that lead to negotiation. Thus, the personnel may disagree over what is the proper placement within the hospital for some patient; believing that, at any given time, he is more likely to improve when placed in one ward rather than in another. This issue is the source of considerable tension between physicians and ward personnel. Again, what is meant by 'getting better' is itself open to differential judgment when applied to the progress—or retrogression— of a particular patient. This judgment is influenced not only by professional experience and acquaintance with the patient but is also influenced by the very concept of getting better as held by the different echelons. Thus the aides—who are laymen—have quite different notions about these matters than do the physicians, and on the whole those notions are not quite equivalent to those held by nurses. But both the nurses and the aides see patients getting better according to signs visible from the patient's daily behaviour, while the psychiatrist tends to relate these signs, if apprehended at all, to deeper layers of personality; with the consequence that frequently the staff thinks one way about the patient's 'movement' while the physician thinks quite otherwise, and must argue his case, set them right, or even keep his peace.

To turn now to another set of conditions for negotiation: the very mode of treatment selected by the physician is profoundly related to his own psychiatric ideology. For instance, it makes a difference whether the physician is neurologically trained, thus somatically oriented, or whether he is psychotherapeutically trained and oriented. The former type of physician will prescribe more drugs, engage in far more electric shock therapy, and spend much less time with each patient. On occasion the diagnosis and treatment of a given patient runs against the judgment of the nurses and aides, who may not go along with the physician's directives, who may or may not disagree openly. They may subvert his therapeutic programme by one of their own. They may choose to argue the matter. They may go over his head to an administrative officer. Indeed, they have many choices of action—each requiring negotiative behaviour. In truth, while physicians are able to command considerable obedience to their directives at this particular hospital, frequently they must work hard at obtaining cooperation in their programming. The task is rendered all the more difficult because they, as professionals, see matters in certain lights, while the aides, as laymen, may judge matters quite differently—on moral rather than on strictly psychiatric grounds, for instance.

If negotiation is called for because a generalised mandate requires implementaton, it is also called for because of the multiplicity of purpose found in the hospital. It is incontestable that each professional group has a different set of reasons for working at this hospital (to begin with, most nurses are women, most physicians are men); and of course colleagues inevitably differ among themselves on certain of their purposes for working there. In addition, each professional develops there his own specific and temporarily limited ends that he wishes to attain. All this diversity of purpose affects the institution's division of labour, including not only what tasks each person is expected to accomplish but also how he manœuvres to get them accomplished. Since very little of this can possibly be prefigured by the administrative rule-makers, the attainment of one's purposes requires inevitably the cooperation of fellow workers. This point, once made, scarcely needs illustration.

However, yet another ground of negotiation needs emphasising: namely, that in this hospital, as doubtless elsewhere, the patient as an 'individual case' is taken as a virtual article of faith. By this we mean that the element of medical uncertainty is so great, and each patient is taken as—in some sense—so unique, that action round and about him must be tailor-made, must be suited to his precise therapeutic requirements. This kind of assumption abets what would occur anyhow: that only a minimum of rules can be laid down for running a hospital, since a huge area of contingency necessarily lies outside those rules. The rules can provide guidance and command for only a small amount of the total concerted action that must go on around the patient. It follows, as already noted that where action is not ruled it must be agreed upon.

One important further condititon for negotiation should be mentioned. Changes are forced upon the hospital and its staff not only by forces external to the hospital but also by unforeseen consequences of internal policies and negotiations carried on within the hospital. In short, negotiations breed further negotiations.

LAY PERSONNEL AND NEGOTIATED ORDER

Before turning to certain important features of negotiation, we shall first discuss the impact of laymen—both personnel and patients— upon the hospital's negotiated order. A special feature of most hospitals is that, although administered and controlled by professionals, they also include among their personnel considerable numbers of non-professionals. This they must, for only in the most affluent establishments could floors be staffed wholly with professionals. The non-professionals set special problems for the establishment and maintenance of orderly medical process.

To suggest how subtle and profound may be the lay influence, we give the following illustration as it bears upon negotiated order. The illustration pertains to the central value of our hospital: returning patients to the outside world in better shape than when they entered. Like everyone else, the aides subscribe to this institutional goal. A host of communications, directed at them, inform them that they too are important in 'helping patients get better'. Yet none of the professionals ascribe an unduly important role to the aides: in the main, aides are considered quite secondary to the therapeutic process. The aides do not agree. They do not contest the point, because in fact the point does not arise explicitly: yet our own inquiry left no doubt that most aides conceive of themselves as the principal agent for bringing about improvement in most patients. The grounds of their belief, in capsule form, are as follows.

Working extensively with or near the patients, they are more likely than other personnel to see patients acting in a variety of situations and ways. The aides reason, with some truth, that they themselves are more likely to be the recipients of patients' conversations and even confidences, because of frequent and intimate contact. They reason, with common sense, that no one else can know most of the patients as well as do the aides. ('I always know more than the nurses and the doctors. We are with the patients almost eight hours, whereas the nurses and doctors don't come in. The nurse reads the charts and passes the medicine'). With due respect to the best nurses—and some are greatly admired—nurses are too busy with their administrative work; and lazy ones just never leave the office! As for the physicians: not only do they make evident mistakes with their patients, and spend scarcely any time with them, but they must even call upon the nurses and aides for information about their patients.

Actually, aides have no difficulty in comprehending that they themselves cannot give shock treatment—only the physicians know how to do that—but we found that our aides could not, with few exceptions, make a clear distinction between what the doctor does when he helps the patient 'by talking' and what they themselves do when they talk with him. Even the aides who have worked most closely with head nurses do not really comprehend that a substantial difference exists between talking and psychotherapy. Hence aides believe that everyone may contribute toward patients' improvement, by acting right toward them and talking properly with them. The most that aides will admit is: 'Sometimes the patients will really talk more about their problems with the doctor than they will with us. Sometimes it's vice versa.' But on the whole those who talk most with patients are the aides.

It does not take much imagination to anticipate what this view of the division of labour implies for the aides' handling of patients. However frequently the aides may attend staff meetings, however frequently they listen to psychiatrists talk about the problems of patients and how to handle patients, they end by perceiving patients in nonpsychiatric (nontechnical) terms and use their own kinds of tactics with patients. Aides guide themselves by many common-sense maxims, and are articulate about these when questioned about how they work with patients. The professional staff generally regards good aides as being very 'intuitive' with patients; but aides are probably no more intuitive than anyone else; it is that their reasoning is less professionalised. Lest this seem to be a characterisation of psychiatric aides alone, we hasten to add that aides on medical services seem to us to think and operate in similar ways.

Turning briefly now to how these nonprofessionals affect the processes of negotiation, one may begin by stating that, like anyone else, they wish to control the conditions of their work as much as possible. Of course, they must negotiate to make that possible: they must stake claims and counterdemands; they must engage in games of give-and-take. Among the prizes are: where one will work, the colleagues with whom one will share tasks, the superiors under whom one will work, and the kinds of patients with whom one will deal. Illustrating from one area only, that of controlling superiors: aides have various means of such control. These include withholding information and displaying varying degrees of cooperativeness in charting or in attending meetings. Aides also are implicated, as are the nurses, in negotiations with the physicians—except that the head nurse tends to carry on the necessary face-to-face bargaining. Since aides have their own notions about how specific patients should be handled and helped, they may negotiate also with the nurses in order to implement those notions. Nurses and physicians, in their turn, need to transact negotiations with the aides: while the physicians usually work through the head nurse, on occasion they may deal directly with an aide. In any event, professionals and nonprofessionals are implicated together in a great web of negotiation. It does not take much imagination to see that this world, and its negotiated order, would be different without nonprofessionals. More important: unless one focuses upon the negotiated character of order, he is most unlikely to note the above kinds of consequential actions and relations.

THE PATIENTS AND NEGOTIATED ORDER

The patients are also engaged in bargaining, in negotiative processes. (As some public-administration theorists have put it, clients are also part of the organisational structure.) Again, a significant aspect of hospital organisation is missing unless the clients' negotiation is included. They negotiate, of course, as laymen, unless they themselves are nurses or physicians. Most visibly they can be seen bargaining, with the nurses and with their psychiatrists, for more extensive privileges (such as more freedom to roam the grounds); but they may also seek to affect the course and kind of treatment—including placement on given wards, amounts of drugs, and even choice of psychiatrist, along with the length of stay in the hospital itself. Intermittently, but fairly continually, they are concerned with their ward's orderliness, and make demands upon the personnel—as well as upon other patients—to keep the volume of noise down, to keep potential violence at a minimum, to rid the ward of a trouble-making patient. Sometimes the patients are as much guardians of ward order as are the nurses, who are notorious for this concern in our hospital. (Conversely, the nursing personnel must also seek to reach understandings and agreements with specific patients; but sometimes these are even collective, as when patients pitch in to help with a needy patient, or as when an adolescent clique has to be dealt with 'as a bunch'.)

An unexpected dividend awaits anyone who focuses upon the patients' negotiations. An enriched understanding of their individual sick careers—to the hospital, inside it, and out of it—occurs. In the absence of a focus upon negotiation, ordinarily these careers tend to appear overly regularised (as in Parsons and Fox, 1952) or destructive (as in Goffman, 1959). When patients are closely observed 'operating around' the hospital, they will be seen negotiating not only for privileges but also for precious information relevant to their own understandings of their illness. We need only add that necessarily their negotiations will differ at various stages of their sick careers.

What Caudill (1952) and Goffman (1957) have written of as patient culture is roughly equivalent to the demands and expectations of the patients; but their accounts require much supplementation by a conception of patients entering, like everyone else, into the over-all negotiative process. How demands and claims will be made and met, by whom, and in what manner—as well as who will make given demands and claims upon them, how, and in what manner—are of utmost importance for understanding the hospital's structure. When patients are long-term or chronic, then their impact upon structure is more obvious to everyone concerned; but even in establishments with speedy turnover, patients are relevant to the social order.

PATTERNED AND TEMPORAL FEATURES OF NEGOTIATION

To do justice to the complexity of negotiative processes would require far more space than can be allowed here. For present purposes, it should be sufficient to note only a few aspects. In our hospital, as elsewhere, the various physicians institute programmes of treatment and care for their patients. Programming involves a mobilisation and organisation of action around the patient (and usually involves the patient's cooperation, even in the psychiatric milieu). Some physicians in our hospital had reached long-standing understandings with certain head nurses, so that only a small amount of communication was necessary to effectuate their treatment programmes. Thus a somatically oriented psychiatrist typically would attempt to get his patients to those two wards where most electric-shock treatment was carried out; and the nurse administrators there understood quite well what was expected in handling 'their type of patients'. It was as if the physician were to say 'do the usual things' (they sometimes did)—little additional instruction being needed. We ourselves coined the term 'house special' (as opposed to '*à la carte*') treatment, to indicate that a patient could be assigned to these wards and handled by the ward staff without the physician either giving special instructions or asking for special favours. However, an original period of coaching the nurses and of reaching understandings was necessary. Consequently when personnel leave, for vacations or permanently, then arrangements must be instituted anew. Even with house special treatment, some discussion will be required, since not every step of the patient's treatment can be imagined ahead of time. The nurses are adept (as in nonpsychiatric hospitals) at eliciting information from the physician about his patient; they are also adept both in forcing and fostering agreements about action *vis-à-vis* his patient. We have watched many a scene where the nurse negotiates for such understandings, as well as many staff meetings that the nurses and aides consciously convert into agencies for bringing recalcitrant physicians to terms. When physicians choose, they can be equally concerned with reaching firm agreements and understandings.

It is important that one realise that these agreements do not occur by chance, nor are they established beween random parties. They are, in the literal sense of the word, patterned. Thus, the somatically oriented physicians have long-standing arrangements with a secretary who is attached to the two wards upon which their patients tend to be housed; this secretary does a variety of jobs necessitated by these physicians' rather medical orientation. The more psychotherapeutically minded physicians scarcely utilise her services. Similarly, the head nurses and the administrative residents attached to each ward reach certain kinds of understandings and agreements, which neither tends to establish with any other type of personnel. These latter agreements are less in evidence when the resident is new; then the nurse in some helplessness turns to the next highest administrative officer, making yet other contracts. Again, when an attending physician is especially recalcitrant, both resident and nurse's aide seek to draw higher administrators into the act, negotiating for support and increased power. This kind of negotiation occurs with great predictability: for instance, certain physicians because of their particular philosophies of treatment use the hospital in certain ways; consequently, their programmes are frequently troublesome for the house staff, who must then seek to spin a network of negotiation around the troublesome situation. When the ward is in high furore, then negotiative activity of course is at its most visible!

In sum: there is a patterned variability of negotiation in the hospital pertaining to who contracts with whom, about what, as well as when these agreements are made. Influencing this variability are hierarchical position and ideological commitments, as well as periodicities in the structure of ward relationships (for instance, because of a rotational system that moves personnel periodically on and off given wards).

It is especially worth emphasising that negotiation—whether characterised as 'agreement', 'understanding', 'contract', 'compact', 'pact' or by some other term—has a temporal aspect, whether that aspect is stated specifically or not by the contracting parties. As one listens to agreements being made in the hospital, or watches understandings being established, he becomes aware that a specific termination period, or date line, is often written into the agreement. Thus a physician after being accosted by the head nurse—who may in turn also be responding to her own personnel—may agree to move his patient to another ward after this specific ward has agreed 'to try for two more days'. What he is doing is issuing to its personnel a promissory note that if things don't work out satisfactorily, he will move his patient. Sometimes the staff breaks the contract, if the patient is especially obstreperous or if tempers are running especially high, and transfers the patient to another ward behind the back of the physician. However, if the patient does sufficiently better, the ward's demands may subside. Or, interestingly, it often happens that later both sides will negotiate further, seeking some compromise: the staff, for instance, wishing to restrict the patient's privileges or to give him stronger drug prescriptions, and the physician giving in on these issues to gain some ends of his own. On less tender and less specific grounds, the physician and the head nurse may reach nodding agreement that a new patient should be handled in certain ways 'until we see how he responds'. Thus there exists a continuum running from specific to quite nonspecific termination dates. But even those explicit and long-term permissions that physicians give to nurses in all hospitals—such as to administer certain drugs at night without bothering to call upon the physicians—are subject to review and withdrawal along with later qualified assent.

It should be added that the very terms 'agreements' and 'understandings' and 'arrangements'—all used by hospital personnel—point up that some negotiations may be made with full explicitness, while others may be established by parties who have scarcely talked. The more implicit or tacit kinds of contracts tend to be called 'understandings'. The difference can be high-lighted by the following contrasting situations: when a resident suggests to a nurse that an established house rule temporarily be ignored, for the good of a given patient, it may be left implicit in their arrangement that he must bear the punishment if administration discovers their common infraction. But the nurse may make this clause more explicit by demanding that he bear the possible public guilt, otherwise she will not agree to the matter. It follows that some agreements can be both explicit and specific as to termination, while others are explicit but nonspecific as to termination, and so on. What might be referred to as 'tacit understandings' are likely to be those that are neither very specific nor very explicitly discussed. When a physician is not trusted, the staff is likely to push him for explicit directives with specific termination clauses.

NEGOTIATION, APPRAISAL, AND ORGANISATIONAL CHANGE

We come now to the full import of the above discussion, for it raises knotty problems about the relationships that exist between the current negotiated order and genuine organisational change. Since agreements are patterned and temporal, today's sum total of agreements can be visualised as different from tomorrow's—and surely as quite different from next week's. The hospital can be visualised as a place where numerous agreements are continually being terminated or forgotten, but also as continually being established, renewed, reviewed, revoked, revised. Hence at any moment those that are in effect are considerably different from those that were or will be.

Now a sceptic, thinking in terms of relatively permanent or slowly changing structure, might remark that from week to week the hospital remains the same—that only the working arrangements change. This contention only raises the further question of what relationship exists between today's working agreements and the more stable structure (of rules, statuses, and so on).

With an eye on practicality, one might maintain that no one knows what the hospital 'is' on any given day unless he has a comprehensive grasp of what combination of rules and policies, along with agreements, understandings, pacts, contracts, and other working arrangements, currently obtains. In any pragmatic sense, this is the hospital at the moment: this is its social order. Any changes that impinge upon this order—whether something ordinary like a new staff member, a disrupting event, a betrayed contract; or whether unusual, like the introduction of a new technology or a new theory—will call for renegotiation or reappraisal, with consequent changes in the organisational order. Mark the last phrase—a new order, not the re-establishment of an old, a reinstituting of a previous equilibrium. This is what we remarked upon earlier as the necessity for continually reconstituting the bases of concerted action, or social order.

That reconstituting of social order, we would hazard, can be fruitfully conceived in terms of a complex *relationship between the daily negotiative process and a periodic appraisal process*. The former not only allows the daily work to get done; it also reacts back upon the more formalised—and permanent—rules and policies. Further elaboration of this point will follow, but first the following illustration taken from our field notes should be helpful. For some time the hospital had been admitting an increased number of nonpaying adolescent patients, principally because they made good supervisory subjects for the residents. As a consequence, the hospital began to get the reputation of becoming more interested in adolescents than previously; also, some attending physicians were encouraged to bring adolescents for treatment to the hospital. Their presence on the wards raised many new problems, and led to feverish negotiative activity among the various actors implicated in the daily drama. Finally, after some months of high saturation with an adolescent population, a middle-level administrative committee formally recognised what was happening to the institution. The committee recognised it primarily because the adolescents, in the mass, were much harder to handle than an equal number of adults. Yet the situation had its compensatory aspects, since adolescents remained longer and could be given more interesting types of therapy. After some debate, the committee decided that no more adolescent patients would be admitted after an additional stated number had been reached. The decision constituted a formal proclamation, with the proviso that if the situation continued, the policy should be reviewed at high administrative levels in light of 'where the institution was going'. The decision was never enforced, for shortly thereafter the adolescent census dropped and never rose again to such dangerous heights. The decision has long since been forgotten, and if the census were again to rise dangerously, doubtless a new discussion would take place rather than an evocation of the old rule.

But this is precisely how more long-standing policy and many rules become established in what conventionally is called 'hospital structure'. In turn, of course, the policies and rules serve to set the limits and some of the directions of negotiation. (This latter proposition is implicit in much of our foregoing discussion on rules and negotiation as well as the patterning of negotiation.) We suggest that future studies of complex relationships existing between the more stable elements of organisational order and the more fleeting working arrangements may profit by examining the former as if they were sometimes a background against which the latter were being evolved in the foreground—and sometimes as if the reverse obtained. What is needed is both a concentrated focus upon, and the development of a terminology adequate to handle, this kind of metaphor. But whether this metaphor or another, the question of how negotiation and appraisal play into each other, and into the rules or policies, remains central.

SUMMARY AND IMPLICATIONS

As remarked at the outset of this paper, the reader must judge for himself whether a model possibly suited to studying psychiatric hospitals might equally guide study and understanding of other types of hospitals. The model presented has pictured the hospital as a locale where personnel, mostly but not exclusively professionals, are enmeshed in a complex negotiative process in order both to accomplish their individual purposes and to work—in an established division of labour—toward clearly as well as vaguely phrased institutional objectives. We have sought to show how differential professional training, ideology, career, and hierarchical position all affect the negotiation; but we have also attempted to show how nonprofessionals may affect the total process. We have outlined important relationships between daily working arrangement and the more permanent structure.

We would argue that this mode of viewing hospitals can be very useful. One reason is that it directs attention to the interplay of professionals and nonprofessionals—*as* professionals and nonprofessionals rather than just in terms of hierarchical position. It forces attention also upon the transactions of professionals, among echelons and within echelons. Properly carried out, the approach will not permit, as in many studies, a focus upon the hospital without cognisance of how the outside world impinges upon what is going on within the hospital: a single hospital, after all, is only a point through which multiple careers stream—including the patients' careers. As suggested in the opening page, the approach also pins one's gaze upon processes of change, and of stability also, providing one assumes that 'no change' must be worked at within the organisation. Among other considerations, it allows focus upon important internal occurrences under the impact of external pressures as well as of internal changes within the establishment. Whatever the purely specific characteristics of psychiatric hospitals as compared with nonpsychiatric ones, it is evident that most of the latter share certain features that make them amenable to our approach. Hospitals are evolving as institutions—and rapidly. They are locales where many different kinds of professionals work—and more are joining the ranks. The very heterogeneity of personnel and of professional purpose, along with the impact of a changing medical technology, bespeaks the kind of world sketched above.[3]

But what of other organisations, especially if sizeable or complex—is this kind of interactional model also relevant to them? The answer, we suggest, is strongly in the affirmative. Current preoccupation with formal organisation tends to underplay—or leave implicit—the interactional features underscored in the foregoing pages. Yet one would expect interactional features to jump into visibility once looked for systematically. We urge that whenever an organisation possesses one or more of the following characteristics, such a search be instituted: if the organisation firstly utilises personnel trained in several different occupations, or secondly, if each contains an occupational group including individuals trained in different traditions, then they are likely to possess

[3] Without drawing the same conclusions, Sayre (1956), a professor of public administration, has suggested similar features of modern hospitals: 'In the health and medical professions together in a hospital these stresses between *organization* and *profession* are made the more complex by a multiplicity of professions, a multiplicity of values and perspectives not easily reconciled into a harmonious organization.... The hospital would seem to be an organizational setting where many semi-autonomous cooperators meet for the purpose of using common services and facilities and to provide services to each other, but in a loosely integrated organizational system.'

somewhat different occupational philosophies, emphasising somewhat different values; then also if at least some personnel are professionals, the latter are likely to be pursuing careers that render them mobile—that is, carrying them into and out of the organisation. The reader should readily appreciate why those particular characteristics have been singled out. They are, of course, attributes of universities, corporations, and government agencies, as well as of hospitals. If an organisation is marked by one or more of those characteristics, then the concept of 'negotiated order' should be an appropriate way to view it.

REFERENCES

CAUDILL, W. *et al.* (1952) 'Social structure and interaction processes on a psychiatric ward', *American Journal of Orthopsychiatry*, **22**, 314–34.

DALTON, M. (1959) *Men Who Manage*, Wiley.

GOFFMAN, E. (1957) 'On the characteristics of total institutions', *Proceedings of the Symposium on Preventive and Social Psychiatry*, Walter Reed Army Institute of Research.

GOFFMAN, E. (1959) 'The moral career of the mental patient', *Psychiatry*, **22**, 123–42.

MEAD, G. H. (1936) 'The problem of society—how we become selves', in *Movements of Thought in the Nineteenth Century*, University of Chicago Press.

PARSONS, T., and FOX, R. (1952) 'Illness, therapy and the modern urban American family', *Journal of Social Issues*, **7**, 31–44.

SAYRE, W. S. (1956) 'Principles of administration', *Hospitals*, 16 January, 1 February.

21

Alan Fox   The social organisation of industrial work

Excerpts from Alan Fox, 'The social organization of industrial work', in Alan Fox, *The Sociology of Work in Industry*, Collier-Macmillan, 1971, pp. 28–47.

1. THE SOCIAL ORGANISATION OF THE ENTERPRISE

As men pursue their experience within the organisation, we may assume a process of explicit or implicit assessment to be taking place as they measure that experience against such aspirations as they may entertain. Clearly their experience has a number of different aspects. It will be assessed by the individual, according to his aspirations, along various dimensions of extrinsic rewards such as money, environmental conditions, status, and social satisfactions; along dimensions of intrinsic rewards such as job interest, challenge, creativity, autonomy and other paths to self-actualisation; and along dimensions of participation in decision-making which may have extrinsic or intrinsic value or both. Before this assessment process is explored, however, we need to define the corresponding constituent elements of the social structure of the work organisation, for it is the individual's location in this social structure (referred to hereafter as 'the social organisation') which determines his experience.

The essence of organisation is regular, standardised and recurrent behaviour. The social organisation therefore consists of patterned uniformities of behaviour which persist for varying lengths of time. The regularities and uniformities are structured into the behaviour by norms—a norm being defined here (as in the *International Encyclopaedia of the Social Sciences*) as 'a rule, a standard, or pattern for action'. It will be assumed for analytical purposes that all organisational behaviour is structured, regulated or guided by some norm or combination of norms. If certain patterned uniformities of behaviour give way to different uniformities, a change in structure has taken place as a result of a change in certain of the norms.

As in the case of the norms which govern behaviour in the wider society, organisational norms are of several different kinds. . . .

2.   SUBSTANTIVE AND PROCEDURAL NORMS

Procedural norms are those rules and understandings which structure and regulate the decision-making methods by which norms are formulated. Substantive norms, emanating from these decision-making procedures, cover . . . every aspect of organisational activities. Of course, the formulation of norms is not the only activity of decision-making procedures. They are also concerned with the application of norms. What this really means is that decisions constantly have to be taken, explicity or implicitly, about which norm or norms are to be used in dealing with a particular situation, problem, or instance. Against the background of this distinction between procedural and substantive norms, we turn now to examine certain necessary components of the social organisation.

Minimally, the social organisation comprises systems of roles, of sanctions and of communications. Without these there is no organisation. . . .

The second major element of the social organisation is the normative system of sanctions through which superordinates seek to regulate and control the behaviour of subordinates. Every sanction has its positive and negative aspects. . . .

What is the basis of the ability to apply sanctions? Here we shall follow Emerson (1962) and Blau (1964) in seeing this ability as deriving from a relationship of dependence in which one person is dependent upon another for the securing or the continued availability of something that he values. The entity to which value is attached may be scarce resources, approval or symbolic rewards, or life itself. . . .

Insofar as managements have control over the supply of whatever men value, they are able to control and regulate behaviour by making a supply available under the threat of withdrawal if the required behaviour is not pursued. They can grant or deny men access to an income—and therefore livelihood. They can adjust the level of that livelihood and manipulate possibilities of promotional advancement. They can bestow or withdraw status. They can transfer men to more satisfying work, and display signs of approval or disapproval as encouragement or threats. In some societies they can recommend the bestowal of state honours. In all societies there are defined circumstances in which they can call upon the civil power and even perhaps the armed services to apply physical force against those who transgress certain norms. . . .

The third and last major basic component of the social organisation is a communications system. . . .

Our notional picture of the basic components of the social organisation therefore includes technological behaviour systems, sets of more general behavioural norms, control mechanisms, a system of sanctions, a status system, and a pattern of communications, all buttressed by relationships of superordination and subordination. We can also abstract from the general behavioural norms the values expected of all participants, and from the communication system the orientation and indoctrination of new members, and introduce a concept of management ideology and its function of serving management goals by socialising members into desired orientations and patterns of behaviour. Management ideology has other functions besides this, as will emerge later, but this is an important one. . . .

Management ideology seeks to legitimise, in the eyes of organisation members, not only the goals defined by the organisation's leaders but also the social organisation which is designed to serve them. By these means it hopes to strengthen its chances of securing willing compliance from its members, which means here not simple obedience, but also a disposition on the part of the subordinate to use whatever discretion he has in decision-making to further the ends of organisational leaders. . . .

3. THE BASES OF LEGITIMACY

. . . We [now] turn to inquire into the possible bases of managerial authority. In other words, by what means do managers seek to induce subordinates to perceive their rule as legitimate, and thus extend willing compliance and cooperation?

We are here concerned with the ideas and values by which management hopes to validate its procedural norms. In this quest for legitimacy, ideologies are pressed into service in the hope of promoting agreement on these values. They are aimed not only at subordinates but also at the wider society in the belief that, if they succeed in modifying expectations of subordinate behaviour at work, social pressures of various kinds will help to induce acceptance by the subordinates themselves.

The types of appeal are many and diverse, varying over time and between countries. They vary, too, according to whether they receive physical or moral support from the state. . . .

But there are, of course, many other kinds of appeal which employers and managers make for support of their rule. They may invoke the Social Darwinist principle that success in the competitive struggle proclaims their fitness and thereby their entitlement to govern, or that their special contribution to national wealth justifies them in their leadership (Bendix, 1956). More recently, in the United States, the focus has been upon the 'modern' 'socially conscious' private enterprise system which, by its success and creative dynamic, its professional orientation of social responsibility as against the old 'exploitative, harsh capitalism', and its enlightened concern with 'human values' (Cheit, 1964), justifies management in their appeal for social support. In the Soviet Union, the source of the manager's formal legitimacy derives from the backing of the Communist Party hierarchy, and the ideological pressure is directed towards ensuring that the hierarchy is accepted as the sole final authority for the proper interpretation of Marxism–Leninism (Granick, 1961).

Alternatively the appeal in the Third World may be to the legitimacy enjoyed by the nationalist regime which liberated the masses from imperialism. In Japan the manager's legitimacy has rested heavily on the persistence of feudal and family values which shaped industry as they shaped other institutions (Abegglen, 1958). Even in Western societies the force of tradition and custom can endow managers with legitimacy in the eyes of their subordinates. This may be important, for example, in explaining the unchallenged writ that may run within long-standing family firms—and equally the sudden collapse of authority that may follow a sudden change in their circumstances.

Charismatic leadership may be important. The position of the charismatic leader rests on an identification between leader and led of such a kind that he is able to crystallise, articulate, and shape the practical expression of normative aspirations among his followers.

. . . In a society where expertise *per se* commands great respect, managers may be able to justify their rule by demonstrating efficiency and superiority of judgment, even where subordinates feel no great enthusiasm for the objectives being pursued. If managers believe that subordinates attach value to such procedural aspirations as 'worker participation', 'democratic involvement', joint decision-making and the like, they may seek to strengthen their legitimacy by modifying the procedural norms accordingly, hoping thereby for the procedural-normative agreement which will mean substantive agreement. A wide range of possibilities exists for procedural change and can be arranged in sequence of significance. Subordinates may receive the right to have information: to protest against decisions; to make suggestions; to be consulted; or to participate directly or through representatives in a joint process of decision-making or collective negotiation. As with all the other possible sources of legitimacy, subordinates may or may not share the relevant values. If they do not, management will gain nothing by such a change. If they do, they may, as we have already noted, value procedural participation for terminal or instrumental reasons or both. A terminal preference reflects ideological or cultural values which may or may not be adequately met by the procedural changes. If the preference is an instrumental one, subordinates will value the new procedural norms—and reward management with the sought-for legitimacy—only insofar as they prove effective for the pursuit of substantive aspirations. Instrumental success may, however, result in the new procedural norms becoming valued for their own sake by promoting such principles as self-respect, dignity and independence.

Insofar as subordinates are—or can be brought to be—strongly committed to the value of a continuously rising material standard of life, managers may hope to strengthen their legitimacy by trying to meet subordinate aspirations in respect of material rewards, welfare, and fringe benefits. Since this is one of the appetites that grow by what they feed upon, it is apt to prove an unstable base for authority. Yesterday's luxuries are today's necessities; the horizons of satisfaction ever recede, and management may find themselves expected to meet aspirations that rise faster than their productive ability—especially when the demands of other constraints are taken into account. Their authority may be correspondingly unstable. This is a specially uncertain base for the reason that material rewards are palpable, precisely measurable, and therefore all too easily comparable. Shifting relationships between rewards can quickly generate a sense of grievance. We also get a sense here of the part that may be played by class or caste divisions which structure and limit aspirations of different groups. As these divisions weaken, aspirational limits weaken with them. Normative references long maintained by custom dissolve, thus giving freer play to the growth of more expansive aspirations.

Finally, insofar as managers perceive the values sought by subordinates to be those of 'integration into the factory social system', or 'personality development', or 'psychological growth', or self-actualisation, they may try to serve them not only by such procedural changes as are mentioned above but also by 'permissive' or 'supportive' supervision, 'employee-counselling' and other types of 'human-relations' programmes . . . , or by changes in job structure. . . . They may combine these with an ideology designed to persuade subordinates and society at large that the industrial organisation is, in essence, a cooperative harmony of common goals which only fools or knaves choose to disrupt, and which thereby renders theirs a legitimate government (Fox, 1966).

4. PATTERNS OF AUTHORITY RELATIONS

All these diverse bases of managerial authority rest on normative agreement upheld by shared values. It follows that should management behave in ways which are based on, or directed towards, values other than those by which subordinates are legitimising management's role, or in ways which fail to embody those values adequately, the authority relationship comes under potential threat. For example, if subordinates are legitimising that role on the basis of management's professed concern first and foremost with employee interests, authority relations will be threatened if management are perceived as giving employee interests low priority. If legitimacy is offered on the basis of management's presumed respect for professional standards, it may not survive an instruction from management that standards be cut in order to gain a short-term competitive advantage. The case is equally clear if we suppose management to issue orders which conflict with a subordinate's moral principles. Thus the shared values promoting legitimacy create a 'zone of acceptance' within which management's writ of authority holds for the subordinate, but outside which their behaviour may be perceived to be, as it were, 'ultra vires'.

But managerial authority may be undermined not only by a failure of management to embody adequately the shared values in their behaviour, but also by a movement away from those values by subordinates. Employees who once acquiesced in the assertion that property rights and the freely consenting equality of the parties to the employment contract legitimised the employer's rule may come to see the situation differently. Experience may dispose them to accept the leadership of those who argue that since the assumption of equality is a mere legal fiction which masks gross economic inequality, the employer's rule and his use of sanctions must be considered illegitimate. The employment relationship will then come to be seen not as based on consent but as essentially coercive in nature. This exercise of power by the employer will be regarded as justifying the mobilisation of counter-power by employees collectively in an attempt to introduce parity in their dealings with him. The more nearly they succeed the less they are likely to experience the relationship as one of coercion.

But given the existence of shared values, the commitment to these values by either side can be strong or weak. This means that there can be strong or weak support for the tacit or explicit agreement on the procedural norms regulating the relationship of subordination. Thus there can be strong or weak authority. Accordingly it may be useful to consider degrees of commitment *to* management rule as being on a common scale with degrees of commitment *against* it. This would give us a continuum ranging from total acceptance of authority at one end to total rejection at the other. Examples of total acceptance are rare in industry, but illustrations may be found in other spheres. Since total acceptance means unquestioning submission to substantive norms or instructions, examples must be found in the utter commitment to the religious or charismatic leader, in the behaviour of suicide troops in war, or in the doctrinal subservience of members of extremist authoritarian political sects. At the other end of the scale, total rejection of authority is an expression of complete normative breakdown. Revolutionaries or extreme militants may completely reject the procedural norms on ideological grounds. Since both procedural and substantive legitimacy are commensurate, and their repudiation of the former is total, it follows that they cannot be appeased by substantive concessions. Indeed, in order to justify their continued militancy, extremists are likely to respond to concessions only by raising their demands, even if only to avoid cognitive dissonance. Their ideology requires them to keep up the fight and they must have something to fight about.

In these polar-type cases the substantive outcome of the particular hierarchical relationship in which he is involved is irrelevant to the subordinate. In these contexts he has no substantive aspirations. But few organisations reveal such extremities. More frequent are situations where commitment to values which either support or reject the established procedural norms, while not total, is nevertheless very strong. Members of some religious sects accept rigorous and detailed regulation of their private life of a sort which they would reject from any other source. Workers in Communist countries may likewise lend themselves to management purposes by exceeding official production norms and readily accepting rationalisation in the manner of 'heroes of labour', 'shock workers' and Stakhanovites (Dobb, 1942). The devoted employee of long standing in the paternalist family firm in the capitalist West may uncomplainingly endure much. Other examples are the members of a *kibbutz* workshop; the leading spirits in a small production cooperative; and fervent nationalist employees in a newly-developing country. Examples of situations displaying strong commitment to values which reject the established procedural norms are naturally more apparent in societies which permit open challenge than in those which do not. In the West one may find the militant shop-floor worker who rejects all or many of the values which support procedural-normative agreement in industrial organisations. He may refuse to acknowledge the rights attached to private property in the means of production; deny that private enterprise serves anybody but property-owners; cherish a contempt for managerial competence, and despise the emphasis on material progress. Clearly if he extends any legitimacy to management at all it will be minimal.

Insofar as authority relations do prevail in the industrial organisations of the West, they are probably most widely characterised, so far as subordinates are concerned, by a low-key acquiescence. Of all the values which can legitimise managerial rule, those which appear to be coming to predominate in these societies are those which relate to substantive aspirations for a continuously rising material standard of life, and to procedural aspirations for participative decision-making machinery through which substantive gains can be made and protected. If this is the case then it suggests a predominantly instrumental and utilitarian type of involvement of the subordinate in the industrial organisation. Etzioni (1961) arrives at the same destination but by a very different conceptual route.

As we have seen, this is apt to prove a somewhat unstable base for authority relations. We must not overlook, however, the degree to which it may be buttressed by the habituated behaviours created by early socialisation. From childhood we are all trained in obedience, though social classes differ sharply in how far their members are trained in giving orders as well as obeying them. As children we are urged to obey parents, teachers, policemen, and public officials simply *because* they are parents, teachers, policemen and public officials. Our mentor may or may not add—'and if you don't you'll be punished'. Even if he does, we are usually left in no doubt that the principal reason why we should obey is that we *ought* to obey; that it is right for the functionary concerned to expect our obedience. We also learn that if punished for transgression we are receiving no less than our just desert. These are lessons in the behaviours appropriate to subordination. The importance of the family, the group, the school, the community, the society at large, in shaping our perceptions of legitimacy is therefore crucial. In the case of any particular individual, of course, socialising influences brought to bear may or may not conform to the predominant pattern.

So far as the majority are concerned, however, by the time they take up employment they are trained to accept that they must work for a living, that this normally involves employment in a privately or publicly owned organisation, and that they there come under a generalised expectation that they will accept the orders of persons appointed to govern them. This generalised expectation is likely to be supported, in the case of private industry, with certain propositions about the 'rights' of 'ownership', and in the case of the public sector, the 'right' of public officials. These expectations and their supporting propositions are likely, for many people, to be only vaguely conceived, and to have the status of traditional rather than rationally evaluated behaviours. Their effect is nevertheless crucial, for they ensure that the employer or manager receives an employee who is already socialised and trained in obedience.

Increasingly, however, over the period of industrialisation these socialising processes have in many societies been supplemented by others offering a less accommodating perspective. Trade unions, while supporting management legitimacy in general and helping to socialise members in the behaviours appropriate to their subordinate roles, have also trained them to reject management prerogative over certain limited types of decision and to support the union in demanding joint decision-making in those spheres. Other values not necessarily generated only by trade unions may also bring new challenges by employee groups to the traditional bases of managerial authority, as when workers increasingly judge the economic system by whether it can supply them with a continuously rising standard of life.

In summary, most work organisations in most societies are likely to be found in the middle ranges of the continuum of power and authority. Only a tiny minority of employees are likely totally to deny all legitimacy to the procedural norms which structure the decision-making roles of those who rule them, and a still tinier minority are likely to offer total submission. The specific basis and strength of authority relations in any given organisation is of course a matter for empirical enquiry, and national patterns vary widely. The values which provide the basis differ considerably and can be found associated in different combinations. The significance of a free market in values is, however, plain to see. Management will have an enormous advantage in maintaining its authority in societies where it enjoys the support of a state apparatus which controls the dissemination and teaching of ideas and values. In other societies managerial authority is permanently under threat from new values or from new interpretations of existing values.

In the West, much of the history of personnel techniques such as profit-sharing, co-partnership, paternalism, industrial 'betterment', industrial welfare, the 'human relations' movement, 'permissive' management and the like, is a record of the search for new, or for the strengthening of old, legitimations. But what happens when the search fails? We need to remind ourselves of the resource available to managers when their authority falters, breaks down, or cannot come effectively into existence because the shared values necessary to uphold normative agreement are only weakly held or have never existed. This resource is, of course, power. In the event that the value-commitment by subordinates is not adequate to uphold the procedural norms of decision-making, management can turn to power.

REFERENCES

ABEGGLEN, J. G. (1958) *The Japanese Factory*, New York, Free Press of Glencoe.

BENDIX, R. (1956) *Work and Authority in Industry: ideologies of management in the course of industrialization*, Wiley.

BLAU, P. M. (1964) *Exchange and Power in Social Life*, Wiley.

CHEIT, E., ed. (1964) *The Business Establishment*, Wiley.

DOBB, M. (1942) *Soviet Planning and Labour in Peace and War*, Routledge & Kegan Paul.

EMERSON, R. M. (1962) 'Power-dependence relations', *American Sociological Review*, **27**, 31–41.

ETZIONI, A. (1961) *A Comparative analysis of Complex Organizations*, New York, Free Press of Glencoe.

FOX, ALAN (1966) *Industrial Sociology and Industrial Relations*, Research Paper 3, Royal Commission on Trade Unions and Employers' Associations, H.M.S.O.

GRANICK, D. (1961) *The Red Executive: a study of the organization man in Russian industry*, Doubleday.

22

Egon Bittner ## The police on skid-row: a study of peace keeping

Excerpts from Egon Bittner, 'The police on skid-row: a study of peace keeping', *American Sociological Review*, **32**, no. 5, October 1967, 699–715.

THE PROBLEM OF KEEPING THE PEACE IN SKID-ROW

Skid-row has always occupied a special place among the various forms of urban life. While other areas are perceived as being different in many ways, skid-row is seen as completely different. Though it is located in the heart of civilisation, it is viewed as containing aspects of the primordial jungle, calling for missionary activities and offering opportunities for exotic adventure. While each inhabitant individually can be seen as tragically linked to the vicissitudes of 'normal' life, allowing others to say 'here but for the Grace of God go I', those who live there are believed to have repudiated the entire role-casting scheme of the majority and to live apart from normalcy. Accordingly, the traditional attitude of civic-mindedness toward skid-row has been dominated by the desire to contain it and to salvage souls from its clutches. The specific task of containment has been left to the police. . . .

Patrolmen who are more or less permanently assigned to skid-row districts tend to develop a conception of the nature of their 'domain' that is surprisingly uniform. . . .

In the view of experienced patrolmen, life on skid-row is fundamentally different from life in other parts of society. . . . Skid-row is perceived as the natural habitat of people who lack the capacities and commitments to live 'normal' lives on a sustained basis. The presence of these people defines the nature of social reality in the area. In general, and especially in casual encounters, the presumption of incompetence and of the disinclination to be 'normal' is the leading theme for the interpretation of all actions and relations. Not only do people approach one another in this manner, but presumably they also expect to be approached in this way, and they conduct themselves accordingly. . . .

What patrolmen view as normal on skid-row—and what they also think is taken for granted as 'life as usual' by the inhabitants—is not easily summarised. It seems to focus on the idea that the dominant consideration governing all enterprise and association is directed to the occasion of the moment. Nothing is thought of as having a background that might have led up to the present in terms of some compelling moral or practical necessity. . . . In this atmosphere, the range of control that persons have over one another is exceedingly narrow. Good faith, even where it is valued, is seen merely as a personal matter. Its violations are the victim's own hard luck, rather than demonstrable violations of property. There is only a private sense of irony at having been victimised. The over-all air is not so much one of active distrust as it is one of irrelevance of trust: as patrolmen often emphasise, the situation does not necessarily cause all relations to be predatory, but the possibility of exploitation is not checked by the expectation that it will not happen.

Just as the past is seen by the policeman as having only the most attenuated relevance to the present, so the future implications of present situations are said to be generally devoid of prospective coherence. No venture, especially no joint venture, can be said to have a strongly predictable future in line with its initial objectives. It is a matter of adventitious circumstances whether or not matters go as anticipated. That which is not within the grasp of momentary control is outside of practical social reality.

Though patrolmen see the temporal framework of the occasion of the moment mainly as a lack of trustworthiness, they also recognise that it involves more than merely the personal motives of individuals. In addition to the fact that everybody *feels* that things matter only at the moment, irresponsibility takes an *objectified* form on skid-row. The places the residents occupy, the social relations they entertain, and the activities that engage them are not meaningfully connected over time. Thus, for example, address, occupation, marital status, etc., matter much less on skid-row than in any other part of society. The fact that present whereabouts, activities, and affiliations imply neither continuity nor direction means that life on skid-row lacks a socially structured background of accountability. Of course, everybody's life contains some sequential incongruities, but in the life of a skid-row inhabitant every moment is an accident. That a man has no 'address' in the future that could be in some way inferred from where he is and what he does makes him a person of *radically reduced visibility*. If he disappears from sight and one wishes to locate him, it is virtually impossible to systematise the search. All one can know with relative certainty is that he will be somewhere on some skid-row and the only thing one can do is to trace the factual contiguities of his whereabouts. . . .

This, then, constitutes the problem of keeping the peace on skid-row. Considerations of momentary expediency are seen as having unqualified priority as maxims of conduct; consequently, the controlling influences of the pursuit of sustained interests are presumed to be absent.

THE PRACTICES OF KEEPING THE PEACE IN SKID-ROW

From the perspective of society as a whole, skid-row inhabitants appear troublesome in a variety of ways. The uncommitted life attributed to them is perceived as inherently offensive; its very existence arouses indignation and contempt. More important, however, is the feeling that persons who have repudiated the entire role-status casting system of society, persons whose lives forever collapse into a succession of random moments, are seen as constituting a practical risk. As they have nothing to forsake, nothing is thought safe from them.

The skid-row patrolman's concept of his mandate includes an awareness of this presumed risk. He is constantly attuned to the possibility of violence, and he is convinced that things to which the inhabitants have free access are as good as lost. But his concern is directed toward the continuous condition of peril *in the area* rather than *for society in general*. While he is obviously conscious of the presence of many persons who have committed crimes outside of skid-row and will arrest them when they come to his attention, this is a peripheral part of his routine activities. In general, the skid-row patrolman and his superiors take for granted that his main business is to keep the peace and enforce the laws on *skid-row*, and that he is involved only incidentally in protecting society at large. Thus, his task is formulated basically as the protection of putative predators from one another. The maintenance of peace and safety is difficult because everyday life on skid-row is viewed as an open field for reciprocal exploitation. As the lives of the inhabitants lack the prospective coherence associated with status incumbency, the realisation of self-interest does not produce order. Hence, mechanisms that control risk must work primarily from without.

External containment, to be effective, must be oriented to the realities of existence. Thus, the skid-row patrolman employs an approach that he views as appropriate to the *ad hoc* nature of skid-row life. The following are the three most prominent elements of this approach. First, the seasoned patrolman seeks to acquire a richly particularised knowledge of people and places in the area. Second, he gives the consideration of strict culpability a subordinate status among grounds for remedial sanction. Third, his use and choice of coercive interventions is determined mainly by exigencies of situations and with little regard for possible long range effects on individual persons.

The Particularisation of Knowledge. The patrolman's orientation to people on skid-row is structured basically by the presupposition that if he does not know a man personally there is very little that he can assume about him. This rule determines his interaction with people who live on skid-row. Since the area also contains other types of persons, however, its applicability is not universal. To some such persons it does not apply at all, and it has a somewhat mitigated significance with certain others. For example, some persons encountered on skid-row can be recognised immediately as outsiders. . . .

Clearly set off from these outsiders are the residents and the entire corps of personnel that services skid-row. It would be fair to say that one of the main routine activities of patrolmen is the establishment and maintenance of familiar relationships with individual members of these groups. Officers emphasise their interest in this, and they maintain that their grasp of and control over skid-row is precisely commensurate with the extent to which they 'know the people'. By this they do not mean having a quasi-theoretical understanding of human nature but rather the common practice of individualised and reciprocal recognition. As this group encompasses both those who render services on skid-row and those who are serviced, individualised interest is not always based on the desire to overcome uncertainty. Instead, relations with service personnel become absorbed into the network of particularised attention. Ties between patrolmen, on the one hand, and businessmen, managers, and workers, on the other hand, are often defined in terms of shared or similar interests. It bears mentioning that many persons live *and* work on skid-row. Thus, the distinction between those who service and those who are serviced is not a clearcut dichotomy but a spectrum of affiliations.

As a general rule, the skid-row patrolman possesses an immensely detailed factual knowledge of his beat. He knows, and knows a great deal about, a large number of residents. He is likely to know every person who manages or works in the local bars, hotels, shops, stores, and missions. Moreover, he probably knows every public and private place inside and out. Finally, he ordinarily remembers countless events of the past which he can recount by citing names, dates and places with remarkable precision. Though there are always some threads missing in the fabric of information, it is continuously woven and mended even as it is being used. New facts, however, are added to the texture, not in terms of structured categories but in terms of adjoining known realities. In other words, the content and organisation of the patrolman's knowledge is primarily ideographic and only vestigially, if at all, nomothetic.

... In the course of making their rounds, patrolmen seem to have access to every place, and their entry causes no surprise or consternation. Instead, the entry tends to lead to informal exchanges of small talk. At times the rounds include entering hotels and gaining access to rooms or dormitories, often for no other purpose than asking the occupants how things are going. In all this, patrolmen address innumerable persons by name and are in turn addressed by name. The conversational style that characterises these exchanges is casual to an extent that by non-skid-row standards might suggest intimacy. Not only does the officer himself avoid all terms of deference and respect but he does not seem to expect or demand them. ...

This kind of expressive freedom is an intricately limited privilege. Persons of acquaintance are entitled to it and appear to exercise it mainly in routinised encounters. But strangers, too, can use it with impunity. The safe way of gaining the privilege is to respond to the patrolman in ways that do not challenge his right to ask questions and issue commands. ...

The explicit refusal to answer questions of a personal nature and the demand to know why the questions are asked significantly enhances a person's chances of being arrested on some minor charge. While most patrolmen tend to be personally indignant about this kind of response and use the arrest to compose their own hurt feelings, this is merely a case of affect being in line with the method. There are other officers who proceed in the same manner without taking offence, or even with feelings of regret. Such patrolmen often maintain that their colleagues' affective involvement is a corruption of an essentially valid technique. The technique is oriented to the goal of maintaining operational control. The patrolman's conception of this goal places him hierarchically above whomever he approaches, and makes him the sole judge of the propriety of the occasion. As he alone is oriented to this goal, and as he seeks to attain it by means of individualised access to persons, those who frustrate him are seen as motivated at best by the desire to 'give him a hard time' and at worst by some darkly devious purpose.

Officers are quite aware that the directness of their approach and the demands they make are difficult to reconcile with the doctrines of civil liberties, but they maintain that they are in accord with the general freedom of access that persons living on skid-row normally grant one another. That is, they believe that the imposition of personalised and far-reaching control is in tune with standard expectancies. In terms of these expectancies, people are not so much denied the right to privacy as they are seen as not having any privacy. Thus, officers seek to install themselves in the centre of people's lives and let the consciousness of their presence play the part of conscience.

When talking about the practical necessity of an aggressively personal approach, officers do not refer merely to the need for maintaining control over lives that are open in the direction of the untoward. They also see it as the basis for the supply of certain valued services to inhabitants of skid-row. The coerced or conceded access to persons often imposes on the patrolman tasks that are, in the main, in line with these persons' expressed or implied interest. In asserting this connection, patrolmen note that they frequently help people to obtain meals, lodging, employment, that they direct them to welfare and health services, and that they aid them in various other ways. Though patrolmen tend to describe such services mainly as the product of their own altruism, they also say that their colleagues who avoid them are simply doing a poor job of patrolling. The acceptance of the need to help people is based on the realisation that the hungry, the sick, and the troubled are a potential source of problems. Moreover, that patrolmen will help people is part of the background expectancies of life on skid-row. Hotel clerks normally call policemen when someone gets so sick as to need attention; merchants expect to be taxed, in a manner of speaking, to meet the pressing needs of certain persons; and the inhabitants do not hesitate to accept, solicit, and demand every kind of aid. The domain of the patrolman's service activity is virtually limitless, and it is no exaggeration to say that the solution of every conceivable problem has at one time or another been attempted by a police officer. . . .

THE RESTRICTED RELEVANCE OF CULPABILITY

It is well known that policemen exercise discretionary freedom in invoking the law. It is also conceded that, in some measure, the practice is unavoidable. This being so, the outstanding problem is whether or not the decisions are in line with the intent of the law. On skid-row, patrolmen often make decisions based on reasons that the law probably does not recognise as valid. The problem can best be introduced by citing an example.

A man in a relatively mild state of intoxication (by skid-row standards) approached a patrolman to tell him that he had a room in a hotel, to which the officer responded by urging him to go to his bed instead of getting drunk. As the man walked off, the officer related the following thoughts: Here is a completely lost soul. Though he probably is no more than thirty-five years old, he looks to be in his fifties. He never works and he hardly ever has a place to stay. He has been on the street for several years and is known as 'Dakota'. During the past few years, 'Dakota' has been seen in the company of 'Big Jim'. The latter is an invalid living on some sort of pension with which he pays for a room in the hotel to which 'Dakota' referred and for four weekly meal tickets in one of the restaurants on the street. Whatever is left he spends on wine and beer. Occasionally, 'Big Jim' goes on drinking sprees in the company of someone like 'Dakota'. Leaving aside the consideration that there is probably a homosexual background to the association, and that it is not right that 'Big Jim' should have to support the drinking habit of someone else, there is the more important risk that if 'Dakota' moves in with 'Big Jim' he will very likely walk off with whatever the latter keeps in his room. 'Big Jim' would never dream of reporting the theft; he would just beat the hell out of 'Dakota' after he sobered up. When asked what could be done to prevent the theft and the subsequent recriminations, the patrolman proposed that in this particular case he would throw 'Big Jim' into jail if he found him tonight and then tell his hotel clerk to throw 'Dakota' out of the room. When asked why he did not arrest 'Dakota', who was, after all, drunk enough to warrant an arrest, the officer explained that this would not solve anything. While 'Dakota' was in jail 'Big Jim' would continue drinking and would either strike up another liaison or embrace his old buddy after he had been released. The only thing to do was to get 'Big Jim' to sober up, and the only sure way of doing this was to arrest him.

As it turned out, 'Big Jim' was not located that evening. But had he been located and arrested on a drunk charge, the fact that he was intoxicated would not have been the real reason for proceeding against him, but merely the pretext. The point of the example is not that it illustrates the tendency of skid-row patrolmen to arrest persons who would not be arrested under conditions of full respect for their legal rights. To be sure, this too happens. In the majority of minor arrest cases, however, the criteria the law specifies are met. But it is the rare exception that the law is invoked merely because the specifications of the law are met. That is, compliance with the law is merely the outward appearance of an intervention that is actually based on altogether different considerations. Thus, it could be said that patrolmen do not really enforce the law, even when they do invoke it, but merely use it as a resource to solve certain pressing practical problems in keeping the peace. This observation goes beyond the conclusion that many of the lesser norms of the criminal law are treated as defensible in police work. It is patently not the case that skid-row patrolmen apply the legal norms while recognising many exceptions to their applicability. Instead, the observation leads to the conclusion that in keeping the peace on skid-row, patrolmen encounter certain matters they attend to by means of coercive action, e.g., arrest. In doing this, they invoke legal norms that are available, and with some regard for substantive appropriateness. Hence, the problem patrolmen confront is not which drunks, beggars, or disturbers of the peace should be arrested and which can be let go as exceptions to the rule. Rather, the problem is whether, when someone 'needs' to be arrested, he should be charged with drunkenness, begging, or disturbing the peace. Speculating further, one is almost compelled to infer that virtually any set of norms could be used in this manner, provided that they sanction relatively common forms of behaviour.

The reduced relevance of culpability in peace keeping practice on skid-row is not readily visible. As mentioned, most arrested persons were actually found in the act, or in the state, alleged in the arrest record. It becomes partly visible when one views the treatment of persons who are not arrested even though all the legal grounds for an arrest are present. Whenever such persons are encountered and can be induced to leave, or taken to some shelter, or remanded to someone's care, then patrolmen feel, or at least maintain, that an arrest would serve no useful purpose. That is, whenever there exist means for controlling the troublesome aspects of some person's presence in some way alternative to an arrest, such means are preferentially employed, provided, of course, that the case at hand involves only a minor offence.

The attenuation of the relevance of culpability is most visible when the presence of legal grounds for an arrest could be questioned, i.e., in cases that sometimes are euphemistically called 'preventive arrests' . . .

Finally, it must be mentioned that the reduction of the significance of culpability is built into the normal order of skid-row life, as patrolmen see it. Officers almost unfailingly say, pointing to some particular person, 'I know that he knows that I know that some of the things he "owns" are stolen, and that nothing can be done about it.' In saying this they often claim to have knowledge of such a degree of certainty as would normally be sufficient for virtually any kind of action except legal proceedings. Against this background, patrolmen adopt the view that the law is not merely imperfect and difficult to implement, but that on skid-row, at least, the association between delict and sanction is distinctly occasional. Thus, to implement the law naïvely, i.e., to arrest someone *merely* because he committed some minor offence is perceived as containing elements of injustice.

Moreover, patrolmen often deal with situations in which questions of culpability are profoundly ambiguous. For example, an officer was called to help in settling a violent dispute in a hotel room. The object of the quarrel was a supposedly stolen pair of trousers. As the story unfolded in the conflicting versions of the participants, it was not possible to decide who was the complainant and who was alleged to be the thief, nor did it come to light who occupied the room in which the fracas took place, or whether the trousers were taken from the room or to the room. Though the officer did ask some questions, it seemed, and was confirmed in later conversation, that he was there not to solve the puzzle of the missing trousers but to keep the situation from getting out of hand. In the end, the exhausted participants dispersed, and this was the conclusion of the case. The patrolman maintained that no one could unravel mysteries of this sort because 'these people take things from each other so often that no one could tell what "belongs" to whom.' In fact, he suggested, the terms owning, stealing, and swindling, in their strict sense, do not really belong on skid-row, and all efforts to distribute guilt and innocence according to some rational formula of justice are doomed to failure.

It could be said that the term 'curb-stone justice' that is sometimes applied to the procedures of patrolmen in skid-rows contains a double irony. Not only is the procedure not legally authorised, which is the intended irony in the expression, but it does not even pretend to distribute deserts. The best among the patrolmen, according to their own standards, use the law to keep skid-row inhabitants from sinking deeper into the misery they already experience. The worst, in terms of these same standards, exploit the practice for personal aggrandisement or gain. Leaving motives aside, however, it is easy to see that if culpability is not the salient consideration leading to an arrest in cases where it is patently obvious, then the practical patrolman may not view it as being wholly out of line to make arrests lacking in formal legal justification. Conversely, he will come to view minor offence arrests made solely because legal standards are met as poor craftsmanship.

THE BACKGROUND OF 'AD HOC' DECISION MAKING

When skid-row patrolmen are pressed to explain their reasons for minor offence arrests, they most often mention that it is done for the protection of the arrested person. This, they maintain, is the case in virtually all drunk arrests, in the majority of arrests involving begging and other nuisance offences, and in many cases involving acts of violence. When they are asked to explain further such arrests as the one cited earlier involving the man attempting to sell the pocket knife, who was certainly not arrested for his own protection, they cite the consideration that belligerent persons constitute a much greater menace on skid-row than any place else in the city. The reasons for this are twofold. First, many of the inhabitants are old, feeble, and not too smart, all of which makes them relatively defenceless. Second, many of the inhabitants are involved in illegal activities and are known as persons of bad character, which does not make them credible victims or witnesses. Potential predators realise that the resources society has mobilised to minimise the risk of criminal victimisation do not protect the predator himself. Thus, reciprocal exploitation constitutes a preferred risk. The high vulnerability of everybody on skid-row is public knowledge and causes every seemingly aggressive act to be seen as a potentially grave risk.

When, in response to all this, patrolmen are confronted with the observation that many minor offence arrests they make do not seem to involve a careful evaluation of facts before acting, they give the following explanations: First, the two reasons of protection and prevention represent a global background, and in individual cases it may sometimes not be possible to produce adequate justification on these grounds. Nor is it thought to be a problem of great moment to estimate precisely whether someone is more likely to come to grief or to cause grief when the objective is to prevent the proliferation of troubles. Second, patrolmen maintain that some of the seemingly spur-of-the-moment decisions are actually made against a background of knowledge of facts that are not readily apparent in the situations. Since experience not only contains this information but also causes it to come to mind, patrolmen claim to have developed a special sensitivity for qualities of appearances that allow an intuitive grasp of probable tendencies. In this context, little things are said to have high informational value and lead to conclusions without the intervention of explicitly reasoned chains of inferences. Third, patrolmen readily admit that they do not adhere to high standards of adequacy of justification. They do not seek to defend the adequacy of their method against some abstract criteria of merit. Instead, when questioned they assess their methods against the background of a whole system of *ad hoc* decision making, a system that encompasses the courts, correction facilities, the welfare establishment, and medical services. In fact, policemen generally maintain that their own procedures not only measure up to the workings of this system but exceed them in the attitude of carefulness.

In addition to these recognised reasons, there are two additional background factors that play a significant part in decisions to employ coercion. One has to do with the relevance of situational factors, and the other with the evaluation of coercion as relatively insignificant in the lives of the inhabitants.

There is no doubt that the nature of the circumstances often has decisive influence on what will be done. . . . For example, a patrolman was directed to a hotel and found a father and son fighting about money. The father occupied a room in the hotel and the son occasionally shared his quarters. There were two other men present, and they made it clear that their sympathies were with the older man. The son was whisked off to jail without much study of the relative merits of the conflicting claims. In yet another case, a middle-aged woman was forcefully evacuated from a bar even after the bartender explained that her loud behaviour was merely a response to goading by some foul-mouth youth.

In all such circumstances, coercive control is exercised as a means of coming to grips with situational exigencies. Force is used against particular persons but is incidental to the task. An ideal of 'economy of intervention' dictates in these and similar cases that the person whose presence is most likely to perpetuate the troublesome development be removed. Moreover, the decision as to who is to be removed is arrived at very quickly. Officers feel considerable pressure to act unhesitatingly, and many give accounts of situations that got out of hand because of desires to handle cases with careful consideration. However, even when there is no apparent risk of rapid proliferation of trouble, the tactic of removing one or two persons is used to control an undesirable situation. Thus, when a patrolman ran into a group of four men sharing a bottle of wine in an alley, he emptied the remaining contents of the bottle into the gutter, arrested one man—who was no more and no less drunk than the others—and let the others disperse in various directions.

The exigential nature of control is also evident in the handling of isolated drunks. Men are arrested because of where they happen to be encountered. In this, it matters not only whether a man is found in a conspicuous place or not, also how far away he is from his domicile. The further away he is, the less likely it is that he will make it to his room, and the more likely the arrest. Sometimes drunk arrests are made mainly because the police van is available. In one case a patrolman summoned the van to pick up an arrested man. As the van was pulling away from the kerb the officer stopped the driver because he sighted another drunk stumbling across the street. The second man protested saying that he 'wasn't even half drunk yet'. The patrolman's response was 'OK, I'll owe you half a drunk'. In sum, the basic routine of

keeping the peace on skid-row involves a process of matching the resources of control with situational exigencies. The overall objective is to
reduce the total amount of risk in the area. In this, practicality plays a
considerably more important role than legal norms. Precisely because
patrolmen see legal reasons for coercive action much more widely distributed on skid-row than could ever be matched by interventions, they
intervene not in the interest of law enforcement but in the interest of
producing relative tranquillity and order on the street.

Taking the perspective of the victim of coercive measures, one could
ask why he, in particular, has to bear the cost of keeping the aggregate
of troubles down while others, who are equally or perhaps even more
implicated, go scot-free. Patrolmen maintain that the *ad hoc* selection
of persons for attention must be viewed in the light of the following
consideration: Arresting a person on skid-row on some minor charge
may save him and others a lot of trouble, but it does not work any real
hardships on the arrested person. It is difficult to overestimate the skid-
row patrolman's feeling of certainty that his coercive and disciplinary
actions toward the inhabitants have but the most passing significance
in their lives. Sending a man to jail on some charge that will hold him
for a couple of days is seen as a matter of such slight importance to the
affected person that it could hardly give rise to scruples. Thus, every
indication that a coercive measure should be taken is accompanied by
the realisation 'I might as well, for all it matters to him'. Certain
realities of life on skid-row furnish the context for this belief in the
attenuated relevance of coercion in the lives of the inhabitants. Foremost
among them is that the use of police authority is seen as totally un-
remarkable by everybody on skid-row. Persons who live or work there
are continuously exposed to it and take its existence for granted. Shop-
keepers, hotel clerks, and bartenders call patrolmen to rid themselves
of unwanted and troublesome patrons. Residents expect patrolmen to
arbitrate their quarrels authoritatively. Men who receive orders, whether
they obey them or not, treat them as part of life as usual. Moreover,
patrolmen find that disciplinary and coercive actions apparently do not
affect their friendly relations with the persons against whom these
actions are taken. Those who greet and chat with them are the very
same men who have been disciplined, arrested, and ordered around in
the past, and who expect to be thus treated again in the future. From all
this, officers gather that though the people on skid-row seek to evade
police authority, they do not really object to it. Indeed, it happens quite
frequently that officers encounter men who welcome being arrested and
even actively ask for it. Finally, officers point out that sending someone
to jail from skid-row does not upset his relatives or his family life, does

not cause him to miss work or lose a job, does not lead to his being reproached by friends and associates, does not lead to failure to meet commitments or protect investments, and does not conflict with any but the most passing intentions of the arrested person. Seasoned patrolmen are not oblivious to the irony of the fact that measures intended as mechanisms for distributing deserts can be used freely because these measures are relatively impotent in their effects.

SUMMARY AND CONCLUSIONS

It was the purpose of this paper to render an account of a domain of police practice that does not seem subject to any system of external control. Following the terminology suggested by Michael Banton (1964), this practice was called keeping the peace. The procedures employed in keeping the peace are not determined by legal mandates but are, instead, responses to certain demand conditions. From among several demand conditions, we concentrated on the one produced by the concentration of certain types of persons in districts known as skid-row. Patrolmen maintain that the lives of the inhabitants of the area are lacking in prospective coherence. The consequent reduction in the temporal horizon of predictability constitutes the main problem of keeping the peace on skid-row.

Peace keeping procedure on skid-row consists of three elements. Patrolmen seek to acquire a rich body of concrete knowledge about people by cultivating personal acquaintance with as many residents as possible. They tend to proceed against persons mainly on the basis of perceived risk, rather than on the basis of culpability. And they are more interested in reducing the aggregate total of troubles in the area than in evaluating individual cases according to merit.

There may seem to be a discrepancy between the skid-row patrolman's objective of preventing disorder and his efforts to maintain personal acquaintance with as many persons as possible. But these efforts are principally a tactical device. By knowing someone individually the patrolman reduces ambiguity, extends trust and favours, but does not grant immunity. The informality of interaction on skid-row always contains some indications of the hierarchical superiority of the patrolman and the reality of his potential power lurks in the background of every encounter.

Though our interest was focused initially on those police procedures that did not involve invoking the law, we found that the two cannot be separated. The reason for the connection is not given in the circumstance that the roles of the 'law officer' and of the 'peace officer' are enacted by the same person and thus are contiguous. According to our observations, patrolmen do not act alternatively as one or the other, with certain actions being determined by the intended objective of keeping the peace and others being determined by the duty to enforce the law. Instead, we have found that *peace keeping occasionally acquires the external aspects of law enforcement*. This makes it specious to inquire whether or not police discretion in invoking the law conforms with the intention of some specific legal formula. The real reason behind an arrest is virtually always the actual state of particular social situations, or of the skid-row area in general.

We have concentrated on those procedures and considerations that skid-row patrolmen regard as necessary, proper, and efficient relative to the circumstances in which they are employed. In this way, we attempted to disclose the conception of the mandate to which the police feel summoned. It was entirely outside the scope of the presentation to review the merits of this conception and of the methods used to meet it. Only insofar as patrolmen themselves recognised instances and patterns of malpractice did we take note of them. Most of the criticism voiced by officers had to do with the use of undue harshness and with the indiscriminate use of arrest powers when these were based on personal feelings rather than the requirements of the situation. According to prevailing opinion, patrolmen guilty of such abuses make life unnecessarily difficult for themselves and for their co-workers. Despite disapproval of harshness, officers tend to be defensive about it. For example, one sergeant who was outspokenly critical of brutality, said that though in general brutal men create more problems than they solve, 'they do a good job in some situations for which the better men have no stomach'. Moreover, supervisory personnel exhibit a strong reluctance to direct their subordinates in the particulars of their work performance. According to our observations, control is exercised mainly through consultation with superiors, and directives take the form of requests rather than orders. In the background of all this is the belief that patrol work on skid-row requires a great deal of discretionary freedom. In the words of the same sergeant quoted above, 'a good man has things worked out in his own ways on his beat and he doesn't need anybody to tell him what to do'.

The virtual absence of disciplinary control and the demand for discretionary freedom are related to the idea that patrol work involves 'playing by ear'. For if it is true that peace keeping cannot be systematically generalised, then, of course, it cannot be organisationally constrained. What the seasoned patrolman means, however, in saying that he 'plays by ear' is that he is making his decisions while being attuned to the realities of complex situations about which he has immensely detailed knowledge. This studied aspect of peace keeping generally is not made explicit, nor is the tyro or the outsider made aware of it. Quite to the contrary, the ability to discharge the duties associated with keeping the peace is viewed as a reflection of an innate talent of 'getting along with people'. Thus, the same demands are made of barely initiated officers as are made of experienced practitioners. Correspondingly, beginners tend to think that they can do as well as their more knowledgeable peers. As this leads to inevitable frustrations, they find themselves in a situation that is conducive to the development of a particular sense of 'touchiness'. Personal dispositions of individual officers are, of course, of great relevance. But the licence of discretionary freedom and the expectation of success under conditions of autonomy, without any indication that the work of the successful craftsman is based on an acquired preparedness for the task, is ready-made for failure and malpractice. Moreover, it leads to slipshod practices of patrol that also infect the standards of the careful craftsman.

The uniformed patrol, and especially the foot patrol, has a low preferential value in the division of labour of police work. This is, in part, at least, due to the belief that 'anyone could do it'. In fact, this belief is thoroughly mistaken. At present, however, the recognition that the practice requires preparation, and the process of obtaining the preparation itself, is left entirely to the practitioner.

REFERENCE

BANTON, MICHAEL (1964) *The Policeman in the Community*, New York, Basic Books.

23

David Sudnow

Normal crimes: sociological features of the penal code in a public defender office

Excerpts from David Sudnow, 'Normal crimes: sociological features of the penal code in a public defender office', *Social Problems*, **12**, 1965, 255–72.

GUILTY PLEAS, INCLUSION, AND NORMAL CRIMES

It is a commonly noted fact about the criminal court system generally, that the greatest proportion of cases are 'settled' by a guilty plea. In the county from which the following material is drawn, over 80 per cent of all cases 'never go to trial'. To describe the method of obtaining a guilty plea disposition, essential for the discussion to follow, I must distinguish between what shall be termed 'necessarily-included-lesser-offences' and 'situationally-included-lesser-offences'. Of two offences designated in the penal code, the lesser is considered to be that for which the length of required incarceration is the shorter period of time. *Inclusion* refers to the relation between two or more offences. The 'necessarily-included-lesser-offence' is a strictly legal notion:

> Whether a lesser offense is included in the crime charged is a question of law to be determined solely from the definition and corpus delicti of the offense charged and of the lesser offense. . . . If all the elements of the corpus delicti of a lesser crime can be found in a list of all the elements of the offense charged, then only is the lesser included in the greater (Fricke, 1961, p. 41).

. . . I shall call *lesser* offences that are not necessarily but 'only' *actually* included, 'situationally-included-lesser-offences'. By statutory definition, necessarily included offences are 'actually' included. By actual here, I refer to the 'way it occurs as a course of action'. In the instance of necessary inclusion, the 'way it occurs' is irrelevant. With situational inclusion, the 'way it occurs' is definitive. In the former case, no particular course of action is referred to. In the latter, the scene and progress of the criminal activity would be analysed.

The issue of necessary inclusion has special relevance for two procedural matters:

A. A man cannot be charged and/or convicted of two or more crimes any one of which is necessarily included in the others, unless the several crimes occur on separate occasions.

If a murder occurs, the defendant cannot be charged and/or convicted of both 'homicide' and 'intent to commit a murder', the latter of which is necessarily included in first degree murder. . . .

B. The judge cannot instruct the jury to consider as alternative crimes of which to find a defendant guilty, crimes that are not necessarily included in the charged crime or crimes.

If a man is charged with 'statutory rape' the judge may instruct the jury to consider as a possible alternative conviction 'contributing to the delinquency of a minor', as this offence is necessarily included in 'statutory rape'. He cannot, however, suggest that the alternative 'intent to commit murder' be considered and the jury cannot find the defendant guilty of this latter crime, unless it is charged as a distinct offence in the complaint.

It is crucial to note that these restrictions apply only to (*a*) the relation between several charged offences in a formal allegation, and (*b*) the alternatives allowable in a jury instruction. At any time before a case 'goes to trial', alterations in the charging complaint may be made by the district attorney. The issue of necessary inclusion has no required bearing on (*a*) what offence(s) will be charged initially by the prosecutor, (*b*) what the relation is between the charge initially made and 'what happened', or (*c*) what modifications may be made after the initial charge and the relation between initially charged offences and those charged in modified complaints. It is this latter operation, the modification of the complaint, that is central to the guilty plea disposition.

Complaint alterations are made when a defendant agrees to plead guilty to an offence and thereby avoid a trial. The alteration occurs in the context of a 'deal' consisting of an offer from the district attorney to alter the original charge in such a fashion that a lighter sentence will be incurred with a guilty plea than would be the case if the defendant were sentenced on the original charge. In return for this manipulation, the defendant agrees to plead guilty. The arrangement is proposed in the following format: 'if you plead guilty to this new lesser offence, you will get less time in prison than if you plead not guilty to the original, greater charge and lose the trial'. The decision must then be made whether or not the chances of obtaining complete acquittal at trial are great enough to warrant the risk of a loss and higher sentence if found guilty on the original charge. As we shall see below, it is a major job of the Public Defender, who mediates between the district attorney and the defendant, to convince his 'client' that the chances of acquittal are too slight to warrant this risk.

If a man is charged with 'drunkenness' and the Public Defender and Public Prosecutor (hereafter P.D. and D.A.) prefer not to have a trial, they seek to have the defendant agree to plead guilty. While it is occasionally possible, particularly with first offenders, for the P.D. to convince the defendant to plead guilty to the originally charged offence, most often it is felt that some 'exchange' or 'consideration' should be offered, i.e., a lesser offence charged.

To what offence can 'drunkenness' be reduced? There is no statutorily designated crime that is necessarily included in the crime of 'drunkenness'. That is, if any of the statutorily required components of drunk behaviour (its corpus delicti) are absent, there remains no offence of which the resultant description is a definition. For drunkenness there is, however, an offence that while not necessarily included is 'typically-situationally-included', i.e., 'typically' occurs as a feature of the way drunk persons are seen to behave—'disturbing the peace'. The range of possible sentences is such that, of the two offences, 'disturbing the peace' cannot call for as long a prison sentence as 'drunkenness'. If, in the course of going on a binge, a person does so in such a fashion that 'disturbing the peace' may be employed to describe some of his behaviour, it would be considered as an alternative offence to offer in return for a guilty plea. A central question for the following analysis will be: in what fashion would he have to behave so that disturbing the peace would be considered a suitable reduction?

If a man is charged with 'molesting a minor', there are not any necessarily included lesser offences with which to charge him. Yet an alternative charge—'loitering around a schoolyard'—is often used as a reduction. As above, and central to our analysis the question is: what would the defendant's behaviour be such that 'loitering around a schoolyard' would constitute an appropriate alternative? . . .

Offences are regularly reduced to other offences the latter of which are not necessarily or situationally included in the former. . . .

When encountering a defendant who is charged with 'assault with a deadly weapon', the P.D. asks: 'what can this offence be reduced to so as to arrange for a guilty plea?' As the reduction is only to be proposed by the P.D. and accepted or not by the D.A., his question becomes 'what reduction will be allowable?' (As shall be seen below, the P.D. and D.A. have institutionalised a common orientation to allowable reductions.) The method of reduction involves, as a general feature, the fact that the particular case in question is scrutinised to decide its membership in a class of similar cases. But *the penal code does not provide the reference for deciding the correspondence between the instant event and the general case; that is, it does not define the classes of offence types.* To decide, for purposes of finding a suitable reduction, if the instant case involves a 'burglary', reference is not made to the statutory definition of 'burglary'. To decide what the situationally included offences are in the instant case, the instant case is not analysed as a *statutorily* referable course of action; rather, reference is made to a *non-statutorily* conceived class 'burglary' and offences that are typically situationally included in it, taken as a class of behavioural events.

... If a defendant is charged with burglary and the P.D. is concerned to propose a reduction to a lesser offence, he might search the elements of the burglary at hand to decide what other offences were committed. The other offences he might 'discover' would be of two sorts: those necessarily and those situationally included. In attempting to decide those other offences situationally included in the instant event, the instant event might be analysed as a statutorily referable course of action. Or, as is the case with the P.D., the instant case might be analysed to decide if it is a 'burglary' in common with other 'burglaries' conceived of in terms other than those provided by the statute.

Burglaries are routinely reduced to petty theft. If we were to analyse the way burglaries typically occur, petty theft is neither situationally or necessarily included; when a burglary is committed, money or other goods are seldom illegally removed from some person's body. If we therefore analysed burglaries, employing the penal code as our reference, and then searched the P.D.'s records to see how burglaries are reduced in the guilty plea, we could not establish a rule that would describe the transformation between the burglary cases statutorily described and the reductions routinely made (i.e., to 'petty theft'). The rule must be sought elsewhere, in the character of the non-statutorily defined class of 'burglaries', which I shall term *normal burglaries*.

NORMAL CRIMES

In the course of routinely encountering persons charged with 'petty theft', 'burglary', 'assault with a deadly weapon', 'rape', 'possession of marijuana', etc., the P.D. gains knowledge of the typical manner in which offences of given classes are committed, the social characteristics of the persons who regularly commit them, the features of the settings in which they occur, the types of victims often involved, and the like. He learns to speak knowledgeably of 'burglars', 'petty thieves', 'drunks', 'rapists', 'narcos', etc., and to attribute to them personal biographies, modes of usual criminal activity, criminal histories, psychological characteristics, and social backgrounds. The following characterisations are illustrative:

> Most ADWs (assault with deadly weapon) start with fights over some girl.
> These sex fiends (child molestation cases) usually hang around parks or schoolyards. But we often get fathers charged with these crimes. Usually the old man is out of work and stays at home when the wife goes to work and he plays around with his little daughter or something. A lot of these cases start when there is some marital trouble and the woman gets mad.

> I don't know why most of them don't rob the big stores. They usually break into some cheap department store and steal some crummy item like a $9.95 record player, you know.

> Kids who start taking this stuff (narcotics) usually start out when some buddy gives them a cigarette and they smoke it for kicks. For some reason they always get caught in their cars, for speeding or something.

They can anticipate that point when persons are likely to get into trouble:

> Dope addicts do OK until they lose a job or something and get back on the streets and, you know, meet the old boys. Someone tells them where to get some and there they are.

> In the springtime, that's when we get all these sex crimes. You know, these kids play out in the schoolyard all day and these old men sit around and watch them jumping up and down. They get their ideas.

The P.D. learns that some kinds of offenders are likely to repeat the same offence while others are not repeat violators or, if they do commit crimes frequently, the crimes vary from occasion to occasion:

> You almost never see a check man get caught for anything but checks —only an occasional drunk charge.

> Burglars are usually multiple offenders, most times just burglaries or petty thefts.

> Petty thefts get started for almost anything—joy riding, drinking, all kinds of little things.

> These narcos are usually through after the second violation or so. After the first time some stop, but when they start on the heavy stuff, they've had it.

I shall call *normal crimes* those occurrences whose typical features, e.g., the ways they usually occur and the characteristics of persons who commit them (as well as the typical victims and typical scenes), are known and attended to by the P.D. For any of a series of offence types the P.D. can provide some form of proverbial characterisation. For example, *burglary* is seen as involving regular violators, no weapons, low-priced items, little property damage, lower class establishments, largely Negro defendants, independent operators, and a non-professional orientation to the crime. *Child molesting* is seen as typically entailing middle-aged strangers or lower class middle-aged fathers (few women), no actual physical penetration or severe tissue damage, mild fondling, petting, and stimulation, bad marriage circumstances, multiple offenders with the same offence repeatedly committed, a child complainant, via the mother, etc. *Narcotics* defendants are usually Negroes, not syndicated, persons who start by using small stuff, hostile with police officers, caught by some form of entrapment technique, etc. *Petty thefts* are about 50–50 Negro-white, unplanned offences, generally committed on lower-class persons and don't get much money, don't often employ weapons, don't make living from thievery, usually younger defendants with long juvenile assaultive records, etc. *Drunkenness* offenders are lower class white and Negro, get drunk on wine and beer, have long histories of repeated drunkenness, don't hold down jobs, are usually arrested on the streets, seldom violate other penal code sections, etc.

Some general features of the normal crime as a way of attending to a category of persons and events may be mentioned:

1. The focus, in these characterisations, is not on particular individuals, but offence types. If asked 'What are burglars like?' or 'How are

burglaries usually committed?', the P.D. does not feel obliged to refer to particular burglars and burglaries as the material for his answer.

2. The features attributed to offenders and offences are often not of import for the statutory conception. In burglary, it is 'irrelevant' for the statutory determination whether or not much damage was done to the premises (except where, for example, explosives were employed and a new statute could be invoked). Whether a defendant breaks a window or not, destroys property within the house or not, etc., does not affect his statutory classification as a burglar. While for robbery the presence or absence of a weapon sets the degree, whether the weapon is a machine gun or pocket knife is 'immaterial'. Whether the residence or business establishment in a burglary is located in a higher income area of the city is of no issue for the code requirements. And, generally, the defendant's race, class position, criminal history (in most offences), personal attributes, and particular style of committing offences are features specifically not definitive of crimes under the auspices of the penal code. For deciding 'Is this a "burglary" case I have before me', however, the P.D.'s references to this range of non-statutorily referable personal and social attributes, modes of operation, etc., is crucial for the arrangement of a guilty plea bargain.

3. The features attributed to offenders and offences are, in their content, specific to the community in which the P.D. works. In other communities and historical periods the lists would presumably differ. Narcotics violators in certain areas, for example, are syndicated in dope rackets or engage in systematic robbery as professional criminals, features which are not commonly encountered (or, at least, evidence for which is not systematically sought) in this community. Burglary in some cities will more often occur at large industrial plants, banking establishments, warehouses, etc. The P.D. refers to the population of defendants in the county as 'our defendants' and qualifies his prototypical portrayals and knowledge of the typically operative social structures, 'for our county'. An older P.D., remembering the 'old days', commented: 'We used to have a lot more rapes than we do now, and they used to be much more violent. Things are duller now in. . . .'

4. Offences whose normal features are readily attended to are those which are routinely encountered in the courtroom. This feature is related to the last point. For embezzlement, bank robbery, gambling, prostitution, murder, arson, and some other uncommon offences, the P.D. cannot readily supply anecdotal and proverbial characterisations. While there is some change in the frequencies of offence-type convictions over time, certain offences are continually more common and others remain stably infrequent. The troubles created for the P.D. when

offences whose features are not readily known occur, and whose typicality is not easily constructed, will be discussed in some detail below.

5. Offences are ecologically specified and attended to as normal or not according to the locales within which they are committed. The P.D. learns that burglaries usually occur in such and such areas of the city, petty thefts around this or that park, ADWs in these bars. Ecological patterns are seen as related to socio-economic variables and these in turn to typical modes of criminal and non-criminal activities. Knowing where an offence took place is thus, for the P.D., knowledge of the likely persons involved, the kind of scene in which the offence occurred, and the pattern of activity characteristic of such a place:

> Almost all of our ADWs are in the same half a dozen bars. These places are Negro bars where laborers come after hanging around the union halls trying to get some work. Nobody has any money and they drink too much. Tempers are high and almost anything can start happening.

6. One further important feature can be noted at this point. . . . The P.D. office consists of a staff of twelve full-time attorneys. Knowledge of the properties of offence types of offenders, i.e., their normal, typical, or familiar attributes, constitutes the mark of any given attorney's competence. A major task in socialising the new P.D. deputy attorney consists in teaching him to recognise these attributes and to come to do so naturally. The achievement of competence as a P.D. is signalled by the gradual acquisition of professional command not simply of local penal code peculiarities and courtroom folklore, but, as importantly, of relevant features of the social structure and criminological wisdom. His grasp of that knowledge over the course of time is a key indication of his expertise. Below, in our brief account of some relevant organisational properties of the P.D. system, we shall have occasion to re-emphasise the competence-attesting aspects of the attorney's proper use of established sociological knowledge. Let us return to the mechanics of the guilty plea procedure as an example of the operation of the notion of normal crimes.

Over the course of their interaction and repeated 'bargaining' discussions, the P.D. and D.A. have developed a set of unstated recipes for reducing original charges to lesser offences. These recipes are specifically appropriate for use in instances of normal crimes and in such instances alone. 'Typical' burglaries are reduced to petty theft, 'typical' ADWs to simple assault, 'typical' child molestation to loitering around a schoolyard, etc. The character of these recipes deserves attention.

The specific content of any reduction, i.e. what particular offence class X offences will be reduced to, is such that the reduced offence may bear no obvious relation (neither situationally nor necessarily included) to the originally charged offence. The reduction of burglary to petty theft is an example. The important relation between the reduced offence and the original charge is such that the reduction from one to the other is considered 'reasonable'. At this point we shall only state what seems to be the general principle involved in deciding this reasonableness. The underlying premises cannot be explored at the present time, as that would involve a political analysis beyond the scope of the present report. *Both P.D. and D.A. are concerned to obtain a guilty plea wherever possible and thereby avoid a trial. At the same time, each party is concerned that the defendant 'receive his due'. The reduction of offence X to Y must be of such a character that the new sentence will depart from the anticipated sentence for the original charge to such a degree that the defendant is likely to plead guilty to the new charge and, at the same time, not so great that the defendant does not 'get his due'.*

In a homicide, while battery is a necessarily included offence, it will not be considered as a possible reduction. For a conviction of second degree murder a defendant could receive a life sentence in the penitentiary. For a battery conviction he would spend no more than six months in the county jail. In a homicide, however, 'felony manslaughter', or 'assault with a deadly weapon', whatever their relation to homicide as regards inclusion, would more closely approximate the sentence outcome that could be expected on a trial conviction of second degree murder. These alternatives would be considered. For burglary, a typically situationally included offence might be 'disturbing the peace', 'breaking and entering' or 'destroying public property'. 'Petty theft', however, constitutes a reasonable lesser alternative to burglary as the sentence for petty theft will often range between six months and one year in the county jail and burglary regularly does not carry higher than two years in the state prison. 'Disturbing the peace' would be a thirty-day sentence offence.

While the present purposes make the exposition of this calculus unnecessary, it can be noted and stressed that the particular content of the reduction does not necessarily correspond to a relation between the original and altered charge that could be described in either the terms of necessary or situational inclusion. Whatever the relation between the original and reduced charge, its essential feature resides in the spread between sentence likelihoods and the reasonableness of that spread, i.e., the balance it strikes between the defendant 'getting his due' and at the same time 'getting something less than he might so that he will plead guilty'.

The procedure we want to clarify now, at the risk of some repetition, is the manner in which an instant case is examined to decide its membership in a class of 'crimes such as this' (the category *normal crimes*). Let us start with an obvious case, burglary. As the typical reduction for burglary is petty theft and as petty theft is neither situationally nor necessarily included in burglary, the examination of the instant case is clearly not undertaken to decide whether petty theft is an appropriate statutory description. The concern is to establish the relation between the instant burglary and the normal category 'burglaries' and, having decided a 'sufficient correspondence', to now employ petty theft as the proposed reduction.

In scrutinising the present burglary case, the P.D. seeks to establish that 'this is a burglary just like any other'. If that correspondence is not established, regardless of whether or not petty theft in fact was a feature of the way the crime was enacted, the reduction to petty theft would not be proposed. *The propriety of proposing petty theft as a reduction does not derive from its in-fact-existence in the present case, but is warranted or not by the relation of the present burglary to 'burglaries', normally conceived.*

In a case of 'child molestation' (officially called 'lewd conduct with a minor'), the concern is to decide if this is a 'typical child molestation case'. While 'loitering around a schoolyard' is frequently a feature of the way such crimes are instigated, establishing that the present defendant *did in fact loiter around a schoolyard* is secondary to the more general question 'Is this a typical child molestation case?' What appears as a contradiction must be clarified by examining the status of 'loitering around a schoolyard' as a typical feature of such child molestations. The typical character of 'child molesting cases' does not stand or fall on the fact that 'loitering around a schoolyard' is a feature of the way they are in fact committed. It is *not* that 'loitering around a schoolyard' as a *statutorily referable behaviour sequence* is part of typical 'child molesting cases' but that 'loitering around a schoolyard' as a *socially distinct mode of committing child molestations typifies the way such offences are enacted*. 'Strictly speaking', i.e., under the auspices of the statutory *corpus delicti*, 'loitering around a schoolyard', requires *loitering, around, a schoolyard*; if one loiters around a ball park or a public recreation area, he 'cannot', within a proper reading of the statute, be charged with loitering around a *schoolyard*. Yet 'loitering around a schoolyard', as a feature of the typical way such offences as child molestations are committed, has the status not of a description of the way in *fact* (*fact*, statutorily decided) it occurred or typically occurs, but 'the-kind-of-social-activity-typically-associated-with-such-offences.' It is not its statutorily conceived features but its socially relevant attributes that gives 'loitering around a schoolyard' its status as a feature of the class 'normal child molestations'. Whether the defendant loitered around a schoolyard or a ball park, and whether he loitered or 'was passing by', 'loitering around a school-yard' as a reduction will be made if the defendant's activity was such that 'he was hanging around some public place or another' and 'was the kind of guy who hangs around schoolyards'. As a component of the class of normal child molestation cases (of the variety where the victim is a stranger), 'loitering around a schoolyard' typifies a mode of com-mitting such offences, the class of 'such persons who do such things as hang around schoolyards and the like'. A large variety of actual offences could thus be nonetheless reduced to 'loitering' if, as kinds of social activity, 'loitering', conceived of as typifying a way of life, pattern of daily activity, social psychological circumstances, etc., characterised the conduct of the defendant. The young P.D. who would object 'You can't reduce it to "loitering"—he didn't really "loiter",' would be repri-manded: 'Fella, you don't know how to use that term; he might as well have "loitered"—it's the same kind of case as the others'. . . .

SOME CONCLUSIONS

An examination of the use of the penal code by actually practising attorneys has revealed that categories of crime, rather than being 'unsuited' to sociological analysis, are so employed as to make their analysis crucial to empirical understanding. What categories of crime are, i.e., who is assembled under this one or that, what constitute the behaviours inspected for deciding such matters, what 'etiologically significant' matters are incorporated within their scope, is not, the present findings indicate, to be decided on the basis of an *a priori* inspection of their formally available definitions. The sociologist who regards the category 'theft' with penal code in hand and proposes necessary, 'theoretically relevant' revisions, is constructing an imagined use of the penal code as the basis for his criticism. For in their actual use, categories of crime, as we have reiterated continuously above, are, at least for this legal establishment, the shorthand reference terms for that knowledge of the social structure and its criminal events upon which the task of practically organising the work of 'representation' is premised. That knowledge includes, embodied within what burglary, petty theft, narcotics violations, child molestation and the rest *actually stand for*, knowledge of modes of criminal activity, ecological characteristics of the community, patterns of daily slum life, psychological and social biographies of offenders, criminal histories and futures; in sum, practically tested criminological wisdom. The operations of the Public Defender system, and it is clear that upon comparative analysis with other legal 'firms' it would be somewhat distinctive in character, are routinely maintained via the proper use of categories of crime for everyday decision making. The proprieties of that use are not described in the state criminal code, nor are the operations of reduction, detailed above.

REFERENCE

FRICKE, C. W. (1961) *California Criminal Law*, Los Angeles, The Legal Book Store.

24

Joan Emerson

Behaviour in private places: sustaining definitions of reality in gynaecological examinations

Excerpts from Joan Emerson, 'Behaviour in private places: sustaining definitions of reality in gynecological examinations' in Hans Peter Dreitzel, ed., *Recent Sociology*, 2, New York, Macmillan, 1970, pp. 73-100.

I. INTRODUCTION

In *The Social Construction of Reality*, Berger and Luckmann (1966) discuss how people construct social order and yet construe the reality of everyday life to exist independently of themselves. Berger and Luckmann's work succeeds in synthesising some existing answers with new insights. Many sociologists have pointed to the importance of social consensus in what people believe; if everyone else seems to believe in something, a person tends to accept the common belief without question. Other sociologists have discussed the concept of legitimacy, an acknowledgment that what exists has the right to exist, and delineated various lines of argument which can be taken to justify a state of affairs. Berger and Luckmann emphasise three additional processes that provide persons with evidence that things have an objective existence apart from themselves. Perhaps most important is the experience that reality seems to be out there before we arrive on the scene. This notion is fostered by the nature of language, which contains an all-inclusive scheme of categories, is shared by a community, and must be learned laboriously by each new member. Further, definitions of reality are continuously validated by apparently trivial features of the social scene, such as details of the setting, persons' appearance and demeanour, and 'inconsequential' talk. Finally, each part of a systematic world view serves as evidence for all the other parts, so that reality is solidified by a process of intervalidation of supposedly independent events.

...In this paper observations of a concrete situation will be interpreted to show how reality is embodied in routines and reaffirmed in social interaction.

Situations differ in how much effort it takes to sustain the current definition of the situation. Some situations are relatively stable; others are precarious. Stability depends on the likelihood of three types of disconforming events. Intrusions on the scene may threaten definitions of reality, as when people smell smoke in a theatre or when a third person joins a couple and calls one member by a name the second member does not recognise. Participants may deliberately decline to validate the current reality, like Quakers who refused to take off their hats to the king. Sometimes participants are unable to produce the gestures which would validate the current reality. Perhaps a person is ignorant of the relevant vocabulary of gestures. Or a person, understanding how he should behave, may have limited social skills so that he cannot carry off the performance he would like to. For those who insist on 'sincerity', a performance becomes especially taxing if they lack conviction about the trueness of the reality they are attempting to project.

A reality can hardly seem self-evident if a person is simultaneously aware of a counter-reality. Berger and Luckmann write as though definitions of reality were internally congruent. However, the ordinary reality may contain not only a dominant definition, but in addition counter themes opposing or qualifying the dominant definition. Thus, several contradictory definitions must be sustained at the same time. Because each element tends to challenge the other elements, such composite definitions of reality are inherently precarious even if the probability of disconfirming events is low.

A situation where the definition of reality is relatively precarious has advantages for the analysis proposed here, for processes of sustaining reality should be more obvious where that reality is problematic. The situation chosen, the gynaecological examination,[1] is precarious for both reasons discussed above. First, it is an excellent example of multiple contradictory definitions of reality, as described in the next section.

---

[1] The data in this article are based on observations of approximately 75 gynaecological examinations conducted by male physicians on an obstetrics-gynaecology ward and some observations from a medical ward for comparison.

Second, while intrusive and deliberate threats are not important, there is a substantial threat from participants' incapacity to perform.

Dramaturgical abilities are taxed in gynaecological examinations because the less convincing reality internalised by secondary socialisation is unusually discrepant with rival perspectives taken for granted in primary socialisation. Gynaecological examinations share similar problems of reality-maintenance with any medical procedure, but the issues are more prominent because the site of the medical task is a woman's genitals. Because touching usually connotes personal intimacy, persons may have to work at accepting the physician's privileged access to the patient's genitals (cf. Lief and Fox, 1963, p. 32). Participants are not entirely convinced that modesty is out of place. Since a woman's genitals are commonly accessible only in a sexual context, sexual connotations come readily to mind. Although most people realise that sexual responses are inappropriate, they may be unable to dismiss the sexual reaction privately and it may interfere with the conviction with which they undertake their impersonal performance. The structure of a gynaecological examination highlights the very features which the participants are supposed to dis-attend. So the more attentive the participants are to the social situation, the more the unmentionable is forced on their attention.

The next section will characterise the complex composition of the definition of reality routinely sustained in gynaecological examinations. Then some of the routine arrangements and interactional manoeuvres which embody and express this definition will be described. A later section will discuss threats to the definition which arise in the course of the encounter. Measures that serve to neutralise the threats and reaffirm the definition will be analysed. The concluding section will turn to the theoretical issues of precariousness, multiple contradictory definitions of reality, and implicit communication.

II. THE MEDICAL DEFINITION AND ITS COUNTER-THEMES

... What happens in a gynaecological examination is part of the common stock of knowledge. Most people know that a gynaecological examination is when a doctor examines a woman's genitals in a medical setting. Women who have undergone this experience know that the examination takes place in a special examining room where the patient lies with her buttocks down to the edge of the table and her feet in stirrups, that usually a nurse is present as a chaperone, that the actual examining lasts only a few minutes, and so forth. Besides knowing what equipment to provide for the doctor, the nurse has in mind a typology of responses patients have to this situation, and a typology of doctors' styles of performance. The doctor has technical knowledge about the examining procedures, what observations may be taken to indicate, ways of getting patients to relax, and so on.

Immersed in the medical world where the scene constitutes a routine, the staff assume the responsibility for a credible performance. The staff take part in gynaecological examinations many times a day, while the patient is a fleeting visitor. More deeply convinced of the reality themselves, the staff are willing to convince sceptical patients. The physician guides the patient through the precarious scene in a contained manner: taking the initiative, controlling the encounter, keeping the patient in line, defining the situation by his reaction, and giving cues that 'this is done' and 'other people go through this all the time'.

Not only must people continue to believe that 'this is a gynaecological examination', but also that 'this is a gynaecological examination going right'. The major definition to be sustained for this purpose is 'this is a medical situation' (not a party, sexual assault, psychological experiment, or anything else). If it is a medical situation, then it follows that 'no one is embarrassed' and 'no one is thinking in sexual terms'. Anyone who indicates the contrary must be swayed by some non-medical definition.

The medical definition calls for a matter-of-fact stance. One of the most striking observations about a gynaecological examination is the marked implication underlying the staff's demeanour toward the patient: 'Of course, you take this as matter-of-factly as we do.' The staff implicitly contend: 'In the medical world the pelvic area is like any other part of the body; its private and sexual connotations are left behind when you enter the hospital.' The staff want it understood that their gazes take in only medically pertinent facts, so they are not concerned with an aesthetic inspection of a patient's body. Their nonchalant pose attempts to put a gynaecological examination in the same light as an internal examination of the ear.

Another implication of the medical definition is that the patient is a technical object to the staff. It is as if the staff work on an assembly line for repairing bodies; similar body parts continually roll by and the staff have a particular job to do on them. The staff are concerned with the typical features of the body part and its pathology rather than with the unique features used to define a person's identity. The staff disattend the connection between a part of the body and some intangible self that is supposed to inhabit that body.

The scene is credible precisely because the staff act as if they have every right to do what they are doing. Any hint of doubt from the staff would compromise the medical definition. Since the patient's non-chalance merely serves to validate the staff's right, it may be dispensed with without the same threat. Furthermore, the staff claim to be merely agents of the medical system, which is intent on providing good health care to patients. This medical system imposes procedures and standards which the staff are merely following in this particular instance. . . .

The medical definition grants the staff the right to carry out their task. If not for the medical definition the staff's routine activities could be defined as unconscionable assaults on the dignity of individuals. The topics of talk, particularly inquiries about bodily functioning, sexual experience, and death of relatives might be taken as offences against propriety. As for exposure and manipulation of the patient's body, it would be a shocking and degrading invasion of privacy were the patient not defined as a technical object. The infliction of pain would be mere cruelty. The medical definition justifies the request that a presumably competent adult give up most of his autonomy to persons often subordinate in age, sex, and social class. The patient needs the medical definition to minimise the threat to his dignity; the staff need it in order to inveigle the patient into cooperating.

Yet definitions that appear to contradict the medical definition are routinely expressed in the course of gynaecological examinations. Some gestures acknowledge the pelvic area as special; other gestures acknowledge the patient as a person. These counter-definitions are as essential to the encounter as the medical definition. We have already discussed how an actor's lack of conviction may interfere with his performance. Implicit acknowledgments of the special meaning of the pelvic area help those players hampered by lack of conviction to perform adequately. If a player's sense of 'how things really are' is implicitly acknowledged, he often finds it easier to adhere outwardly to a contrary definition.

A physician may gain a patient's cooperation by acknowledging her as a person. The physician wants the patient to acknowledge the medical definition, cooperate with the procedures of the examination, and acknowledge his professional competence. The physician is in a position to bargain with the patient in order to obtain this cooperation. He can offer her attention and acknowledgment as a person. At times he does so.

Although defining a person as a technical object is necessary in order for medical activities to proceed, it constitutes an indignity in itself. This indignity can be cancelled or at least qualified by simultaneously acknowledging the patient as a person.

The medical world contains special activities and special perspectives.

Yet the inhabitants of the medical world travel back and forth to the general community where modesty, death, and other medically relevant matters are regarded quite differently. It is not so easy to dismiss general community meanings for the time one finds oneself in a medical setting. The counter-themes that the pelvic area is special and that patients are persons provide an opportunity to show deference to general community meanings at the same time that one is disregarding them.

Sustaining the reality of a gynaecological examination does not mean sustaining the medical definition, then. What is to be sustained is a shifting balance between medical definition and counter-themes. Too much emphasis on the medical definition alone would undermine the reality, as would a flamboyant manifestation of the counter-themes apart from the medical definition. The next three sections will suggest how this balance is achieved.

III. SUSTAINING THE REALITY

The appropriate balance between medical definition and counter-themes has to be created anew at every moment. However, some routinised procedures and demeanour are available to participants in gynaeco- logical examinations. Persons recognise that if certain limits are ex- ceeded, the situation would be irremediably shattered. Some arrange- ments have been found useful because they simultaneously express medical definition and counter-theme. Routine ways of meeting the task requirements and also dealing with 'normal trouble' are available. This section will describe how themes and counter-themes are embodied in routinised procedures and demeanour.

The pervasiveness of the medical definition is expressed by indicators that the scene is enacted under medical auspices. The action is located in 'medical space' (hospital or doctor's office). Features of the setting such as divisions of space, decor, and equipment are constant reminders that it is indeed 'medical space'. . . . The staff wear medical uniforms, don medical gloves, use medical instruments. The exclusion of lay persons, particularly visitors of the patient who may be accustomed to the patient's nudity at home, helps to preclude confusion between the contact of medicine and the contact of intimacy (cf. Glaser and Strauss, 1965, p. 162).

Some routine practices simultaneously acknowledge the medical definition and qualify it by making special provision for the pelvic area. For instance, rituals of respect express dignity for the patient. The patient's body is draped so as to expose only that part which is to receive the technical attention of the doctor. The presence of a nurse acting as 'chaperon' cancels any residual suggestiveness of male and female alone in a room.

Medical talk stands for and continually expresses allegiance to the medical definition. Yet certain features of medical talk acknowledge a non-medical delicacy. Despite the fact that persons present on a gynaecological ward must attend to many topics connected with the pelvic area and various bodily functions, these topics are generally not discussed. Strict conventions dictate what unmentionables are to be acknowledged under what circumstances. However, persons are exceptionally free to refer to the genitals and related matters on the obstetrics-gynaecology service. If technical matters in regard to the pelvic area come up, they are to be discussed nonchalantly.

The special language found in staff-patient contacts contributes to depersonalisation and desexualisation of the encounter. Scientific-sounding medical terms facilitate such communication. Substituting dictionary terms for everyday words adds formality. The definite article replaces the pronoun adjective in reference to body parts, so that for example, the doctor refers to 'the vagina' and never 'your vagina'. Instructions to the patient in the course of the examination are couched in language which bypasses sexual imagery; the vulgar connotation of 'spread your legs' is generally metamorphosed into the innocuous 'let your knees fall apart'.

While among themselves the staff generally use explicit technical terms, explicit terminology is often avoided in staff-patient contacts. The reference to the pelvic area may be merely understood, as when a patient says: 'I feel so uncomfortable there right now', or 'They didn't go near to this area, so why did they have to shave it?' In speaking with patients the staff frequently uses euphemisms. A doctor asks: 'When did you first notice difficulty down below?' and a nurse inquires: 'Did you wash between your legs?' ...

Sometimes the staff introduce explicit terminology to clarify a patient's remark. A patient tells the doctor, 'It's bleeding now', and the doctor answers, 'You? From the vagina?' Such a response indicates the appropriate vocabulary, the degree of freedom permitted in technically oriented conversation, and the proper detachment. Yet the common avoidance of explicit terminology in staff-patient contacts suggests that despite all the precautions to assure that the medical definition prevails, many patients remain somewhat embarrassed by the whole subject. To avoid provoking this embarrassment, euphemisms and understood references are used when possible.

Highly specific requirements for everybody's behaviour during a gynaecological examination curtail the leeway for the introduction of discordant notes. Routine technical procedures organise the event from beginning to end, indicating what action each person should take at each moment. Verbal exchanges are also constrained by the technical task, in that the doctor uses routine phrases of direction and reassurance to the patient. There is little margin for ad-libbing during a gynaeco-logical examination.

The specifications for demeanour are elaborate. Foremost is that both staff and patient should be nonchalant about what is happening. According to the staff, the exemplary patient should be 'in play': showing she is attentive to the situation by her bodily tautness, facial expression, direction of glance, tone of voice, tempo of speech and bodily movements, timing and appropriateness of responses. The patient's voice should be controlled, mildly pleasant, self-confident, and impersonal. Her facial expression should be attentive and neutral, leaning toward the mildly pleasant and friendly side, as if she were talking to the doctor in his office, fully dressed and seated in a chair. The patient is to have an attentive glance upward, at the ceiling or at other persons in the room, eyes open, not dreamy or 'away', but ready at a second's notice to revert to the doctor's face for a specific verbal exchange. Except for such a verbal exchange, how-ever, the patient is supposed to avoid looking into the doctor's eyes during the actual examination because direct eye contact between the two at this time is provocative. Her role calls for passivity and self-effacement. The patient should show willingness to relinquish control to the doctor. . . . The self must be eclipsed in order to sustain the definition that the doctor is working on a technical object and not a person.

The physician's demeanour is highly stylised. He intersperses his examination with remarks to the patient in a soothing tone of voice: 'Now relax as much as you can'; 'I'll be as gentle as I can'; 'Is that tender right there?' Most of the phrases with which he encourages the patient to relax are routine even though his delivery may suggest a unique relationship. He demonstrates that he is the detached profes-sional and the patient demonstrates that it never enters her mind that he could be anything except detached. . . .

The doctor needs to communicate with the patient as a person for technical reasons. Should he want to know when the patient feels pain in the course of examination or information about other medical matters, he must address her as a person. Also the doctor may want to instruct the patient on how to facilitate the examination. The most reiterated instruction refers to relaxation. Most patients are not suffici-ently relaxed when the doctor is ready to begin. He then reverts to a primitive level of communication and treats the patient almost like a young child. He speaks in a soft, soothing voice, probably calling the patient by her first name, and it is not so much the words as his manner which is significant. This caressing voice is routinely used by hospital staff members to patients in critical situations, as when the patient is overtly frightened or disorientated. By using it here the doctor heightens his interpersonal relation with the patient, trying to reassure her as a person in order to get her to relax.

Moreover even during a gynaecological examination, failing to acknowledge another as a person is an insult. It is insulting to be entirely instrumental about instrumental contacts. Some acknowledgment of the intimate connotations of touching must occur. Therefore, a measure of 'loving' demeanour is subtly injected. . . . The doctor conveys this loving demeaour not by lingering or superfluous contact, but by radiating concern in his general manner, offering extra assistance, and occasionally by sacrificing the task requirements to 'gentleness'.

In short, the doctor must convey an optimal combination of impersonality and hints of intimacy that simultaneously avoid the insult of sexual familiarity and the insult of unacknowledged identity. The doctor must manage this even though the behaviour emanating from each definition is contradictory. If the doctor can achieve this feat, it will contribute to keeping the patient in line. In the next section, we will see how the patient may threaten this precarious balance.

IV. PRECARIOUSNESS IN GYNAECOLOGICAL EXAMINATIONS

Threats to the reality of a gynaecological examination may occur if the balance of opposing definitions is not maintained as described above. Reality in gynaecological examinations is challenged mainly by patients. . . .

Failure to maintain a poised performance is a possible threat in any social situation. Subtle failures of tone are common, as when a performer seems to lack assurance. Performers may fumble for their lines: hesitate, begin a line again, or correct themselves. A show of embarrassment, such as blushing, has special relevance in gynaecological examinations. On rare occasions when a person shows signs of sexual response, he or she really has something to blush about. A more subtle threat is an indication that the actor is putting an effort into the task of maintaining nonchalant demeanour; if it requires such an effort, perhaps it is not a 'natural' response. . . .

Certain lapses in patient's demeanour are so common as hardly to be threatening. When patients express pain it can be overlooked if the patient is giving other signs of trying to behave well, because it can be taken that the patient is temporarily overwhelmed by a physiological state. The demonstrated presence of pain recalls the illness framework and counters sexual connotations. Crying can be accredited to pain and dismissed in a similar way. . . .

Some threats derive from the patient's ignorance of how to strike an acceptable balance between medical and non-medical definitions, despite her willingness to do so. In two areas in particular, patients stumble over the subtleties of what is expected: physical decorum (proprieties of sights, sounds, and smells of the body) and modesty. While the staff is largely concerned with behavioural decorum and not about lapses in physical decorum, patients are more concerned about the latter, whether due to their medical condition or the procedure. Patients some-times even let behavioural decorum lapse in order to express their concern about unappealing conditions of their bodies, particularly discharges and odours. This concern is a vestige of a non-medical definition of the situation for an attractive body is relevant only in a personal situation and not in a medical one.

Some patients fail to know when to display their private parts un-ashamedly to others and when to conceal them like anyone else. A patient may make an 'inappropriate' show of modesty, thus not grant-ing the staff the right to view what medical personnel have the right to view and others do not. But if patients act as though they literally accept the medical definition this also constitutes a threat. If a patient insists on acting as if the exposure of her breasts, buttocks, and pelvic area are no different from exposure of her arm or leg, she is 'immodest'. The medical definition is supposed to be in force only as necessary to facilitate specific medical tasks. . . . Patients who misinterpret the licence by exceeding its limits unwittingly challenge the definition of reality.

V. NEUTRALISING THREATENING EVENTS

Most gynaecological examinations proceed smoothly and the defintion of reality is sustained without conscious attention. Sometimes subtle threats to the definition arise, and occasionally staff and patient struggle covertly over the definition throughout the encounter. The staff take more preventive measures where they anticipate the most trouble: young, unmarried girls; persons known to be temporarily upset; and persons with reputations as uncooperative. In such cases the doctor may explain the technical details of the procedure more carefully and offer direct reassurance. Perhaps he will take extra time to establish personal rapport, as by medically related inquiries ('how are you feeling?' 'do you have as much pain today?'), personal inquiries ('where do you live?'), addressing the patient by her first name, expressing direct sympathy, praising the patient for her behaviour in this difficult situation, speaking in a caressing voice, and affectionate gestures. Doctors also attempt to reinforce rapport as a response to threatening events.

The foremost technique in neutralising threatening events is to sustain a nonchalant demeanour even if the patient is blushing with embarrassment, blanching from fear, or moaning in pain. The patient's inappropriate gestures may be ignored as the staff convey, 'We're waiting until you are ready to play along.' Working to bring the scene off, the staff may claim that this is routine, or happens to patients in general; . . . The staff may verbally contradict a patient, give an evasive answer to a question, or try to distract the patient. By giving a technical explanation or rephrasing in the appropriate hospital language something the patient has referred to in a non-medical language way, the staff member reinstates the medical definition.

Redefinition is another tactic available to the staff. Signs of embarrassment and sexual arousal in patients may be redefined as 'fear of pain'. Sometimes sexual arousal will be labelled 'ticklishness'. . . .

Humour may be used to discount the line the patient is taking. At the same time, humour provides a safety valve for all parties whereby the sexual connotations and general concern about gynaecological examinations may be expressed by indirection. Without taking the responsibility that a serious form of the message would entail, the participants may communicate with each other about the events at hand. They may discount the derogatory implications of what would be an invasion of privacy in another setting by dismissing the procedure with a laugh. If a person can joke on a topic, he demonstrates to others that he possesses a laudatory degree of detachment. . . .

While in most encounters the nurse remains quietly in the background, she comes forward to deal actively with the patient if the definition of reality is threatened. In fact, one of the main functions of her presence is to provide a team member for the doctor in those occasional instances where the patient threatens to get out of line. Team members can create a more convincing reality than one person alone. Doctor and nurse may collude against an uncooperative patient, as by giving each other significant looks. If things reach the point of staff collusion, however, it may mean that only by excluding the patient can the definition of reality be affirmed. . . .

Perhaps the major safeguard of reality is that challenge is channelled outside the examination. Comments about the unpleasantness of the procedure and unaesthetic features of the patient's body occur mainly between women, two patients or a nurse and a patient. Such comments are most frequent while the patient gets ready for the examination and waits for the doctor or after the doctor leaves. The patient may establish a momentary 'fellow-woman aura' as she quietly voices her distaste for the procedure to the nurse. 'What we women have to go through' the patient may say. Or, 'I wish all gynaecologists were women'. Why? 'They understand because they've been through it themselves.' The patient's confiding manner implies: 'I have no right to say this, or even feel it, and yet I do.' This phenomenon suggests that patients actually have strong negative reactions to gynaecological examinations which belie their acquiescence in the actual situation. Yet patients' doubts are expressed in an innocuous way which does not undermine the definition of reality when it is most needed.

To construct the scene convincingly, participants constantly monitor their own behaviour and that of others. The tremendous work of producing the scene is contained in subtle manoeuvres in regard to details which may appear inconsequential to the layman. Since awareness may interfere with a convincing performance, the participants may have an investment in being as unself-conscious as possible. But the sociologist is free to recognise the significance of 'inconsequential details' in constructing reality.

VI. CONCLUSION

In a gynaecological examination the reality sustained is not the medical definition alone, but a dissonance of themes and counter-themes. What is done to acknowledge one theme undermines the others. No theme can be taken for granted because its opposite is always in mind. That is why the reality of a gynaecological examination can never be routinised, but always remains precarious.

The gynaecological examination should not be dismissed as an anomaly. The phenomenon is revealed more clearly in this case because it is an extreme example. But the gynaecological examination merely exaggerates the internally contradictory nature of definitions of reality found in most situations. Many situations where the dominant definition is occupational or technical have a secondary theme of sociality which must be implicitly acknowledged (as in buttering up the secretary, small talk with sales clerks, or the undertaker's show of concern for the bereaved family). In 'business entertaining' and conventions of professional associations a composite definition of work and pleasure is sustained. Under many circumstances a composite definition of action as both deviant and unproblematic prevails. For example, while Donald Ball (1967) stresses the claim of respectability in his description of an abortion clinic, his material illustrates the interplay of the dominant theme of respectability and a counter-theme wherein the illicitness of the situation is acknowledged. Internally inconsistent definitions also are sustained in many settings on who persons are and what their relation is to each other.

Sustaining a sense of the solidness of a reality composed of multiple contradictory definitions takes unremitting effort. The required balance among the various definitions fluctuates from moment to moment. The appropriate balance depends on what the participants are trying to do at that moment. As soon as one matter is dealt with, something else comes into focus, calling for a different balance. Sometimes even before one issue is completed, another may impose itself as taking priority. Further, each balance contains the seeds of its own demise, in that a temporary emphasis on one theme may disturb the long-run balance unless sub-sequent emphasis on the counter-theme negates it. Because the most effective balance depends on many unpredictable factors, it is difficult to routinise the balance into formulas that prescribe a specific balance for given conditions. Routinisation is also impractical because the particular forms by which the themes are expressed are opportunistic. That is, persons seize opportunities for expression according to what would be a suitable move at each unique moment of an encounter. Therefore, a person constantly must attend to how to express the balance of themes via the currently available means.

Multiple contradictory realities are expressed on various levels of explicitness and implicitness. Sustaining a sense of solidity of reality depends on the right balance of explicit and implicit expressions of each theme through a series of points in time. The most effective gestures express a multitude of themes on different levels. The advantages of multiple themes in the same gesture are simultaneous qualification of one theme by another, hedging (the gesture lacks one definite meaning), and economy of gestures.

Rational choices of explicit and implicit levels would take the follow-ing into account. The explicit level carries the most weight, unless countered by deliberate effort. Things made explicit are hard to dismiss or discount compared to what is left implicit. In fact, if the solidification of explication is judged to be non-reversible, use of the explicit level may not be worth the risk. On the other hand, when participants sense that the implicit level is greatly in use, their whole edifice of belief may become shaken. 'I sense that a lot is going on underneath' makes a person wonder about the reality he is accepting. There must be a lot he does not know, some of which might be evidence which would undermine what he currently accepts.

The invalidation of one theme by the concurrent expression of its counter-theme must be avoided by various manoeuvres. The guiding principle is that participants must prevent a definition that a contradiction exists between theme and counter-theme from emerging. Certain measures routinely contribute to this purpose. Persons must try to hedge on both theme and counter-theme by expressing them tentatively rather than definitely and simultaneously alluding to and discounting each theme. Theme and counter-theme should not be presented simultaneously or contiguously on the explicit level unless it is possible to discount their contradictory features. Finally, each actor must work to keep the implicit level out of awareness for the other participants.

The technique of constructing reality depends on good judgment about when to make things explicit and when to leave them implicit, how to use the implicit level to reinforce and qualify the explicit level, distributing themes among explicit and implicit levels at any one moment, and seizing opportunities to embody messages. To pursue futher these tentative suggestions on how important explicit and implicit levels are for sustaining reality, implicit levels of communication must be explored more systematically.

REFERENCES

BALL, D. W. (1967) 'An abortion clinic ethnography', *Social Problems*, **14**, Winter, 293–301.
BERGER, P., and LUCKMANN, T. (1966) *The Social Construction of Reality*, Doubleday.
GLASER, B., and STRAUSS, A. (1965) *Awareness of Dying*, Chicago, Aldine Publishing Co.
LIEF, H. I., and FOX, R. C. (1963) 'Training for "detached concern" in medical students', in H. I. Lief, *et al.*, eds., *The Psychological Basis of Medical Practice*, Harper & Row.

SECTION 5

Perspectives on organisations

The final section of the book deals with two issues which underlie most of what has gone before.

The first issue, as discussed by David Weeks (25), is that of trying to draw out some relevant distinctions with regard to the various approaches adopted in the study of organisations. In fact, as Weeks points out, critical distinctions abound in the literature on organisations. What is more problematical is to discern a pattern amongst these distinctions. His article is devoted to uncovering such a pattern.

The distinctions discussed fall into three main groups: theoretical, methodological, and substantive. The various distinctions (or dichotomies) in each of these groups are then examined in terms of whether they tend towards a deductive, determinist model of social explanation, or alternatively to an inductive, voluntaristic model. Weeks maintains that a pattern along these lines can be discerned. Furthermore, he suggests that we can also distinguish two underlying and contrasting sets of assumptions about man and society corresponding to the two sides of the deductive-inductive, determinist-voluntarist, dichotomies. The contrasting assumptions reflect the dialectical quality of social life. On the one side man is seen to be a resultant of his organisational environment in terms of both social constraints and psychological endowment. On the other side, the focus is on man as a creator of his organisational environment.

Of course, there is a great deal of overlap in these sets of assumptions, just as there is in the various approaches that Weeks dichotomises. Some of these are noted in the article. It is pointed out that the various distinctions do not represent logical opposites, but rather they offer alternative perspectives, different ways of viewing social behaviour in organisations. Too often, however, one or other perspective has been adopted in research on organisations without conscious awareness of the assumptions and likely consequences of that choice.

The second underlying issue to which this Section addresses itself, is concerned with the relation of such assumptions to the values and interests of the organisation theorist. This is discussed by Martin Albrow (23) in his article 'The study of organizations—objectivity or bias?'

Albrow charges that organisation theory, by seeking to bring advice to the administrator and at the same time provide a generalising approach to the study of organisations, seems to cast doubt on the separation of fact and value in social science and to deprive the sociologist of any distinctive contribution to the analysis of organisations. For example, he points out that a science which instructs managers to treat organisational structure as contingent only on their own conception of its purpose is not only misguided in its empirical analysis of organisations, but it is also taking sides in a struggle for power. The only solution is for the sociologist to study organisations in the same open-ended way, and within the same general theoretical perspective, as he would utilise to study societies. And remembering what was said in Section 1 about new forms of control and multinational corporations, it gives added force to his comment that: 'To argue that organizations must be studied as societies is scarcely paradoxical when a score of companies have power and income surpassing independent states and activities transcending national boundaries, and when nations may be more dependent on one product, be it tobacco, sugar, or oil, than many an organization.'

Appropriately, Albrow's final appeal is for a recognition of the distinctiveness of the two perspectives of 'organization theory' and the sociology of organisations. For the justification for the unconventional selection of articles presented in this book derives from the conviction we share with Albrow that the sociologist 'cannot accept the conceptual framework of the organization theorist as setting the limits to his research interests in organizations'.

25

David R. Weeks   Organisation theory—
some themes and dis-
tinctions

An original article prepared for this volume[1]

INTRODUCTION

Basically this paper consists of a comparison and discussion of a number of ideas which have gained prominence in the sociological literature on complex organisations. In some ways they are rather a mixed bag for they deal with very general approaches to social phenomena, prescriptions for research procedures as well as concrete classifications of actual organisational situations. One major point they have in common is the way they are frequently used by organisational theorists to channel their research in general but discernable directions. In this sense they are one step removed from such questions as, why does organisation X function more efficiently than organisation Y? or, how did individual Z come to exercise such power in the organisation? How we answer such questions as these will largely depend on the way we start looking at organisations. For example there are no automatic criteria for assessing organisational efficiency or the degree of power wielded by any individual. When we make statements about efficiency or power we are already employing general concepts about the nature of organisations and these ideas will strongly influence the kind of answer we look for. The ideas considered below are some of the most commonly used 'orienting'

[1] I should like to thank Professors David Hickson and Charles Perrow, and Dr David Silverman as well as the editors for their comments on an earlier draft of this paper, but should like to make clear that none of the above are responsible for the views expressed.

approaches and concepts used by writers on organisations. By studying these ideas we are not merely playing with words, for by deciding to follow one course rather than another we generate important consequences for our practical understanding of how organisations work.

The body of theory and research which today we loosely term organisation theory arose from a variety of different intellectual concerns which have been of particular interest to social scientists in the last 150 years. Two major strands of development have been the study of bureaucracy, as an element in broader political analysis, and the study of industrial management, mainly from the point of view of improving management performance as indicated by greater industrial efficiency and productivity (Mouzelis, 1968). The distinctions between these two areas of study have gradually become less significant and theorists have studied 'industrial bureaucracy' (Gouldner, 1954), as well as governmental agencies from the perspective of 'management' problems (Blau and Scott, 1963).

As organisation theory has evolved there has been an increased awareness of the social complexity of the phenomena under study. The organisation is a very important mediating institution between the wider societal culture and the individual social actor. One consequence of the complexity involved is that organisations can be studied on several different levels, that is, they can be analysed in terms of sets of descriptive and explanatory concepts which have no easy and direct relationship to one another. For example, the economic climate within which an organisation operates has important consequences for the working opportunities, satisfactions and general conditions experienced by groups and individuals within the organisation. When we remember, however, that the economic climate is both a constraint on, and, a consequence of, an organisation's activities, the intervening organisational processes of interpretation and decision making complicate to an enormous degree the possibility of moving from very general statements about economic conditions to statements concerning the effects on individual workers.

One way of coming to grips with the complexity involved has been to restrict empirical research to specific and fairly limited areas of interest. In this way there have developed specialised research fields such as administration science, management theory, decision-making theory, industrial and organisational psychology and social psychology, each with their own journals and professional associations. Each of these modes of analysis brings with it its own set of concepts and research methods which determine the focus of analysis and circumscribe the data collection, in terms of its assumed theoretical relevance and empirical manageability. In a situation where reality is believed to be extremely complex, research interests and findings are like jigsaw pieces clustered at various points, comprising but not completing the whole picture. The irony is that we can have no knowledge of the over-all picture without knowledge of specific elements, but once we have built up the whole picture the individual pieces in a sense become redundant.

On this basis the selection of research variables must remain essentially arbitrary. It involves us picking on various ideas, attempting to apply them in research and then deciding whether they are useful after all. In this context 'useful' may mean: confirm what we expect to find, or, reveal interconnections or correlations over a wide range of empirical cases. To refer back to our jigsaw analogy it is as if we are forced to pick the pieces in an arbitrary manner without being able to select them in terms of their relevance to the complete picture. The more of the picture we get completed however the more accurate and relevant are our choices likely to be.

The choice of starting point of any research on organisations is determined by a number of factors: the reseacher's beliefs about his own professional competence based on his education and training; the problem he wants to solve, which may be practical or theoretical; and what he considers are the most important (determining) variables operating in the situation. In this way a fairly distinct rift has developed between those researchers into organisations who focus their attention on the role of management and worker performance, and who often aim to formulate theories and practices which will increase managerial control and hopefully result in greater organisational efficiency and effectiveness, and those researchers who mainly study 'worker behaviour' concentrating particularly on industrial conflict and the nature and degree of commitment which workers feel towards the firm. This second emphasis has largely been within the province of industrial sociology and psychology.

This difference in initial approach reflects different assumptions about the nature of organisational behaviour particularly with regard to the distribution of social power within organisations, a point we shall consider below. In fact critical distinctions abound in the literature on organisations and it is to the problem of trying to discern a pattern amongst them that the rest of this paper is devoted.

SOCIAL STRUCTURE AND ORGANISATIONAL ANALYSIS

The sociological analysis of organisations confronts the same problems with regard to the nature of social structure as does sociology in general.

One difference perhaps lies in the relatively bounded nature of organisational phenomena making organisational research empirically more manageable, but this refers to a difference in the scale of the problem, not to a difference in essence.

The major problem is to account for the dialectical quality in social life in a scientific manner, given that scientific explanation and prediction are our aim. This involves coping with the observation that man is both a result of his social/organisational environment as well as a participating creator of that social/organisational environment. There is thus a constant tension between our view of man as constrained by social influences, Durkheim's 'social facts', and our view of man as an autonomous being capable of superceding such man-made restrictions and creating new situations and bases for social organisation. In Roy's analysis of 'Banana time' (reading 13), for example, we see a work group constrained by work schedules and technology yet able to generate a distinct culture with its own unique set of symbols and norms, any disruption of which has important consequences for work output and other members of the organisation. These two aspects of social existence provide a fundamental basis for distinguishing between different theoretical approaches to organisations.

Individual theories rarely concentrate solely on one side of the picture. To totally ignore the innovative and constructive aspects of behaviour in organisations would be to largely ignore social change. To ignore the many constraints which the individual has placed on his behaviour —what Berger and Luckmann call 'objective social reality'—and which he is relatively powerless to change, would be to discount the possibility of constructing a structural sociology, capable of generating wide ranging theoretical propositions.

In looking at particular theories, what we see is a degree of emphasis towards one aspect of the picture rather than the other. Research methods and theoretical concepts will tend to vary accordingly. While the tendency from one perspective is to concentrate on the collection and analysis of statistical data, using more or less refined techniques of quantitative measurement, the other perspective tends to investigate social behaviour as much as possible in the situation of its creation and development through detailed analysis employing techniques of participant observation. These different modes of analysis are clearly asking different questions about broadly the same kinds of phenomena and as a result the answers and explanations arrived at tend to be rather different.

SOME IMPORTANT CONCEPTUAL DISTINCTIONS IN ORGANISATION THEORY

A number of recurring conceptual distinctions commonly provide channels along which organisational research is pursued. These distinctions offer a significant choice in terms of where we focus our attention, the kind of data we consider to be relevant, and, related to this, the way we go about collecting that data. The distinctions we discuss here do not of course constitute an exhaustive list. Rather, they are chosen because of their common and influential employment in the literature and because they seem to fairly represent other distinctions not discussed. They may be divided into three main groups: theoretical distinctions, methodological distinctions, and substantive distinctions.

Theoretical distinctions represent fundamental assumptions about the nature of social behaviour and the nature of organisation. They provide a set of interrelated principles and definitions which serve conceptually to organise selected aspects of the empirical world, in our case the empirical world of organisations. Such choice of assumptions, however implicit, is necessary in all sociological reasearch for it determines the kind of data selected and collected: that is, it provides a criterion of relevance, a basis on which we can build the substantive superstructure.

Methodological distinctions are not concerned with building substantive knowledge as such but rather they deal with the procedures by which such knowledge is generated, in particular with regard to research procedures. Finally, substantive distinctions relate directly to the empirical world by describing and categorising the social phenomena under study.

In drawing distinctions of these various kinds, the terms which we juxtapose one against the other do not represent logical opposites, rather they offer alternative perspectives, different ways of viewing social behaviour and organisation.

(a) *Theoretical distinctions*

In this section we shall review five sets of distinctions (or dichotomies) which vary in scope and precision. The distinctions are; System *v.* Action; Universalist *v.* Particularist; Formal *v.* Informal; Unitary *v.* Pluralist; Structure *v.* Process.

System v. *Action*. This first distinction in a way sets the tone for all the others in that they are all in some way variations on this main theme. The system approach to analysing social phenomena and organisations has several forms but perhaps the most influential in sociological terms is the kind drawn from the structural-functionalism of Talcott Parsons.

The main concern of this approach is with society or an organisation as a whole. Parsons (1956) defines an organisation as 'a social system which is organized for the attainment of a particular type of goal; the attainment of that goal is at the same time the performance of a type of function on behalf of a more inclusive system, the society'. The workings of the system are explained by postulating the existence of various societal or organisational 'needs' or functions which have to be met to ensure the health and survival of the social organism. The internal elements of the system are held to be operating more or less in unison to meet these needs. This equilibrium maintaining mechanism working within the system copes with any conflict or other disruptive threats which endanger the general stability.

From this brief sketch of one system approach we can note that it operates at a very high level of generality, employing concepts, such as societal or organisational 'needs', which may be very difficult to operationalise and test. Because of the highly abstract formulation, much has to be taken-for-granted and broad assumptions made about how actual people fit into the conceptual framework. If these assumptions and concepts are valid however, it would provide us with an enormously powerful body of social theory in terms of its predictive capacity.

It is against this abstractness that the action approach makes its stand. The argument is that only by actual observation and research into the social actions which constitute the fabric of our social existence, and the meanings which are associated with those actions, can we hope to represent at all faithfully the nature of social order and change.

We can highlight this difference by looking at psychiatric hospital organisation as viewed from these two perspectives. In Parsons' terms the function of the hospital is 'integrative'. As Scott (1959) explains, 'The integrative organization functions to see to it that members of society *do* in fact manifest the same values and expectations within allowable limits and, if they do not, to win them over or expel them' (p. 388). We see here a fairly rigid boundary drawn round any research study, the nature of the organisation has been defined in advance and the remaining problem is to map out exactly how it achieves its goal or fulfils its function. In contrast to this the action approach adopted by Strauss *et al.* (reading 20), suggests that the complexity of the organisation's functioning can only be understood by close and careful scrutiny. Their orienting premise defines the hospital as 'a locale where personnel, mostly but not exclusively professionals, are enmeshed in a complex negotiative process in order both to accomplish their individual purposes and to work—in an established division of labour—toward clearly as well as vaguely phrased institutional objectives' (p. 318).

Thus these two perspectives start from quite different assumptions and with somewhat different aims. The system approach views the whole, locating individual social action according to its place within that whole, whilst the action approach begins with the social act and attempts to construct more general propositions by a process of accumulation (for a much fuller treatment of this issue see Silverman, 1968 and 1970).

Universalist v. *Particularist.* This distinction, common in organisation theory, concerns the relative generality of theoretical propositions. The universalist approach aims to uncover a body of general principles and techniques applicable to all organisations with regard to such issues as task allocation, the general control of work, and motivation and reward at work. In other words the search is for general 'logic of organizational functioning' and this perspective has clear points in common with the system approach in its aim of developing a general theory.

One such attempt which has had considerable and enduring influence was put forward by Frederick W. Taylor (1970) with his ideas on 'scientific management'. By applying the principles of scientific analysis to the operations of an organisation Taylor believed greater efficiency would naturally result. This approach meant disregarding the possibility of conflicts arising in organisations because of a clash of values between various groups. For Taylor conflict between workers and owners and managers could only result from bad management for it was self-evident to him that the prosperity of the individual man was tied to the prosperity of the firm. Armed with this faith the difficulties faced by all organisations could be overcome by applying the appropriate techniques.

The particularist approach however advocates a more specific attack on the problem of organisational control. It argues that different organisations face different problems, or contingencies, they exist in different circumstances and this makes the search for general solutions a rather doubtful pursuit. It is only by concentrating on the particular conditions in which an organisation exists that an appropriate solution can be found. The aim of the search may be the same as the universalist approach, for example, more effectiveness, greater efficiency, but the assumptions about where and how to look for such a goal are quite different. In terms of its more limited scope and openness of approach the particularist perspective shares common ground with the action orientation (for further discussion of this point see Child, 1973).

Formal v. *Informal*. This distinction has a long history in organisation theory and provided the basis for early criticisms of the scientific-management school. The formal aspects of an organisation are often represented by such indices as the 'organisation chart' and statements made by powerful organisation members about how the organisation is supposed to operate (see Argyris, reading 5). This approach adopts a similar view of individual action as the system approach; action is largely seen as a derivative of more general needs or demands.

Critics of organisational theories which concentrate on formal aspects argue that to assume organisations function according to their official charters involves an important misrepresentation of reality and a resulting inadequacy in any theoretical propositions derived from such data. In line with the action approach a focus on the informal aspects of organisational behaviour involves a more open perspective, although there are important difficulties to be faced when we try to clearly distinguish the nature of informal behaviour.

Four main usages of the term informal have been distinguished by Mouzelis (1968). Firstly informal behaviour may simply mean deviations from expectations, but this begs the question of: whose expectations? If there does not exist within an organisation a clear explicit rule or procedure to deal with a situation, and presumably such rules or procedures would constitute the formal structure, then it becomes extremely difficult to say whether behaviour is formal or informal. Behaviour involving deviation from one set of expectations could simultaneously involve conforming to another set of different expectations.

A second meaning of informal behaviour may refer to that behaviour which is irrelevant to the organisation's goals. This interpretation poses exactly similar problems to those just discussed. To speak of an organisation's goals usually means talking in fairly general terms, for example, to make normal profits or service clients adequately may be typical goals. On this basis the distinction between formal and informal behaviour becomes difficult to draw in any general way.

Thirdly, informal behaviour may refer to the unanticipated consequences of social action. If a wage incentive scheme fails to achieve the management's aims of higher productivity, lower turnover, *et cetera*, this failure may be attributed to effects of informal behaviour on the part of the work force. This explanation tends to assume a common belief about the anticipated consequences of such a wage policy. Managers expecting one set of consequences may well define any failure in terms of informal behaviour but this same behaviour may have been just what a worker or shop-steward expected. In their case, any compliance with management intentions may be unanticipated or informal behaviour. Thus, in this way, informal behaviour is always relative to a particular and partial set of expectations.

Lastly, informal behaviour may be taken to mean real or concrete activity; actual behaviour rather than assumptions about what should happen. If we adopt this approach the distinction between formal and informal largely disappears for we are talking then about the way behaviour is related to situations and motivations, rather than about what is supposed to happen. For this reason, and others suggested above, the validity of the distinction between formal and informal aspects of organisations has been seriously questioned.

Unitary v. *Pluralist*. This distinction refers to a basic analytic framework used to depict the nature of coordinated activity in organisations; it also provides a basis for ideologies supporting or opposing that coordination. This distinction is particularly relevant when discussing industrial relations.

From the unitary perspective the organisation is viewed rather like a team or family. All the members are held to share common basic values and perceptions. Although individuals may exhibit different ambitions and aspirations this occurs within the framework of common values: a general consensus is assumed. Thus workers engaged in provoking and supporting conflict are held to be acting irrationally, that is, against their own self-interest. In this situation those with authority are justified in exercising coercive control over deviants in the deviants' own interests. Also, by maintaining the essential consensus and unity of the organisation, not only is productivity maximised but so is the worker's satisfaction with his job. This was the message from the Human Relations school in their analysis of organisations. As Lupton (1971) has noted, 'It is highly probable that it is this felicitous conjunction of the efficiency criterion and the human happiness criterion within a single body of doctrine that make for that doctrine's ready acceptance' (p. 17).

One consequence of adopting a unitary perspective is that top and middle management are clearly seen as the initiators and controllers of organisational functioning. As Etzioni (1958) points out, 'these élites occupy crucial positions in the organizational structures and the decision-making processes' (p. 308). Such groups are seen as the determiners of others' behaviour rather than as being determined by others. As a result there have developed theories on managerial psychology where such topics as leadership and communication and negotiating skills are researched and taught as appropriate managerial techniques.

In this way the general study of organisational reality becomes bounded by implicit assumptions concerning the distribution of organisational authority and its legitimacy. In brief, managers act; workers react.

A different picture of organisations is revealed when the pluralist perspective is adopted. Here the organisation is depicted as a coalition of individuals and groups with their own aspirations and perceptions. Conflict is accepted as a likely consequence of these competing interests. The scope and depth of such conflict may be assessed according to various criteria but in many instances the conflict is assumed to be resolvable, that is, there is a belief in the existence of a set of deep-lying common values that favour 'conciliation' and 'an honourable settlement'. The manner in which such agreements are said to be reached also implies a rough balance of power between the competing parties. On this basis the trade union movement is seen as a constructive force channelling problems of conflict into a negotiable form.

The role of the worker also tends to occupy a more important place with research directed towards the type and consistency of commitment which workers reveal to their organisation. In this area some interesting research on job satisfaction and industrial bargaining has been reported by Daniel (1973). He has shown that different aspects of the job role are important at different times. Thus during wage negotiations concern is greatest with regard to the extrinsic rewards to be gained from work, whilst after a settlement intrinsic factors concerned with the performance of the job itself tend to assume prominence. In other words, the 'vocabularies of motivation' change from one context to another, a variation often not considered in unitary and managerial conceptions of worker behaviour but one which is clearly important for understanding organisational functioning.

As may be inferred from what has already been said, choice of framework, as a model of organisational functioning, will have important consequences for the conception and practice of industrial relations. According to Fox (1973), the Industrial Relations Act of 1972 adopts a unitary perspective, whilst the Donovan Report of 1968, on Trade Unions and Employers' Associations, adopted a markedly pluralist approach. One crucial difference between these perspectives can be seen in relation to the assumed appropriateness of legal intervention in the settlement of industrial negotiations and disputes. Whilst the Industrial Relations Act created a new and complex set of laws and legal machinery, the Donovan Report largely discounted the effectiveness of legal sanctions as a means of controlling industrial relations behaviour.

Structure v. *Process*. This common distinction in sociology generally

also arises in the sociological analysis of organisations. Structure refers
to the basic regularities and more or less constant factors which enable
us to distinguish organisations as spatially and temporally distinct
entities. This fundamental stability allows us to describe the nature and
coordination of task allocations and the exercise of authority as
enduring identifiable features. There are many dimensions along which
structure might be measured in a variety of ways. Among the most
common classifications are those based on organisational size, complexity (the division of labour and authority), and formalisation (the
centralisation of power and general rigidity). These factors provide the
backdrop against which organisational behaviour can be observed,
that is, they represent a network of constraining conditions.

When we turn to the notion of process, we leave the rather static
picture presented by a structural analysis and concentrate on the
mechanisms employed for doing and achieving things within the
particular organisation structure. Major points of interest here are:
the nature of power and conflict in organisations and issues involving
leadership, decision making and communication. In other words the
focus is on purposeful social behaviour and, in this way, the study of
such processes has much in common with an action approach.

It is clear that organisations possess both structural and processual
elements and therefore the two aspects of this distinction do not exist
in direct conflict. One important problem, however, arises over the
question of causal primacy. Does the organisation's structure largely
determine the outcome of the processes involved or is the structure
constantly undergoing change as a result of the processual flux which
signifies the organisation's functioning? One answer to this question is
that the two aspects are in constant interaction. But this is not a very
satisfactory answer when we wish to explain the causes of specific
events or changes. In terms of the system/action dichotomy a concentration on structure has more in common with the system approach
whilst a concentration on process has clear links with the action
approach.

We can now consider these five major distinctions just outlined as a
whole and attempt to assess the relationships between them. If we take
the left hand side of each dichotomy we have the terms: System,
Universalist, Formal, Unitary, and Structure. These terms have certain
common associations and two interrelated aspects are particularly
important.

First, they all subscribe, to some extent, to a deductive model of social
explanation. Once the general theoretical framework has been established the task of research is seen as filling out empirically the empty

categories in the largely preconceived conceptual plan. Now it can be argued that all scientific theories employ a deductive approach to some extent since they start from an initial general conjecture and then work out its empirical validity through a process of confirmation and refutation. Theories do vary however in the initial degree of openness or closedness they display. In their traditional form, system and universalist theories are probably the most closed, whilst formal, unitary and structural theories are more open. By openness we mean the attempt to derive analytic categories from the available data rather than simply collecting data in terms of an *a priori* categorisation.

Second, all these theoretical terms share a deterministic bias; by this we mean that social action is largely taken as a derivation of the higher-order propositions analysing the system or structure concerned. A conceptual scheme emphasising explanatory concepts like 'need' and function, or stressing the influence of formal structure, organisational consensus, or size, places a high value on a logical system of classification concerning these fairly abstract features. The adequacy of any such classification for describing actual organisations is seen as a secondary and mainly empirical problem. The emphasis, in terms of our social dialectic is on the picture of man as a resultant of his social/organisational environment.

If we now consider the terms on the other side of the dichotomies a rather different picture emerges. The terms involved here are: Action, Particularist, Informal, Pluralist and Process. The common qualities which these terms share parallel those just considered.

First, all the terms imply an inductive model approach to the problem of social explanation. Although some initial presuppositions are necessary in terms of the choice of what is to be studied, the theoretical ideas themselves are grounded, to a much greater extent, in the empirical phenomena under study. The discovery process is a cumulative one, building up the theoretical structure piece by piece.

Second, much greater significance is attributed to the social actions of individuals in shaping society or the organisation, the bias is away from determinism and towards voluntarism, and the concepts employed mirror this emphasis. By investigating the way cultural symbols and social norms and conflicts are created, maintained and changed in the organisational environment, the stress is on the empirical adequacy of the terms employed and not on their logical or classificatory inclusiveness. These terms highlight the other aspect of our social dialectic, that side depicting man as an innovator and creator of his social/organisational environment. Having distinguished between these theoretical dichotomies in this general way we can now turn to the methodological and substantive distinctions to see if the pattern we have suggested is continued there.

(b) *Methodological distinctions*
There are two sets of distinctions to be considered in this section; Functionalist *v.* Historical and Comparative Analysis *v.* Case Study.

Functionalist v. *Historical.* By the term functionalist we may mean a number of somewhat different things. In this context functionalist analysis is taken to mean the kind of analysis which concentrates on the interrelationships believed to hold between elements of a system or structure. On this basis a unified organisation theory would concentrate on describing and explaining various functional problems that all organisations are said to face. Such problems would include: recruiting, training, socialising and motivating personnel; coping with the relationships between the organisation's goals and inner needs in the context of a changing environment; satisfying the need to obtain resources from outside the organisation (see Etzioni, 1958). This kind of analysis is based firmly in the present, the existing functional problems provide the focus for analysis.

Historical analysis, in the broad sense in which the term is used here, does not imply a direct opposition to functional analysis. Certainly some functional analyses are historical in that they employ historical data. Historical also implies however, a concern with formulating theory relating to the development of a particular social phenomenon, not simply with its current state. This development perspective is missing from much functional analysis.

To return to the area of industrial relations, a functional analysis might concentrate on the economic, social and political relationships which the parties involved in the bargaining have to one another. The consequences of a move by one part may be analysed simply in terms of the functional result it has for the problem involved. From an historical viewpoint any move may be analysed not simply in terms of its current effects but also as a result of a bargaining history that has developed between the parties.

Comparative Analysis v. *Case Study.* These terms are closely linked to the two just discussed. As defined above the aims of a functionalist analysis imply use of comparative data in order to arrive at a theory applicable to a wide range of organisations. The common functional problems faced by organisations are held to be more significant than the individual differences which exist between organisations and on this basis we can see that comparative analysis is allied to both functionalist and system approaches.

The case study approach has more in common with the historical perspective. Tracing the development of historical trends often involves concentrating on a single organisation or industry and the initial aim of the case study is not to produce a general, abstract theory of organisational functioning but rather to arrive at a more detailed understanding of a specific situation. In this respect there are common links with an action approach.

In mapping out the relationship between Functionalist *v*. Historical and Comparative Analysis *v*. Case Study we have merely noted some major tendencies. Although Functionalist and Comparative analysis and Historical and Case study approaches have been linked together, this does not imply that Functionalist-Case study and Historical-Comparative analysis approaches are impossible or worthless but merely that they are less common combinations in the study of organisations.

(c) *Substantive distinctions*

The distinctions discussed in this section relate to actual research findings describing organisations or to comments on such research. Two dichotomies are considered; Mechanistic *v*. Organismic, and High specificity of role prescription *v*. Low specificity of role prescription.

Mechanistic v. *Organismic*. This distinction, as developed by Burns and Stalker (1968), refers to two types of management organisation. Under the mechanical regime the organisation is highly specialised with precise specification of job roles. The role of authority within the organisation is largely concerned with maintaining conformity to these precise divisions of position and function. This type of social organisation closely resembles Weber's ideal type of rational-legal bureaucracy and is particularly suited to stable conditions of operation both inside and outside the organisation.

The organismic type of management organisation displays quite different qualities. Here there is a flux of continual adjustment of task roles to meet new requirements. Authority relations are much less rigid and the communications network much more diverse. This form of organisation is said to deal more effectively with unstable conditions, where new problems arise requiring creative solutions outside the scope of the more rigid, specialised spheres of competence found in traditional mechanistic organisations.

Special problems occur when changing conditions suggest a change in organisational functioning from one pattern to the other. Burns and

Stalker note that the transition from the mechanistic to the organismic pattern is only achieved with difficulty, the legacy of the old pattern imposing itself on any attempt at change. Given this situation the maximising of organisational effectiveness can be seen as a complex and enduring problem.

High specificity of role prescription v. *Low specificity of role prescription*. This distinction, drawn by Hickson (1966), following an extensive review of the literature on organisational structure, identifies two poles in such analyses: one focusing on high specificity of role prescription as a central feature of organisations, the other focusing on low specificity of role prescriptions as a central feature.

Organisations can be seen as varying along this high-low specificity dimension and different theorists associate the location of an organisation along this dimension with other important structural variables. This is of critical importance in designing organisational structures since the division of labour and distribution of authority are clearly fundamental elements affecting organisational effectiveness.

Although this specificity dimension is, explicitly or implicitly, widely used in the literature, it remains ambiguous in research terms. To overcome this problem Hickson suggests that 'measurements of degree of specificity are needed, first to verify the variations discerned by general observation, second to test hypotheses about the kinds of organisation in which differing specifications occur, and third to test hypotheses relating group and individual variables to structure' (Hickson, 1966, p. 235).

We can now review the methodological and substantive distinctions just considered in relation to the pattern outlined for the theoretical distinctions. If we take the left hand side of each dichotomy we have the terms: Functionalist, Comparative Analysis, Mechanistic and High specificity of role prescription. From our discussion of these terms we can note that they all, to a greater or lesser extent, employ a deductive approach to social explanation; that is, they move from the general to the particular. Once the conceptual framework has been formulated, whether in methodological or substantive terms, elements of social behaviour appropriate to that framework can be deduced. The terms employed also tend to be deterministic, emphasising formal and rational aspects of research and practical organisational planning.

On the other side of the dichotomies the terms are: Historical, Case Study, Organismic and Low specificity of role prescription. Our discussion of these terms suggested an inductive approach to social explanation and greater concern with empirical variety as an element in theory construction. Greater weight is also given to the voluntaristic aspects of social behaviour, for example, in the study and explanation of social conflict.

The general pattern covering all the distinctions is summarised in Table 25.1.

TABLE 25.1. *Distinctions between approaches to organisations*

Distinctions:	Deductive, determinist approach	Inductive, voluntaristic approach
Theoretical	System	Action
	Universalist	Particularist
	Formal	Informal
	Unitary	Pluralist
	Structure	Process
Methodological	Functionalist	Historical
	Comparative Analysis	Case Study
Substantive	Mechanistic	Organismic
	High specificity of role prescription	Low specificity of role prescription

A critical concept in the background throughout the above discussion has been that of an organisation's 'environment'. If the environment is defined in terms of constraining factors on an organisation's activities then organisations have to deal with both external and internal environments. Externally, governmental and market factors clearly play a major role in determining organisational development and, at a more abstract level, as we have seen, societal 'needs' are sometimes considered of crucial importance.

Technology has also been regarded by many writers as a major influence on organisational structure, particularly in the work of Woodward and her associates. Perhaps the most important internal aspect influencing organisational development has been that attributed to the psychological endowment of man himself. Theorists such as Argyris (1964) have discussed the idea of human 'psychological needs' and the way in which these are satisfied or frustrated by organisational structures or demands. In the same way as inadequate technology or insufficient markets will limit an organisation's effectiveness so will social arrangements that do not provide for psychological needs. Ideas such as these lie at the basis of alternative sets of assumptions concerning research into organisations.

SOME ASSUMPTIONS UNDERLYING ORGANISATION THEORIES

We can distinguish two sets of assumptions of a very general nature which provide takeoff points for organisational research. They correspond to the distinction we have drawn between the two sides of our dichotomies in terms of deductive/inductive, determinist/voluntarist approaches and concepts. They also reflect the dialectical quality of social phenomena.

The first set focuses on the picture of man as a result of his organisational environment in terms of both social constraints and psychological endowment. They are:

1. That the structural and functional similarities of organisations are more important than the cultural differences existing between organisations.
2. That the social context (core values and norms) within which organisations develop is more important than the particular development of each organisation.
3. That the above mentioned similarities of organisations persist over time and that changes occur in a fairly consistent and uniform manner.
4. That there exists a body of more or less precise principles, the rational and continued application of which will enable desired organisation goals to be attained (i.e. a logic of organisational functioning).
5. That management control is effectively achieved by the implementation of formal organisational rules.

The second set focuses on the picture of man as a creator of his organisational environment. The central issues and assumptions can be summarised as follows:

1. That processual aspects of organisations are more important than abstract notions of structural interdependence.
2. That socially generated specific situational meanings are the basis for understanding control in organisations; the study of formal rules and order provides only a partial and inadequate picture.
3. That 'vocabularies of motivation' (psychological needs) do not remain consistent but vary according to social and organisational context.

Clearly a very important question concerns the relationship between these two sets of assumptions. They are related in one particularly important way which brings out a central issue for all organisation theory. If we concentrate on man as a creator of his organisational environment we must also bear in mind that one man's behaviour may act as a possible constraint on someone else's activity, and so, in this sense, the second man's behaviour is partially determined by the first man's social activity. This is especially the case with regard to the generation and application of rules in an organisation. Thus although we may not be able to predict with absolute precision the reaction to such rules we also cannot deny that they do exist and have important effects on organisational members' behaviour.

The central issue is that of authority, or rather, power and its legitimation, and this topic has held a central place in the history of organisation theory. By studying the forms of social power and related ideological legitimations we can attempt to understand the relationship between: various forms of societal rationalisations (e.g. criteria of 'market efficiency' or 'in the public interest'), the role of technology in achieving product output goals and changing management style, and the reaction of organisational members in terms of their acceptance or rejection of such ideological goals and influence in differing contexts.

Recent attempts to cope with such complexity have been labelled 'contingency theory', although throughout the history of organisation theory many authors have noted the variety of 'contingencies' which influence organisational functioning. Major modern proponents of such a theory, Lawrence and Lorsch, start with the premise 'that organisational variables are in a complex interrelationship with one another and with conditions in the environment' (Lawrence and Lorsch, 1967, p. 157). The main aim of such theory remains, however, to uncover a logic of effectiveness, not in the wide ranging sense of system or universalist theory, but in terms of a more particularist consideration of the organisational context under study.

This kind of theory has been criticised by Child (1973) on a number of grounds. Although he sees such theory as a move in the right direction in terms of coming to grips with the social complexity of organisational functioning, the conceptualisation of the key variables is criticised as too mechanistic. For not only do the same organisational structures yield different results and different structures similar results, but the goals of similar organisations vary to an important degree. Thus, 'Decision making about organisation is not simply a matter of accommodating to operational contingencies. It is equally a political process into which other considerations, particularly the expression of power holders' values, also enter' (p. 240). This is extremely significant, for as Child suggests, 'a failure to recognize that management faces both a legitimatory and a technical problem is perhaps the most serious theoretical deficiency in present day contingency theories of organization' (p. 251). The values of powerful organisation members, and sociologists who study organisations, are therefore crucial factors in determining the nature and direction of research into organisational functioning.

CONCLUSION

The purpose of this paper has simply been to suggest an ordering of some of the main issues involved in sociological theorising about organisations. The coverage of such issues has been brief and partial. In particular the ethnomethodological critique of established sociological approaches to organisations has been omitted (for a sample of the ethnomethodological approach and research see the articles by Bittner, Zimmerman, Sudnow and Emerson in this Reader). The ideas considered in this paper fall within the category which Douglas (1971) would term 'macroanalysis', and although they subscribe to a mode of sociological explanation which Douglas believes untenable, he does recognise the considerable significance of such studies: 'It is only some form of analysis of general patterns and structures that enables us to know what is going on across the far reaches of our social world in a way that will enable us to achieve our goals in that world' (p. 11).

Given that major orienting assumption, we have suggested that a wide range of conceptual distinctions common in organisation theory display a discernable pattern, a relationship involving different approaches to social explanation and conceptualisation. From such differing perspectives we suggested that two sets of asssumptions concerning the study of organisations could be drawn and that these reflected the basic dialectical quality of social phenomena. Of critical importance in understanding the relationship between these two approaches was the notion of environment and the analysis of social power. Although no solution to the dialectical puzzle is offered, it is suggested that particular consideration of these two areas is crucial, for they focus on both the technical and legitimatory aspects of organisational functioning and only by considering these twin themes can organisation theory become 'practical' in every sense of that term.

REFERENCES

ALBROW, M. (1968) 'The study of organizations—objectivity or bias?', *Penguin Social Sciences Survey*, Penguin Books pp. 146–67 (also no. 26 in this Reader).
ARGYRIS, C. (1964) *Integrating the Individual and the Organization*, Wiley.
ARGYRIS, C. (1971) *The Applicability of Organizational Sociology*, Cambridge University Press.

BERGER, P., and LUCKMANN, T. (1967) *The Social Construction of Reality*, Allen Lane.

BITTNER, E. (1965) 'The concept of organization', *Social Research*, **32**, 239–255 (also no. 17 in this Reader).

BLAU, P. M. (1968) 'Theories of organization', in *International Encyclopaedia of the Social Sciences*, New York, Free Press of Glencoe.

BLAU, P. M., and SCOTT, W. (1963) *Formal Organizations*, Routledge & Kegan Paul.

BROWN, R. (1973) 'Sources of objectives in work and employment', in Child, ed. (1973) pp. 17–38.

BURNS, T., and STALKER, G. M. (1968) *The Management of Innovation*, 2nd edn, Tavistock.

CHILD, J. (1973) 'Organization: a choice for man', in Child, ed. (1973) pp. 234–55.

CHILD, J., ed. (1973) *Man and Organization*, Allen & Unwin.

DANIEL, W. W. (1973) 'Understanding employee behaviour in its context', in Child, ed. (1973) pp. 39–62.

DENZIN, N. K. (1971) 'Symbolic interactionism and ethnomethodology', in Douglas, ed. (1971) pp. 259–84.

DOUGLAS, J., ed. (1971) *Understanding Everyday Life*, Routledge & Kegan Paul.

ELDRIDGE, J. E. T. (1973) 'Industrial conflict: some problems of theory and method', in Child, ed. (1973) pp. 138–84.

ETZIONI, A. (1958) 'Industrial sociology: the study of economic organizations', *Social Research*, **25**, 303–24.

FOX, A. (1973) 'Industrial relations: a social critique of pluralist ideology', in Child, ed. (1973) pp. 185–233.

GOULDNER, A. W. (1954) *Patterns of Industrial Bureaucracy*, New York, Free Press of Glencoe.

GRUSKY, O., and MILLER, G. A. (1970) *The Sociology of Organizations*, New York, Free Press of Glencoe.

HICKSON, D. (1966) 'A convergence in organization theory', *Administrative Science Quarterly*, **11**, 224–37 (also no. 7 in this Reader).

KATZ, F. E. (1968) 'Integrative and adaptive uses of autonomy: worker autonomy in factories', in F. E. Katz, *Autonomy and Organization*, Random House (also no. 12 in this Reader).

LAWRENCE, P. R., and LORSCH, J. W. (1967) *Organization and Environment*, Harvard University Press.

LUPTON, T. (1971) *Management and the Social Sciences*, Penguin Books.

MANNING, P. K. (1971) 'Talking and becoming: a view of organizational socialization', in Douglas, ed. (1971).

MAYNTZ, R. (1964) 'The study of organizations', *Current Sociology*, **13**, no. 3, pp. 94–157.

MOUZELIS, N. P. (1968) *Organization and Bureaucracy*, Chicago, Aldine.

PARSONS, TALCOTT (1956) 'Suggestions for a sociological approach to the theory of organizations—I and II', *Administrative Science Quarterly*, **1**, 63–85.

PUGH, D., ed. (1971) *Organization Theory*, Penguin Books.

SCOTT, F. G. (1959) 'Action theory and research in social organization', *American Journal of Sociology*, **64**, no. 4, pp. 386–95.

SILVERMAN, D. (1968) 'Formal organizations or industrial sociology: towards a social action analysis of organizations', *Sociology*, **2**, 221–38.

SILVERMAN, D. (1970) *The Theory of Organizations*, Heinemann.

STRAUSS, A., SCHATZMAN, L., EHRLICH, D., BUCHER, R., and SABSHIN, M. (1963) 'The hospital and its negotiated order', in Elliott Friedson, ed., *The Hospital in Modern Society*, New York, Free Press of Glencoe (also no. 20 in this Reader).

PARKER, S., BROWN, R., CHILD, J., and SMITH, M. (1967) *The Sociology of Industry*, Allen & Unwin.

TAYLOR, F. W. (1970) 'Scientific management', in Grusky and Miller, eds. (1970) pp. 45–52.

TURNER, B. (1971) *Exploring the Industrial subculture*, Macmillan.

WOODWARD, J. (1965) *Industrial Organization: theory and practice*. Oxford University Press.

WOODWARD, J., ed. (1970) *Industrial Organization: behaviour and control*, Oxford University Press.

ZWERMAN, W. L. (1970) *New Perspectives on Organization Theory*, Westport, Greenwood.

26

Martin Albrow   The study of organisations
                     —objectivity or bias?

Excerpts from Martin Albrow, 'The study of organizations—objectivity or bias?' in Julius Gould, ed., *Penguin Social Sciences Survey*, Penguin Books, 1968, pp. 146–67.

One of the most stimulating recent developments in sociology has been the growing attention given to organisations. Power, authority, the division of labour, rules of behaviour, social control, all difficult to isolate for study in society, present themselves universally in organisations and with much greater clarity and definition. The problems of organisation recur in such varied social units as firms, civil services, armies, hospitals, universities, and trade unions, and therefore involve issues which transcend the concerns of the experts on any one of these organisations. They involve an awareness of the distinctive contribution sociologists may make to the understanding of social life. The 'sociological standpoint' insists that human beings must be studied in respect of how they actually act rather than how they might ideally act. This standpoint when applied to problems of organisation produces a literature which is distinctive to sociology and which in my view stands at the traditional core of that discipline.

Yet however fervently the sociologist may stress the distinctiveness and the virtues of his approach to the study of organisations, he has to face the fact that any organisation he begins to analyse will almost certainly already possess a literature of its own. Manuals of rules, instructional handbooks, descriptive treatises, eulogistic histories, even advertising material are sources of information the sociologist ignores at his peril. Even where this literature is patently concerned with giving instructions and advice to members of an organisation it is by no means

Ans that made 'A' — philosophical.

irrelevant to the sociologist's task of dicovering the facts and accounting for them. For such advice is rarely arbitrary; its force will depend upon an intimate acquaintance with the facts of the organisation and a clear idea of what kind of counsel would be necessary and welcome.

Here the problem of objectivity becomes pressing. How can a social scientist, committed to the belief that to be objective is to be free from moralising and to avoid recommending courses of action, avail himself of a literature which is so plainly involved in a particular set of values? That sociology should be value-free is taken by most sociologists to be axiomatic. This is certainly a worthwhile aim but how elusive it is is not always or fully recognised. Too often people take the profession of faith in value-freedom as a sufficient safeguard against partiality and preaching. And if such faith is regarded as sufficient it is because the founders of sociology, in particular Max Weber, are held to have dispelled the taint of value so that their successors can work absolved from this original sin of social research. My argument is that such optimism is excessive. The problem of objectivity is endemic in social science. Crude and obvious forms of bias and wishful thinking are expunged only to be replaced by more subtle ones. The sociologist, far from asserting that he has 'attained' objectivity, must be prepared to struggle towards it with every development in his field. The 'recentness' of research, its technical and conceptual sophistication, do not guarantee immunity to bias.

Is this too pessimistic an account? Let us look at the standard answer to this problem. In a tradition which goes back to Weber it is commonly held that there are certain conditions under which 'prescriptions' may be incorporated into a value-free sociology. Injunctions which involve stating what means are necessary for the attainment of specific, given goals may be considered as comprising straightforward generalisations about the relations of two or more variables. If prescriptions are capable of being translated into the form 'given this goal, the following actions are necessary for its achievement', the sociologist may be exempted from the charge of preaching. All 'ought' statements must, on this view, be converted into 'if and then' statements. For example, the sociologist may wish to consider the proposition 'the executive ought to ensure maximum communication with employees'. If this advice is directed at executives he can assume that it involves a hidden premiss, 'if the executive wishes to maximize productivity'; and he can then go on to assume that behind this lies an empirical generalisation, i.e. 'productivity and comunication are related in such a way that increases in the latter result in increases in the former'.

However, this procedure is deceptively easy and has severe limitations. Let us examine the case of the Human Relations Movement in industrial management. Under the aegis of Elton Mayo, who became the leading spokesman for the Movement, a long series of investigations at the Western Electric Company's works near Chicago in the twenties and thirties of this century were interpreted as providing the empirical foundations for certain recommendations to management, i.e., that improved communications between workers and managers, more cooperation between them in making decisions, and a greater concern for satisfying the social needs of the workers would improve production more than would the use of financial incentives. The Human Relations Movement has frequently been criticised (e.g. Friedman, 1955; Bendix and Fisher, 1949; Krupp, 1961, chap. 3). What follows is simply a schematic account of these criticisms which focuses on the problem of value-freedom.

In the first place, no science for management can assume that production, or indeed any other managerial objective, exists in a vacuum. It is a characteristic of social action that no objective is 'given' in isolation from other objectives. The limits on the attainment of an objective are set not only by the availability of means but also by criteria which determine what means are acceptable. These criteria frequently stem from goals which are independent of the objective from which the analysis began. Thus managers may well have goals other than high production, e.g. profit, industrial peace, the preservation of power and privilege. Explicit recommendations to management may either ignore these while tacitly taking them into account, or else neglect them completely—in which case the proffered advice may well have consequences which managers would deplore. In neither case is the advice what it seems to be; in the former it amounts to whitewashing, in the latter to imposing a policy on management. Secondly, a general assumption behind the advice is that if the interest of managers and workers can be made to coincide production will be increased. Such a coincidence may well be rare. Managers and workers may have such deep divisions of interests that no amount of communication and schemes for participation will secure harmony. The recommendations are then open to two further charges; that the conditions which would make them applicable are very limited rather than universal, and that where those conditions do not exist the advice within the industrial situation will not function as a boost to productivity but rather as a programme of propaganda for management to demonstrate to the world its good intentions.

From this example it is clear that information which stems from a concern to develop maxims of conduct cannot easily be incorporated into a neutral and objective social science by the mere affirmation of value-freedom and the routine translation of 'ought' statements into 'if and then' statements. For criticisms levelled at the Human Relations Movement do not amount simply to the charge of covert involvement in managerial values. They relate also to the substantive results of the research programme. The prescriptions for the attainment of a specific goal necessarily involve the prescriber in a much wider complex of value judgments. Furthermore, the generalisations upon which the policy suggestions are based, epitomised in Mayo's claim that they possess 'significance equally for a factory on the Volga or for another on the banks of the River Charles' (Friedman, 1955, p. 325), are shown to be far more limited in their scope than their authors assume.

The story of the Human Relations Movement may be regarded as a cautionary tale for those who are too sanguine about the chances of objective social science. It can equally be seen as encouraging those who wish to rid sociology of evaluative elements, since the criticism to which the Movement has been subjected might itself seem to indicate an advance towards objectivity. Indeed, a heightened consciousness of the biases stemming from the intrusion of practical concerns into empirical research would appear to be a welcome by-product, providing the sociologist with additional safeguards when analysing material concerned to instruct and advise managers and administrators. But this would be to underestimate the changes which have taken place in the instructional literature itself. For over and above the treatises concerned with particular types of organisation there has developed a discipline known as 'organisation theory' which aims to systematise, supplement and advance the knowledge contained in such work in order to help managers and administrators to make better decisions. In its concern to analyse the logic of organisational decisions, organisation theory aims to bring advice to the administrator to the level of an applied science; and in its generalising approach to the study of organisations it appears simultaneously to take on the mantle of sociology. It seems both to cast doubt on the separation of fact and value in social science and to deprive the sociologist of any distinctive contribution to the analysis of organisations.

At this point, to clarify the relation of fact and value in organisation theory, I turn to the classic statement of the scope of organisation theory by its most distinguished exponent. In *Administrative Behaviour*, Herbert Simon (1957) lays great stress on two points. First, he argues that it is impossible to assess organisational problems adequately within the context of one type of organisation. Organised behaviour is a feature of many different organisations and the findings of research must be interpreted in the widest possible frame of reference. Second, he launches a sustained attack on the traditional maxims of administrative conduct, the principles of specialisation, unity of command, span of control, and departmentalisation. He contends that the conditions under which these principles are to be applied are never adequately specified. They purport to have a timeless validity when in fact even in the narrow confines of the industrial firm, to which they most clearly relate, their application is ambiguous. Simon's criticism of earlier theories of administration points to the same kind of flaws as were found in the Human Relations Movement, i.e. that the so-called general principles of action recommended were derived from the experience of a very restricted number of organisations—and a very restricted type as well. He proposes to reverse this situation by developing a science of organisations in general and to offer advice which would be appropriate to a particular situation only.

At this point, however, a crucial qualification must be made. Simon's emphasis on the difficulty of making prescriptions brings him to a position where the role of prescription in organisation theory almost vanishes. He contends that the principles of administration amount only to the directing of the administrator's attention to fundamental aspects of organisation which he might otherwise have neglected. No general injunction such as 'unity of command must be ensured' is valid, but it is always of relevance to direct the administrator's attention to the problem of unity of command and the information that has been collected on this issue. Organisation theory is thus formulated as the study of the categories that are relevant to the making of administrative decisions. This makes the relation of the organisation theorist to the organisation far more complex than hitherto. He is no longer the purveyor of ready-made solutions to unambiguous problems set for him by the administrator. His task is one of illumination. His position may be likened to that of the psychotherapist helping the patient come to terms with problems which he only dimly perceives without professional help. Like the therapist, the organisation theorist eschews injunctions to act and hopes to lead the administrator to the position where he is able to decide for himself on an analysis of the situation in which he himself has participated.

As Simon develops it, organisation theory aims to assist men in the running of organisations by building up a set of empirical propositions of wide validity and at the same time refining the terminology used to analyse organisations. From organisation theory, managers and administrators can expect both a widening of knowledge about how organisations work and a clarification of the concepts which guide their action. They are not handed ready-made solutions but rather the means to discover them.

But for the sociologist the development of organisation theory poses a problem. Here is a literature which stems from the needs of practical men and which quite openly aims to assist them to achieve their objectives. Yet in the pursuit of this task it goes far beyond the level of a recipe book for managers. It has reached a more sophisticated understanding about the relations of prescription and social research than the Human Relations Movement did, and in its comparative and generalising approach bids fair to pre-empt anything the sociologist might have to offer in the way of a distinctive contribution to the understanding of organisations. Organisation theory appears to take over the sociologist's programme of research and for good measure to link it with practical needs. It is perhaps small wonder that the attractiveness of such a prospectus should have led sociologists to avoid tiresome demarcation disputes between disciplines, to overlook the question of practical involvement, and to identify their research objectives with those of organisation theory. My argument in what follows aims to show that this identification of the sociological approach with organisation theory is invalid. The perspective of a theory designed to assist the administrator cannot be merged into an approach which has no concern with the application of its results. The two spheres of interest may frequently overlap, they each have their value, but to confuse them is to allow a persistent bias to intrude.

One of the best illustrations of this identification of the two perspectives is provided by a definition of the organisation which has become orthodox among sociologists and organisation theorists alike. It is defined as a social unit explicitly established for the achievement of specific goals. To achieve these goals an extensive division of labour is needed—one in which each member of the organisation has a prescribed task. This complex division of labour is governed by a formal authority structure and a set of rules and regulations which are normally written down. The social units which this definition has been made to cover are as varied as firms, hospitals, universities, prisons, political parties, governmental departments, trade unions, armies, and voluntary associations.[1]

---

[1] In sociology this viewpoint received most authoritative support from T. Parsons (1960), p. 17: 'As a formal analytical point of reference, primacy of orientation to the attainment of a specific goal is used as the defining characteristic of an organization which distinguishes it from other types of social systems. This criterion has implications for both the external

This seems a relatively innocuous and uncontroversial formulation. But I want to show here that the central position of the organisational goal in this conception reflects the necessary interest of the theorist concerned to improve administrative decision, and that a valid sociological definition applicable to the organisations I have mentioned would differ considerably by emphasising at least four major points; namely, that organisational goals are not normally specific, that formal procedures are more than simply expressions of organisational goals and those goals are regularly implemented in ways other than through formal procedures, that the behaviour of groups within the organisation is not simply a function of organisational position, and that the notion of the specific goal as the origin and cause of the organisation is an unhistorical myth. In other words, the argument will be that this is not a definition of real organisations but of a hypothetical or idealised situation to which a theorist concerned with improvements and future states might wish them to tend. Such ideal formulations are invaluable in the context of organisation theory but a bias results if sociologists employ them uncritically as defining existing situations.

1. The requirement of the orthodox definition that the goal of an organisation should be specific leads to a host of problems, for it is commonly very difficult to get an agreed statement from members of an organisation as to its goal. This is particularly evident in such organisations as hospitals, prisons, or universities. Fundamental dilemmas as to whether the organisation exists to promote cure or medical advance, punishment, reform, or restraint, teaching or research, are apparent to all involved (e.g. Stanton and Schwartz, 1954; Galtung, 1961). Such dilemmas may be resolved by different people in different ways within the same organisation, and each will have considerable latitude to interpret the organisational purpose in his own way. Even within the industrial firm, which is often thought of as having a single and exceptionally clear-cut purpose, there may be multiple and competing objectives. Thus, one investigator analysed company policy statements and found that profit was supplemented or even replaced as an objective by commitments to consumers, the personnel of the firm, corporate growth, technological progress, and society in general (Shubik, 1964).

relations and the internal structure of the system referred to here as an organization.' The implicit qualification, 'As a formal analytical point of reference', is omitted in later writers who offer the goal-attainment definition of an organization in even more extreme form. See P. M. Blau and W. R. Scott (1963), p. 1: 'An organization has been established for the explicit purpose of achieving certain goals'; and also A. Etzioni (1964), p. 3: 'Organizations are social units (or human groupings) deliberately constructed and reconstructed to seek specific goals'.

Now the goal-oriented conception of the organisation set out above makes the organisation's structure dependent on its relation to the specific goal. A clear-cut programme devoted to the achievement of an end is seen as only possible if the end is conceived with clarity and precision. Confusion on objectives entails confusion on means. But the orthodox view of organisations regards their structure as a means for the achievement of the organisational goal. If, in the words of Mason Haire (1962), the goals of organisations are multiple, vague, and unweighted in relation to each other, then organisations should continually be faced with confusion and disruption. In fact, organisations persist with relatively stable structures in spite of recurrent conflict as to the nature of their goals. Organisational structure must therefore be dependent on factors other than its relation to goals.

What are these factors? Behaviour which is bound by formal rules may originate otherwise than in agreement on a common goal. Co-operation may result from a situation where actors have divergent goals but recognise that each can only obtain his own objective on the basis of an exchange of contributions to the requirements of others. This may be governed by explicitly formulated rules. (The law of contract is an example.) On this basis it would therefore be quite possible to view organisations as collections of such coalitions as much as collectivities orientated to a specific goal. This fact seems to have led at least one writer to drop the orthodox definition of the organisation and to substitute 'If several persons agree to follow a certain set of rules we shall say... that they are members of an organization.' He recognises that the concept of goals presents great difficulty ('if psychologically even a single man may lack consistency of goals, what to say of a group of several?') and regards the choice of any particular goal to gauge organisational efficiency as basically arbitrary. One can measure the profits of a business corporation 'without postulating this to be the goal of any of the executives or stockholders' (Marschak, 1959, pp. 307, 311). But this solution can scarcely be accepted. Rules are a universal feature of social life. A definition of this kind fails to identify the distinctive characteristics of organisations. Nonetheless, this does at least underline the fact that it is possible to think of organisational structure without reference to goals as the major determinant.

In a situation where the members of an organisation themselves disagree as to what constitutes the organisational goal, the requirements of the orthodox definition can seriously prejudice an objective account. At its worst, the student's determination to impute clear-cut goals can lead him to the point where he is actually siding with one party or the other in saying what the objective ought to be. This is obvious if we consider the case of a political party. The statement 'the Labour Party's objective is the increase of equality' is simply a masquerade of an empirical statement. Even if it were accepted by all members of the Party its very generality would make it the topic of fervent political debate. Certainly it will be treated by the members of the organisation in the way it deserves to be, as a contribution to the argument about what the policy of the party ought to be. . . .

2. As mentioned in the last section, the instrumental conception of organisational structure leads to a misinterpretation of the place of formal procedures. Indeed, the fact that rules and regulations are very frequently not the expression of organisational purpose but result from the intervention of outside bodies is scarcely considered. Take the case of safety regulations, contractual agreements, compulsory insurance and all the rules which stem from the activity of trade unions. These rules are obviously *not* the expression of organisational purpose: rather they may appear to the members as limits on the implementation of that purpose. Not even the extreme proponent of *laissez faire* would claim that they stem from enlightened self-interest on the part of the organisation rather than from outside interference. An odd feature about this neglect of the extra-organisational determination of rules is that it was sharply emphasised by one of the founding fathers of organisation theory, Charles Barnard. For him, the churches and the state were dominant organisations: 'all subordinate organisations may be described as incomplete and dependent' (Barnard, 1938, chap. 8). As will be seen later, in other respects also a return to Barnard would be advantageous.

Just as formal procedures which originate from outside the organisation tend to be regarded as being determined by the organisation, so also those formal procedures which are, strictly, internally determined tend to be regarded as the only way in which organisational purpose is expressed. In both cases formal procedures and organisational structure are regarded as coterminous. This is not the place to review the abundant and often illuminating literature on informal patterns within organisations. But its over-riding concern is to establish that informal patterns of behaviour may work to the benefit or detriment of the formal structure. The implication is that formal structure potentially contains within itself its own capacity to implement organisational purpose. The informal elements are extrinsic helps or hindrances. In two respects this is an inadequate formulation of the relations of formal and informal elements.

Normally the formal structure of an organisation is held to comprise two elements, the authority system determining who gives orders to whom, and rules and regulations governing work procedures. In respect of the authority structure, it has been pointed out by Parsons (1960b) that the orders transmitted may well demand on the part of the recipient a competence which will be outside the experience of the person giving the order. For example, instructions from a headmaster with a degree in history to a teacher whose qualifications are in mathematics must necessarily be ill defined in content, and the teacher receiving the instructions may well be the best person to determine whether they have been implemented. The authority structure of an organisation can well be regarded as internal to the organisation, although, as will be seen later, this must be severely qualified. But the experience and competence of an individual can never entirely be 'internal' in this sense. For, quite obviously, he can bring it to and take it away from the organisation. This kind of competence cannot be conferred by fiat. It is not a mere help or hindrance to the authority system—it is intrinsic to its operation. The formal transmission of orders demands informal implementation.

This intimate relation between 'formal' and 'informal' elements operates also in respect of work governed by rules rather than orders. It is a matter of logic and not experience that is it impossible for a rule to determine the conditions under which it is implemented. It is the agent's perception and interpretation of a situation which decides whether or not the application of a rule is justified. Compliance with a rule therefore is not removed from the area of disputable judgment. Formal organisation is not facilitated or distorted by individual judgment and discretion; these are necessary preconditions for its operation. This is why 'pure' administration—if conceived of as the execution of completely rule-determined activity—cannot exist. Many of the complaints against bureaucracy stem from this misconception, the belief that the execution of policy can and ought to be completely routinised. Reinhard Bendix (1949, p. 12), in a study of American civil servants, argues strongly against this belief. Too great a compliance with statutory rules is popularly denounced as bureaucratic. 'Too great a reliance on initiative in order to realise the spirit, if not the letter, of the law is popularly denounced as an abuse of power, as interfering with legislative prerogative.' Administrative judgment and discretion is an essential part of administration and, as Bendix shows, a product of so-called informal elements—professional ethics, group solidarity, relations with the public, social status, and many other factors.

3. My argument so far has been that the goals of organisations are not necessarily single, precise or specific. Rules in an organisation may have

other functions than the implementation of a 'goal'. However, this still leaves the question of how we are to account for formal structures which do not depend on the intervention of outside bodies and which persist in spite of conflict on goals. Certainly there is no need to view formal rules and authority as determined by their relation to a specific goal. After all, formalised rules and authority may develop in a society and there is no need to refer to an over-riding purpose to explain them. Usually sociologists attempt to explain such structures by reference to the demands of competing groups. There is no reason to think that organisational structure may not be interpreted in the same way.

Certainly one of the earliest complaints against the theories of the Human Relations Movement was that it was unable to conceive of the interests of the members of the organisation as being determined by any other social unit. In Friedmann's (1955) words,

> The firm is suspended in a void, in a social vacuum . . . but the complexity of the firm derives chiefly from the fact that at the same time as each worker belongs to various collectivities within the works, he also belongs to larger external collectivities such as trade union, social class, and nation (pp. 322–3).

This has clear consequences for the goal-oriented conception of the organisation. The individual's commitment to his organisational role will depend partly on how that role is 'evaluated' in his society and on how his other group affiliations put him in a position to make demands of the organisation, to negotiate on his commitment, and to take an independent view of the organisational purpose. Thus members of the organisation may put job-security at the very centre of the organisational goal structure, and commitment to any other goal may be regarded as a price to be paid. Alternatively, it may be the case that an organisational goal is treated by the various social groupings in the organisation as purely instrumental in obtaining their own purposes.

These points are best exemplified by the outstanding recent study by Michel Crozier (1964) of two governmental agencies. He shows that the formal authority system of these bodies is determined by the organisational structure of the whole sphere of public services in France and by the hierarchic demands and expectations of French society rather than by necessities imposed by the implementation of the agencies' goals. Production workers, administrative officers and maintenance workers are all members of strata that are protected from each other by rules which express their relative power positions. In this situation the scope for managerial decision is limited. Does the manager appear as the powerful maximiser of productivity envisaged in the goal-attainment model of the organisation? No. His task is to arbitrate and mediate between groups jockeying for position. The rules develop not so much from managerial purpose but from the need of human groups to protect themselves from that purpose.

4. Finally, we must examine a myth about the origins of organisations. The organisational goal is presented as an objective common to a large number of individuals moved to organise themselves to secure its attainment. Take one such account:

> If the accomplishment of a task requires more than a handful of men to work together they cannot simply proceed by having each do whatever he thinks needs to be done: rather they must first get themselves organized. They establish a club or a firm, they organize a union or a political party, or they set up a police force or a hospital (Blau and Scott, 1963, p. 1).

Another version relates how 'an organization comes into being whenever a group of people recognize that a synergistic effect will result from the proposed co-operative group action', and 'every religion, every great movement, every company, every organization at its very genesis began in the mind of one man' (Lloyd, 1962, pp. 29, 34). Now it is true though trivial that individuals must always be involved in some institution but whether this primordial conception of a purpose is an adequate account of the origins of an organisation seems doubtful.

These accounts are altogether too like the social contract theory of the origins of the state and society. At some point of time, never specified, individuals conceive an objective with uncommon unanimity and clarity to live an organised social life. But just as the social contract theory has been rejected on account of its rationalism, its individualism and its lack of historicity, so must this account of the origins of organisations be rejected. Their formulation of rules and goals is in fact a long and tortuous progress. It is rarely possible to indicate a point of time at which they begin. If organisations have founders, and nearly always the 'foundation' amounts to the reorganising of existing organisational elements, it is rare for them to have the slightest conception of how the organisation is to develop. Of course some organisations may have a relatively clear-cut and abrupt beginning. The founders of a residents' association may have a simple, single purpose in common, e.g. the exclusion of coloured residents; but this kind of single, specific, 'common' purpose is not to be found in the dominating organisations of government and industry.

If we consider the state or the great industrial corporation it is remarkably difficult to trace their origins back to a common purpose.

Their present highly complex structures are related to a multiplicity of purposes which arise in the course of the organisation's development.

Furthermore, to emphasise a common originating purpose blinds us to another important fact. This is that organisation may originate in the imposition of one group's purpose on another. The parallel with social contract theory is again quite close, i.e. it minimises the importance of constraint. Workers in early factories scarcely 'got themselves organized'. The goal-attainment perspective persistently tends to minimise conflict. With regard to March and Simon, one critic has said 'they have ignored centuries of highly documented instances of economic, social and political conditions of conflict taken from the concrete records of government and industry. If their analysis is correct there should never be a union' (Krupp, 1961, p. 164).

It is ironic that a discipline so recent, and in many respects highly developed, should fall victim to an antiquated philosophy of man in society. Rationalism involves an over-emphasis on the differentiating characteristics of the human animal, in particular the possession of reason, to the extent that it is seen as the explanation and essence of all that is truly human and destined to triumph over the animal elements in man. We only have to substitute, 'the rational attainment of the organizational goal' for 'reason', and 'organization' for 'human being' to see this as an account of rationalism in the study of organisations. The lesson of modern historiography and psychology is that while rationality may be the distinguishing mark of human beings it is not an unmoved mover but depends on a variety of social conditions. Far from being in necessary conflict with the animal elements in man it is an organising factor in their expression. As far as organisations are concerned a similar advance in insight will come if we jettison the myth of the original goal and recognise that organisations possess all the social characteristics of collectivities over and above their special features of goal achievement.

What conception of the organisation should replace the orthodox model? One possible source of misunderstanding should be dispelled at once. While common conceptions of the functioning of goals within organisations have been criticised, at no point has the argument denied that such goals may indeed exist. It is fundamental to the analysis of organisations that a distinction can be made between action of an individual in a private capacity and his action in an organisational role (cf. Haworth, 1959). Members of any organisation refer to purposes to legitimate their action—they impute their action not to themselves but to the organisation. For that reason a distinction can be drawn between official and unofficial action. What has been criticised is the notion that official action can be interpreted as flowing exclusively and unambiguously from a predetermined specific goal.

In formulating a more objective concept of the organisation, three elements in Barnard's classic *The Functions of the Executive* (1938) should be noted. He defines a formal organisation as 'a system of consciously co-ordinated activities of two or more persons' (p. 81). This has the advantage of being wider in scope than definitions which emphasise the specific goal—although it may be that its scope is too wide for it to be accepted without modification. In addition, he stresses the multiple nature of organisational goals, and emphasises that authority is a relationship depending on the beliefs of those who accept it. To bring these elements together and to add another we may refer to an important contribution by E. Wight Bakke (1959). He takes Malinowski's notion of the Charter and applies it to organisations. For him, the 'Organizational Charter' is 'basically a set of ideas shared by the participants which may or may not be embodied in written documents' (p. 38). These ideas include goals, values, symbolic elements, beliefs in what the organisation stands for, which facilitate and legitimise interpersonal activities in the organisation. I would add the important qualification that there is no reason why members of the organisation should have equal shares in the charter.

The following definition of an organisation may be suggested: organisations are social units where individuals are conscious of their membership and legitimise their cooperative activities primarily by reference to the attainment of impersonal goals rather than to moral standards. In a subject congested with definitions a strong argument has to be made for suggesting a new one. It is hoped that in the light of what has gone before its rationale is clear. In brief, this formulation has three major advantages over the conception of organisations as created for the attainment of specific goals. In the first place, while it still emphasises the importance of goal attainment as the distinctive characteristic of organisations it does not assume unity, specificity, or *causal* efficacy as attributes of organisational goals. Secondly, by stressing the legitimising functions of goals in an organisation it avoids regarding goals as the property of any one stratum. All members contribute to conceptions of legitimacy. For example, if in an organisation service to the community has hitherto been regarded as the legitimising principle *par excellence*, managerial efforts to set up profitability as the prime objective may well be regarded by most members as illegitimate. In this situation a sociologist is not in a position to take sides. A science which instructs managers to treat organisational structure as contingent only on their own conception of its purpose is not only misguided in its empirical analysis of organisations but also taking sides in a struggle for power. Thirdly, the relevance of conventional sociological analysis to organisations is more obvious. Societies also have legitimising principles. For sociologists they are to be accounted for by such variables as power, conflict, class, status, the division of labour, and culture. However, in contrast to organisations the legitimising principles of action in society are usually moral standards.

Thus, in relations as varied as those between friends, relatives, politicians and the public, the judiciary and accused persons, individuals regularly justify their actions by reference to notions of right, justice, propriety, equality, or fairness. In the wider society such reference may well be regarded as sufficient justification; in an organisation actions need justification primarily by claims to success in achieving an objective. Of course this distinction allows for intermediate cases. In a society at war, goal attainment is so highly emphasised that it does no violence to language to call such a society an organisation, and moral standards may frequently be invoked in organisations. To argue that organisations must be studied as societies is scarcely paradoxical when a score of companies have power and income surpassing independent states and activities transcending national boundaries, and when nations may be more dependent on one product, be it tobacco, sugar, or oil, than many an organisation.

It may well be thought surprising that a plea should need to be made for sociologists to study organisations as societies. Regular definitions of sociology as the scientific study of society would lead one to expect that sociologists would in any case be vocationally inclined in that direction. Their proneness to the biases outlined here is therefore plainly in some need of explanation. The most likely reason is not that organisation theory has been uncritically admired. It is rather that sociologists have adhered to an inadequate 'general' theory. This 'theory' identifies research into society with analysis of the concept of a social system and accounts for the integration of that system by attributing to it a set of central values.

It has been all too easy for sociologists to adapt this way of thinking to organisations simply by substituting organisation for society and organisational goal for central values. This may be illustrated briefly by reference to two essays on organisational analysis which cover similar ground. Both Alvin Gouldner (1959a) and Amitai Etzioni (1960) have criticised what, respectively, they call 'the rational model' and 'the goal model' of organisations. At first sight they are making the same kind of objections to an over-emphasis on organisational goals as have been set out in this article. But as an alternative all they suggest is what they term 'the natural system' or 'the system model'. For Etzioni this means that analysis of the organisation in terms of its success in achieving its stated goal (which he argues is unrealistic, since organisations never achieve their goals completely) gives way to comparison of organisations in terms of their relative success in goal achievement and an assessment of their optimum distribution of resources in the light of the general requirements of systems for survival. Etzioni believes this excludes the normative orientations of the goal model. But it is difficult to see how this tallies with an insistence on assessing an optimum distribution of resources. Goal attainment remains as the central measure in organisational analysis even though it may be viewed in a more realistic light.

Similarly, Gouldner (1969a) argues that the system model emphasises an equilibrium of parts within which the goal is but one factor, but simultaneously concedes that this formulation exaggerates the integration of the organisation around the goal. He takes issue with Parsons on this very point and asserts, 'the statement that an organization is oriented toward certain goals often means no more than that these are the goals of its top administrators or that they represent its societal function, which is another matter altogether' (p. 420). Yet, oddly enough, after pinpointing the deficiencies of both the rational and natural system models, all Gouldner calls for is an attempt to bring the two together rather than a break from them. Neither author draws the conclusion that if the system concept fails to do justice to the sociological facts of multiplicity and vagueness of goals, the extra-organisational determination of authority, the societal locus and independent power of the organisation's members, their constant redefinition of organisational structure—then so much the worse for the system concept.

Of course, if this argument is valid it supports the criticism that the system concept is used too hastily and with misleading consequences in sociology (cf. Lockwood, 1956). If organisations cannot simply be conceived of as integrated by means of the specific goal, how much more unlikely it is that societies can be conceived of as integrated solely by means of basic values. If goal determination, formal rules, and authority structure must first be considered as independent factors before being considered as elements of a whole, known as 'the organisation', then *a fortiori* the relation of social facts to a much vaguer entity termed 'society' must also be regarded at the outset of any research as problematical.[2] So we come round to one of the points which I made at the

[2] It is somewhat strange that elsewhere both Etzioni and Gouldner develop implicitly this third view of the strategy of organizational analysis. Thus Etzioni (1961) virtually dispenses with the concept of system and proceeds by taking one variable, compliance, and examining its connections

outset, that the study of organisations has direct theoretical consequences for general sociology.

Let me, finally, take up one broader issue. It has been assumed
throughout that there are at least two perspectives on the study of
organisations, one known as organisation theory, concerned basically
with the improvement of organisational efficiency, and another, the
sociology of organisations, devoted to discovering the causes and consequences of various types and features of organisations. While the
whole argument has been designed to show that the two perspectives
may not be confused, it has never been suggested that either in itself is
invalid. The organisation theorist is concerned to help managers and
administrators. By contrast, the perspective of the sociologist is 'impractical'. His search is for understanding, untrammelled by the needs
of men of affairs. Therefore he cannot accept the conceptual framework
of the organisation theorist as setting the limits to his research interests
in organisations.

But this appeal for a recognition of the distinctiveness of the two
perspectives is not a demand that organisation theorist and sociologist
must set up intellectual apartheid. On the contrary, the subtlety of the
relations between the two perspectives shows that each must have a close
understanding of the other. The organisation theorist is bound to take
cognizance of any contribution to knowledge about organisations, regardless of the motives from which it springs. In his search for
value-freedom the sociologist must constantly re-examine the relations
between practical discourse and his own language of analysis.

---

with others, while Gouldner (1959b) argues at a theoretical level for a
revival of the factor approach.

REFERENCES

BAKKE, E. W. (1959) 'Concept of the social organization', in Haire, ed. (1959).
BARNARD, C. (1938) *The Functions of the Executive*, Harvard University
Press.
BENDIX, R. (1949) *Higher Civil Servants in American Society*, University of
Colorado Studies.
BENDIX, R., and FISHER, L. H. (1964) 'The perspectives of Elton Mayo', in
A. Etzioni, ed., *Complex Organizations*, Holt, Rinehart & Winston.
BLAU, P. M. and SCOTT, W. R. (1963) *Formal Organizations*, Routledge & Kegan
Paul.
CROZIER, M. (1964) *The Bureaucratic Phenomenon*, Tavistock.
ETZIONI, A. (1964) *Modern Organizations*, Prentice-Hall.

ETZIONI, A. (1961) *A Comparative Analysis of Complex Organizations*, New York, Free Press of Glencoe.

ETZIONI, A. (1960) 'Two approaches to organizational analysis: a critique and a suggestion', *Administrative Science Quarterly*, 5.

FRIEDMANN, G. (1955) *Industrial Society*, New York, Free Press of Glencoe.

GALTUNG, J. (1961) 'Prison: the organisation of a dilemma', in D. R. Cressey, ed., *The Prison*, Holt, Rinehart & Winston.

GOULDNER, A. W. (1959a) 'Organizational analysis', in R. K. Merton *et al.*, eds., *Sociology Today*, New York, Basic Books.

GOULDNER, A. W. (1959b), 'Reciprocity and autonomy in functional theory', in L. Gross, ed., *Symposium on Sociological Theory*, Row, Peterson.

HAIRE, M. (1962) 'What is organized in an organization', in Haire, ed., (1962).

HAIRE, M., ed. (1959) *Modern Organization Theory*, Wiley.

HAIRE, M., ed. (1962) *Organization Theory in Industrial Practice*, Wiley.

HAWORTH, L. (1959) 'Do organizations act?', *Ethics*, **70**, 59–63.

KRUPP, S. (1961) *Pattern in Organization Analysis*, New York, Chilton.

LLOYD, L. E. (1962) 'Origins and objectives of organizations', in Haire, ed. (1962).

LOCKWOOD, D. (1956) 'Some remarks on the social system', *British Journal of Sociology*, **7**.

MARSCHAK, J. (1959) 'Efficient and viable organizational forms', in Haire, ed. (1959).

PARSONS, TALCOTT (1960a) 'A sociological approach to the theory of organizations' in *Structure and Process in Modern Societies*, New York, Free Press of Glencoe.

PARSONS, TALCOTT (1960b) 'Some ingredients of a general theory of formal organizations', in *ibid*.

SHUBIK, M. (1964) 'Approaches to the study of decision-making relevant to the firm', in W. J. Gore and J. W. Dyson, eds., *The Making of Decisions*, New York, Free Press of Glencoe.

SIMON, H. (1957) *Administrative Behaviour*, 2nd rev. edn, New York, Macmillan.

STANTON, A. H., and SCHWARTZ, M. S. (1954) *The Mental Hospital*, New York, Basic Books.

Subject Index

Author Index